"*Witnessing is indeed a process that involves experiencing the ?
survivors and their children is an area that we need to continua
that needs repeated witnessing—it is all areas of trauma. The P?
of the therapist with the survivor, which in turn helps widen th
their continuing influences. This witnessing makes possible re:*

—Henry Krystal, ?

"*Witnessing—most readily thought of in terms of the Holocaust—is actually a vital intersubjective phenomenon that is central to the way that the interpersonal process facilitates individual consolidation and
growth. As does a clinical analysis, so does this piercingly wise study of witnessing engage the reader in
the active emotional experience of learning, leading one to know from both inside and outside, to understand from new depths. The contributions within this work expose not only the impact of trauma but,
importantly, how the very act of witnessing is itself essential to life, to change, and to growth. It was so
for me and I believe will be so for others: The reader of this powerful contribution will learn and will be
enriched by the learning.*"

—Warren S. Poland, M.D., author, *Melting the Darkness*

"*Part memoir, part ethnography, part depth-psychology, and part documentation of an event of human
history where mountains of evil and occasions of sorrow met like never before, is a stunning addition
to the Holocaust-related literature. Distinguished psychoanalysts have joined hands with poets, painters, geriatricians, professors of English, and performing artists to produce a powerful collage of human
suffering and resilience. The book is, at times, painful to read but never does it cease to be engaging and
illuminating about the informative role played by those who have faced such suffering first-hand. It gently
but firmly takes our hand and invites us to join the circle of witnesses to a great human tragedy. The book
therefore serves both clinical and humanitarian purposes!*"

—Salman Akhtar, M.D., Jefferson Medical College, Pennsylvania

"*Thank you to Nancy Goodman and Marilyn Meyers for the gift of* The Power of Witnessing. *Once you
start this remarkable book, you don't want to put it down. That may seem very surprising when you are
reliving and witnessing one of the worst examples of narcissistic rage and human destruction the world
has ever seen. In some ways it is still beyond comprehension. However, you realize as soon as you start
reading some of these descriptions that we owe it to every single person in the book (and elsewhere) who
has suffered like this not only to read their story but to honor their ability to finally tell the world what
they have suffered and lost. We must witness all of this and bear the pain. By being there with them and
sharing it word for word, we can feel that we are doing our part in helping them not to feel alone and helping the world not to forget. When Dori Laub describes wanting to hug each person after they have given
their testimony of their Holocaust experiences, I had the same experience as I finished each chapter. The
sense of intimacy was profound. I thank Nancy and Marilyn for this incredible privilege and what they
have given the world.*"

—Carolyn S. Ellman, Ph.D., editor, *The Modern Freudians*

"*As I began to read this book I thought that I didn't want to feel what others had witnessed. Then I
thought perhaps I am too ashamed by my fascination with the views that may be provided by those who
witnessed these horrors. I now realize that all of my expectations were set ajar by the depth of humanity
of the authors' experiences. Rather than turn away in horror I found that I was provided new hope that
even in the most terrible of circumstances other human beings can offer something that makes one proud
of our species. All who want to be reminded of the honor of life and the valor of some fellow beings should
read these deeply moving accounts and new conceptualizations.*"

—Steven J. Ellman, Ph.D., author, *When Theories Touch*

"The Power of Witnessing *is a rich, disturbing, provocative, startling but ultimately inspiring collection
of essays related to the Holocaust by some of the leading thinkers of our time on some of its key issues. We
encounter incredible stories of cruelty, elevating ones on how to rise above it, and the challenge of retelling those stories. Though the focus on one level is the Holocaust, on another level it is really about the
human condition. The book holds up a mirror for us to see ourselves—whether we are students or faculty
on campus, those involved in interfaith relations or simply wish to reflect on the follies of man. Anyone
who believes in our common humanity must take a long, hard look into this mirror. I am grateful to the*

contributors for allowing us this privilege. Read this book if you wish to confront the human condition and discover ways of transcending it."

—Akbar Ahmed, Ph.D., Ibn Khaldun Chair of Islamic Studies, American University

"Nancy Goodman and Marilyn Meyers have contributed a gripping collection—told by survivors of the Holocaust and the witnesses to their testimonies—about the power of witnessing. These highly personal essays are an important addition to the growing 'literature of testimony.' There can never be too many. Goodman, Meyers, and the authors in their book affirm that the power of witnessing lies in the restoration of humanity born in the process of the telling and the receiving of the horrors that mark this period in our collective history. The spiral of witnessing—across generations and consulting rooms, in the narratives, poetry, and images—leaves so much more than 'a trace.'"

—Rachel Peltz, Ph.D., Psychoanalytic Institute of Northern California

"In demonstrating The Power of Witnessing, *Goodman and Meyers illuminate the many subtle—and often surprising—aspects of this under-theorized topic. Without adhering to one dominant theoretical position, but resonating with several, a fundamental thread connects the varied chapters: our omnipresent need for a witness and the traumata that result from its absence or loss. This is a book about loss—individual and collective—and thus an exercise in mourning. But, more importantly, it is a profound testament to the healing powers of acknowledging, accepting, and absorbing the past through the mediation of witnessing. The reciprocal psychological changes in both witness and witnessed are revealingly articulated with courage and honesty by all who participated in this project. The process of mediation that allows terror of real experience to become symbolized, given voice, and shared are multiple, and multiply represented here: visual images, awake and dreaming; poetry; music; lists of names; memories and stories. Although the Holocaust is at its center,* The Power of Witnessing *speaks to a wider audience, and especially to those who seek to help others transform loss into hope for a future."*

—Bonnie Litowitz, Ph.D., Chicago Institute for Psychoanalysis

"The Power of Witnessing, edited by Nancy Goodman and Marilyn Meyers, invites us to revive the horror, the outrage, and the violence done to blameless people during the Holocaust—and to their descendents. As the contributors to this book vividly demonstrate, the acts of witnessing that cause us to remember are not on behalf of a just revenge for injustice done; they remind us to do the work necessary within ourselves and our societies to do everything possible to ensure that its like will never happen again. The book combines oral history and psychoanalytic insight with moral persuasion."

—Charles Hanly, Ph.D., President, International Psychoanalytical Association

"As an artist and as the only daughter to Holocaust survivors, I celebrate the publication of The Power of Witnessing. *Those of us raised in the presence of absence understand the necessity not only to 'remember' but to find a way of healing. There is no question that the writings in this book—whether coming from a psychoanalytic understanding or the beauty of a Myra Sklarew poem—emphasize finding a way to make peace with loss, to come full circle and allow the survival of beauty to live on."*

—Mindy Weisel, artist, Washington, DC

"Let me begin by saying I was reluctant to read this book. I anticipated it would be depressing and traumatizing. How wrong I was. In their edited book, The Power of Witnessing, *Drs. Goodman and Meyers illustrate the importance of witnessing as an agent in healing. By using the experiences of authors who tell the story of their own trauma or witnessing the trauma of others during the Holocaust, the editors have broadened our understanding of witnessing to all important life events. At a time in our modern history when we are exposed to so many traumas in the world, it is especially important we not become immune but instead listen and try to understand the human effect these experiences have on individuals, groups, and society. All who want to help expand the human experience of others and themselves, whether they are psychotherapists, parents, teachers, or loving friends, should read this book."*

—Joyce Lowenstein, Ph.D., psychologist

"A deeply moving and important work. Goodman and Meyers' book brings together an exceptional group of papers which constitute a succession of Odysseys. Together they create a vivid testimony to human resilience in the face of essentially unimaginable terror and sadism. Through their nightmares and those confronted by each contributor, we learn just why the Holocaust is timeless and belongs to everyone and just why we must attend to all such new incidents with vigilance and inward questioning, balanced by the imperative we remain curious."

—David Tuckett, M.A., M.Sc., University College London

"Nancy Goodman and Marilyn Meyers' edited book, The Power of Witnessing, offers us a compelling and moving array of testimonies to the Holocaust. Through prose, poetry, film, and art, these distinguished authors allow us to witness the Holocaust and reflect on the long shadow it has cast on future generations. Each contributor provides an important window into this haunting and profoundly disturbing time in our history. As therapist editors, Goodman and Meyers bring a deep understanding of the necessity and power of witnessing—to know what was previously unknowable."

—Kerry L. Malawista, Ph.D., co-author of The Bereaved Therapist

"'There is nothing one man will not do to another.' Those words were written by the poet Carolyn Forche. It's the last line of her poem 'The Visitor' and it's separated or perhaps imprisoned on the page by white space. I've always found Forche's words haunting. There are some things I cannot even imagine. One is the Holocaust. Looking back on my life, I believe this word first became part of my vocabulary because of my mother. Growing up in the South Bronx in the 1950s, my mother worked in the Manhattan garment industry. Her employer and some of her fellow workers were Jewish. My mother was also a regular patron of small Jewish businesses in the Bronx, places where we purchased our food and clothes. Over counters, stories were shared and my mother came home with things she told me to never forget. Maybe this was my introduction to the importance of witnessing. What pain and silence was not hidden from my childhood eyes? Reading The Power of Witnessing made me think about memoir writing. The need to discover courage beneath the flesh. How does one find the strength to give testimony and the power not to forget? We live in an era of erasure. One click of a button can delete almost anything. And this is why the reflections and interviews in The Power of Witnessing contain not just the songs of survival but more the resiliency of living that can only be found in the human heart. There is such a thing as family and after all this suffering we must remember how to love. This is what we owe each other. Hopefully it will protect us from the trauma."

—E. Ethelbert Miller, Director, African American Resource Center, Howard University

"Goodman and Meyers' groundbreaking book takes us on a journey where we grapple with the unthinkable horrors of the Holocaust. Their narrative, holding this richly diverse, edited collection of stunning memoirs and incisive essays, details their own encounters with first-person accounts and images of the brutality of the Holocaust. They pay close attention to the challenge of witnessing. The Power of Witnessing gives readers a vehicle to engage with the incomprehensible cruelty of the Holocaust and the hope of a greater capacity to be present with the suffering and pain of others."

—Elizabeth Fritsch, Ph.D., President, New York Freudian Society

"Nancy Goodman and Marilyn Meyers have edited an important book, deeply moving and in many parts painful to read, helping us to reflect on the different aspects of the process of witnessing: its meaning and significance for the traumatized person as witness but also for the successive generations as listener and as secondary witness. This is particularly important in a time where the last survivors of the Holocaust are dying out. Remembering the Holocaust, we need to return to the witness's individual memory in order to not neglect the horrific, catastrophic, and traumatic experiential quality in the process of its historical description and classification."

—Werner Bohleber, Ph.D., editor, Psyche

"This is a project of enormous reach, informed, most importantly, by a generous and empathic impulse to gather as many perspectives as possible for the purpose of reawakening attention to testimony, as opposed to dulling our collective interest through a dry academic recounting. It celebrates perhaps the most important action we can partake in as citizens living in the shadow of catastrophe: the dynamic and moral act of witnessing. This book reminds us of the great good that has come from that collective mission to keep memory alive through testifying and transmission, through cultural expression that's actively engaged with both historical archives and personal imagination. As a playwright and producer of Jewish theater, I find strength in its honoring the role of the witness and the power of collective witnessing—after all, isn't that what a theater audience is, a gathering of witnesses engaged in a collective act of empathy? I have a special appreciation for the chapters that specifically point to theater, film, photography, literature, and crafts as their own powerful transformational acts, finding redemptive byproducts in the creation and cultural responses to the Shoah, as we engage with history anew and afresh every time we experience a work of art drawn from the act of authentic witnessing. This is a compendium I'll keep returning to over the years, drawing inspiration and a grounding sense of the authentic. As we grow ever more distant from the Holocaust in time, vivid witnessing will keep its presence in our consciousness close, rich, and as real as we can possibly imagine."

—Ari Roth, Artistic Director, Theater J

"The Power of Witnessing is an important contribution derived from the Holocaust. Nancy Goodman and Marilyn Meyers are well-respected psychoanalysts who have carefully studied the effects, direct and indirect, of witnessing the Holocaust. They clarify powerful ramifications not only for the survivors but for their children, relatives, and friends, illustrating vividly the power of witnessing such a grotesque degradation. Its extreme nature has led to impacts in a variety of fields and has lasting significance. The contributors to the book are very capable, and a particularly significant piece is an interview with Professor Irvin Staub. One hopes that this book will have far-reaching effects on those who care about our common humanity."

—David A. Hamburg, M.D., President Emeritus, Carnegie Corporation of New York

"This is the book for adults who have an interest in the Holocaust and who know very little about it, and for people dealing with the effects of trauma caused by the very people who they thought were their friends and neighbors. It testifies to the healing power of talking about the shame of being a victim and the loss of faith in other people and the social system that a horror like the Holocaust leaves in its wake."

—Fanya Gottesfeld Heller, author, *Love in a World of Sorrow*

"The Power of Witnessing is an overview of the teeming world of Jewish culture before the Holocaust and a living tribute to the memory of those who did not survive."

—Aaron Lansky, President, Yiddish Book Center

"Reading The Power of Witnessing was a deeply moving and enriching experience. I was obliged to relive the wrenching and inconsolable crying of my mother and her brothers when, at the end of World War II, they found out that all of their family had disappeared in Nazi concentration camps. It was an unimaginable pain that they could never recover from and which I have not forgotten, as I will never fail to remember the assassinations, injury, and terror that we Peruvians suffered during the years of violence in our country. The magnificent and brave effort of Nancy Goodman and Marilyn Meyers to bring together a series of writings, of others as well as their own, that testify from different perspectives to the horror of the Holocaust, allows the reader to experience firsthand the power of witnessing."

—Moisés Lemlij, M.D., Peruvian Psychoanalytic Society

The Power
of Witnessing

Reflections, Reverberations,
and Traces of the Holocaust

Trauma, Psychoanalysis, and the Living Mind

Edited by
Nancy R. Goodman and Marilyn B. Meyers

Routledge
Taylor & Francis Group
New York   London

Routledge
Taylor & Francis Group
711 Third Avenue
New York, NY 10017

Routledge
Taylor & Francis Group
27 Church Road
Hove, East Sussex BN3 2FA

Printed in the United States of America on acid-free paper
Version Date: 20111017

International Standard Book Number: 978-0-415-87902-6 (Hardback) 978-0-415-87903-3 (Paperback)

Library of Congress Cataloging-in-Publication Data

The power of witnessing : reflections, reverberations, and traces of the Holocaust /
    edited by Nancy Goodman, Marilyn Meyers.
        p. cm.
    Includes bibliographical references and index.
    ISBN 978-0-415-87902-6 (hardcover : alk. paper) -- ISBN 978-0-415-87903-3 (pbk. :
    alk. paper) -- ISBN 978-0-203-85276-7 (e-book
    : alk. paper)
        1. Holocaust, Jewish (1939-1945)--Historiography. 2. Holocaust, Jewish
    (1939-1945)--Personal narratives--History and criticism. 3. Holocaust
    survivors--Biography--History and criticism. 4. Holocaust, Jewish
    (1939-1945)--Influence. 5. Memory--Social aspects. I. Goodman, Nancy (Nancy R.)
    II. Meyers, Marilyn (Marilyn B.)

D804.348.P69 2012
940.53'18--dc23   2011037872

Visit the Taylor & Francis Web site at
http://www.taylorandfrancis.com

and the Routledge Web site at
http://www.routledgementalhealth.com

Contents

Preface: An Invitation

Nancy R. Goodman and Marilyn B. Meyers

You are invited to join in the power of witnessing. The power of witnessing opens a place in your mind and brings about a feeling of connection with others. We recognize that we are bringing you into contact with the terror of the Holocaust and with all mass and individual trauma. We also firmly attest that engaging with the power of witnessing is uplifting and inspiring. The power of witnessing creates space in which courage, resilience, and connection are discovered. In the writings in this book, you will find remarkable narrative, poetry, scholarship, artwork, and stories of dedication to metabolize and symbolize psychic pain. We hope you feel sustained, as we have, by being part of a witnessing community.

OUR PERSONAL JOURNEY

We feel that coming to know the trauma of the Holocaust, and indeed all trauma, is very personal because of the resonances felt within oneself. We write here about our journey in conceiving of the book, gathering contributors, and thinking, writing, and feeling over the last 3 years. Psychoanalytic therapists learn by allowing transmissions into their own minds of patients' conscious and unconscious fears and wishes. The activation of these counterfeelings and fantasies are then used to understand deeply. In personal statements, we speak of our inner experiences— associations, memories, previously undiscovered connections, and profound feelings. These personal reflections have helped to uncover and reveal the power of witnessing.

We are aware that our difficulties in confronting our own psychic wounds and ruptures when getting close to the genocide of the Shoah are very real and also small compared to those of the survivors themselves. We feel privileged to be witnesses and to learn so much about witnessing itself. We felt throughout our work on this project that we were more keenly cognizant of how to help our patients because we were intimately discovering how witnessing awakens fear and space for knowing, reflecting, and relationship.

We began by committing to meet twice a week. We made "to do" lists about contacting possible participants. We cleared off a bookshelf for our already extensive library of Holocaust, trauma, and witnessing literature. Over the next 3 years, our collection swelled far beyond the capacity of our bookshelves. We consistently received "recommendations" from Amazon and friends for Holocaust and trauma books. We were amazed at what we found on the Internet. Marilyn began to collect relevant newspaper articles, and they appeared almost weekly. We received positive responses to our invitations to write for the book. We went to New York to talk with Dori Laub, Sophia Richman, Arlene Kramer Richards, and Arnold Richards. Marilyn had met Edgar and Hana Krasa at a performance of the *Defiant Requiem* on site at the Terezín Ghetto, and we traveled to Boston to interview them.

We knew we were on our way. The project had momentum. We experienced oscillations between excitement, manic states, and despair at beginning this project. Eventually, we wondered if it would ever be "done." We soon came to the realization that being done is not possible. This, of course, was the point of the whole enterprise—we could not be done, could not revive the dead, and we would endure all of the states of mind ignited by this project and complete the book. It was difficult to bear all that we were discovering. It was gratifying and actually wondrous to find so many colleagues and friends who wanted to be witnesses with us. At times, we felt guilty that we were so excited about the work and about the intimacy of our work with each other and our colleagues. As contributions came in, we could not believe their depth of meaning and evocation of feeling.

At times, we found ourselves almost unable to tolerate the pain of details described in written materials, in testimonies, in historic facts. These included accounting of numbers of those killed, images in films, maps of the rail network to concentration camps, and phrases used in documents. We also both wanted to know more and wanted to help others know. Certain materials were more approachable and gave us ways into the project. At these times, we were able to feel and cry and speak of fear. Daniel Mendelsohn's *The Lost: A Search for Six of Six Million* (2006) captivated both of us and helped us feel we could develop this book. Mendelsohn articulates the idea of specificity that allows true empathic resonance with one person, one family, one moment. There were times when the totality of the Holocaust overwhelmed and when a particular, singular event described in a testimony or narrative became a place of despair. We found often the sense of shame of belonging to a group of people who could be so hated and abandoned.

Moving forward to read more and write more brought about activity, learning, and thinking that made us proud. At times, we actually laughed and realized it was okay to laugh. We gave ourselves permission to turn toward and to turn away from the intense trauma of taking in the Holocaust. At one point when we were exchanging our numerous nightmares, Marilyn said, "I wish I would dream about Paul Newman." Nancy eagerly agreed (we are dating ourselves), and we gave ourselves permission to feel alive and joke. We entertained each other remembering Larry David's irreverent episode on *Curb Your Enthusiasm* when he invited two survivors to dinner. The story is that he and a friend wanted two survivors to meet. At the dinner, one survivor is a Holocaust survivor and one is from the reality television show *Survivor*.

We agreed that photographs were the worst, too real, too terrible. Nancy was certain that she had seen photographs at the age of 3 that made her a witness then and there: "What I felt impressed me was the look in the eyes of emaciated people staring at the camera—something I wanted to know about and something resonating with a lonely place in my childhood experience." We know this is what our parents saw in newsreels and what we each had seen when learning about the Holocaust, and that psychic trauma about the Holocaust was transmitted to us as children. At times, we wondered if it was all right to be witnesses when we were not directly survivors or children of survivors. We spoke of this to Dori Laub, and he said, "What difference does it make? You are witnesses." We realized that everyone is a witness. The Holocaust is timeless and belongs to everyone. Once it is known, it is in the mind. We are all descendants of the Holocaust and need to witness and be witnessed to maintain a living mind.

Nancy's Nightmares

Marilyn says it is time to start writing. I have a nightmare the night before our meeting to talk about writing—I keep playing with it as "righting." There is no righting of the Holocaust. Dori tells me that the core is always being approached when there is the desire to know; knowing is cathected even though the emptiness, the horror, the agony, the totality, the individual experience cannot be completely entered. We will try. This is a special project capturing the reciprocity that occurs when there is witnessing between people. To me this reciprocity seems as close as attuned breathing between mother and infant. We meet at our Tuesday time, and Marilyn says again that it is time to begin writing. I begin to cry. I had a dream last night, a nightmare; it must be related. I woke up so worried, maybe there is truth in the dream:

> I dream I am going outside of my house on a walk and that I am naked and do not know I am naked, and when I realize it I know I have Alzheimer's and will have to stop working, and I do not want to stop working, and I feel so bad for my kids and husband and patients knowing how sad they will be to see me disappear.

Associations: Maybe I really do have Alzheimer's—that would mean I am losing my mind. I think I have a wish not to be able to know and remember and want to lose my mind before I further face the Holocaust and my own traumas. There were so many naked women who did not survive the Holocaust. Is it really all right to write and be alive? I realize that being able to have my dream and to talk about it and to cry with Marilyn recognizes the possibility of writing our book. A few weeks later I have a second dream—an unspeakable terror dream:

> I dream that I am with my grandchildren, feeling the absolute gratitude that they are in my life. We are near water. One of them falls into the water, and I jump in to grab this baby and I cannot. The baby slips through my hands, and the water is too dark to see into. I am beyond horrified and want to die. This is impossible. I cannot bring this pain to others.

I tell Marilyn that I have had another nightmare. The pain of it was on my face. I realize I am identifying with the way survivor parents would not want to tell their children stories of their Holocaust experience. I do not ever want to tell my children this dream. But this dream is not a true event; having the dream and knowing it is "only" a dream separates me from the Holocaust survivor who did not have the privilege to have a nightmare and know it was solely a nightmare. Being able to symbolize what is terrifying and to be able to tell another who listens is being found and pulled out of the water.

Marilyn's Nightmares

Nancy and I drive together to BWI (Baltimore Washington International) Airport for our trip to Boston to meet with Edgar and Hana. We have time before the flight to have a cup of coffee in the diner at the airport. We are both in a heightened state of anxiety and excitement at the impending meeting. I am keenly aware that I know Edgar and Hana from several meetings and performances of the *Defiant Requiem*, and that Nancy has not yet met them. This trip is a leap of faith for her. Among the clanging of dishes and the smell of freshly brewed coffee, I tell Nancy my dreams of the night before:

> I am lying in the bed with someone who comes in with medical adhesive tape. I am not sure if it is me or someone else. Someone comes in with medical adhesive tape, putting the tape on my skin, looking for evidence—like I am going to be accused of something ... like finding something subtle on my skin ... the

person who is doing it (I want to say like a Nazi) ... something bad is going to happen if they find whatever they are looking for on my skin.

In a second dream that same night:

I think it is me in the dream, I am not sure. I am with a child, and the child needs to have its nails clipped. The child is not a baby, not a toddler; it is hard to know the age. The clipping of the nails is being done in secret. I have to gather up the nail clippings because if anyone sees them, it is bad, dangerous.

We both know that these dreams pertain to our work. We associate together to the dreams. Being skinned ... lampshades ... something penetrates the skin, patting the hand could be soothing, the contrast is danger. ... The skin is sensitive, it's fragile, skin heads, foreskin, boundary ... danger ... secrecy ... being discovered ... the Wannsee protocol. ... What will we discover? What bad things will happen? What can we hold onto? What will slip away? What is unspeakable? What must be spoken? We also know that there will be many more dreams/nightmares.

Over time, we had many more painful experiences and dreams. We discovered that once we got through these dark places, further momentum always developed. When we reached the point of sending our work out to colleagues for editorial feedback, we had some truly excruciating nightmares, often involving endless searching and death. We told friends and colleagues we were going to include our nightmares in the book. Our husbands each told us about nightmares they had as children in hearing about the Holocaust. Some thought maybe our nightmares should not be included; we are not direct survivors. We knew our nightmares were as witnesses once removed and knew they were important resonances. We actually did not mind having these responses as witnesses. It is what we do and want to do as therapists—to help bring knowing that is transformational once it takes place. It is good psychic work. Nancy called Dori Laub, telling him she was having nightmares and wanted to know if he has nightmares when he is writing. He tells her: "I always have nightmares."

NANCY'S PERSONAL REFLECTION

Each individual who approaches knowing of the Holocaust is willing to see and feel and forge a painful path to the edge of the nothingness of the Shoah. It is on the edge of this abyss that a turning away or a turning toward or, it is hoped, oscillations of both can take place. When I was a psychology intern and on the staff at Connecticut Valley Hospital in

Middletown, Connecticut, I participated in a weekly clinical seminar led by Dori Laub. I quickly asked him to supervise my therapies with young adult schizophrenic patients. This was in 1978. Dori was already involved with thinking about Holocaust testimony and working with Laurel Vlock, his partner in founding the Yale Video Archives of Holocaust Testimony. He invited me to read some materials and took me to the first showing of the first testimony videos to a gathering of members of the Jewish community of Holocaust survivors in and around New Haven, Connecticut. This night really got into my psyche because of the clashing of two impressions: the truths of horrible things that people were revealing about their experiences some 35 years earlier during the Holocaust and the truth of celebration, including food, hugging, and excitement. Adult children of survivors were saying they had not previously heard these stories from their parents. That night, survivors had eagerness and a special sparkle in their eyes. I had always felt frightened to see the numbers tattooed on survivors' arms, and I was now drawn to them and their stories identifying with their aliveness and what was being created in the archive project.

I realize now that my projections onto survivors included the wish not to know because of humiliation about my own vulnerabilities and desire to disidentify. In my family, the Holocaust was treated as something distant that happened over there and to them. This was similar to the way grandparents spoke of their origins. They all acted like life began when they got to Chicago. There was no idea of having come from anywhere except, "oh, the old country," a place without name and not worth knowing. Living in Chile, in 1967–1968, before the terror could be imagined, taught me how quickly societies can change and jeopardize life. I also saw firsthand and felt pride about the determination of my husband, Louis Goodman, to assist and rescue persecuted scholars in Latin America during the 1970s and after. Intervening for individuals matters.

Becoming a witness to Holocaust survivors, and most importantly becoming a witness to the Archives Project and Dori's belief in witnessing, helped me face the depths of my own mind in my personal analysis in which I was deeply immersed during this time. Something so important was taking place; those who knew terrifying helplessness were moving toward action: telling, recording for posterity, creating, thinking up new forms of expression, and making a community full of all human emotion. These impressions are lasting and help me understand dualities in my patients' minds and in my own: fear and conquest, terror and celebration, aloneness and being with.

When I moved to Bethesda, Maryland, in 1982, Dori took me to a reunion of Holocaust survivors held in Washington, D.C. Again, this was compelling. Everyone was so busy searching for others they had lost track of. People were rushing to monitors that displayed names in hope of finding friends and relatives. I helped with a testimony interview and had a sense of never wanting to say good-bye to the woman who entrusted me to be her witness. I sat in an auditorium listening to speeches, including a remarkably poetic, emotionally full address by Elie Wiesel. A lasting scene in my mind is of what happened in the parking lot when the event was over. There were hundreds of buses, all looking the same in an eerie yellowish fogginess from the parking lot fixtures. When the speeches were over, people were rushing around in the parking lot looking for their bus—their transportation home. Elderly men and women were frantically speaking with their European accents to bus drivers trying to find the right bus. I felt an awful tension—what if someone, anyone, all of us, got on the wrong bus, what if you could not find the right bus, what if you missed your bus and were left behind? I was left with guilt and helplessness at not being able to help all these old people in the shadows of that reunion night. Also from that night, I felt the thrill of reunion, of what Dori calls a "homecoming," in which people can find each other and remember things together. As I write this, I realize how deeply I will miss the accents of survivors, who hold the truths of their terrifying experiences, along with their courage to live and speak as well. They will not live forever. I feel grief. I am again so glad for the voices on video and, in my mind, of people willing to let others know them.

In 2007, I learned more about witnessing from two experiences. I organized a conference for the New York Freudian Society, Washington, D.C., Program, bringing together Dori Laub and Akbar Ahmed, an anthropologist and Muslim scholar, to dialogue about fear and trauma. As children, Dori had been transported to a concentration camp and Akbar had been on a train following "ghost trains" during the partition of India. In their life's work, each became a witness for societal trauma and ruptures for individuals. They had respect for each other. I also attended the International Psychoanalytic Association Congress in Berlin, Germany, to present my paper on the film, *Schindler's List* (see Chapter 20). This was my first trip to Germany, a place my parents had always referred to as someplace no one should ever visit (until my Dad got his first BMW). All over Berlin, there are efforts to memorialize the terrible atrocities of the Holocaust. I found this profoundly emotionally moving. I was really in a place where the ideas for the extermination of all Jewish people was "thought" of (sic) and a place where the two-square-block Memorial to the Murdered Jews of Europe had been built (see Chapter 19) almost next to the center of German government, the Reichstag. The first time my husband and I walked among the stellae making up the monument, I heard myself tell him that I did not like the material of the blocks; it did not reflect light like the marble wall of the Vietnam Memorial in Washington, D.C. I then realized how brilliant the architect, Peter Eisenman, was in choosing this deadly, unresponsive-to-light material. I could feel the paradox of knowing the death of the genocide and knowing the creative metaphoric representation in downtown Berlin. This helped inspire my desire to organize and write for this book.

I know that finding the power of witnessing through this book has made me a better and more willing witness to pain of my patients, myself, and others in general. While I was working on writing this book and being so open to the suffering of human beings, I read a review of the book *The Eyes of Willie McGee: A Tragedy of Race, Sex, and Secrets in the Jim Crow South* by Alex Heard (2010). Descriptions of violence and torture really shook me to the core. One description was of a group of people not only committing the horror of lynching a black man, but also deciding to block his nostrils so that the smoke would not make him unconscious, and he would have to feel himself being burned. I had nightmares for many nights thinking of the terror and searing pain. Most of all, I could not bear, and still cannot bear, the idea that someone thought of doing this, and others agreed and even more watched. I realized that I was more deeply witnessing the pure atrocities of slavery and hatred because of my willingness to be open to the Holocaust. I think this makes me more human and more desirous of recognizing hatred and naming it as such. It is okay to have nightmares to be more human. It is important to know the unbearable.

My personal experience of my psychoanalysis leads me to know, at the core of myself, the importance of having a profound connection to a sense of someone, the analyst, the witness, who is always willing to know and to be with. This shores up my sense that I will always be willing to struggle to know my patients and to continue to know myself and family, even and especially when there is great fear and grief. Once found, this becomes an internalized place that continues throughout one's life. Any disruption in it is shattering and full of endless grief.

The absence of a felt perception that one matters, or having moments of experience that are disavowed by others, produces a sense of annihilation, need to dissociate, and an emptiness in the psyche. We know from the descriptions of Renee Spitz that abandoned babies can enter a state of anaclitic depression and marasmus in which they destroy themselves. Having been a premature infant separated from my mother at birth to reunite 3 months later with a mother who had trauma and grief in her mind has given me deep intimate knowledge of the need for finding, holding, and containment in order to face and ameliorate something felt as too painful.

MARILYN'S PERSONAL REFLECTION

In retrospect, I realize that my professional interest in the Holocaust has spanned close to 20 years. My personal relationship with the Holocaust dates back to my early teens and perhaps earlier. I read the diary of Anne Frank; I saw the play on Broadway and the movie many times. Throughout my life, I have had an almost insatiable appetite for Holocaust books and movies. In 1994, I co-chaired the spring meeting of the Division of Psychoanalysis (39) of the American Psychological Association and organized a panel at the Holocaust Museum in connection with this conference. Dori Laub and Eva Hoffman were among those who participated and spoke about witnessing at that conference. Subsequently, I have remained immersed in studying the witnessing of the Holocaust. Together with Nancy and Beatrice Smirnow, I presented papers on the use of film to portray the trauma of the Holocaust and its aftermath. I have written on work with couples with a Holocaust history and given papers on that work (Meyers, 2005). I have only recently fully examined the reasons for my motivation behind these professional activities.

My grandparents came to the United States in 1905 by boat; they left Vilna, Lithuania, on a ship from Odessa, Russia, and landed on Ellis Island. They were fleeing the pogroms in the shtetls of Czarist Russia. The men were escaping service in the Czar's army. The women were seeking safety from the rape and pillaging. Most of all, anti-Semitism was rampant, and the Jews were not safe in their own homes and villages. They came to the United States with other immigrants—to the "promised land." Along with others, they were intent on leaving their painful history behind and starting fresh in America. It was the land of opportunity. On arrival, they immediately enrolled in classes to learn English. They were determined to assimilate. Their names are registered at Ellis Island.

When I was in junior high school, I had an assignment to interview an interesting person. I chose my paternal grandfather, Louis Band (his name had been "Americanized" from the original, Leiser Gaitleband). As he lay in his bed in the nursing home, I sat with him for hours, writing down the story of his life. It was, in retrospect, my first foray into bearing witness and taking testimony. Through my time with him, I came to see him as a real, multifaceted person, rather than "Grandpa." I never pursued learning my paternal grandmother's story. I think that I unconsciously knew that she carried a lot of trauma and unmourned losses. Perhaps I was frightened of opening wounds and retraumatizing her or of experiencing trauma secondhand. Many years later, I have come to understand more about this. Writing this book has brought me in deeper contact with the impact that my immigrant family has had on me. This is not only the Holocaust losses, about which I knew little consciously, but also their own courage and determination in making a new life in America.

My father's mother was widely seen as smart, politically astute, and strong. Often, she was referred to as a "woman before her time." She was the person to whom the extended family turned when seeking wisdom for complex family issues. My father has told me a story about my grandmother that sheds some light on the origins of my interest and subsequent work on this book and other Holocaust-related projects. Sometime after the end of World War II, my grandmother received a letter from "the old country."

I can picture my grandmother in her faded print housedress and apron. In my mind, she is surrounded by her children—Shirley, Sydney, Abe, Bertha, Irving—Louis (my grandfather), and my parents, Molly and Jack. They are all seated around the large dining room table, which served as a family gathering place as well as for sharing meals. There is an old-fashioned lace tablecloth covering the table; a faint smell of cooking cabbage wafts from the kitchen. My grandmother had strong but weathered hands, evidence of a hard life. She had a serious demeanor but was also loving and warm. She had something of the old world aura. As she opened the letter, read it silently, and wept, my father asked, "What was that?" She folded the letter and said, "You don't want to know." To this day, despite repeated efforts, we have not been able to find out the contents of that letter or what happened to my grandmother's family. The best we can surmise is that her family was executed in the killing fields of Lithuania. When I see the torturous photographs of these killing fields—dead bodies piled in ditches dug by the victims—I feel quite certain that there were the murdered members of my grandmother's family. However, I cannot know for sure. There is not a trace. I have come to realize that I absorbed her traumatic losses wordlessly. Perhaps that is the "trace." I knew something about her that never got put into words, and I will never know.

In the 1980s and 1990s, my father and his sister attempted to find out the fate of their relatives. They had limited success. They were able to construct a genealogy of my grandfather's family. I have examined this "family tree" numerous times. Each time I look at it, I realize that I enter a dissociated state. I literally cannot focus my gaze. Intermittently, I am able to focus and see. The clear recognition of my family's losses in the Holocaust is traumatic and overwhelming for me. At least 12 members of the family are listed as "killed by the Nazis." Some have the name of the camp in which they died, and others do not. In some odd way, I find it comforting to know the place where they died, although I still cannot know the specifics or have an image of the person in my mind. There are missing branches of the family tree, never to be known. There are endings without context. I think of the idea of a phantom limb, but this does not convey or capture the experience. When I look at this family tree, I feel untethered—a vaguely floating feeling. This is traumatic knowledge without any sense of comfort or narrative. I close the book, both literally and metaphorically. I know something that I cannot know; I know that I will never know. All of these people—members of my family—are named but remain unknowable. I cannot hold the information in my mind. The knowing is elusive and fragmentary. It becomes a blur of not knowing, and yet I feel compelled to know. Somehow, when the place is identified, I feel better. What does this mean, and how do I make sense or bring order to these stories?

Just recently, as I have been working on this book, I realized that I had not explored or thought about what became of my mother's family. I am shocked and embarrassed that I had never thought about this. I was very close to my maternal grandfather (Abraham Levine), and it did not occur to me until that moment that he had no family that I knew of. My image of him instantly shifted. The warm, kind man who I knew as a child became shrouded in loss. I think now that the sadness that he carried registered for me. Is it also this recognition that drives me to this project? He bore a presence that had both tragedy and intense love for my mother, her sister, and me. Both aspects of him were always present.

Perhaps this project is an effort to bridge the gaps in my family, to make connections in a deeply felt way. The "facts" of the losses may never be known, but the feelings can be. Like many therapists, I am compelled to know the "unknowable" and ask questions, to put the pieces of the puzzle together, with the knowledge that there will always be gaps and absences.

In bringing this reflection full circle, when my father died in February 2011 at the age of 95, I came into the possession of family photographs and other memorabilia. Actually, there were four large cartons for me to explore. It came to me in bold focus that my father was a committed witness and archivist. This shed light on my own commitment to witnessing. Further exploration of this treasure trove led to the discovery of the full copy in Yiddish and partial translation of a memoir written by my grandmother's uncle, Shmuel Horowitz. (It includes a note: "The proceeds of this publication is to be used to go to the support and help of the Central Yiddish Craftsmen's organization in Vilna.") Shmuel Horowitz was a locksmith, known for his artistry in his work, as well as a labor organizer of artisans. He was described in a letter by an unnamed person as a "slight, thin man with constantly blackened, calloused hands due to filing, sweating and hammering. His face often covered with oil and soot. Yet this same man had a strong feeling for beauty, for fine antiques and for artistically perfected objects." The author of this letter went on to say that "Horowitz died two years before World War II, thereby being spared from the martyrdom of the Vilna Jews."

The translation of Horowitz's memoir is handwritten and difficult to read; however, it contains a fascinating look into a particular aspect of the life of the Jewish artisans of Vilna in those years. The complex internal political dynamics play out within the context of the upheaval surrounding the city of Vilna. The material in the cartons also contained a translation of a letter to Shmuel Horowitz dated September 22, 1915, written from Moscow by L. M. Antonakolsy, a renowned artist from Vilna. This letter was in response to receipt of an issue of the journal produced by the artisans of Vilna. Antonakolsy stated his admiration of Horowitz for this accomplishment "in spite of the extremely difficult circumstances and events of recent years."

I recently purchased a book *The Last Days of the Jerusalem of Lithuania* (2002). This is a book that contains the diaries of Herman Kruk, a librarian in Vilna, documenting the annihilation of the Jewish community of Vilna—the Jerusalem of Lithuania. At the beginning of the book, there is a poem written by Herman Kruk, dated March 24, 1944. It was originally written in Yiddish and was found among his other writing.

For Future Generations

Neighbors in Camp Klooga often ask me
Why do you write such hard times?
Why and for whom? ...
For we won't live to see it anyway.
I know I am condemned and awaiting my turn,
Although deep inside me burrows a hope for a miracle.
Drunk on the pen trembling in my hand,
I record everything for future generations:
A day will come when someone will find
The leaves of horror I write and record.
People will tear their hair in anguish,
Eyes will plunge into the sky
Unwilling to believe the horrors of our times.
And then these lines will be a consolation
For future generations, which I, prisoner,
Kept in my sight, things
I recorded, fixed faithfully
For me it is superfluous,
For future generations I leave it as a trace.
And let it remain though I must die here
And let it show what I could not live to tell.
And I answer my neighbors:
Maybe a miracle will liberate me.
But if I must die, it must not die with me—
The time of horrors I leave for future worlds.
I write because I must write—a consolation in my time of horror:
For future generations I leave it as a trace.[1]

Six months after writing this poem, Kruk made his final entry in his diary, hours before he was shot to death. He managed to bury his diaries before his death. For the moment, my personal search ends here. I write out of a need to write—to bear witness. My motivation is still not entirely clear to me, but I feel compelled to do so.

---

[1] From Kruk, H., *The Last Days of the Jerusalem of Lithuania*. © 2002 Yale University Press. Reprinted with permission.

REFERENCES

Heard, A. (2010). *The eyes of Willie McGee: A tragedy of race, sex, and secrets in the Jim Crow South*. New York: HarperCollins.

Kruk, H. (2002). *The last days of the Jerusalem of Lithuania* (B. Harshav, Ed.). New Haven, CT: Yale University Press.

Mendelsohn, D. (2006). *The lost: The search for six of the six million*. New York: HarperCollins.

Meyers, M. (2005). When the Holocaust haunts the couple: Hope, guilt and survival. In *Psychoanalytic perspectives on couple work* (Vol. 1, pp. 43–55). London: Society of Couple Psychoanalytic Psychotherapists.

Acknowledgments

We thank all of the contributors who were willing to open their hearts and minds to the Holocaust, genocide, and mass trauma and to write for the book. Every single person who has provided witnessing in histories, memoirs, and artistic representations of the Holocaust, mass trauma, and individual trauma provided courage for us in our work. Witnessing helps make more witnessing. Dori Laub holds a special place in our minds and in this book. His work guided us. Kristopher Spring at Routledge believed in the project from the beginning and helped us along the way. His presence was essential during every phase of the project. We are so lucky that he has accompanied us on this journey. Marsha Hecht, our project editor, was invaluable in helping us bring this book to completion. Kathy Quakenbusch transcribed all of the interviews (Laub, Krasa, Richards, Staub) with diligence and accuracy. Tamar Schwartz worked to get the permissions for publishing all of the poems included in the book. Bruce Zimmerman worked on many of the photographs of artworks to have them reflect the importance of these records of witnessing. We are grateful to all of these people. The book would not have come into being without them.

Nancy R. Goodman and Marilyn B. Meyers

I have received love and support throughout this project. I am grateful to Louis Goodman, my husband, who believes in the book and in me. I thank my children and grandchildren for their existence in my life and the joy they give me: Elizabeth Goodman and David Brown and Ella, Isaiah, and Julian; Jennifer Goodman and Fred Yturralde and Kaia and Sophia. My mother and father, Mildred Clein Rosenthal and Robert H. Rosenthal, have always given me permission to learn—thank you. Diane Rosenthal, my sister, is there when I need her along with Dan Friedlander and their family: Michael and Lisa Friedlander with Jack and Adeline; David Friedlander and Jaqueline Schmidt. All of the Goodmans across all generations provide me with a village of family: William and June, Vivienne, Michael, Ana, Kelric, Lyssa, Jessica, Henry, Somers, Felicia, Helen, Daisy, Kitty, John, Douglas, Susan, Glen, Sasha, Yaniv, Dahlia, Rebecca, and Joshua.

I am so fortunate to have an enduring relationship with my friend and coeditor, Marilyn Meyers. You enrich my life every day. I thank my friend and colleague Arlene Kramer Richards for being with me and helping me understand deeply. Dori Laub provides inspiration in so many ways: his writing, the interview, receiving phone calls, and sharing his wisdom. I am deeply grateful to my analyst, Stanley Stern. Laurie Kaslove, Kerry Malawista, and Katalin Roth came and sat with me to go over drafts when I most needed it. I thank Paula Ellman, Harriet Basseches, Leslie Johnson, Henri Parens, Donna Blank, Raquel Berman, Gloria Burgess, Batya Monder, and Beth Reese for attending to me and my writing and validating my efforts. The courage and fortitude of patients reinforce for me the way pain can be felt, narrated, and lived out in the therapy, eventually leading to an ability to create life, both internally and in the world with others. It is not easy traveling through territories of terror, and I am so grateful for the accompaniment of others who have also been willing to know.

Nancy R. Goodman

It is almost impossible to know where to begin. I must express my gratitude to my husband, Alan, for his patience, forbearance, and support during this project. I know that I was preoccupied, and he understood that and believed in me throughout. My children, Linn and Eric, and Eric's wife Sabine, hold me in their minds in my personal and professional pursuits. My mother, father, and entire extended family have always believed in me. I have had an incredible gift in my life to be thought of as a person of value. My only regret is that neither of my parents is here to witness this book. My own history of Holocaust losses has been clarified for me in this work and leads me to be grateful to the memory and sad for the losses that family members and vast numbers of others signify.

Friends and colleagues were kind enough to read various drafts of my writing. Their responses were creative and helpful, but most of all, validating and supportive. Among those are Amy Antonelli, Sally Bloom-Feshbach, Kathy Camicia, Ann Devaney, Rona Eisner, Stephanie Green, Hallie Lovett, Joyce Lowenstein, Steve Schulman, Rosemary Segalla, Damon Silvers, Barbara Smilow, Mike Stadter, and Pat Strongin.

The privilege offered to me to enter into the private world of my patients is beyond words. Their pain and their triumphs inspire me and make me a fuller human being. I believe that this book is in large measure a product of those encounters over the past years.

None of this could have come to fruition without my dearest friend, colleague, sister I never had, fellow traveler and soul mate, Nancy Goodman. We shared laughter, tears, arguments, despair, and joy. We not only survived but we prevailed.

Marilyn B. Meyers

Contributors

Harriet I. Basseches, PhD, ABPP, FIPA, recently completed a four year term as a trustee of the International Psychoanalytic Association (IPA). She is a former president of the New York Freudian Society (NYFS), the Confederation of Independent Psychoanalytic Societies (CIPS), and the North American Psychoanalytic Societies Confederation (NAPsaC). She is a training and supervising analyst and on the permanent faculty of the NYFS. She is co-editor with Paula Ellman and Nancy Goodman of *Battling the Life and Death Forces of Sadomasochism: Theoretical and Clinical Perspectives* (Karnac, 2013). She maintains a private practice of psychoanalysis and psychoanalytical psychotherapy in Washington, D.C.

Elsa Blum, PhD, is a psychotherapist and artist with an interest in the psyche and in the world of art and images. One example of these combined interests is her co-authored book (with H. Blum and J. Amati-Mahler), *Psychoanalysis and Art: The Artistic Representation of the Parent/Child Relationship* (International Universities Press, 2004).

Bridget Conley-Zilkic, PhD, is research director for the World Peace Foundation at the Fletcher School at Tufts University. She previously worked as research director for the U.S. Holocaust Memorial Museum's Committee on Conscience. She led the Museum's research and projects on contemporary threats of genocide, including curating an interactive installation "From Memory to Action: Meeting the Challenge of Genocide Today." She received a PhD in comparative literature from Binghamton University in 2001 writing about cultural responses to humanitarian interventions in Bosnia and Haiti.

Paula L. Ellman, PhD, ABPP, is a training and supervising analyst in the New York Freudian Society, Washington Program, as well as an assistant professor of psychology at George Washington University's PsyD Program, a board member of the Confederation of Independent Psychoanalytic Societies and faculty of the New York Freudian Society. She has written and presented papers on listening, femininity and female psychology, enactment, and sadomasochism. Recent publications are "Enactment: Opportunity for Symbolizing Trauma" (Ellman & Goodman, 2012) in A. Frosch (Ed.), *Absolute Truth and Unbearable Psychic Pain: Psychoanalytic Perspectives on Concrete Experience* (Karnac, 2012) and *Battling the Life and Death Forces of Sadomasochism: Theoretical and Clinical Perspectives* (Karnac, 2013; Eds. with Harriet Basseches and Nancy Goodman). She has a private practice in psychoanalysis and psychotherapy in North Bethesda, Maryland and Washington, DC.

Susan S. Elmendorf, LICSW, BCD, has recently retired. She was a training and supervising analyst and a permanent faculty member of the Psychoanalytic Training Institute of the New York Freudian Society. She was also on the faculty of the Washington School of Psychiatry. She was a clinical social worker and psychoanalyst in private practice in Washington, DC, specializing in intensive individual therapies with adults.

Nancy R. Goodman, PhD, is a supervising and training analyst and permanent faculty member with the New York Freudian Society, Washington, DC Program, and the International Psychoanalytic Association. She writes on female development, analytic listening, Holocaust trauma and witnessing, film and psychoanalysis, enactments, and sadomasochism. Her most recent publications include "Enactment: Opportunity for Symbolizing Trauma" (Ellman & Goodman, 2012) in A. Frosch (Ed.), *Absolute Truth and Unbearable Psychic Pain: Psychoanalytic Perspectives on Concrete Experience* (Karnac, 2012) and "Nancy Goodman Wonders What Is Normal in Myth and Psychic Reality" (2010) in Moises Lemlij (Ed.), *IPA Electronic Newsletter,* December 2010. She is co-editor with Harriet Basseches and Paula Ellman of *Battling the Life and Death Forces of Sadomasochism: Theoretical and Clinical Perspectives* (Karnac, 2013). She maintains a full time psychoanalytic practice in Bethesda, Maryland.

Dr. George Halasz, MD, is a consultant child and adolescent psychiatrist and adjunct senior lecturer, School of Psychology and Psychiatry, Faculty of Medicine, Nursing and Health Sciences, Monash University in Australia. He has written extensively on the experience of the "second generation" of Holocaust survivors and is contributor to Kathy Grinblat's *Children of the Shadows: Voices of the Second Generation* (University of Western Australia Press, 2002). He has written and co-edited three books and a number of chapters and journal articles on a range of developmental and psychiatric disorders. He served on the editorial board of the *Australian and New Zealand Journal of Psychiatry* (1992-2004) and is currently on the editorial board of *Australian Psychiatry*. Since 2007 he has been on the Cunningham Dax Collection's Steering committee and working group for the art exhibition, "Out of the Dark: The Emotional Legacy of the Holocaust."

Geoffrey Hartman, PhD, is Sterling Professor Emeritus of English and Comparative Literature at Yale University, and was faculty advisor and project director of the Fortunoff Video Archive for Holocaust Testimonies, helping to bring it to a permanent residence at Yale University. He has written numerous books on topics ranging from criticism, texts, culture, deconstruction, poetry, formalism, Judaica, and the Holocaust, including *The Longest Shadow: In the Aftermath of the Holocaust* (University Press, 1996) and a memoir about his life as a scholar, *A Scholar's Tale: Intellectual Journey of a Displaced Child of Europe* (Fordham University Press, 2007).

Renée Hartman is a poet and an artist. A survivor of Bergen-Belsen, her recent book *Wounded Angels* (Porlock Press, 2007) contains poetry arising from her Holocaust experience and her ability to put deep feeling into words and imagery.

Elaine Neuman Kulp Shabad, PsyD, is a psychologist, poet, and painter. Her clinical work focuses on serving as a witness to unconscious and conscious hopelessness, anxiety, losses, and longings. She is in private practice in Chicago, specializing in the trauma of infertility struggles.

Dori Laub, MD, is a child survivor and a psychoanalyst dedicated to witnessing the Holocaust and other genocides. He has written over 50 articles related to witnessing, testimony and clinical experience with survivors and children of survivors of the Holocaust and other mass traumas, and is the co-author, with Shoshana Felman, of *Testimony: Crises of Witnessing in Literature, Psychoanalysis and History* (Routledge, 1992). He developed the first Holocaust video archives with Laurel Vlock in 1979 (now the Fortunoff Video Archive for Holocaust Testimonies at Yale University). In addition, Dr. Laub is the Deputy Director of Trauma Studies in the Genocide Studies Program at Yale University. He maintains a private practice in New Haven, Connecticut and in Middletown, Connecticut.

Clemens Loew, PhD, is a psychoanalyst and co-founder of the National Institute for the Psychotherapies, New York City, where he teaches and supervises and serves on the board of directors. He has published numerous articles and books on psychoanalytic work and his Holocaust experience. He is in private practice; he sees couples and individuals and has an interest in Holocaust survivors and their children. In addition, he has exhibited his photography and sculpture in New York City and New Jersey.

Gail Humphries Mardirosian, PhD, is professor in the Department of Performing Arts at American University in Washington, DC. She received a Fulbright Senior Scholar award (2008-2009) allowing her to pursue the performance of a recently rediscovered play, *The Smoke of Home.* Under her directorship, the play was performed in the barracks of Terezín, for the first time in the summer of 2009. She has directed over 135 plays and is the author of many articles that focus on the use of arts-based teaching/ learning as a mechanism for social justice and equity in the classroom.

Margit Meissner is a Holocaust survivor, born in Austria and raised in Prague. She escaped the Nazis via France and Spain and in 1941 came to the United States where she worked in the U.S. Office of War Information during WWII and was employed by the U.S. Army of Occupation in Nuremberg in 1947 to re-educate Nazi youth. She subsequently spent 20 years working for the Montgomery County, Maryland school board, spearheading the integration of handicapped children into the general education program, and is presently a volunteer translator and guide at the U.S. Holocaust Memorial Museum in Washington, DC. She is the author of *Margit's Story* (Schreiber, 2003), a memoir.

Marilyn B. Meyers, PhD, is on the faculty of the Washington School of Psychiatry, where she teaches and supervises in the postgraduate Clinical Program on Psychotherapy Practice. She is President of the Section on Couples and Families of the Division of Psychoanalysis (39) of the American Psychological Association. She has a longstanding interest in working with Holocaust survivors and their children. Her publications include "When the Holocaust Haunts the Couple: Hope, Guilt and Survival" in *Psychoanalytic Perspectives on Couple Work* (2005) and "Am I My Mother's Keeper? Certain Vicissitudes in the Mother–Daughter Relationship Concerning Envy" in *The Mother–Daughter Relationship* (Jason Aronson, 2008). In addition she has presented papers on the use of film to illustrate the aftermath of massive trauma and the inter-generational transmission of Holocaust trauma. She maintains a private practice in Bethesda, Maryland where she sees individuals and couples.

Henri Parens, MD, FACPsa, is Professor of Psychiatry at Thomas Jefferson University, training and supervising analyst (adult and child) at the Psychoanalytic Center of Philadelphia. He has authored over two hundred publications, including ten books and nine co-edited books, five scientific films, one documentary, and one television series for CBS (thirty–nine half-hour programs).The recipient of many honors, his principal research and prevention efforts include areas of development of aggression in early childhood, the prevention of violence and malignant prejudice and the prevention of experience-driven emotional disorders.

He developed the 4-volume set *Parenting for Growth*. Dr. Parens is a Holocaust survivor and has written a memoir, *Renewal of Life: Healing from the Holocaust* (Schreiber, 2004). His numerous books include *Handling Children's Aggression Constructively: Toward Taming Human Destructiveness* (Jason Aronson, 2010), *The Development of Aggression in Early Childhood* (Jason Aronson, 2007), and *The Unbroken Soul: Tragedy, Trauma, and Resilience* with Harold Blum and Salman Akhtar (Eds.), (Jason Aronson, 2008).

Arlene Kramer Richards, EdD, is a psychoanalyst and a poet. She is a training and supervising analyst with the New York Freudian Society and the International Psychoanalytic Association and Fellow of IPTAR. She is currently faculty at the NYFS and Tongji Medical College of Huazhong University of Science and Technology at Wuhan, China. Her psychoanalytic writings help clarify issues of female development, perversion, loneliness, and the internal world of artists and poets. Most recent publications include "Gambling and Death" in E. Ronis and L. Shaw (Eds.), *Greed, Sex, Money, Power and Politics* (IPPress, 2011) and "Little Boy Lost" in Anne Adelman and Kerry Malawista (Eds.), *The Bereaved Therapist: From the Faraway Nearby* (Columbia University Press, 2012). She recently published a book of poetry, *The Laundryman's Granddaughter: Poems by Arlene Kramer Richards* (IPPress, 2011) and a book of selected papers *Psychoanalysis: Listening to Understand: The Collected Papers of Arlene Kramer Richards,* Ed., Nancy Goodman (IPBooks, 2012). She is in private practice in New York City.

Arnold Richards, MD, is a training and supervising analyst at the New York Psychoanalytic Institute and on the faculty of Tongji Medical College of Huazhong University of Science and Technology at Wuhan, China. He was editor of the *Journal of the American Psychoanalytic Association (JAPA)* from 1994 to 2003 and founding editor of the *American Psychoanalyst*. He served as Chairman of the YIVO Institute of Jewish Research and presently serves on the board of directors. He has co-edited four major festschrifts (Brenner, Arlow, Bergman, and Etchegoyan) and has written more than one hundred articles. Most recently he edited *The Jewish World of Sigmund Freud* (McFarland Press, 2010). He was a recipient of the 2000 Sigourney Award and with Arlene Kramer Richards was honored by the Mental Health Division of the UJA in New York. He delivered the A. A. Brill Memorial Lecture of the New York Psychoanalytic Society and the 50th annual Leo Baeck Memorial Lecture. He organized the first Yiddish film festivals in New York City (1972 and 1973). Currently, Dr. Richards is Editor-in-Chief of www.InternationalPsychoanalysis.net

Sophia Richman, PhD, ABPP, is a psychoanalyst, painter, and writer. In addition to maintaining a private practice in New York and New Jersey, she is a supervisor at the New York University Postdoctoral Program in Psychotherapy and Psychoanalysis, a supervisor and training analyst at the Center for Psychotherapy and Psychoanalysis of New Jersey and a faculty member of the Stephen A. Mitchell Center for Relational Studies. Dr. Richman's memoir, *A Wolf in the Attic: The Legacy of a Hidden Child of the Holocaust* (Routledge, 2002), won the 2003 Award for Scholarship from the Jewish Women's Caucus of the Association for Women in Psychology. She has published a number of professional articles in the area of trauma and creativity and is currently working on a book titled *Mended by the Muse: Creative Transformations of Trauma* to be published by Routledge.

Katalin Eve Roth, JD, MD, is an internist and educator in Washington, D.C. She is a board certified specialist in geriatrics and palliative medicine at George Washington Medical Faculty Associates and is assistant professor of medicine at the George Washington School of Medicine and Health Sciences, where she is director of the Division of Geriatrics and Palliative Medicine and leads courses in medical ethics. Throughout her career she has been committed to physician involvement and advocacy for the health of communities and vulnerable populations. She is a member of the Asylum Network of Physicians for Human Rights and co-founded the GW Bread for the City Human Rights Clinic in Washington, DC in 2005. She currently serves as a volunteer physician and member of the board of directors of Bread for the City. She is also a physician volunteer with Somos Amigos Medical Missions on medical missions in the Dominican Republic.

Nina Shapiro-Perl, PhD, is an award winning film producer and anthropologist. She currently holds the position of Filmmaker-in-Residence at American University in Washington, DC. She has produced films that document the lives of working men and women, the unseen and unheard. She debuted her documentary film, *Through the Eye of the Needle: The Art of Esther Nisenthal Krinitz*, at the Washington Jewish Film Festival in December 2011 winning the Audience Favorite Documentary prize.

Myra Sklarew is professor emerita at American University in Washington, DC and former president of Yaddo Artist's Community. Early work at Yale University School of Medicine in frontal lobe function and memory has given root to a current project, "Holocaust and Construction of Memory." She has written many books of poetry including *Harmless* (Mayapple Press, 2010), *The Witness Trees* (Cornwall Books, 2000, 2008, a bilingual edition with Yiddish translation by poet David Wolpe), and *Lithuania: New & Selected Poems* (Azul Editions, 1995, 1997). She is also the author of *Over* *the Rooftops of Time: Jewish Stories, Essays, Poems* (SUNY Press, 2003) and with Bruce Sklarew, she co-edited *The Journey of Child Development: The Selected Papers of Joseph D. Noshpitz* (Routledge, 2010). Her honors include the PEN Syndicated Fiction Award and the National Jewish Book Council Award in Poetry.

Ervin Staub, PhD, is an emeritus professor of psychology at the University of Massachusetts, Amherst and founding director of its doctoral concentration in the psychology of peace and violence. He has won many awards and widespread recognition for his work and has written numerous books and hundreds of professional articles. He has worked on reconciliation in Rwanda, Burundi, and the Congo. His books include *The Roots of Evil: The Origins of Genocide and other Group Violence* (Cambridge University Press, 1989), *Overcoming Evil: Genocide, Violent Conflict, and Terrorism* (Oxford University Press, 2011), and *The Roots of Goodness: Inclusive Caring, Moral Courage, Altruism Born of Suffering and Active Bystandership* (Oxford University Press, 2012).

Introduction

Nancy R. Goodman and Marilyn B. Meyers

> I recognize three separate, distinct levels of witnessing in relation to the Holocaust experience: the level of being a witness to oneself within the experience, the level of being a witness to the testimonies of others, and the level of being a witness to the process of witnessing itself.
>
> **Dori Laub (1992, p. 75)**

In this book, we honor the power of witnessing and how it brings about space in the mind and between people for revealing trauma, pain, sorrow, endurance, and motivation. We bring the power of witnessing to the Holocaust to illustrate how remarkable it is when narrative and symbol are created to reveal truths of experience in the most awful of circumstances. We believe that in opening up the process of witnessing, we are helping to keep the knowledge of the Holocaust alive and learning to extend witnessing to the world of psychoanalytic treatments and to contemporary atrocities and genocides. The presentations by contributors demonstrate how the power of witnessing results in revelation and transformation. At all times, from the distant past to the present, we believe that anyone who bears witness has in mind a sense of an other who is not only willing to know but is also passionately wanting to know.

We have gathered together contributions from psychoanalysts, psychoanalytically oriented therapists, scholars, poets, filmmakers, and artists. Their commentaries are exquisitely personal and intimate. Each author makes contact with atrocity and with human courage and capacities. The authors stay as close as they can to knowing of the Shoah and other mass and individual terrors. They absorb, feel, and think about what has transpired and what is taking place within them. The chapters in the book demonstrate the depths of human experience and how to convey it to others. Reflections, descriptions, poetic narratives, and artwork are invitations to find the living mind that the power of witnessing makes possible.

The writing here will resonate in the minds of the readers who are willing to know about pain, grief, and fear. They will also discover the inspiration of belonging to a witnessing community. It is striking and exceptional to find the presence of unbearable truths and acts of witnessing capable of reaching one's heart. Hope, resilience, and courage reside in the power of witnessing that can be brought to the past and then be brought to the future to help prevent and curtail mass and individual trauma.

THE STRUCTURE OF THE BOOK

The book is divided into five parts: "A Triptych of the Power of Witnessing," "Reflections," "Reverberations," "Traces," and "Links."

A Triptych of the Power of Witnessing

In Chapter 1, Nancy Goodman gives definition to the way the power of witnessing works by showing how witnessing brings about knowing of what is often referred to as unknowable, the "tremendum" of the Shoah. Witnessing is presented as embedded in the intimate exchange between minds wanting to know. While trauma is always present, the process of witnessing brings about a "living surround" where symbolism emerges. An interview with Dori Laub about the inception of the Yale Video Archives of Holocaust Testimonies (now the Fortunoff Video Archive for Holocaust Testimonies at Yale University) is included. In Chapter 2, Marilyn Meyers presents historic and psychic timelines of witnessing, stressing the ways witnessing opens and closes over time. She traces the various forms that witnessing has taken from the beginning of the Nazi atrocities to the present. In the third chapter, Nancy develops the metaphor of the "Anti-Train," providing a symbol representing a place of containment and relationship with others from which the horror of the Nazi trains can become known. The Anti-Train provides a location for readers of this volume to gather together as witnesses. We welcome you.

Reflections

The contributors to this section all experienced the Holocaust as children and have been active witnesses of the Holocaust. They show here how the ability to reflect on their experiences continues to evolve.

Dori Laub writes about becoming a witness from early childhood, when he was caught up in the Holocaust with his mother and father in a concentration camp. He has relentlessly pursued witnessing ever since. He invites the reader to accompany him as he revisits early memories and the development of his professional involvement as a co-creator of the Yale Video Archives of Holocaust Testimonies and as a psychoanalyst treating and writing about trauma. His personal reflections are infused with the feeling inherent in being a lifelong witness carrying thousands of survival stories within him.

Geoffrey Hartman helped bring the Video Archives of Holocaust Testimonies to Yale University, where it has gained a permanent presence. He has had an intimate relationship to the archives since its inception. As a scholar of "texts," he here gets inside the testimonial event, revealing its potency. He describes the way the survivor is part of the audience, the need for a testimonial alliance, the spirit of the interviewing, and the way showing videotaped testimony lessens the risk of "secondary trauma."

Henri Parens reflects on the very personal experience of writing his memoir. He began telling his story as he turned 70, which coincided with the 60th anniversary of his mother's deportation to Auschwitz. In this chapter, he reveals how he communicates to family and young people about the Holocaust. In his psychoanalytic work, he has devoted his life to the study of resilience to trauma and aggression in children. He brings wisdom born of his experience to this piece.

Sophia Richman describes how writing her memoir of being a hidden child became a crucially important way for her to find her voice and be a witness to herself. During her time in hiding, she was instructed to be silent for fear of revealing her father's presence, "the wolf in the attic." She used her creative talent as a child to conjure up an imaginary friend, a witness of her own making. Many years later, this act of writing led to further reflection and exploration for her and her understanding of the psychoanalytic therapeutic encounter.

Reverberations

In this section, we have contributions directly addressing the ways in which the trauma of the Holocaust is transmitted across time and across generations. Massive trauma, such as the Holocaust, leads inevitably to reverberations that are both within the individual psyche and shared with others. Our contributors to this section include survivors, their children, and other family members.

Myra Sklarew tells us about her remarkable relationship with her cousin Leiser, who survived the atrocities in Lithuania perpetrated by the Nazis. She and Leiser maintained a connection through phone calls for 9 years (1999–2008) until his death. They sometimes spoke as often as nine times a day. Myra was in Washington, D.C., and Leiser was in Zurich, Switzerland. She was his very passionately present witness, and he became able to speak to her about what was deep in his soul. Artwork by Leiser's wife, Ada, is generously offered in this piece.

George Halasz has struggled to face the impact that the trauma suffered by his family in the Holocaust has had on him. He writes about "relational trauma" and his efforts to understand his relationship with his mother through her video testimony. He adapted techniques used in mother–infant studies to examine his facial and nonverbal responses. As a psychiatrist interested in making contact with the traumas of his patients, he here focuses on the experience of fragmentation and dissociation and what he calls "reparative moments" when in the presence of trauma.

Renée Hartman returned to Bergen-Belsen in 2009, the concentration camp where she and her sister, who was deaf, had been imprisoned as children. She reveals in her writing the many levels of experience called up by this trip. She reminds us that today there are no names to go with the photos of the children, nor of all who are buried in the mass graves at Bergen-Belsen. She describes her memories of the past, the present-day landscape at the camp, and a dream about her mother.

Katalin Roth memorializes her father, Miklós. She writes of the reverberations of his Holocaust experience in Hungary on her and her children. She describes moments of life before, during, and after the Holocaust as the family made a new life in the United States. Her father's resilience and love of his family are felt. There are moments of poignant remembering and discovery of secrets that carry pain. The connections made across generations are revealed through her narrative.

Margit Meissner, at the age of 16, rode a bicycle out of Paris to escape the Nazis. She recollects her life as an adolescent who was becoming a young woman in the context of needing to survive. Margit's writing captures the way she felt then and now. She describes some of her current experiences as a guide at the United States Holocaust Memorial Museum. When called on, she travels to teach about the Holocaust.

Marilyn Meyers writes about the Terezín Ghetto, the *Defiant Requiem*, and the centrality of music to lift the spirits of the prisoners in that terrible place. Life in Terezín symbolizes the creative forces that helped to counteract the horrors of the Holocaust. The interview with Edgar and Hana Krasa, both survivors of Terezín, serves as a centerpiece for this chapter. Edgar and Hana talked with us for hours and showed us the room in their home filled with artwork from friends who were witnesses while in the ghetto.

Elaine Neuman Kulp Shabad shares a poem that she wrote about her Uncle Joe, a survivor of Auschwitz. The poem illustrates her admiration of this man, who in a brief moment acted to escape the Nazis by a clever turn. Her commentary about the poem and a painting done to honor her mother add to our understanding of the impact of these traumatic losses on her family.

Clemens Loew writes of his deeply felt relationship with his father. Feelings about his father came alive as he sculpted his image. He last saw his father at the age of 4 as his father was taken to Auschwitz, never to return. He acts as witness to his own creation of a work of art to memorialize his father.

Marilyn Meyers tells about her family member, Shira, whose story of survival was told in whispers when Marilyn was a child. The story has been seared in her mind as one of mystery and terror. Shira, born in 1942, was given to another family, who cared for her as their own as her parents were deported to Auschwitz. After the war, her uncle located her and took her from the rescuers. The story is told from the perspective of a witness to a nonwitnessed event.

Traces

In this section, we provide contributions that emphasize and highlight the use of art forms and how they carry intense recognition of the horrors of the Holocaust. The chapters present poetry, needlework, photography, film, and theater. These forms of symbolization allow for knowing that which is beyond comprehension in words alone. This section also honors the destruction of Yiddish culture and the poets and writers who were murdered during the Nazi genocide.

Arlene Kramer Richards writes about Holocaust poetry and her responses to it. She brings together poems that affect her deeply as they pierce the darkness of the Holocaust. The poems and her writing give evidence of the way despair can be symbolized to reveal the human heart. The poets are witnesses, Arlene is a witness to them, and her writing brings us into witnessing the endurance of poetry.

Nina Shapiro-Perl tells us about making the film *Through the Eye of the Needle: The Art of Esther Nisenthal Krinitz*. The artwork shown in this chapter represents Esther serving as her own witness to her journey of terror and survival. These stunningly beautiful needlework panels are honored by Shapiro-Perl in her quest to create a film about Esther and her art in order to be a witness to the witness and to bring this work to a wider audience.

Elsa Blum brings us witnessing through the lens of her camera and her reflections on what was captured in the imagery. She uses her artistic eye and her inner eye to reveal the powerful presence of the Monument to the Murdered Jews of Europe in the center of Berlin. The monument itself is an act of witnessing, and her exquisite photographs show the mix of life and death that exist when memorial monuments are erected.

Nancy Goodman writes of the lessons she learned in her study of sequencing and imagery in the film *Schindler's List*. Nancy describes the way Spielberg used the camera to change focus between scenes of overwhelming anomic trauma and scenes that allow affects to be felt. It is these oscillations that permit the viewer of the film to absorb enough of the trauma to bring about and maintain the capacity to be a witness.

Gail Humphries Mardirosian writes of her commitment to theater as a conduit for giving voice to trauma. She emphasizes the transformational power of theater as an avenue to seeing and knowing trauma. Specifically, she shares her experience of directing the recently discovered play, *The Smoke of Home*, which had been written in the Terezín Ghetto. The theater in the confines of the Terezín Ghetto provided sustenance to the spirits and souls of the prisoners.

Arnold Richards writes about the destruction of the Yiddish culture. He memorializes the murdered poets and writers by listing their names so we can know of their existence. Both the writers and their audience were annihilated. He uses the image of the "holes in the doorposts," where mezuzahs used to be, to represent the absence of the Yiddish way of life that resulted from the Holocaust. He writes about his childhood and family and how the Shoah became known to him.

Links

We conclude the book with essays that bring the power of witnessing into other realms. Our study of witnessing in relation to the Holocaust helps define the witnessing function that takes place in psychoanalytic psychotherapies. Furthermore, the power of witnessing is linked to witnessing of contemporary mass trauma. Witnessing helps ensure that genocide and atrocity cannot be denied, and that there are ways to identify the march to genocide and to interrupt it. Our intent is to emphasize that apprehending the Holocaust helps the mind become open to other individual and mass traumas.

Marilyn Meyers brings the concepts of witnessing the Holocaust to clinical work with trauma. She reviews the development of the concept of trauma, including the evolution of the identification of war trauma, post-traumatic stress disorder, and clinical concepts of working with trauma. She utilizes a model for "knowing" and "not-knowing" as a framework for working with psychic trauma. In her vivid clinical material, she shows how trauma gets into the mind and how therapeutic work takes place.

Nancy Goodman, Harriet Basseches, Paula Ellman, and Susan Elmendorf formed a study group to understand their psychoanalytic work with patients immediately following the terrorist attacks of 9/11. Living in the Washington, D.C., area lent a particular sense of imminent danger that they and their patients felt. Under the press of trauma, images of the Holocaust often appeared in their patients' minds and in their minds. The group functioned as a witnessing group helping to contain their fears and their therapeutic work.

Bridget Conley-Zilkic brings our exploration of the power of witnessing full circle as she includes the struggle to link the uniqueness of the Holocaust with other genocidal atrocities. She curated the exhibit "From Memory to Action" at the Holocaust Museum. She writes poignantly of her witnessing of genocide and atrocity and emphasizes the essential nature of making an emotional connection that she hopes will lead to positive action.

Nancy Goodman and Marilyn Meyers interviewed Ervin Staub, who has written extensively about how to recognize the evil of genocide and mass trauma and how to prevent and overcome it. His ideas make a profound link between the power of witnessing and learning about contemporary atrocities. In this interview, he shared his ideas on bystandership and his own personal experience during the Holocaust. Active bystanders, his nanny Macs and Raoul Wallenberg, risked their lives to bring survival to him and his family. He discussed many of his concepts and reflected on how being a hidden child affected him.

REFERENCE

Laub, D. (1992). An event without a witness: Truth, testimony, and survival. In S. Felman & D. Laub, *Testimony: Crises of witnessing in literature, psychoanalysis, and history* (pp. 75–92). New York: Routledge.

Part I

A Triptych of the Power of Witnessing

Chapter 1

The Power of Witnessing

Nancy R. Goodman

INTRODUCTION

Witnessing is a powerful force that allows massively traumatic experiences to become known and communicated. In this chapter, I describe how witnessing of the Holocaust takes place to give definition to the way a witnessing process develops and evolves. Contact is made with the Holocaust and with the remarkable ways Holocaust survivors, and all who witness, have been able to represent the horror to others. In particular, survivors' affirmations of their humanity are so moving and impressive that they create in us a determination to know more about how witnessing takes place even though there will be pain endured in doing so. When concentration camps were liberated, the world learned about genocide and unimaginable inhumanities. It is the power of witnessing that is able to break through the barriers erected in the mind when facing fear and terror and then is able to engender ways to convey what took place to others. Over and over again, the essence of witnessing is found to rest in a connection between people. Many survivors have recorded how they "lived to speak." They kept alive a sense that someone would be able to listen. Without witnessing, the most terrible of events can remain untold, leaving a place of negation and 'nothing' in the mind and in the historic record. When the psyche is overwhelmed with helplessness, the story may remain unsymbolized and fragmented until a witness is present who says, "I want to know." Then, the power of witnessing helps give birth to the narrative.

There are important lessons to be learned from the study of witnessing of the Holocaust. Knowing how witnessing of the Holocaust takes place helps fortify desire to witness other genocides and mass traumas. When a blind spot in the eye (and I) is constructed to hide from the inhumanities of the Holocaust, it is also likely to operate in obfuscating knowledge of other mass atrocities and traumas. It is the power of witnessing that can overcome the terror of seeing and allow blindness to diminish. As a psychoanalyst, I am aware that the traumatic places in my patients' minds, and in all human beings, are better attended to by understanding the power of witnessing and the way it functions. As Marilyn and I read each contribution to this volume, we learned more and more about the ways witnessing elicits meaningful, direct, thoughtful, and poetic articulation of human experiences of rupture and terror. These examples of witnessing reinforce a belief that the "nothing" of mass trauma and of moments of trauma can become important stories for both internal communication and dialogue with others.

Dori Laub, a psychoanalyst, child survivor, and co-founder of the Yale Video Archives of Holocaust Testimonies (now the Fortunoff Video Archive for Holocaust Testimonies), has written extensively about Holocaust trauma and the way it becomes known through testimony and in psychoanalytic therapies (1992a, 1992b, 1998, 2005; Laub & Auerhahn, 1989, 1993). By welcoming the objective and subjective facts of what has transpired, it is the presence of the witness that is the essential element for bringing the unspeakable into existence. Those who study mass trauma, annihilation terror, abuse, and neglect show repeatedly the importance of establishing a safe relationship for bringing nascent trauma stories into being (Bohleber, 2010; Caruth, 1995, 1996; Davies & Frawley, 1994; Herman, 1992; Laub, 1992a). Once telling takes place, the trauma and the way it has settled in the mind can be reflected on. The story can then evolve, bringing depth to witnessing within oneself and with others.

HOW THE POWER OF WITNESSING WORKS: IMPORTANCE OF SPACE, HOLDING, CONTAINMENT, AND GRIEF

Throughout this project, I have been thinking about how to depict the way the power of witnessing makes it possible to tell about the very most terrible of events. How does the place of too much become titrated enough to become a spoken place? The idea of space, space within the mind and space between people, is particularly important for comprehending what brings about movement in the mind. A view opens because someone else is willing to see as well.

The contact made during witnessing seems resonant with what occurs between a mother and her infant when continuous interactions accrue over time (Beebe, 1986; Beebe, Knoblauch, Rustin, & Sorter, 2005; Schore, 1994; Stern, 1985). Daniel Stern (1985) states: "The central idea [is] that internal objects are constructed from repeated, relatively small interactive patterns derived from the microanalytic perspective. ... They are constructed from the patterned experience of self in interaction with another" (p. xv). The power of witnessing exists in this fearless willingness to know and to be known as it is transmitted back and forth. It gains its potency through the dynamics of a system of micro-communications engendering new possibilities. I believe these micro-communications take place continually between analyst and patient in psychoanalytic treatment as unconscious fantasy, frightening wishes, imagined punishments, and overwhelming affects are discovered. In the intimate process of the dialogue, the type of holding defined by Winnicott (Abram, 1996; Winnicott, 1956, 1971) and the containment and alpha functioning (taking in and processing) defined by Bion (1962, 1984) come to exist, making inroads into what could not previously be known. For Winnicott, holding could lead to development of a transitional space, a play space. I see the type of space created by witnessing to be where description, metaphor, and reflection arise. Intense affects, terror, hatred, shame, aloneness, and grief can begin to be felt, named, and shared.

DEAD SPACE AND LIVING SURROUND

I present here a picture I have come to see in my mind of the way the power of witnessing opens space. Bohleber (2010) points out that we need to resort to metaphor when attempting to knit together meaning where it has been disrupted, as with the Holocaust. I develop a dynamic metaphor made up of two elements: the dead space and the living surround. In choosing the term *dead space* to refer to the traumatized place, I am influenced by Green's (1993) concept of the "dead mother," the mother who does not respond and places in the baby an internal sense of a "no one," a painful place of nonexistence rather than an internal aliveness.

The Holocaust places a dead place in the individual and in humanity. This traumatic place is so dark and dense. It has no pulsation, no breathing, no flexibility. Sometimes, it is solid like cement, separate from all else that is alive in the mind; sometimes, it oozes out and invades other places in the mind. Sometimes, it has narrative, or at least fragments of narrative, but cannot be told as if the telling itself would wound self and other too deeply; sometimes, it is completely unsymbolized. The density I am imagining as a defining feature of the dead space indicates that both the horrific known and the too much unknown are present. This is how I have come to think of the way huge, unremitting traumas of all kinds get into the mind. It is in the minds of survivors, and it will likely exist as a smaller point of dead space in the minds of even distant witnesses, including the readers of this volume.

In turn, I have come to think of the power of witnessing as the force providing a clearing away and lighting for a living surround near the dead space where an opening, the new space, develops and takes hold. There may be pathways to the edge of the silent or actively volcanic abyss. My favored imagining is of a circular surround, first narrow and over time widening and perhaps, here or there, penetrating, mining, and refining the dead space. There can now be communication between the trauma and the living mind. Whatever form it takes, it begins with someone claiming loudly and forcibly, "Let us visit this place together." In this way, the dense overgrowth blocking access to the dead space is trampled, becoming a place for growth and fertilization of mind with narrative, building of monuments, and lasting conversation both with others and within oneself. As more knowing takes place, there is expansion of the living surround and in turn further penetration of the dead space. The dead space and the living surround inform each other.

Sometimes, there is an attempt to compartmentalize who trembles from knowing the Holocaust—just survivors and their children, just Jewish people—but the Holocaust belongs to all of humanity and will arouse fear in all. The power of witnessing also belongs to all who can find the inspiration of the living surround. When there is a living surround, the mind can make a story, describe, and even over time reflect on what has taken place and how it resides in the psyche. Reflection is important. It is a developmental landmark for the child to look in the mirror and to see "that is me." The child is realizing something about a separate and individual identity. When the trauma becomes a witnessed trauma, it can be mirrored back, becoming a more recognized part of oneself. Around the dead space, survivors, writers, scholars, and artists do think and find ways to bring impressions and accounts to us. These may be in the form of descriptions of gruesome atrocities and through constructions of evocative, often-heartbreaking imagery. This is what can happen when the power of witnessing is active. Throughout this book, we find this duality repeatedly—there is the too much of absolute trauma, and there is the finding of words and symbols when witnessing takes place that brings the horror, learning, and the human spirit into being.

Does the traumatic place become so infused with light that it ceases to exist? I think not. In fact, the desire to eradicate it entirely, and the fantasy that it can disappear, may be a kind of identification with the perpetrator who would hide a cemetery, as if all the death never happened. Witnessing confirms that it happened, it must not be eradicated, there is a way to let others know, and there is always grief. Grief is one of the ingredients making up the substance of the dead space that needs to be released. I think that so much that is evocative in the contributions in this book—poetry, reflections, art forms, scholarship—arrives as the witness producing them passes through private grief and horror. This grief is as eternal as grief can be. It is extraordinary. It contains an amount of sadness equal to the number of stars in the Milky Way. It can be mourned, maybe, one star at a time. I think that in what I am calling the living surround grief can become a felt grief. This grief feels awful, and it feels affirming. Grief itself can release the poetry needed to express the feel of what has happened. Once there is this opening, opening to the grief of others also expands. The Holocaust can never be transformed—but through the power of witnessing, the mind gains expressiveness and greater capacity to see contemporary mass and individual trauma and the desire to intervene. It is worth enduring the suffering and hard work of witnessing to make the living surround because it is here the mind can think and symbolize and feel and where others can be invited also to witness. It is here that contact is made with oneself and with others.

THE HOLOCAUST: CAN IT BE KNOWN?

The Holocaust, as an entity, is itself too hot a burning fire, too cold a frozen place, and too threatening to sanity to take in completely. I choose to use metaphoric language because this is often the only way to enter the world of horror. During the Nazi reign in Germany (1933–1945), 6 million Jewish people were slaughtered in a genocide and millions of others as well. Techniques of destruction were developed that defy ideas of humanity. It is almost impossible to truly think about one extermination camp, one furnace, one mother or father being torn from each other and their children, killing of babies, unbearable thirst and hunger, instances of abject humiliation, and every moment of the extermination of 6 million individuals and the attempts to eradicate their culture as well. Contained in the Holocaust are methods of madness and proclamations distorting what is rational and intelligible. It is only through bringing witnessing to this "tremendum" that the horror of the Holocaust takes enough shape to be at least partially known and communicated to others. Ervin Staub (see Chapter 26) is a persistent believer that the Holocaust, other genocides, and all mass killings can be and must be approached for study. His books contain evidence of the importance of witnessing to define *The Roots of Evil* (1989) and the possibility of *Overcoming Evil* (2010).

The Holocaust is often referred to as unthinkable because it requires bringing such devastation into one's mind and into the minds of others. It is so large, massive, and destructive. Basically, there is no template for the totality of what took place. In our interview with Laub (2008), he used ideas of a "black hole," "the core," and the "empty circle" to represent what is at the center of the survivor's experience: "From the survivor perspective [the core] is fraught with terror and with loss and sadness, and this may be a little bit insurmountable, but mostly it is being surmounted. But there will be always a circle, an empty circle somewhere." Grotstein (1990) writes about patients living with equivalents of the "black hole" phenomenon he relates to analytic despair. He defines the central element to be meaninglessness. "The absence of the 'floor' of meaningfulness exposes the 'black hole'" (p. 382). In my way of thinking, the dead space at the center can breathe just a little bit once it has been witnessed and in many ways must also remain as a monument to the horror that has transpired.

TRAUMA

It is deeply frightening to see and feel the tortuous scenes that were perpetrated on the Jewish population of Europe by the Nazis. There is always trauma in this territory of reckoning. Facing trauma is difficult; facing Holocaust trauma is intensely difficult. Psychoanalysts refer to trauma as "psychic helplessness," a state of being completely overwhelmed. Trauma hurts so much—it entails experiences of shock, a breaking through of a usual ego barrier, altered perceptions, affect overload, a sense of fragmentation, depersonalization, and dysregulation (A. Freud, 1967; S. Freud, 1896, 1919; Herman, 1992; Krystal, 1978; Tarentelli, 2003; van der Kolk, McFarlane, & Weisaeth, 2007). Color, size, space, and sense of time may appear altered, surreal, foggy, compressed, or expanded. Sound may be suspended or cacophonous. Psychic helplessness and annihilation anxiety (Hurvich, 2003, 2011) can be accompanied by the sense of dissolving and eternally falling. The fearful images and fantasies in the intrapsychic world of wishes and fears no longer have any boundary with the external world of terror. The external too much has crashed through, and now the internal might not be contained. Catastrophe seems a certainty.

There is psychological impact as well for those who come to know the traumatic through witnessing. This is known as secondary trauma, vicarious trauma (McCann & Pearlman, 1990), or countertransference to the traumatic and will likely take place as the reader is drawn into the pages of this book. There is resonance to the trauma being witnessed. This is inevitable. Mastering and symbolizing what is felt is reassuring that one is courageous and that the mind functions. Empathy creates a sense of being in touch with others. There may be reviving of one's own traumatic experiences that now can be recognized, put into words, and worked through. Being determined to witness and know is hard work. The receiving of the transmission of the traumatic experience and its sequelae include activation of grief and loss. This is true for all who are willing to witness. It is inevitable to be anxious when witnessing mass trauma as it is passed from one person to the other (Apprey, 2003, 2006; Faimberg, 2005; Kogan, 1995, 2007). There is also something remarkable about being able to receive these most human of stories and to honor that they have happened and deserve to be known.

INSPIRATION FROM THOSE WHO WITNESS

Survivors demonstrate that places of activity and discovery are very much alive in their minds along with their traumatic truths. Very simply, this is inspirational. Many survivors of the Holocaust, and those who study the Holocaust, narrate, symbolize, and represent the intimate knowledge of horrors that lives within them. It is not an illness or a pathology to be a survivor and to have awful rememberings inside along with resilience. It is not shameful. It is what happens when mass murder, atrocity, abuse, and neglect take place and affect real people. Survivor testimonies are sometimes raw descriptions of atrocity, depravity, death, and dying. Memoirs tell the story and reflect on the meaning it has attained in one's life. Survivors of the Holocaust lead the way by showing how we can feel and think. If it cannot get in, it cannot be thought about, digested as true, and then used to help arouse desire to be watchful and prevent a repetition of it.

Each person who is willing to live with knowing of the Holocaust signals the possibility of witnessing to others. The power of witnessing is then transmitted from one to another. The transmission of this possibility of mind becomes stamped in the mind so that other mass traumas and individual traumas will not be denied. This is the powerful force of witnessing, bringing about the possibility of returning structure of thought and meaning to the mind after it has been so annihilated.

ACTS OF WITNESSING

From witnessing of the testimonial events of others, including those of the authors in this book, it becomes clear that a witnessing process can be established. When Renée Hartman (Chapter 10) responded to our invitation to write for the book, she told me that her husband, Geoffrey Hartman (Chapter 5), had accepted an invitation to speak at a Holocaust conference at Bergen-Belsen. She had not previously considered returning to the concentration camp where she and her sister had been imprisoned. She told me: "I will go with him. I cannot let him go alone." The simple statement, "I cannot let him go alone," produced such deep feeling in me, and still does. Renée held Geoffrey in her mind so completely, with empathy for her husband and for all who "went alone." She allowed herself to accompany him on a return to "her" concentration camp and then to write about it for this book. This is witnessing in the fullest way possible.

In Berlin at the International Psychoanalytic Congress in 2007, I attended a panel on the topic of children and grandchildren of both Holocaust survivors and Nazi perpetrators. The cases and situations discussed were compelling engendering personal stories from those in the audience. A young man stood up and told how his parents had caused him distress and pain by the way they dealt with their Shoah experience. Henri Parens (Chapter 6) rose to speak in the front of the room and faced the audience, stating: "I am one of those parents whose Holocaust experience has burdened his sons. I apologize to the children of survivors for the pain we have brought into your lives." The entire audience breathed differently when he made this simple and direct acknowledgment, and many allowed tears to flow as he brought empathy to all who come after the "parents" who lived through the annihilating. Parens (2004) considers this "bringing of pain" to be an inevitable outcome and emotional truth of being a survivor parent.

These two examples show the centrality of an empathic connection when witnessing takes place. Once there is "a witnessed event," it can be visited by others and witnessed further. Our contributors provide evidence of this in all of their writings as they revisit and reflect on their own Holocaust experience or visit the experience of others bringing it to us.

THE UNWITNESSED EVENT: ANNIHILATION OF MEANING

There is a particular annihilating force when others are present and do not acknowledge the inhumanity in front of them. This creates the "unwitnessed event." Laub (1992b) sees the way that the Holocaust went unwitnessed as a basic aspect of the breach of trust in the world that took place. I turn to a variety of sources on the Holocaust to depict the full meaning of the unwitnessed event. A moment of trauma is intensified and perhaps even petrified when there is decimation of a sense of being within reach of a helping other. A major scarring that is placed in the mind is not only the absence of others but also the knowledge that the others who were there would not respond. This type of absence is perhaps the most untenable aspect of traumatic experience, causing complete rupture in belief in a world where one matters and is recognized. Many of my therapy patients have this wound from the awful moments when they came to realize this particular type of absence in relation to their parents. When we speak of genocide, this includes a recognition that one's family, entire social system, and culture were also allowed to be annihilated (Richards, see Chapter 22).

Inactions of others who appear to be present but have turned away define the position of the passive bystander (Staub, 1989, 2011; see Chapter 26). Staub (1989) recounts an incident that emphasizes the lack of active bystandership in relation to the events of the Holocaust. Protests were organized in Germany to fight the policy of euthanasia of those considered less than pure, including children, elderly, and the mentally ill. "Members of the Catholic Church, relatives of victims, and other Germans spoke out. … After more than a year of rising public clamor and 70,000 to 100,000 dead, the program was discontinued. Few voices, however, were raised against the mistreatment of Jews" (p. 125). Knowing that there was such little protest against increasingly destructive policies against the Jewish citizenry of Germany and then Europe claims the Holocaust as historically and shockingly unwitnessed. The results of the struggle to establish a witnessing process are all the more profound because of the previous absence.

Wiesenthal (1969) describes what he felt when the eye of the onlooker held hate:

> You could read on the faces of the passersby that we were written off as doomed. The people of Lemberg had become accustomed to the sight of tortured Jews and they looked at us as one looks at a herd of cattle being driven to the slaughterhouse. At such times, I was consumed by a feeling that the world had conspired against us and our fate was accepted without a protest, without a trace of sympathy. (p. 13)

In his book *Neighbors: The Destruction of the Jewish Community in Jedwabne, Poland* (2001), Jan Gross presents an example of the specific betrayal of breaking the belief that one's suffering matters to others. He brings us starkly to the truths of how "one day, in July 1941, half of the population of a small East European town murdered the other half—some 1600 men, women, and children" (p. 7). The last group of Jews was sealed in a barn, which was then set on fire while others watched. (The word *Holocaust* is synonymous with fire; in Greek, *hólos* refers to "whole" and *kaustós* refers to "burnt.") There is now in the mind the wrenching truth that the others, once neighbors, deadened their eyes and deafened their ears.

RECIPROCITY OF MINDS: CONCEPTUALIZING THE POTENT PROCESS OF WITNESSING

Each and every act of witnessing is vitalizing as it breaks through a wall of traumatic helplessness and silence. Being able to see and know what happened to individuals feels respectful, courageous, and as one of our contributors, Myra Sklarew (Chapter 8) stated to us, "a privilege." As a teller and listener engage, a place is made for the story to evolve with the knowledge that each will feel deep emotion and be vulnerable. The witness to the original witness sends a signal, conscious and unconscious, that he or she is ready to receive the story and all that will be awakened. It is this reciprocity of minds that makes the narrative appear and makes it possible to return to it repeatedly over time. It is important to acknowledge that there will be moments of turning away and losing each other. There is also a feeling of discovery and conquest as the story is told. According to Laub (1992a) "re-externalization of the event can occur and take effect only when one can articulate and *transmit* the story, literally transfer it to another outside oneself and then take it back again, inside" (p. 69, emphasis in original). It is in this reciprocity of minds, receiving and transmitting, that symbolization is birthed to exist now with the shattering that had taken place.

Laub (1992a) describes the listener as "implicitly" saying: "For this limited time, throughout the duration of the testimony, I'll be with you all of the way, as much as I can. I want to go wherever you go, and I'll hold and protect you along the journey" (p. 70). In my understanding, the "with" of the witnessing relationship then allows fluctuations to take place between the nothingness of being overwhelmed and the something of a valued and transmittable narrative. There is now someone alongside of when there was "no one." There is room for what Laub calls "the nonmetaphorical" (p. 70) statements of actualities. The process takes place within a "felt" representation in which the receiver of the traumatic story is alive and wanting and ready. I also know from therapeutic work with patients that all the intrapsychic layers of feelings and fantasies about the trauma become more conscious as the story develops. For the second generation, the sadness for the parent's trauma and the hatred of the existence of the trauma can be narrated as well.

Laub (1992a) underscores how

> bearing witness to a trauma is, in fact, a process that includes the listener. For the testimonial process to take place, there needs to be a bonding, the intimate and total presence of an *other*—in the position of one who hears ... the witnesses are talking *to somebody*: to somebody they have been waiting for for a long time. (pp. 70–71, emphasis in original)

Being a witness implies that one is ready to take on this knowing of the importance of the victim "having waited a long time," with all of its conscious and unconscious implications of who and what has been missing for so long. In personal communications to us, Laub sees the witness as "passionate" in willingness to know. The witnessing process is thus dependent on the hearer's readiness and continued presence. Such a witnessing process can be actualized, for example, in psychoanalytic treatments and in the video archive format. Development of an internal representation of "someone wanting to know" allows a symbolizing capacity to develop within one's psyche and with others. This may lead as well to discovery of how desymbolizing has entered defensive usage in regard to intrapsychic conflicts as if one does not have a right to deep passions and hatreds and must erase them before they can fully exist.

The feel of the traumatic is likely to be woven into witnessing itself. There is always enactment as well as narrative, especially as something traumatic becomes symbolized. The traumatic story and all the fantasies gathered around it become visible and defined by first appearing in interactions that become named (Ellman & Goodman, 2012; Frosch, 2012; Kogan, 2007; Loewald, 1975). The way of telling, writing, or representing may bring disruption and fragmentation. Langer (1991), who has studied the Fortunoff Video Archive for Holocaust Testimonies, notes that there are times when the process both breaks down and unfolds. The sense of being accompanied is the element helping to knit back together a place for return and evolution of communication. This is how the process begins and is kept going during testimonial events. In his book *Holocaust Testimonies: The Ruins of Memory* (1991), Langer presents a conceptualization of memory attempting to capture the many levels of revelation he observed. There is never one state of self or of mind taking place when the real survivor speaks to the interviewer, the camera, and the future audiences who will watch the video. He writes of "deep memory," "anguished memory," "humiliated memory," "tainted memory," and "unheroic memory." In his descriptions of the person who is testifying and in the witnesses, he finds evidence of the "double existence" and "double reality." He discovers that "several currents flow at differing depths in Holocaust testimonies" (p. xi). The moments of "unshielded truth" he witnessed brought him to use the language of Blanchot (1986) that remembering "falls outside of memory." He describes moments that "pierced the skin of memory" and here says he had been influenced by the writing of Delbo (1995). For Langer, all of these forms of memory and remembering are found in the video testimonies, and I postulate are true in all witnessing.

THE HISTORIC AND EVOLVING CONCEPT OF WITNESS IN HOLOCAUST STUDIES AND IN PSYCHOANALYSIS

In its most basic definition, a witness is someone who is present for an event and can then testify to what has taken place. The word *witness* has been used by scholars, archivists, and memoirists of the Holocaust. It sometimes appears in the phrase of "bearing witness" or referenced in the language of survivors giving of testimony. For example, Des Pres (1976), in his book *The Survivor: An Anatomy of Life in the Death Camps*, emphasizes that survivors speak of wanting to live in order to tell what was happening and not let the truth die. In his book *Survival in Auschwitz: The Nazi Assault on Humanity* (1958/1996), Primo Levi described his desire to speak of his concentration camp experience in the following way: "The need to tell our story to 'the rest,' to make 'the rest' participate in it, had taken on for us, before our liberation and after, the character of an immediate and violent impulse, to the point of competing with our other elementary needs. The book has been written to satisfy this need: first and foremost, therefore, as an interior liberation" (p. 9). The use of "our" and "us" helps us understand how he managed not to be completely alone. He never lost the idea that there was someone to receive his story, and indeed the Russian liberators almost immediately asked him and his ever-present friend and fellow scientist, Leonardo de Benedetti, to record what they could in the *Auschwitz Report* (2006).

The historian Christopher Browning, in his book *Collected Memories: Holocaust History and Postwar Testimony* (2003), refers to "the emergence of "Holocaust consciousness" and the construction of the concept of the "Holocaust survivor" as distinct from the undifferentiated mass of camp victims" (p. 38). We see the terms *witness* and *testimony* coming from the individualizing of Holocaust survivors, each with an important personal story and often one they wanted to bring to the world through active witnessing. In their book *Bearing Witness: A Resource Guide to Literature, Poetry, Art, Music, and Videos by Holocaust Victims and Survivors* (2002), Rosen and Apfelbaum recognize that their 195 pages of examples of witnessing are daily augmented by more memoirs, works of art, and video archives. In her book, *The Era of the Witness* (2006), Annette Wieviorka, a French historian, describes how the idea of witness to the Holocaust developed, changed over time, and produced a paradigm for witnessing of other events. She identifies the Eichmann trial, which took place in Jerusalem in 1961, as pivotal in solidifying a valuing of the term *witness* because, in regard to the Holocaust, it now carried legal significance.

The idea of witness has become a way of thinking about what transpires in psychoanalytic psychotherapy when working with dimensions of trauma and the interpersonal and intersubjective field of patient and therapist. Poland (2000) describes witnessing as a function of the analyst as "one who recognizes and grasps the emotional import of the patient's self-exploration in the immediacy of the moment, yet who stays in attendance without intruding supposed wisdom—at least not verbally" (p. 18). He sees interpreting and witnessing going "hand in hand, each facilitating the other" (p. 18). Donnel Stern (2010) focuses on what turns unformulated experience into formulated experience during psychoanalytic treatments: "I believe that the need for witnessing became visible first in this context [of trauma] because it was in the impact of trauma that some of the most damaging effects of the *absence* of the witness were first observed" (p. 110, emphasis in original).

Felman (1992) considers witnessing to be an essential ingredient in Freud's uncovering of unconscious processes demonstrated in his reflections on his own dream, "the Irma dream." She sees Freud creating "the revolutionized clinical dimension of the *psychoanalytic dialogue*, an unprecedented kind of dialogue in which the doctor's testimony does not substitute itself for the patient's testimony, but *resonates with it*, because, as Freud discovers, *it takes two to witness the unconscious*" (p. 15, emphasis in original). The witnessing function is active in all psychoanalytic treatments, within the mind of both the analyst and the patient and within the dyad. It is this powerful force that breaks through defensive shields, allowing knowing of fearful interior unconscious fantasies and traumas to occur.

Establishing the sense of witnessing by other and by self is a crucial aspect of addressing the terrible anxieties about knowing and becoming known.

Fear can be aroused by external and internal traumas of all kinds. There is always the question: "Will you be able to be with me as I try to tell you who I am?" These moments of individual fear are not the Holocaust. Yet, it is study of witnessing of the Holocaust that can be brought to them to better understand the important place of the witnessing function in treatment. In many ways, the unconscious itself, a place where primitive fantasies and memories have been stored away, is a terrifying place in the mind until there is the therapeutic witness who values its discovery.

BRINGING HOLOCAUST NARRATION TO LIFE: THE FORTUNOFF VIDEO ARCHIVE FOR HOLOCAUST TESTIMONIES

A leap in bringing about witnessing to the Holocaust took place in 1979 when Laurel Vlock, a journalist, and Dori Laub, a psychoanalyst and child survivor, invited Holocaust survivors to record their memories on videotape. This was a new form of taking testimony, and no one was sure what would happen. It soon had the support of the community of Holocaust survivors in New Haven, Connecticut, and, with the help of Geoffrey Hartman, was established at Yale University in 1981. We look here at the development of this format for the giving and receiving of testimony by Holocaust survivors and what it reveals about the power of witnessing. Survivors had been writing down their personal accounts and had been interviewed in various ways before, on audiotape and for written archives. Here, video was used to capture survivors' personal stories, including their facial expressions and tone of voice. Within 2 years, 200 testimonies had been taken. With a grant from the Fortunoff Foundation, the Fortunoff Video Archive for Holocaust Testimonies became a permanent part of Yale University's Department of Manuscripts and Archives, located at Sterling Memorial Library. The archive now contains over 4,000 interviews and is available for study. Excerpts from the interviews can be viewed on their Web site (http://www.library.yale.edu/testimonies).

There were many survivors in the New Haven community, and at that time, years after liberation of the concentration camps, it was feared that stories would die with the survivors. There was a sense of urgency. The time to bring the terribleness of the Holocaust to life was now. This was not a formal psychological study but a way to allow individuals, many who had never spoken of their ordeals, to take up the invitation to do so. During the interviews, almost always with two interviewers, survivors were allowed to find their way and allow an unfolding of their stories. The format for gathering survivor accounts has become a part of the way history is preserved and provides scholars material for thinking and writing about the meaning of testimony and of remembering.

In our 2008 interview with Dori Laub, he told us that he experienced an immediate enlivenment in his own mind. He described his subjective experience as follows:

> That first evening—not only coming alive, but I recognized I came home. It was an arrival. My own witnessing. Here it was ... I wasn't singular, it wasn't sort of a little boy riding in the desert. There is a whole other chorus of voices, of people who do the same thing, and it goes on. ... It is in many, it is unknowingly in many, and you just have to create it.

On the first night of this new project, Dori Laub and Laurel Vlock met in Dori's office with cameramen and video equipment. Four people agreed to be part of the first round of taping. Renée Hartman (Chapter 17) was one of the first participants to present her testimony. At that time, tapes allowed 20 minutes of recording, and Dori and Laurel gave themselves an hour and a half to conduct the four interviews. No one knew what would happen. What transpired was astounding to everyone present. Once the frame of the situation was established and the desire to record for history expressed, a space for a very personal story appeared. Not only are narrative and memories recorded, but the way an individual human being finds his or her way (recalling, hesitating, moving backward and forward, finding fragments, describing, and feeling) appears as well. Stillness and movement on individuals' faces take place moment by moment along with the deep effort and felt accomplishment taking place in front of the camera with interested and determined witnesses. We do not think we would now be writing about witnessing if the event of the Video Archives Project had not taken place.

INTERVIEW WITH DORI LAUB: DEVELOPMENT OF THE FORTUNOFF VIDEO ARCHIVE

The following is taken from an interview with Dori Laub (DL) by Nancy Goodman (NG) and Marilyn Meyers (MM) on October 18, 2008. Dori traveled from New Haven and Nancy and Marilyn traveled from Washington, D.C. We met in New York City at the apartment of Arlene Kramer Richards and Arnold Richards, surrounded by large glass windows overlooking Manhattan. The reader of this interview will likely feel the amazement that accompanied the discovery of the testimonial process on that first night. The power of witnessing is felt along with the horror of what is being revealed. During this interview, Dori also described later re-interviewing with survivors and the way evolution of witnessing takes place over time.

DL: Laurel Vlock called and said, "I have a film crew, you have to find people to interview tonight." It was in my first private office across the street from the mental health center. I think I was already completely in private practice, and I might have already graduated from the Institute in 1979, so there was a readiness to go on my own now and do something not traditional, maybe not consciously. I thought it would be half-hour interviews. We would start at 7 or 8 o'clock and be finished at 10. I called Renée H. and said: "Renée, you have to come." We had collaborated a little bit before when she helped me write something. She said yes. Eva B. was a friend of mine, and we had gone together to meetings on the Holocaust. I called Arthur S., who at that time was the director of the Jewish Federation, and he called Leon W., and Sally H. was the fourth person. So the last patient leaves. I have this little waiting room and a nice office. In the videos, you can see the office furniture in the picture, with me sitting in a simple chair which had a groove here because of years and years of patients scratching it, and the cameramen come, very professional, but they take over, rearranging the office for the camera, and trying to set the tone. I was a little worried about that, the tone. ... I wanted to project something that is authentic, not for television. But, you know, I let them set up, they were quite proficient, and we spaced the survivors. We were thinking of three-quarters of an hour for each appointment with maybe 30 minutes of interviewing. That is what we expected.

And Eva B. comes in. She is the first person I interviewed. We did it with videotape; and the scenes begin to come. The particular scenes are of being stripped naked in Auschwitz by men, by German soldiers, and the young girl's awkwardness, having to walk naked, and how powerfully this was in the room, her own witness, so it was not necessarily the most gruesome scenes, but what was set in her mind as a moment, and experience, the nakedness, and she was the girl with her mother. They probably both were naked, severe awkwardness, a naked girl and a fully dressed armed soldier walking around. What is it like? And then, the hair being shaved. She's even more naked. This is what I remember. The interview didn't last a half hour. I think it went over an hour. And I could sense that we set something in motion. And, it was a beginning. We started with life at home, with growing up. We suggested to imagine like you are sitting in your living room and there's a photo album with those old photos that are brown, before photos were black and white. "Open the photo album and tell me what you see, and what comes to your mind." It was a visual invitation, and on the sort of—run this in your mental movie house, and watch the movie and tell me what you see. Not what you read in books, but what you watch in your own movie.

NG: And, it just opened.

DL: That's what it is. It opened and it had a course, it had a direction, it had movement.

MM: It became a narrative.

DL: And, it became a narrative. It flowed. Sometimes I could sense a point where it has difficulty, and that's where I intervened. And of course, a primary task was to coordinate the work with my co-interviewer, who was a journalist and used to asking questions. We developed a wonderful way of communicating. Whenever I wanted her to stop, I would take her hand and she stopped. And we developed a way of sort of waiting and holding. Sometimes a word is enough. I remember scenes of each interview. I don't remember the whole narrative, but Eva B.— the first interview. One thing that was memorable was that the video tapes at that time lasted only 20 minutes. So every 20 minutes, we needed a break, and the videotape had to be changed.

NG: What would happen during that changeover? Was it quiet?

DL: No, no, no. The interviewer would say: "My God, how can you remember all that?" We were allowing ourselves to speak about the wonderment and the awe that we felt and would say, "Please say more." We didn't expect that. It was a surprise for everybody. At that time, I still didn't notice the photographer. Later on, I realized how much power they had. The camera crew members were crying. From where they were in the background, they could not do anything, they couldn't say anything. But they zoomed in and out. Their emotions, their experience, informed the zooming—when they wanted to zoom out, and when they wanted to zoom in.

NG: But, you hadn't known what would come out in their speaking.

DL: No. I definitely did not expect these moments, like the naked girls walking and their heads shaven and the men in the Auschwitz barracks and the Nazi soldiers walking by and looking at them. The interviews lasted longer and I didn't expect the initiative and, sort of, the agency that carried on the narrative like pausing and then saying ... and the next day, this is what happened. Yeah, I expected maybe fragments; but no, there were lengthy, profound moments of being there, and there was movement. There is the interview with the man who became a baker. He may have been the second interview. He was a very philanthropic man. I remember more because I've shown it so many times. But what struck me so much was his talking about the hunger and then all he wanted to do was eat and he was so hungry. And, he described the ghetto and how he would go down to steal a slice of bread. It was just a strange narration. He spoke at first in the third person: "He would go down and try to steal bread from his sister's ration," and then he said, "I did it. I can't believe that I did it, but, I did it."

So I told you about Eva, I told you about Leon, and then there was Renée H. It was completely unforgettable. She had a completely deaf sister. The parents had been sent to Auschwitz, and the children were desperately trying to join them and begged the Slovak police to reunite them with their parents. They were put on the train. And, she had to be the spokesperson for the completely deaf sister. And you know, this whole particular experience of having to be the ears and the voice of the completely deaf sister and taking care of her. They were, I don't know, 10, 11 years old, or something. And she describes the arrival in Bergen-Belsen. The parents had been sent to Auschwitz. Of course, there are no parents, no reunion, nothing. For years after the war, she believed she would be reunited with her parents who must be in hiding and would get in contact. She says, "I did not experience liberation because I had typhoid and I was unconscious." And what was most striking is how she talks about the two worlds inside her that run parallel, the world of those days and today, and says, "I do not want to connect them, I want to keep them separate, and they have been separate." This is the unexpected, to formulate it in this way—to convey these two different worlds.

NG: She might have kept two worlds, but she was willing to talk about it, as long as they didn't touch too much, I guess, in her soul or something. Had Renée ever given a testimony before?

DL: No, no one had.

NG: So, back to the first night. There's a camera, there's the office, there's you and Laurel Vlock, and the chair with the little ridge in it, and a time frame, and she begins telling you all of this?

DL: She begins telling and reflecting. They were all reflecting, not only telling news but reflecting. And this was so unexpected. The last one was Sally H. and very unforgettable because she talked of being in a slave labor camp. She saw trains passing by, passenger trains—and, how she imagined herself being a passenger on one of the trains, and seeing the camp from the train. And this sort of in-between position of inside–outside, you know, there's creativity in that, to have it available while even in the camp to be able to make it, to imagine that you are not in, you're out, you're observing, and there is witnessing in that. So I particularly remember her for that, for that metaphor.

NG: That's a wonderful metaphor.

DL: And we didn't stop at 10, I think we went until 2 in the morning, and we were completely overwhelmed by what had just happened. Also the sense of intimacy experienced in those interviews, and the inevitable hug at the end, and so you create a bond for life with that. And yes, I do forget the stories, but whenever we meet, the story seems to be picking up again. Often, I don't remember, which is probably my way of protecting myself.

NG: You have heard so many stories. You have to protect yourself, I think.

MM: And yet they're inside you.

DL: They're inside me. I don't think I could—I haven't transformed them into some intellectual database that I can assess as one, two, three.

MM: No, it's not that.

DL: They're not that. They're not that. That's how they're different, and you know I forget names, I forget which camp the survivor was in.

MM: Well, it doesn't matter really, right? Or your description of Renée H., how she has this kind of wall between the two, the before and the after, and she says I don't want to connect them.

DL: The camp and the other life.

MM: The camp and the other life, so it's walled off in some way. And yet, you describe this other person, watching herself on the train. It's a different kind of, different kind of disconnect, different kind of dissociation.

DL: Well, I hesitate to use the word *dissociation*.

MM: Okay, I do, too. As I said it I was hesitating.

DL: I think we need to come up with terminology that better fits this experience—much of the terminology.

MM: Yes.

NG: Well, you started talking about the child who has traumatic experience or something that catches their attention or creates a certain kind of attention. I don't know if I even want to use the word *trauma*, but something happens where there's a certain kind of attention. You're on the fringe of something. It's hard to describe, and I do think it deserves more struggle for language. It makes me think of being in this apartment. I mean, you look at this vista over Manhattan and it gives you, me, a slight vertigo. I'm the only one staring out the window feeling a slight vertigo. You can see so much, but are you grounded or not, and it makes things more vivid in a way. But there's a special experience, and then that gets transformed, or you use it so it's like being on a train at the same time that you're watching—Freud used the metaphor of the train for analysis, that you're looking out the window and—he was afraid to catch trains.

DL: Just in my own work, that first evening was like a homecoming. I found that this process that I had known in myself and sometimes pushed aside and re-found in the Yom Kippur War was there, and it was very powerfully there and in so many ways.

NG: A homecoming?

DL: To myself, to the witness in me. There were others, I mean we shared something that we all kept doing it quietly and unbeknownst to ourselves even, and unknown to anybody, but we all were so, so much connected to it. This was part of our lives. Even though if you could build, decide to build a wall, it still was very much part of our lives and there was something very much in common, in that sense it was a homecoming.

NG: I remember you invited me to go to the first night when you showed the tapes and I was nervous. What would it be like? And everyone was so excited and talking and hugging.

DL: Yes, the excitement when we presented this, in you and others, it was a sense of homecoming for Jewish people, and not only Jewish people.

NG: But that's important. Say more about that, it isn't just Jewish people.

DL: No, I think it has something to do with the truth that is central to the authenticity and refuses trivia ... such authenticity might capture the imagination of interviewers who are not Jews. They become completely involved and dedicated. And then, all of the sudden, later we found that the liberators, who knew everything, came out of the woods. They had not talked for 40 years, not even to their families, and they had suffered from nightmares. This whole history and with its imprints, came alive and had a place and most of all had an impact on life.

NG: Well, it opens a world for everyone to be able to speak the truth and it's like a language. You arrive someplace where—that's the language I've known. I've always known it, and there are other people who speak it.

DL: The other people speak it. There's a community, a nation, not necessarily an ethnic nation, that speak this language. Now, for me the last confirmation, not the last, but one of the most extreme confirmations were the psychotic patients that I recently interviewed in mental hospitals in Israel that were beyond reach. And I thought, they are reachable, and when they gave interviews of an hour, and nobody expected them to last more than 5 minutes. And they hugged, and they stopped and when they could not speak, they stuttered, and they wanted so much to speak. And if they couldn't I would tell them their story, places I knew of, and they would say yes or no, and confirm or disconfirm what was right.

EVOLUTION OF WITNESSING: RE-INTERVIEWING

This part of the transcript involves a description of a re-interview with one of the first four survivors who had given testimony on the first night of taping. It represents a vital part of a witnessing process; namely, that once there is space for the story to begin, it can evolve more. The space opened during the first night as Leon W. spoke with Dori Laub and Laurel Vlock. The re-interview took place almost 30 years later. Leon W. was very aware that he was old and had little time to tell even more deeply about his Holocaust memories and reflections. In many ways, it had taken this long for some of his deepest psychic pain to be added to his own narrative. There

was a sense of continuing between Dori and Leon, indicating again that a
wanting to continue hearing helps bring about a desire to continue telling.

DL: Okay. It was in 2005, 2006, we did a project, an interview of 20 survivors in the New Haven area and some came from New York, for the
International Slave Labor Project, with 550 interviews from all over
the world, a small portion Jews, but Ukrainians, Slovaks, Slovenians,
Czechs, Hungarians. So my role was to interview 20 in New Haven,
preferably I re-interviewed people I had interviewed before.

NG: Re-interviewing.

MM: Oh wow.

NG: Now that's very interesting.

MM: So these people now were much older?

DL: Yes, much older. So I was able to re-interview eight whom I had interviewed before. Many had died; many moved into old age homes in
Florida. One of the people we interviewed was Leon W. Incidentally, I
didn't remember the stories in many. And one I had completely forgotten
that I had interviewed him. He told me during the interview, you have
interviewed me. You can look me up in your catalog, yes, it was me.

NG: Because you didn't recognize him?

DL: No, how do you deal with traumatic stories?

MM: Uh-huh. So it's the knowing and not knowing.

DL: Yeah. When I watched the tape, I remembered everything. I went to
see the tape again. I am carrying out a project to compare three old
interviews with the later interviews.

NG: Absolutely, that's so interesting, with time intervening.

DL: So Leon W. agreed to be interviewed again, luckily. He said, "I'm 85
or 86, my memory is bad, my health is bad, I won't be able to do it,"
and "What shirt should I wear?" An hour before the interview, he still
wasn't sure he was coming. And maybe I exerted pressure a little. "It's
important that you do it." And he came. Finally he came. The first
interview in 1979 was an hour. We also didn't know how to deepen
it. We were given separate fragments. This time, I knew how to wait
through the silences. This time, the interview was two and a half hours.
The man who before could hardly speak was now speaking, and the
story deepened very much. It was more nuanced and layered. It was not
from his sister that he stole the bread, it was from his mother, because
parents are strong and can take everything, so it wouldn't hurt them.
And the bread stealing was much more extensive as he did it for the
whole family. His family was a line of bakers for generations, so when
in the Lodz ghetto they were in the Jewish administration, and they
had their own baker in the community. He took bread while it was put
out to cool at night. He inserted two sticks, extracted a loaf of bread
every night, and brought it home. And somebody caught wind that this

bread was missing, and they put bars on the window. So he devised a stick with a knife tied to the top of it, two sticks. Cut up the bread, and would extract the pieces. Later he figured out a way to make a pouch that connected to his trousers, where he would put in flour to bring home. He was caught and thrown into prison. And then he was forced to be the one that had to gather the feces from all the latrines. It's called the fecalist.

NG: Could you say that again?

DL: It was called the fecalist, in other words, his work as a punishment was to clean out the manholes and bring the sewage to a dumping ground.

MM: That was his punishment for taking the bread and the flour?

DL: For stealing bread. And his luck was he was taken out of the ghetto in July 1944 and sent to a labor camp. They needed labor in Germany. They needed men, and so, that's how he made it, working—and then he said, "And the worst thing of the whole war and the whole, for me, I can't talk about it and I don't want to talk about it, I'm not going to talk about it." But I already knew to wait; and, it took him about 2 minutes, and he said: "It was going back to Lodz, and waiting for 5 months, and nobody returned. My mother and sister, they were all gassed." Okay, so this is how testimony evolves, over the years, and this has been my experience.

NG: Could we pause for a minute? It's like, oh my goodness. It's the story of waiting. It's really ... why do you think he could tell it later? His age? That he knew he wouldn't get another chance? That he couldn't even, he couldn't even allow himself to remember or feel that 20 years before? Who knows, I guess, who knows? But there it was.

DL: I've tried to understand; we've published, my wife and I, a brief paper on that, on revisiting testimonies. First of all, it was clear to both of us we would never meet again. And I think the process set in motion 25 years ago continued in one way, and he had many encounters; he spoke many times and he was interviewed many times. There were many people who found him and wanted to know him. He talked to me a little bit about that. It's another piece of integration, there was that, people who wanted to know him, and it's also life and a sort of legacy, and it's sort of a layering that began to happen even about what was the most cruel. And what really was crucial was that nobody came back, and he was there waiting. If he had to clean up the sewage, it's terrible, but so what? If he was beaten, it was hurting, but so what? I listened to David Boder's interviews from 1946. They are full of incredible sadistic acts by the Nazis, and details like cutting, nailing a nail through tongue, hanging from all kinds of places. These details begin to fade, and what comes into fuller expression is something of the person's experience of the pain. Now, the details are the news, the immediate. More of the losses or the terror that crystallizes, that's what evolves and it comes out and is around, shapes more of a story.

In this revisiting of a testimony, Dori showed how a core pain of the Holocaust experience can take such a long time to be told. Here, Leon W. spoke about the most terrible feeling of all. As he waited in his "hometown," no one came back. He gave us a gift of expression because it is precisely the inability to bring back 1 of the 6 million murdered Jews that is so deeply felt and calls out for symbolizing. Leon W. evolved his story within the context of people, including Dori, wanting to know him, waiting for his recollections and valuing them. Dori told us that the event of the interview created a "bond for life" with the "inevitable hug." We invite our readers to join in the sense that a bond is made among witnesses. Knowing there is a bond helps the power of witnessing to begin and to continue later in time. Dori also described how when meeting again, years later, "the story seems to be picking up again." A powerful witnessing process can stay in the mind and accompany individuals through self-discovery and the continuing bond with those across generations who are receiving the story.

REFERENCES

Abram, J. (1996). *The language of Winnicott: A dictionary of Winnicott's use of words.* London: Karnac.

Apprey, M. (2003). Repairing history: Reworking transgenerational trauma. In D. Moss (Ed.), *Hating in the first person plural: Psychoanalytic essays on racism, homophobia, misogyny, and terror* (pp. 1–27). New York: Other Press.

Apprey, M. (2006). Difference and the awakening of wounds in intercultural psychoanalysis. *Psychoanalytic Quarterly, 75,* 73–93.

Beebe, B. (1986). Mother-infant mutual influences and pre-cursors of self-object representations. In J. Masling (Ed.), *Empirical studies of psychoanalytic theories* (Vol. 2, pp. 27–48). Hillsdale, NJ: Analytic Press.

Beebe, B., Knoblauch, S., Rustin, J., & Sorter, D. (2005). *Forms of intersubjectivity in infant research and adult treatment.* New York: Other Press.

Bion, W. R. (1962). *Learning from experience.* New York: Basic Books.

Bion, W. R. (1984). *Second thoughts.* New York: Basic Books.

Blanchot, M. (1986). *The writing of the disaster* (A. Smock, Trans.). Lincoln: University of Nebraska Press.

Bohleber, W. (2010). *Destructiveness, intersubjectivity, and trauma: The identity crisis of modern psychoanalysis.* London: Karnac.

Browning, C. R. (2003). *Collected memories: Holocaust history and postwar testimony.* Madison: University of Wisconsin Press.

Caruth, C. (Ed.) (1995). *Trauma: Explorations in memory.* Baltimore: Johns Hopkins University Press.

Caruth, C. (1996). *Unclaimed experience: Trauma, narrative, and history.* Baltimore: Johns Hopkins University Press.

Davies, J. D., & Frawley, M. G. (1994). *Treating the adult survivor of childhood sexual abuse: A psychoanalytic perspective.* New York: Basic Books.

Delbo, C. (1995). *Auschwitz and after.* New Haven, CT: Yale University Press.

Des Pres, T. (1976). *The survivor: An anatomy of life in the death camps.* New York: Oxford University Press.

Ellman, P., & Goodman, N. (2012). Enactment: Opportunity for symbolizing trauma. In A. Frosch (Ed.), *Absolute truth and unbearable psychic pain: Psychoanalytic perspectives on concrete experience.* London: Karnac.

Faimberg, H. (2005). *The telescoping of generations: Listening to the narcissistic links between generations.* London: Routledge.

Felman, S. (1992). Education and crisis, or the vicissitudes of teaching. In S. Felman & D. Laub (Eds.), *Testimony: Crises of witnessing in literature, psychoanalysis, and history* (pp. 1–56). New York: Routledge.

Felman, S., & Laub, D. (1992). *Testimony: Crisis of witnessing in literature, psychoanalysis, and history.* New York: Routledge.

Freud, A. (1967). Comments on trauma. In S. Furst (Ed.), *Psychic trauma* (pp. 235–246). New York: Basic Books.

Freud, S. (1896). The aetiology of hysteria. In J. Strachey (Ed., & Trans.), *The standard edition of the complete psychological works of Sigmund Freud* (Vol. 3, pp. 189–221). London: Hogarth Press.

Freud, S. (1919). Introduction to psycho-analysis and the war neuroses. In J. Strachey (Ed., & Trans.), *The standard edition of the complete psychological works of Sigmund Freud* (Vol. 17, pp. 206–215). London: Hogarth Press.

Frosch, A. (Ed.). (2012). *Absolute truth and unbearable psychic pain: Psychoanalytic perspectives on concrete experience.* New York: Karnac.

Green, A. (1993). *The dead mother: The work of Andre Green* (G. Kohon, Ed.). London: Routledge.

Gross, J. (2001). *Neighbors: The destruction of the Jewish community in Jedwabne, Poland.* Princeton, NJ: Princeton University Press.

Grotstein, J. (1990). Nothingness, meaninglessness, chaos, and the "Black Hole" II—The Black Hole. *Contemporary Psychoanalysis, 26,* 377–407.

Herman, J. L (1992). *Trauma and recovery: The aftermath of violence from domestic abuse to political terror.* New York: Basic Books.

Hurvich, M. (2003). The place of annihilation anxieties in psychoanalytic theory. *Journal of the American Psychoanalytic Association, 51,* 579–616.

Hurvich, M. (2011). New developments in the theory and clinical application of the annihilation concept. In A. B. Druck, C. Ellman, N. Freedman, & A. Thaler (Eds.). *New Freudian synthesis.* London: Karnac.

Kogan, I. (1995). *The cry of the mute children: A psychoanalytic perspective of the second generation of the Holocaust.* London: Free Association Press.

Kogan, I. (2007). *The struggle against mourning.* Lanham, MD: Aronson.

Krystal, H. (1978). Trauma and affects. *Psychoanalytic Study of the Child, 33,* 81–116.

Langer, L. (1991). *Holocaust testimonies: The ruins of memory.* New Haven, CT: Yale University Press.

Laub, D. (1992a). Bearing witness or the vicissitudes of listening. In S. Felman & D. Laub, *Testimony: Crises of witnessing in literature, psychoanalysis, and history* (pp. 57–74). New York: Routledge.

Laub, D. (1992b). An event without a witness: Truth, testimony, and survival. In S. Felman & D. Laub, *Testimony: Crises of witnessing in literature, psychoanalysis, and history* (pp. 75–92). New York: Routledge.

Laub, D. (1998). The empty circle: Children of survivors and the limits of reconstruction. *Journal of the American Psychoanalytic Association, 46,* 507–529.

Laub, D. (2005). From speechlessness to narrative: The cases of Holocaust historians and of psychiatrically hospitalized survivors. *Literature and Medicine, 24,* 253–265.

Laub, D., & Auerhahn, N. C. (1989). Failed empathy: A central theme in the survivor's Holocaust experience. *Psychoanalytic Psychology, 6,* 377–400.

Laub, D., & Auerhahn, N. C. (1993). Knowing and not knowing massive psychic trauma: Forms of traumatic memory. *International Journal of Psychoanalysis, 74,* 287–302.

Levi, P. (1996). *Survival in Auschwitz: The Nazi assault on humanity* (S. Woolf, Trans.). New York: Touchstone Books. (Original work published 1958)

Levi, P., & Benedetti, L. (2006). *The Auschwitz report* (J. Woolf, Trans.). New York: Verso. (Original work published 1946)

Loewald, H. W. (1975). Psychoanalysis as an art and the fantasy character of the psychoanalytic situation. *Journal of the American Psychoanalytic Association, 23,* 277–299.

McCann, I. L., & Pearlman, L. A. (1990). Vicarious traumatization: A framework the psychological effects of working with victims. *Journal of Traumatic Stress, 3*(1), 131–149.

Parens, H. (2004). *Renewal of life: Healing from the Holocaust.* Rockville, MD: Schreiber.

Poland, W. S. (2000). The analyst's witnessing and otherness. *Journal of the American Psychoanalytic Association, 48,* 17–34.

Rosen, P., & Apfelbaum, N. (2002). *Bearing witness: A resource guide to literature, poetry, art, music, and videos by Holocaust victims and survivors.* Westport, CT: Greenwood Press.

Schore, A. N. (1994). *Affect regulation and the origin of the self: The neurobiology of emotional development.* Hillsdale, NJ: Erlbaum.

Staub, E. (1989). *The roots of evil: The origins of genocide and other group violence.* New York: Cambridge University Press.

Staub, E. (2011). *Overcoming evil: Genocide, violent conflict, and terrorism.* New York: Oxford University Press.

Stern, D. B. (2010). *Partners in thought: Working with unformulated experience, dissociation, and enactment.* New York: Routledge.

Stern, D. N. (1985). *The interpersonal world of the infant: A view from psychoanalysis and developmental psychology.* New York: Basic Books.

Tarentelli, C. B. (2003). Life within death: Towards a metapsychology of catastrophic psychic trauma. *International Journal of Psychoanalysis, 84,* 915–928.

van der Kolk, B. A., McFarlane, A., & Weisaeth, L. (Eds.) (2007). *Traumatic stress: The effects of overwhelming experience on mind, body, and society.* New York: Guilford Press.

Wiesenthal, S. (1969). *The sunflower: On the possibilities and limits of forgiveness.* New York: Schocken Books.

Wieviorka, J. A. (2006). *The era of the witness* (J. Stark, Trans.). Ithaca, NY: Cornell University Press.

Winnicott, D. W. (1956). *Through paediatrics to psychoanalysis.* New York: Basic Books.

Winnicott, D. W. (1971). *Playing and reality.* London: Tavistock.

Chapter 2

Historic and Psychic Timeline

Opening and Closing the Space for Witnessing

Marilyn B. Meyers

INTRODUCTION

Time is dynamic, not static; one moment leads to another. Like a pebble in a stream or waves on the shore, time cannot be permanently captured, stopped, or reversed. Any rupture leaves its mark. In the context of the Holocaust, there was a catastrophic immeasurable rupture in the fabric of the society and in the psyches of those who experienced or bore witness. The Holocaust has been characterized as representing an experience that is "epochal"; that it occurred at a specific point in time has a monumental impact on both history and the individuals (Engelman, Day, & Durant, 1993).

In this section, I trace the complex nature of the witnessing of the Holocaust—the opening and closing that has occurred within different historic contexts over the years. I emphasize the degree to which the socio-cultural context may or may not have served as a receptive container at various times since the end of the war and up to the present time. The progression of this opening and closing is not linear or uni-directional. I am encompassing the internal (intrapsychic), interpersonal, and societal aspects of witnessing. The relationships and dynamic interactions between these seemingly disparate elements are complex and shifting. Explicit and implicit signals were communicated at various times to speak or not to speak, to know or not to know. The examples of witnessing are arranged in roughly chronological order; however, it is readily apparent and important to recognize that this chronology does not capture the complexity—the movement back and forth over time. All of these examples serve to emphasize the presence of an internal/imagined witness when there is no "real" witness present.

If we think about those individuals who felt compelled to record their experiences by keeping diaries in the Warsaw Ghetto, producing art, writing poetry, and performing music in Terezín, we recognize that the minds of those individuals possessed the idea of a witness. In addition, there was a community of witnesses in these places to enhance and support the need to bear witness. For those individuals who survived the Holocaust, the aftermath presented a challenge to both remember and live life in the present. For the survivors, the existence of a receptive societal context played a central role in whether space was open to knowing.

In the first section, I investigate the early acts of witnessing in the immediacy of the Nazi reign of terror. I posit that any person facing the threat of annihilation who chose to bear witness had in mind a willing recipient—someone who would want to know; thus, an internal witness was held in mind. Then, I present instances of witnessing that occurred over the years immediately following the war and up to the present. In addition to witnessing by victims/survivors, I include witnessing by perpetrators and bystanders. The forms of witnessing vary: diaries, artwork, poetry, oral testimony, film, memorials, and museums.

For example, the immediacy of the diaries that were written at the time that events occurred captured specific and distinct moments in time and inherently assumed a willing witness. The person who wrote a postcard to be tossed from the train as it was headed for Auschwitz was psychically in a state of terror and despair and hoped that someone would want to know. The person who wrote a memoir 60 years after the war had the capacity for self-reflection that comes with developmental maturity and distance from the trauma. The individual maturational process and distance from the trauma thus allow for space in the mind that may not have been possible in the midst of the horrors. Several of the contributors to this book wrote their memoirs many years after the traumatic events; they attribute the willingness and capacity to write at that time to the wish to communicate to their children and grandchildren. Furthermore, there were those who took testimony and bore witness in the immediate aftermath of the war (David Boder, Edward R. Murrow, General Eisenhower, and others). For the most part, with some exceptions, the 1950s were largely marked by a closing down of willingness to know the horrors. However, there were relatively isolated examples of openness. One significant example was the establishment of Holocaust and Ghetto Remembrance Day in Israel in 1951. The name was later changed to Yom Hashoah (Devastation and Heroism Day), thus recognizing the broader significance of the day. On this national holiday, there are candle lightings, poetry readings, speakers, prayers, and singing. At 10:00 a.m. on the holiday, sirens sound, and everyone stops what they are doing for moments of remembrance.

THE FIRST WITNESSES

The first witnesses of the Holocaust were the victims who were writing to others and recording what was happening in the immediacy of the events.

They were appealing for help and leaving evidence for the future in the face of most certain death. Terence des Pres (1976) wrote of survivors:

> The "world" to which the survivor speaks is very much a part of their condition as witnesses. They speak *for* someone, but also *to* someone and the response they evoke is integral to the act they perform. And here an unexpected ambiguity arises. As a witness the survivor is both sought and shunned; the desire to hear his truth is countered by the need to ignore him. (p. 41)

This tension between the desire to know and the horror at knowing is inevitable. However, that knowing and not knowing coexist simultaneously along the continuum of the desire and need to know and the turning away from the horror. This exists in the minds of both the survivors and the witnesses. The tension and dynamic balance between the two poles shift over time.

Amid the horrors, there were people who were determined to speak the truth. They were able to hold in their minds the existence of a willing witness who would believe them and be receptive to knowing the atrocities. Referring to diaries that were written in the early stages of the war, Saul Friedlander (1997) wrote: "Beyond their general historical importance ... personal chronicles are like lightening flashes that illuminate part of a landscape" (p. xv). One survivor (Leon Thorne) stated, "I dare not hope that I will live through this period, but I must work as though my words *will* come through" (des Pres, 1976, p. 40). Telling the truth at that time was both necessary and traumatic; it remains so to today.

Two young people, Anne Frank and David Graber, felt the urgent need to record their experiences with the expectation and hope that others would know. There are, however important differences—Graber knew that he was destined to die, whereas Anne Frank lacked this awareness and remained hopeful to the end.

Anne Frank: An Icon of Witnessing

The Diary of a Young Girl (Frank & Pressler, 1996) stands in a category of its own as an example of witnessing as events unfolded. She began writing in June 1942, and her last entry, more than 2 years later, was on August 1, 1944. Along with her parents, sister, and the others hiding in the secret annex, she was arrested on August 4, 1944. Anne Frank's astute observations of the interactions within the closed circumstances of hiding have been read by millions worldwide. The diary was first published in 1947, with numerous subsequent versions. The publication of her diary was compelling to many adolescent girls in the 1950s.

She wrote as a typical adolescent girl struggling with her relationships to her parents, herself, and others. The diary took on a different tone as the danger became clear and the living arrangements in the cramped attic took their toll. Anne, who would have celebrated her 80th birthday in 2009, died alongside her sister, Margot, of typhus in Bergen-Belsen just days before liberation. Both her mother and father had been sent to Auschwitz, where her mother died but her father survived.

On July 15, 1944, Anne wrote:

> It is utterly impossible for me to build my life on a foundation of chaos, suffering, and death. I see the world being slowly transformed into a wilderness. ... I feel the suffering of millions. And yet when I look up at the sky, I somehow feel that everything will change for the better, that this cruelty will end, that peace and tranquility will return once more. (p. 333)

She wrote these words as a young girl, still hopeful, without knowledge of the impending catastrophe.

Lawrence Langer (2006) wrote that, "The sequel to (Anne Frank's) diary, in which she would have recorded her reaction to her 'deathlife' after Auschwitz and Bergen Belsen, remains one of the much-missed unwritten books of Holocaust literature" (p. xii). One must wonder how she would have seen the world had she survived into adulthood having witnessed the starvation, death, and disease of Bergen-Belsen and deaths of her mother and sister. Her hiding place, the Anne Frank house, remains a place of pilgrimage for millions of people. The filmmaker George Stevens Jr. described meeting Otto Frank in Amsterdam in 1957 while preparing for the film based on *The Diary of Young Girl*. In that meeting, Otto Frank described the day when the Gestapo discovered the hiding place. According to Mr. Frank, the Gestapo *Oberscharführer* Karl Silberbauer emptied Mr. Frank's briefcase on the floor. Silberbauer gathered up the silverware and other "valuables" but left the diary on the floor. Subsequently, Miep Gies hid the pages of the diary in an unlocked drawer; she was intent on preserving the diary and reasoned that the Nazis would not be interested in anything in an unlocked drawer. Thus, through a series of random unremarkable events, one of the most significant works of witnessing was preserved for the world. Anne Frank's voice and spirit have lived on in the minds of millions worldwide. She symbolizes hope in the midst of despair, in the eyes of some having been idealized; she does, however, "communicate" to the world.

In keeping with the perspective of the psychic timeline regarding witnessing, a recent memorialization of Anne Frank took a different form. In her diary, she wrote of her pleasure in seeing the chestnut tree from her hiding place. Saplings from this tree have been collected by the Anne Frank Foundation and distributed to 11 sites. One of the sites is Little Rock

Central High School in Arkansas; the sapling will be planted between two trees that were in place at the time of the battle for desegregation. The executive director of the Anne Frank Center stated that this was meant to highlight the "consequences of intolerance" (*New York Times*, 2009, p. A22). Thus, the acts and forms of commemorating and witnessing continue to evolve as metaphoric and symbolic representations.

Witnessing in the Warsaw Ghetto

Another example of witnessing during the horrific events occurred within the Warsaw Ghetto. A massive effort to bear witness was implemented by the Polish historian Emmanuel Ringelblum. He accumulated testimonies and reports from the Jews of the Ghetto by writers, artists, and journalists. The results of these efforts grew into a resistance organization and what came to be known as the Oyneg Shabes Archive (Kassow, 2007). In addition to the collection of material written by those in the Ghetto, there were meal tickets, tickets for performances, and decrees issued by the Nazis. The archives were sealed in milk cans and metal boxes and systematically buried by Ringelblum and his fellow witnesses. The Warsaw Ghetto was destroyed by the Nazis after the uprising in 1943. "In the minds of the Nazis, not only did the Jews themselves have to disappear, the very environment in which they lived also had to be eradicated. The Ghetto became a desert of stones" (Wieviorka, 2006, p. 7).

Eventually, in 1946 and 1950 portions of the archive were disinterred:

> The diggers moved carefully. It was slow and dangerous work. Where the Warsaw Ghetto once stood was now a scene of total destruction. … They dug deep tunnels under the debris, built ventilation shafts, and pushed long metal probes through the rocks and bricks. And then a probe hit something solid; a tin box covered in clay and tightly bound in string—then nine more. (Kassow, 2007, p. 1)

The sum total of what was found amount to approximately 27,000 pages of documents. More documents are still being uncovered.

Within the Ghetto, David Graber, a 19-year-old, wrote these words:

> What we were unable to cry and shriek out to the world we buried in the ground. … I would love to see the moment in which the great reassure [sic] will be dug up and scream to the world. So the world may know all. So the ones who did not live through it may be glad and we may feel like veterans with medals on our chest. We would be the fathers, the teachers and educators of the future. … But no, we shall certainly not live to see it, and therefore I write my last will. May the treasure fall into good hands, may it last into better times, may it alarm

and alert the world to what happened in the twentieth century. ... We may now die in peace. We fulfilled our mission. May history attest for us. (p. 3)

WITNESSING BY BYSTANDERS

Concurrent with the first witnesses, there were bystanders. Bystanders often stood by passively, although some passive witnesses also recorded events as they occurred. The presence of passive bystanders challenges our notion of a willing witness. How do we understand the mind of the passive bystander? It is beyond the scope of this book to attempt close examination of the bystander/rescuer phenomenon; however, one instance that illustrates the chronicling of the assassination of thousands of Jews without intervening is that of Kazimir Sakowicz. Further in this book we present portions of an interview with Ervin Staub, one of the leading scholars of the bystander phenomenon. He has written extensively on the complex forces that contribute to the choice to act or not on behalf of those who are being victimized (e.g., Staub, 1989).

Kazimir Sakowicz, a Polish journalist who lived in the Ponary forest outside Vilna, Lithuania, where 60,000 Jews were rounded up in 1941 and shot, took minutely detailed extensive notes of what was happening in the forest. His notes were reconstructed by Rachel Margolis (1999), one of the few survivors of these massacres. Margolis located scraps of paper that had been hidden in empty bottles and other places. Sakowicz had observed the atrocities while hiding in the attic of his home. His observations were written in a journalistic style, without elaboration or emotion. Recording these events was extremely dangerous and in its own way an act of courage.

The following is an entry from his diary:

> August 26, 1941: Eighty-eight people were shot, of whom 6 women. The majority, as can be seen from their clothing, etc. did not come from Wilno, but from outside the city, from the small towns. And so Ponary has become something of a central base. ... During August there were shootings on the 1st, 2nd, 6th, 8th, 11th, 16th, 22nd, 23rd, and 26th: all together, 10 days, 2000 people shot. ... The Shaulists were already saying that there would be as many shot in one day as were shot in the whole month of August. And that is how things turned out. (p. 22)

Sakowicz persisted in his writing up until the day he died. The circumstances of his death are not clear. He was shot, possibly accidentally, during an encounter between the German forces and the Soviet troops as they advanced. In contrast to Heinrich Himmler's statement that he was determined to hide the evidence of the crimes of Nazi Germany, "This is a glorious day in our history but it never has been or never will be written down" (Nuremberg Documents, PS-1919), Sakowicz was determined, as a bystander, to record the events. We can only guess at what was in Sakowicz's mind as he wrote; he did not act as a rescuer, but acted to record events for the sake of remembrance so that the world would know what happened in that terrible place. There are still pages missing from his diary, yet to be uncovered. In contrast to Sakowicz, there were many bystanders who were either complicit or passive.

WITNESSING BY PERPETRATORS

Another challenge to comprehension is the role of perpetrators as witnesses. Our minds, and those of many others (e.g., Daniel Goldhagen, 2000; Robert Jay Lifton, 2000), are challenged and horrified by the sadistic, perverse, evil, psychotic acts of the perpetrators. We find ourselves overwhelmed and numbed in our efforts to absorb the reality of the acts of unspeakable brutality perpetrated by the Nazis and to attempt to comprehend the minds of the perpetrators. Numerous scholars have sought to comprehend acts of cruelty toward others (e.g., Bandura, Barbaranelli, Caprara, & Pastorelli, 1996). Bandura (1999) invoked the notion of "moral disengagement," which is useful in explicating the complex factors that can lead to victimizing the other. In this section, I offer three examples of witnessing by perpetrators: a letter written by a German soldier, a description of the Wannsee Conference, and the Topography of Terror Museum in Berlin.

A German Soldier

In mid-July 1942, a reserve officer wrote a letter home:

> In Bereza-Katuska, where I stopped at noon, they had just shot 1300 Jews the day before. They were taken to a pit outside the city, then men, women and children had to take off all their clothes and were finished by shots to the neck. The clothes were disinfected and then reused. I am convinced, if the war lasts longer, it will become necessary to make sausages out of the Jews and feed them to the Russian prisoners of war or the trained Jewish workers. (Kipp, 2007)

In light of the thesis that bearing witness must assume the mind of a willing witness, it is stunning that young men such as this were giving testimony of their experiences to the folks back home. What were they thinking? Was he expecting his mother to write back and say, "I am so

happy to hear from you?" Or had the capacity to think and feel been annihilated? Did the mind go dead in having reached some limit in the capacity to think and feel? Did they have in mind an "other" who could bear
to know such things, or were they attempting to rid themselves, evacuate
the toxicity of their experience? We are not likely to know and numerous
scholars continue to explore these questions.

The Wannsee Conference

In January 1942, a gathering of top-level Nazis took place. This meeting
was conducted under the leadership of *SS-Obergruppenführer* Heydrich
and is referred to as the Wannsee Conference (Protocol). The text of the
meeting is based on the official translation by the U.S. government that was
prepared for evidence at the Nuremberg trials. The transcript is chilling
to read. At the beginning of the meeting, Heydrich asserted that the purpose of the meeting was to come up with the "final solution to the Jewish
problem." An accurate tabulation of all of the Jews of Europe was presented, country by country, with a bottom line of 11 million. The central
points, followed by detailed discussion, were (a) the expulsion of the Jews
from every sphere of life of the German people and (b) the expulsion of the
Jews from the living space of the German people.

The following is one small excerpt: "Jews must be removed ... as quickly
as possible, since it is here that the Jew as an epidemic carrier represents an
extreme danger." Our assumption of a willing witness (or self-witness) is
profoundly challenged by the contents of this meeting. We can only assume
a black hole in the minds of these perpetrators. Much has been written on
the topic of the minds of the perpetrators, and I do not delve into that here.
Reading these words, uttered in a matter-of-fact tone, brings us to a terrifying realization of what can happen when the thinking and moral mind
shuts down. From this perspective it seems incomprehensible that there can
be such a total absence of comprehension of the "other" as human.

Witnessing the Perpetrators:
Sixty-five Years after the War

In May 2010, the Topography of Terror Museum in Berlin (referred to as a
site of memory) was constructed on what was once the key headquarters for
the Secret Police. The site is regarded as the "primary object" in the documentation of the atrocities committed by the Nazis. The museum incorpo-
rates the foundations of the former House Prison operated by the SS. The
permanent exhibits (Documentation Center) in the building are chillingly
explicit. The specificity relies little on the familiar grim photographs of
the dead and emaciated people in the concentration camps, although such
photographs are there. More specifically, this is a place where the viewer

is confronted with the incomprehensible, yet seemingly inevitable, development of mass genocide by seemingly ordinary men. The museum arrives at no conclusion and does not attempt to provide a means of understanding the minds of the perpetrators. In fact, that appears to be the very point of the exhibits. Such minds cannot be understood. It is, however, significant that this museum was constructed in the era when the history of the atrocities is increasingly being documented in Germany.

WITNESSING AT LIBERATION

The newspaper articles and radio broadcasts that came out at the time of liberation, which in themselves were acts of witnessing, occurred within a context of the shock of recognition and an imperative to know by some individuals. Often, however, those accounts fell on deaf ears. General Dwight David Eisenhower ordered every American soldier who was not on the front lines and was in the area to visit Buchenwald at the liberation. Many of the American soldiers who were there never spoke about what they saw. As part of a tour of Buchenwald and other camps organized by General Eisenhower, Joseph Pulitzer wrote: "There are still Americans who are saying that 'this talk of atrocities is all propaganda.'" Pulitzer later mounted an exhibition of life-size photomurals of the camps. He entitled the exhibit "Lest We Forget." Along with this exhibition, he showed a documentary film of the camps (Abzug, 1985, pp. 132–135).

In April 1945, the prominent journalist Edward R. Murrow broadcast from Buchenwald. He possessed the fortitude and courage to speak directly of his experience. This broadcast was heard by millions:

> If you are at lunch, or if you have no appetite to hear what the Germans have done, now is a good time to switch off the radio, for I propose to tell you of Buchenwald. ... There surged around me an evil-smelling horde. Men and boys reached out to touch me; they were in rags and the remains of uniform. Death had already marked many of them. ... As we walked out into the courtyard, a man fell dead. Two others—they must have been over sixty—were crawling toward the latrine. I saw it but will not describe it. ... Dr. Heller asked if I would care to see the crematorium. He said it wouldn't be very interesting because the Germans had run out of coke some days ago and had taken to dumping the bodies into a great hole nearby... (Abzug, 1999, p. 198)

Murrow acknowledged that his report might offend people but refused to turn away.

This description mirrors what we have felt at various points in our work. Murrow's report from Buchenwald paints a picture as stark and horrifying as possible. In some sense, his words are more shocking than a photograph. The limit of looking and knowing is reached. It may be thus, no surprise that the world wanted to turn a blind eye. Many, however, also felt and continue to feel the need to push on and to know.

IMMEDIATE POSTWAR YEARS

In the immediate aftermath of liberation and the end of the war, there was virtual silence surrounding the Holocaust. Just as the documents of the Warsaw Ghetto and other places of atrocities were buried, so were many of the facts and often the memories (Abzug, 1985). This was not, however, universally true. In contrast, 20 high-ranking Nazis were brought to trial just months after the end of the war in November 1945 at the Nuremberg Trials (otherwise known as the International Military Tribunal). The film of the trial, *Nuremberg: Its Lesson for Today*, was suppressed and not made available to the public. In a letter to General Lucius D. Clay, American Military Governor of Germany, Assistant Secretary of War Howard C. Petersen, wrote: "The very way in which the trial was set up ... and the evidence which it produced constitute an historical document that should be of use ... in schools and universities for many years to come." In spite of this sentiment, the film lay dormant until 2009 when a group of filmmakers managed to locate it, restore it, and methodically translate it (http://www.nurembergfilm.org).

David Boder, a psychologist born in Latvia, traveled to Europe in the immediate aftermath of the war to record testimony by many survivors of the genocide. He collected over 100 interviews using primitive recording methods. His pursuit of these interviews may, in fact, be the first example of systematic witnessing of survivors (Boder, 1949). The transcripts of those interviews, while long lost to public view, are now available on the Internet (http://voices.iit.edu/).

Many GIs who had witnessed the camps at the time of liberation took pictures of what they saw. These were largely dismissed. One of the men, Philip Carlquist, who did take photographs of the camps, showed his pictures to his wife and said, "They were such terrible pictures that, when I got home, my wife destroyed them. She tore them up. She couldn't believe it; she tore them up" (Abzug, 1985, p. 127).

In April 2010, 120 veterans who had liberated concentration camps visited the U.S. Holocaust Memorial Museum in honor of the National Days of Remembrance. One of these veterans described an encounter with a severely emaciated survivor that had "haunted him for 65 years." He said, "It was 50 years before I was able to speak about it to anybody, even my wife and kids. [Speaking about it] was like a 50-ton weight off my shoulders" (Gowen, 2010, p. B1).

Immediately after the war, Primo Levi wrote a report at the request of the Soviet government on the conditions in Auschwitz (Levi & de Benedetti, 2006). This full report was subsequently lost to the world until very recently. Thus, even official documents of the deadly conditions in the concentration camps were somehow "lost." The world engaged in a conspiracy of silence. The survivors and the world wanted to put memory aside and get on with their lives.

THE 1960S: "THE ERA OF WITNESSING"

The Eichmann Trial

The capacity to give testimony and bear witness opened up dramatically at the time of the trial of Adolph Eichmann. Some scholars of the Holocaust assign a dramatic turn in the willingness to witness to this trial (Wieviorka, 2006); however, earlier efforts to bear witness served as precursors to the trial. The trial took place in Jerusalem in 1961, following Eichmann's capture. Survivors confronted the perpetrator face to face, and the proceedings were televised worldwide. Mass denial was no longer possible. The trial was pivotal in bridging the divide in Israel between the past and the present.

One of the witnesses at the trial of Adolph Eichmann was the author Yahiel Dinor. He used the name Ka-tzenik—the meaning of which is "prisoner" in the language of the concentration camp. When asked about his name at the trial, he replied: "It was not a pen name. ... This is a chronicle of the planet Auschwitz. ... Time there was not like it is here on earth. ... The inhabitants had no names, they had no parents nor did they have children." The prosecutor, Gideon Hausner, showed Dinor an inmate's uniform. "Is this what you wore there?" Dinor responded: "This is the garb of the planet called Auschwitz." In leaving the witness stand, unable to answer any more questions, Dinor fell to the floor and fainted. The session was adjourned and resumed later.

We can only surmise the psychological impact of that moment. What was Dinor's state of mind in the context of the testimony facing Eichmann? Perhaps that moment overwhelmed his senses and lead him to retreat to a state of "nonbeing." At that moment, he could not bear serving as his own witness.

METAPHORIC FORMS OF WITNESSING

From early on, there were forms of witnessing in metaphor. Within the Terezín Ghetto, for example, there was art, poetry, and music. Museums, memorials, sculpture, and films are among the later forms of witnessing. I include here Yad Vashem; the film *Shoah*; the oral testimony of the Fortunoff Video Archives at Yale; the Holocaust Museum in Washington, D.C.; and the Memorial for the Murdered Jews of Europe. This is far from a complete representation of the extensive repertoire of the symbolic representations of the horrors of the Holocaust. We consider the museums to be metaphorical as they signify much more than exhibition spaces for objects; the architecture of these museums elicits a visceral experience that far exceeds merely observing the exhibits.

Yad Vashem

In 1953, Yad Vashem, the memorial to the Jews in Israel, was established. Since then, this memorial has been the primary site of remembrance in Israel and perhaps the world. The name itself has become symbolic of remembering. This building represents more than a museum. It stands as both a symbol and a concrete place of remembrance and study. The architecture is both welcoming and foreboding. No one is spared the stark realities. The sequence of the rise of anti-Semitism leading up to the Holocaust is told and shown in frank and exhaustive detail. The stories encompass both the sweep of historic events and the personal details of those who were murdered and those who survived. It is not possible to be at Yad Vashem and not be deeply affected by the experience.

Film

The medium of filmmaking has been utilized to witness and allow witnessing to occur with a relatively tolerable distance. Some of the films that serve this purpose are *Schindler's List*, *Shoah*, *Sophie's Choice*, *Enemies: A Love Story*, *Life Is Beautiful*, *Defiance*, and many others. Nancy Goodman writes about *Schindler's List* in this volume (see Chapter 20).

The filmmaker Claude Lanzmann worked for 11 years, from 1974 to 1985, to fulfill his vision for witnessing the Holocaust in the film *Shoah*. This film differs from all other Holocaust films in its unique approach to the act of witnessing. It does not contain footage of the horrific events, but rather consists of interviews in the present. "The film offers a disorienting vision of the present, a compellingly profound and surprising insight into the complexity of the relation between history and witnessing" (Felman & Laub, 1992, p. 205). The film accomplishes many tasks on multiple levels. It engages the viewer as a witness to witnessing. The film consists of interviews with survivors, perpetrators, and bystanders. Lanzmann used a method for the interviews, which are conducted in the interviewee's own language (French, German, Sicilian, English, Hebrew, Yiddish, and Polish); thus, a translator was needed for most of the interviews. The members of the viewing audience are placed in a complex dynamic whereby the witness is being interviewed by Lanzmann, and the translator acts as an intermediary. A strange pacing results from this as the film unfolds. However, the methods used by Lanzmann do not evoke defensive distancing, but rather inescapable intimacy with the horrific. Much of that intimacy owes itself to the fact that the witnessing is enacted by actual participants as well as by Lanzmann's emphasis on the specific. For instance, he inquires: "Was the weather very cold? What were the [gas] vans like? What color?" (p. 219). There is no escape from the specific.

Oral Testimony

One of the most prominent and influential forms that witnessing and remembering took was the establishment of the Fortunoff Video Archive at Yale University. The project began with 183 testimonies taken in 1981. It has grown to over 4,300 testimonies. Further in this book, Dori Laub, who together with Laurel Vlock began that project, reflects on the early phases of that undertaking and the experience of pursuing that endeavor over the years (see Chapter 4). This project has had wide influence on the concept of witnessing and opened the pathway for many documentaries, books, research articles, teaching, and research projects. Laub has written extensively on witnessing (e.g., Felman & Laub, 1992) and is considered one of the leading thinkers on this topic. The Yale Fortunoff Archives model of taking testimony has been applied to survivors of other atrocities, such as the Cambodian genocide, ethnic cleansing in Bosnia, and others.

The Holocaust Museum in Washington, D.C.

The U.S. Holocaust Memorial Museum was completed in 1993. It occupies a prominent place on the National Mall in Washington, D.C., and receives millions of visitors each year. The vast majority of visitors are not Jewish; in fact, many visitors think it is simply another museum on the mall and are witnesses by happenstance. The museum serves as an educational center as well as provides direct evidence of the Holocaust. The monumental accomplishment of this museum is that it succeeds in engaging the visitor on multiple levels. It is experiential—the visitor receives a piece of paper that identifies a person from the Holocaust, and the visitor is invited to take on that identity. Did the person survive or perish? The visitor then enters an elevator that is austere and evocative of a tomb. People are quiet. On the top level, the visitors are funneled through a narrow area that stirs the feeling of danger and apprehension. After the exhibits in the museum, there are large video screens of oral testimony by survivors. The genius of this museum is that it melds the unimaginable scale of the atrocities with the specificity of the individual stories.

The museum also connects in a very concrete way with the experiences of survivors. In our interview with Hana and Edgar Krasa (see Chapter 13), we learned that a dress belonging to Hana's mother had been on exhibit at the Holocaust Museum. The dress had the infamous yellow star sewn on it. Hana had recently received the dress from the museum and told us that she could not bring herself to open the package. Her son, however, was eager to see the dress again. Michael Berenbaum, who served as director of the U.S. Holocaust Memorial Museum, has stated that the museum plays a role in the "Americanization of the Holocaust." In his view, the "story had to be told in such a way that it would resonate not only with the survivor in New York and his children in San Francisco, but with the black leader from Atlanta, a Midwestern farmer, or a northeastern industrialist" (Wieviorka, 2006, p. 124). In more recent years, the Holocaust Museum has been active in addressing such current atrocities as Darfur, Rwanda, and Bosnia. Bridget Conley-Zilkic (Chapter 25) addresses the participation of the Holocaust Museum in addressing recent genocides.

The Memorial for the Murdered Jews of Europe

Sixty-five years after the end of the war, the Memorial for the Murdered Jews of Europe in Berlin was completed. It is widely admired for its symbolic impact. The language used to designate the memorial is notable: The euphemisms of *perished* or *lost* have been eliminated and replaced by the word *murdered*. The memorial consists of 2,711 rectangular concrete blocks. The site covers close to 5 acres in the center of Berlin, just steps from the Brandenburg Gate. There are no demarcated boundaries to the memorial. There is, however, a sense of relief and reorientation when finding the edges. The surface on which you walk is uneven in all directions, both vertically and horizontally, leading to a feeling of vertigo. The experience of walking through is visceral—evoking anxiety and disorientation. The museum under the memorial contains a darkened room in which reproductions of postcards illuminated from below are laid out on the floor. There is a space in this room to see the messages, read them, and linger above a card with eyes caste down and to use the darkness of the room as a cushion for feeling and knowing. The cards contain simple messages, some asking relatives for help, others expressing the hope that the horrors will be believed. The poet Miklos Rodnotti wrote this postcard, which is on display in the Museum:

> I fell beside him and his corpse turned over, tight already as a snapping string; shot in the neck—and that's how you'll end too—I whispered to myself; lie still, no moving. Now patience flowers in death. Then I could hear—*Der spricht noch auf*, above and very near. Blood mixed with mud was drying on my ear.

Rodnotti was murdered in western Hungary. His remains were exhumed from a mass grave, and the poem was found in a notebook in his jacket. Elsa Blum writes about her photographic documentation of her visit to this memorial in the "Traces" section.

WITNESSING IN THE 21ST CENTURY

In the 21st century, there are fewer and fewer survivors of the Holocaust left to bear witness. The child survivors are now adults in their 60s and 70s. There is clearly a race against time and death for the survivors. On a daily basis, the newspapers are reporting the obituaries of survivors, rescuers, and perpetrators. Consequently, both the necessity and the opportunity for new levels and perspectives of witnessing present themselves. The expansion of our capacity to bear witness in many forms also serves to inform the perspective on atrocities and genocides in the present times. While the Nazis were determined to leave no trace of the Jews of Europe and the culture of the Jewish people, they did not succeed in that effort. The remains, the traces, exist, not only because there were survivors, but also because of the determination to have the facts known. This determination now extends into the present with the conviction that we must know the terrible, unspeakable acts that can be committed by man against man. Ervin Staub (1989) wrote about recognizing and preventing genocide. He emphasized both the prevention of violence through contact with the "other" and the role of testimony in the reconciliation and healing process in modern atrocities.

CONCLUSION

In this chapter, I reviewed a process—the relationship between witnessing and the context in which that witnessing occurs. I posit that those individuals who felt compelled to record their experiences contemporaneous with the genocide, in words, artwork, or poetry, were holding in mind a willing witness—someone who would want to know. This "internal" other provided hope and a sense of not being utterly alone in the face of imminent death. I then traced the trajectory of witnessing over the years and up to the present time. A complex relationship between the opening and closing of witnessing exists as a result of many factors that interact on multiple levels. Explicitly, I highlighted the intrapsychic dyad, the interpersonal willingness to know and the societal capacity to receive. While early in the postwar years there were some who were determined to take testimony and bear witness, there were others who turned a blind eye.

The psychic timeline will continue to be in a complex dynamic relationship to the events of history. It is our intention and hope that our work in this book will contribute to our knowledge and understanding of this multidirectional relationship between individual traumatic experiences and the capacity for there to be willing witnesses, both as individuals and in the broader society. The witnessing, itself, takes many forms—diaries, poetry, art, museums, moments of remembrance, and historic writing. Words are necessary, but perhaps not enough. We emphasize, in addition, the importance of the metaphoric acts of remembrance.

An article in *Smithsonian* magazine entitled "Can Auschwitz Be Saved?" (Curry, 2010) sheds light on this. This death camp has been declared a UNESCO (United Nations Educational, Scientific, and Cultural Organization) World Heritage Site. This designation is usually assigned to places of beauty and culture for the purpose of preservation. The article focuses on the dilemma of how to preserve the camp. Auschwitz itself covers 50 acres, and Birkenau (the satellite camp) covers more than 400 acres. In the year 2009, more than 1 million people visited Auschwitz. The director of the Auschwitz Museum is quoted as saying, "Auschwitz is a place of memory, but it's not just about history—it's also about the future." The central debate highlighted in the article is whether to allow the ravages of time to occur as a symbol of the atrocities or to preserve the camp. Mounds of hair cut from the prisoners' heads as they were led to the gas chambers have been preserved as evidence; however, over the years, the hair has decayed. It has been decided to allow for the natural decay rather than try to preserve these human remains. The memorial design committee approved a design that would allow the ruins to crumble in order to "confront oblivion." This proposal was vehemently rejected by survivors, who felt that the plan did not represent remembrance sufficiently. The historian Robert Janvan Pelt stated, "It's a place that constantly needs to be rebuilt in order to remain a ruin for us."

That debate captures the central dilemma and paradox of the psychic timeline as it refers to the Holocaust. Sixty-five years after liberation, there are few survivors remaining to serve as their own witnesses; the ongoing task of remembering is left to be honored by others. How do we do this? Do we create "theme parks"? Do we face the "nothingness"? Do we attempt to find some middle ground that honors both the atrocities and the survival? There is no simple answer to these questions.

As we enter the 21st century, we are faced with new challenges to these issues. This remains a process without an end point. In our process of writing and editing this book, we were deeply aware that we would never bring our work to a close. We know that we would not and perhaps never would be "finished." The task is too great, the monstrosity too incalculable ever to be fully comprehended.

REFERENCES

Abzug, R. H. (1985). *Inside the vicious heart: Americans and the liberation of Nazi concentration camps.* New York: Oxford University Press.

Abzug, R. H. (1999). *America views the Holocaust, 1933–1945: A brief documentary history.* New York: Palgrave Macmillan.

Bandura, A. (1999). Moral disengagement in the perpetration of inhumanities. *Personality and Social Psychology Review, 3*(3), 193–209.

Bandura, A., Barbaranelli, C., Caprara, G. V., & Pastorelli, C. (1996). Multifaceted impact of self-efficacy beliefs on academic functioning. *Child Development, 67*(3), 1206–1222.

Berger, J. (2009). For Ann Frank's tree, 11 places to bloom. *New York Times,* A22.

Boder, D. P. (1949). *I did not interview the dead.* Urbana: University of Illinois Press.

Curry, A. (2010). Can Auschwitz be saved? *Smithsonian,* Feb. 2010.

Des Pres, T. (1976). *The survivor: An anatomy of life in the death camps.* New York: Oxford University Press.

Engelman, T. C., Day, M., & Durant, S. (1993). The nature of time and psychotherapeutic experience: When treatment duration shifts from time-limited to long-term. In S. Rutan (Ed.), *Psychotherapy for the 1990s* (pp. 119–137). New York: Guilford Press.

Felman, S., & Laub, D. (1992) *Testimony: Crises of witnessing in literature, psychoanalysis, and history.* New York: Routledge.

Frank, O., & Pressler, M. (Eds.) (1996). *Diary of a young girl.* New York: Anchor Press.

Freidlander, S. (1997). *Years of persecution.* London: Orion House.

Goldhagen, D. (2000). *Hitler's willing executioners: Ordinary Germans and the Holocaust.* New York: Vintage.

Gowan, A. (2010). Concentration camp liberators gather in Washington. *Washington Post,* April 15, 2010.

Kassow, S. D. (2007). *Who will write our history?* Bloomington: Indiana University Press.

Kipp, M. (2007). The Holocaust in the letters of German soldiers on the Eastern Front (1939–1944). *Journal of Genocide Research, 9*(4), 601–615.

Langer, L. (2006). *Using and abusing the Holocaust.* Bloomington: Indiana University Press.

Levi, P., & de Benedetti, L. (2006). *The Auschwitz report.* New York: Verso.

Lifton, R. J. (2000). *The Nazi doctors: Medical killing and the psychology of genocide.* New York: Basic Books.

Margolis, R. (1999). *The Ponary diaries: A bystander's account of a mass murder, 1941–1943* (Y. Arad, Ed.). New Haven, CT: Yale University Press.

Staub, E. (1989). *The roots of evil: The origins of genocide and other group violence.* New York: Cambridge University Press.

Wieviorka, A. (2006). *The era of the witness.* Ithaca, NY: Cornell University Press.

Chapter 3

The "Anti-Train"

A Metaphor for Witnessing

Nancy R. Goodman

INTRODUCTION

When trying to grasp the realities of the Holocaust and of all mass trauma, a witnessing process is essential to allow the story to enter one's mind and to be able to hold on to one's sanity. A force, an anti-trauma force, is needed to counter the overwhelming impact felt when facing absolutely horrifying events. There must be a belief that there is a receiver of the story, internal or external, who will be unwavering in listening and will accept its truth. This is necessary as well for development of a witnessing process in psychoanalytic therapies when facing terrors in the mind, and I thank my patients for teaching me in depth about this. I develop here a metaphor, the "Anti-Train," to represent the power of witnessing. You are invited to enter this place as you also become a witness and join with others. In my descriptions, you will find a special location for partnership and valuing of finding out what happened and how the stories can be told. As a symbol, the features of the Anti-Train embody the attributes put forth in Chapter 1 considered essential for creation of witnessing: the desire to know, holding, containing, and absorbing of the inevitable annihilation terror.

The idea of the Anti-Train grew out of the experiences we had making contact, over and over again, with the terrible events of the Holocaust and making contact with those we invited to participate in our community of witnesses. We were continually amazed at their evocative writings. One day, when Nina Shapiro-Perl (see Chapter 18), Marilyn, and I were talking about contributors' enthusiasm to write for the book, I said I thought we were forming something I wanted to call an "Anti-Train." We now had a symbolic representation for the power of witnessing. Others quickly intuited the significance of both the *Anti* and the *Train*. The *Anti* refers to a forceful determination to overcome the fear induced by viewing the impossible occurrences of the Holocaust; the *Train* forms an immediate link to the Nazi transports carrying the Jewish population of Europe to their deaths and doing so in absolutely inhumane ways.

Even to begin to know the hideous truths about this genocide and all terrifying events, mass and individual, this place of Anti-Train is required. When getting lost, it is essential to feel one can find a home again where others are waiting, or it can seem that there is little reason to hold oneself together. The Anti-Train represents the place where being 'with' exists. To show how the place of the Anti-Train functions to make a witnessing process, I present my imaginings about the Anti-Train and stories of actual Nazi trains. By entering the world of the Anti-Train, the traumatic feel of the Nazi trains can be faced. I invite the reader to the restorative environment of the Anti-Train as I also bring you to truths of the annihilating Nazi trains.

The details of the structure of the Anti-Train metaphor bring about space and maintain a barrier between the events of the Holocaust and the viewing of the Holocaust. From the interior of the train, there is choice about when and for how long to look out of the window at the landscape of the Nazi death machine. The windows and the movement of the train provide framing of what is being seen so that a sense of seeing and not seeing and seeing again is established. This type of altering of focus is an essential aspect of being able to perceive and process overwhelming anxiety. The enormity of the trauma felt when experiencing raw perceptions is, at least momentarily, kept outside, giving some opportunity to cushion the impact within the movement of the train and the presence of companions doing their own viewing and processing. The capacity to believe that narration, making a story with words and symbols that are bound in a sense of time, is strengthened in the feel of being with others who want to hear perceptions and emotional responses. In this small way, the Holocaust remains outside, and the experience of knowing, taking place with others, is inside the Anti-Train. This is obviously a wished-for reality that does not exist when immediately traumatized and one is inside the trauma and the trauma is inside one's experience. When truths about the Holocaust break through, despair and grief are deeply felt, and the state of being traumatized crashes through stability, making distinction between inside and outside almost impossible. Terror annihilates, and the certainty of annihilation terrorizes. And yet, trauma is also absorbed enough to continue the journey. With the containment of trauma taking place on the Anti-Train, one can bear the affects ignited by this living nightmare and wounding.

Seventy years have passed since liberation of the concentration camps. Survivors have led full lives even when the most terrible of traumas remain within their psychic life. They have found the courage to speak and to find words and images for revealing their terror. Knowing and feeling that there are witnesses revivifies a link to others and to thinking about how to speak these truths.

NAZI TRAIN I

Two years after his liberation from Auschwitz, Primo Levi published his account of his experience in the Lager. His book was first published in Italian in 1947 under the title *Se Questo è un Uomo* (*If This Is a Man*) and translated into English in 1958. In this book, under the title, *Survival in Auschwitz* (1996), Levi describes his journey in February 1944 from the detention camp of Fossoli to Auschwitz. His writing is direct, articulate, and slightly removed. His portrayals provide clear knowledge of the events. In the sensations of his remembrance, we are almost there. Reading every word and sentence of his descriptions brings the reader into direct contact with the "too much" and "too little" of the Nazi train. Yet, his willingness to find a way to convey his experience helps bring us aboard the Anti-Train by providing us with a manuscript we appreciate. We want to witness his witnessing. As readers allow his descriptions to resonate within, consciously and unconsciously, they can say to themselves: "It is possible to create a way to tell."

> But, on the morning of the 21st we learned that on the following day the Jews would be leaving. All Jews, without exception. Even the children, even the old, even the ill. (p. 14)
>
> And night came, and it was such a night that one knew that human eyes would not witness it and survive. (p. 15)
>
> With the absurd precision to which we later had to accustom ourselves, the Germans held the roll-call. At the end the officer asked, 'Wieviel stück?' The corporal saluted smartly and replied that there were six hundred and fifty 'pieces' and that all was in order. (p. 16)
>
> There were twelve goods wagons for six hundred and fifty men; in mine we were only forty-five, but it was a small wagon. Here then, before our very eyes, under our very feet, was one of those notorious transport trains, those which never return, and of which, shuddering and always a little incredulous, we had so often heard speak. Exactly like this, detail for detail: goods wagons closed from the outside, with men, women and children pressed together without pity, like cheap merchandise for a journey towards nothingness, a journey down there, towards the bottom. This time it is us who are inside. (pp. 16–17)
>
> We suffered from thirst and cold; at every stop we clamored for water, or even a handful of snow, but we were rarely heard; the soldiers of the escort drove off anybody who tried to approach the convoy. Two young mothers, nursing their children, groaned night and day, begging for water. Our state of nervous tension made the hunger, exhaustion and lack of sleep seem less of a torment. But the hours of darkness were nightmares without end. (p. 18)

And then, Levi describes the end of the journey—the arrival.

> In less than ten minutes all the fit men had been collected together in a
> group. What happened to the others, to the women, to the children, to
> the old men, we could establish neither then nor later: the night swal-
> lowed them up, purely and simply. ... We know that of our convoy no
> more than ninety-six men and twenty-nine women entered the respec-
> tive camps of Monowitz-Buna and Birkenau, and that of all the others,
> more than five hundred in number, not one was living two days later.
> (pp. 19–20)

Is it possible to really think about what he is telling us? Primo Levi's
words of witnessing bring us to something that is almost unbearable. It is
tempting to divide up the statements with commentary to take in what
is happening. The transport itself was for "nights and days." Such a simple
statement lets us know that these nights and days are special in their reference to devastation. Something had to be endured and for a long time.
Would it help to try to think about specific phrases, such as "even the
children, even the old, even the ill"? The word *even* contains the astonish-
ment, and yet we do not get to stop there. What do we do with the starkness of the use of the word *pieces* in referring to the 650 human beings in
the train cars? Stopping at these specific places sometimes brings a more
traumatic feel than going on to the next sentence. Levi provides us with
poetic descriptions showing what can be narrated while reaching deeply
into the psyche, arousing felt terror. An example is his question: "What
happened to the others, to the women, to the children, to the old men, we
could establish neither then nor later: the night swallowed them up, purely
and simply."

At the beginning of his finding a way to record memories of the transport, Levi presents the overriding question of how to survive knowing the
Holocaust: "And night came, and it was such a night that one knew that
human eyes would not witness it and survive." How did he find the ability to give this type of testimony, to open his mind to himself and to let us
in? Throughout his time in Auschwitz, he was with his friend and fellow
scientist, Leonardo de Benedetti. On liberation, they were both asked by
the Russians to chronicle living conditions in Auschwitz, and they did so
together, writing *The Auschwitz Report* (Levi & Benedetti, 2006). In many
of his descriptions of the inhumanity of his conditions, he refers to "we."
I speculate he was keeping in his mind an idea of someone who cared to
know how he was knowing. I am very aware that this sense of a "we" must
be constructed and sustained with all psychoanalytic patients to find fears
and creativities in their minds and in my own mind.

ANTI-TRAIN I

Each person incurring the emotional impact of knowing mass trauma needs a place of Anti-Train in his or her mind. My imagined Anti-Train is elegant and comfortable with high-back chairs and soft light shining through creamy etched crystal fixtures and lamps. There are colleagues and friends to be with who respect the desire to be alone. On this train, there is modern technology, providing Internet access at all moments for searching into the world of cyberspace, where Holocaust primary and secondary sources are on view. You can hear and see survivors and children of survivors giving testimonies. Filming of the liberation of concentration camps is on the Internet. Wondrous acts of witnessing appearing in paintings, poems, novels, sculptures, and monuments can be found and appreciated. I can read about the kindertransports that carried children away from family, often forever, to safety in Britain. I need an extensive psychoanalytic library for comfort. I can locate reading concerning therapeutic development of a listening environment effective for hearing psychic pain and ways to understand how to help transform and heal terrible trauma. The vitality of these topics provides comfort, wisdom, and hope. There is too much to find and never enough to sate the need to search further and to try to comprehend. On the Anti-Train, the sources of information can all be approached alone, in a private place, or in the company of others who also search.

The interior of my Anti-Train has dark wood, shiny brass, velvet, and thick carpet. The sound of the train moving along the tracks is rhythmic and soothing, with an occasional low whistle-sound being emitted. This is an idealized train for sure, probably inspired from 1940s films and perhaps from picking up a relative at the Chicago Union Station or a trip to grandparents in Miami and memories of hearing distant freight trains from my childhood bedroom windows. It stays in my mind in opposition to newsreel footage of transports that carried Jews to their deaths. I am certain that these Nazi trains were also placed in my mind in childhood and existed in the minds of my Jewish parents and my society, often to be disavowed, denied, and felt as shameful. When there is momentum to know the landscape of the Holocaust and the existence of an Anti-Train in the mind, Nazi trains and the details of the terrible journeys on them can come more into view.

NAZI TRAIN II

The train as icon of the Holocaust appears repeatedly in memoirs and histories of the Nazi period. Families are rounded up and taken from their homes and are further divided, pushed into separate lines and onto different cattle cars. We know that these trains traveled along the many tracks throughout Europe leading to concentration camps. On these trains, there was no ventilation, no temperature control, no food, no water, no light, no toilet, no room to lie down. It was often days before the trains arrived at their destinations. They went in one direction full and came back empty. Many people died on these trains.

These Nazi trains represent the force of death and inhumanity, making it almost impossible to think of the inside of the train car or the inside of the passengers' minds as they recognized how they were forgotten people. On January 20, 1942, at the Wannsee Conference, named for the suburb of Berlin where it took place, a group of Nazi officials signed a document in which the murder of 11 million Jewish people was laid out with bureaucratic precision. The television film *Conspiracy* (Pierson, 2001) is acted as a believable docudrama showing the Wannsee "conversation" taking place at an elegant dining table in a beautiful villa. It is a luncheon; there is conversation about the wine and the food; there is counting of the numbers of Jews in various countries; the "final solution" for the Jewish population is agreed upon. It is absolutely impossible to accept the existence of this document and to recognize that reason and logic were used so perversely to justify the planned murder of the 11 million Jewish people counted on the lists distributed around the table. It was also decided to destroy every possible remnant of Jewish culture. Trains were the method of transport to facilitate the bringing about of the goal of genocide.

Visitors to the Holocaust Museum in Washington, D.C. walk through a train car as they progress through the exhibits in the museum. The walk through is quite easy, with an entrance and exit clearly visible, belying the claustrophobia in the mind thinking of the possibility of being in such a train car. It is extremely chilling to see maps of the network of train tracks in Europe leading to concentration camps, labor camps, and detention camps. Acknowledging the movement of these trains through the cities, towns, villages, farmlands, and forests of Europe brings about harsh reckoning of how many people were carried to their death while silent others watched.

Trains are often powerful images in film portrayals of the Holocaust. The opening sequence in Steven Spielberg's film production of *Schindler's List* (1993) shows smoke wafting up from a candle on the table of a Jewish family celebrating Shabbat (see Chapter 20). The soft gray smoke melds into the spewing smoke coming from a train stack. A scene in Lanzmann's almost 9½-hour film *Shoah* (1985) shows Polish men demonstrating a gesture of death they made to the Jews on the trains that passed by. They put their arm and hand up to their necks with a quick horizontal movement indicating slaughter.

ANTI-TRAIN II

Nighttime on the Anti-Train is particularly noteworthy because of the reflective capacity of the windows to give access to the terrible darkness of night while mirroring the peopled interior space. Reference to darkness is often made by authors writing about the Holocaust. For example, Geoffrey Hartman (Chapter 5), who joined us on this Anti-Train, titled his book of essays *The Longest Shadow: In the Aftermath of the Holocaust* (1996). Elie Wiesel wrote his personal account of the Holocaust in his book, *Night* (1960), first published in French as *La Nuit* (1958). The witnessing environment of the train car allows room to feel and fosters a capacity to take in the genocide that took place outside the windows and now is also in one's mind. The space within the train allows one to think and feel about the Holocaust and the special place of being a witness both to others and to one's own psychic resonances of trauma.

On the Anti-Train, one is not completely alone. Contact with others is always available. The reflections of self and others in the glass, which separates inside from outside, lends possibility for acknowledgment and the beginning of absorption of what is being seen. This special experience of the reflecting window of the train car is also a place in the mind where inner sight of the Holocaust fluctuates between unknowable and knowable, between nothing and something, and between muteness and speaking. The activity of the day—the research, discussions, actual excitement of new discoveries and ways to transform them into told truths—is present as well as quiet solitude. Different perspectives are available. At times, activity may be a kind of manic covering over of sadness and traumatizing states of deadness. Mostly, the Anti-Train is a place of creativity and dialogue sometimes fueled by the need to conquer despair and by the energy of being alive with others. There is the promise that others want to know and want to make links between one and another. When these links are made, there can also be links within one's own mind, allowing approach to what verges on the too terrible. The type of micro-unconscious signaling that knowing is wanted and tolerable to someone else keeps the forces of the Anti-Train moving.

NAZI TRAIN III

The historian Sir Martin Gilbert recorded the history of transports in his book, *Final Journey: The Fate of the Jews in Nazi Europe* (1979). Many chapters are about specific transports (e.g., "Journey to Lublin," "The City of Lodz," "France: Convoy No. 1," "The Jews of Holland"). Some titles are about particular people or groups ("Nobody Came Back … ," "Sophia's Story," "The Children's Convoys"). The titles themselves are almost unreadable in their reference to so many people being carried to their deaths. Each chapter contains details of the names of individuals and cities and villages and of numbers referring to time, size of train car, and people on each car. In Gilbert's own words:

> I have tried to tell the stories of individuals, as well as of communities. On their own, the statistics are powerful and terrible. But the story of the Nazi attempt to murder the Jews of Europe concerned individual people; people with names, families, careers and futures, for millions of whom no one survived to mourn, or to remember. (p. 7)

I use excerpts from his chapter "A Single Train" to continue illustrating the difficulty of being a witness to the Nazi train and the need for the Anti-Train to mobilize the power of witnessing to do so. This chapter is three pages long with over half of the space used for photographs taken by a Polish photographer asked by the Germans to record the events of the day of July 31, 1940. Olkusz was a Polish village with 6,000 inhabitants, half of whom were Jewish. There was a 600-year-old history of Jewish life in this town, which the German troops entered on September 5, 1939. As the Jewish populations of nearby areas were brought to Olkusz, the population increased by 800. A ghetto area was established near the town at the end of 1941. There were hangings and deportations to labor camps, reducing the population by over 1,000. Gilbert's use of detail is shown here as he describes the Nazi's determination to find every single Jewish inhabitant of this village and send them to their deaths.

> As the Jews of Olkusz were being deported seven Olkusz-born Jews, who had been living for some years in France, were arrested in Paris and taken to Drancy. The first to be sent to Auschwitz on 5 June 1942 was the forty-two-year-old Jacob Goldfield. Two months later Malka Rorcfeld was deported with her fifteen-year-old daughter Fryda. Of these seven Olkusz-born Jews, the last to be deported from Paris, the sixty-two-year-old Maurice Stark, reached Auschwitz at the end of March 1944.
>
> Meanwhile, in July 1942 the able-bodied men left in Olkusz were sent to labour camps. Then all the Jews still in the town, more than a thousand women, old men, children, cripples and the sick, together with their rabbi, were deported to Auschwitz: a single train, and a brief journey, only sixty-four kilometers, the sole aim of which was to destroy a whole community.
>
> Following this final deportation, twenty Jews were left in Olkusz to "clear up" the ghetto. All the belongings of its former inhabitants were taken as booty by the occupation forces. Then those twenty were themselves deported to Auschwitz, and murdered. The Jews of Olkusz were no more. (p. 180)

How is it possible to conceive of the idea that a policy was developed to find every Jewish man, woman, and child from this village, to ensure their deaths, to record each detail about it, and to photograph it? What part of this story of "a single train" is able to sink into our minds? I find it helpful to think about the working of the historian and of the prescience of the photographer, who made a second set of prints. Martin Gilbert somehow could bear to write chapter after chapter, wanting to find as many names of individuals as he could to give memory to their lives. Thinking of his determination in this book, and in all of his many Holocaust books (see www.martingilbert.com), helps transmit an Anti-Train to our minds. The historian and photographer here are witnesses helping to make witnessing possible. By adding material to be placed in the library of the Anti-Train, they help create the elements of holding and containment making up the essence of the Anti-Train itself.

ANTI-TRAIN III

Survivors who have written and spoken their stories and created artistic representations lead the way in giving permission to create. They are the first to construct an Anti-Train for the rest of us. Witnessing begets further witnessing, and witnessing feels alive. The Holocaust is pure Thanatos (death instinct); the capacity to witness with others is a dynamic libido (life instinct). Everyone on board is fully aware that there are traumatizing moments, deeply felt and at times barely containable. Each individual can decide when to connect with the landscape of the Holocaust and when and how to take a break. In this way, the Anti-Train provides the basic necessities for witnessing to take place. There are others who want to know and communicate, providing capacity for self-determined movement of the mind toward and away from that which is emotionally overwhelming.

Freud (1913) also set forth the image of the train as a metaphor for the way the unconscious and what is terrifying in it can be viewed and brought into contact with the conscious mind. The analyst was to instruct the patient as follows: "So, say whatever goes through your mind. Act as though for instance, you were a traveler sitting next to a window of a railway carriage and describing to someone inside the carriage the changing views which you see outside" (p. 135). In mining fuller meaning of the train trope for Freud, Lewin (1970) expanded the technical advice to beginning analysands to the realm of how a window to the outside is also the window to the inside, the psychic journey. There is thus an ongoing relation between discovering the outside, what is seen, and discovering the inside of one's mind. In this use of the metaphor, it is recognized that the outside visual scene and felt sense of the scene is a projection of something in the mind. The psychoanalytic process involves coming to see, feel, and reflect on what is deep in one's mind by first bringing it into a place where it can be found with the therapist. In regard to external traumatic realities, they are first outside and then evermore both inside and outside. The trauma of the Holocaust gets inside quickly, and when the outside cannot be reflected on, neither can the inside of one's own experience, leaving blank spaces. On the Anti-Train, an individual develops the ability to look outside and look at the internal subjective responses taking place.

In the transcript of our conversation with Laub (see Chapter 1), he spoke of a testimony story in which a survivor recalled using the idea that she was on a passing train seeing the inmates of the concentration camp, of which she was one. She developed an idea of her Anti-Train, the witnessing place from which she as victim could be seen. Each time a survivor tells about his or her Nazi train experience, the survivor has created an Anti-Train within, first a place to be put into words and later a place receiving reflection and some working through: "This really happened; this really can be known; this can be known with another and has meaning." Laub (personal communication, 2008) told us about a trip he made by train to Germany in 1994 to give a talk. He was robbed of his wallet, passport, and train tickets and was very upset and felt "back in that place" without identity. He tried to talk to people in his coupé, who did not respond. "I could not stand it, and went, and found myself a coupé without anyone in it. Ten minutes later a young woman joins me and says: 'I want to keep you company. I saw what happened. ... I am uncomfortable with how these people aren't helping you.'" She became his witness. The story holds dread and reawakening of Holocaust trauma until the witness appears. With witnessing, it can become a train that is felt in a different way. The trauma is still there and is attenuated by the willingness of the witness to stay with the experience of the traumatized person.

The idea of the Anti-Train is used to convey how a witnessing process takes place and helps sustain a capacity to take in the horrific and traumatizing actualities of the Holocaust. Acts of witnessing help maintain the environment of the Anti-Train by communicating the possibility that precisely that thing that feels too much to know needs to be known and can be known in some way. These contrasting truths—that there is an Anti-Train and there is the Nazi train—are beautifully illustrated in writings of Charlotte Delbo. In her book *Convoy to Auschwitz: Women of the French Resistance* (1965/1997), Delbo witnesses the 230 women political prisoners who were with her on a transport from Compiègne to Auschwitz on January 24, 1943. She wrote what she was able to find about the life and death of each woman. Most of these biographies are brief since only 49 of the women survived. She found an Anti-Train in her mind, writing her remarkable poetry trilogy *Auschwitz and After* (1995), first appearing in French in 1946. Through her writing, she helps us ride on the Anti-Train, joining with the process of witnessing. In her first poem, "Arrivals and Departures," her writing moves between descriptions we can imagine (allowing us space on the Anti-Train) and descriptions we can barely tolerate (views of the Nazi trains). For example, she takes us into the transport train with this phrase: "There's a little girl who hugs her doll against her chest, dolls can be smothered too" (p. 7). She has miraculously found a way to convey what is impossible to fully know and gives us an image in which we find the familiar with body and emotional resonance, "a little girl who hugs her doll," and the terribleness of "smothered too." Delbo exquisitely combines senses of what we know in ordinary ways with what she tells us about the extraordinary as she brings us close to the realities of the transports.

> People arrive. They look through the crowd of those who are waiting, those who await them. They kiss them and say the trip exhausted them.
>   People leave. They say good-bye to those who are not leaving and hug the children. (p. 3)

As we read and take in Delbo's description, it is clear that this is something we all know. It is familiar. Then she brings us to the traumatic.

> But there is a station where those who arrive are those who are leaving
>   a station where those who arrive have never arrived, where those who have left never come back.
>   It is the largest station in the world.
>   This is the station they reach, from wherever they came.
>   They got here after days and nights
>   having crossed many countries
>   they reach it together with their children, even the little ones who were not to be part of this journey (p. 3)[1]

Each contributor to this volume has found an Anti-Train in his or her mind and has helped to create an Anti-Train for this book. Indeed, each chapter is a train car—one after the other, separate but connected—in the Anti-Train of this book. It is gratifying to have each reader join with others to help sustain the Anti-Train.

---

[1] From Delbo, C., *Auschwitz and After.* © 1995 Yale University Press. Reprinted with permission.

REFERENCES

Delbo, C. (1995). *Auschwitz and after*. New Haven, CT: Yale University Press. (Original work published 1946)

Delbo, C. (1997). *Convoy to Auschwitz: Women of the French resistance* (C. Cosman, Trans.). Boston: Northeastern University Press. (Original work published 1965)

Freud, S. (1913). On beginning the treatment (further recommendations on the technique of psychoanalysis I). In J. Strachey (Ed. & Trans.), *The standard edition of the complete psychological works of Sigmund Freud* (Vol. 12, pp. 121–144). London: Hogarth Press.

Gilbert, M. (1979), *Final journey: The fate of the Jews in Nazi Europe*. London: Allen and Unwin.

Hartman, G. A. (1996). *The longest shadow: In the aftermath of the Holocaust*. New York: Palgrave.

Lanzmann, C. (Director). (1985). *Shoah* [Motion picture]. France: Historia.

Levi, P. (1996). *Survival in Auschwitz: The Nazi assault on humanity* (S. Woolf, Trans.). New York: Touchstone Books.

Levi, P., & Benedetti, L. (2006). *The Auschwitz report* (J. Woolf, Trans.). New York: Verso.

Lewin, B. D. (1970). The train ride: A study of one of Freud's figures of speech. *Psychoanalytic Quarterly, 39*, 71–89.

Pierson, F. (Director). (2001). *Conspiracy* [Motion picture]. United States: HBO.

Spielberg, S. (Director). (1993). *Schindler's list* [Motion picture]. United States: Universal Pictures.

Wiesel, E. (1960). *Night*. New York: Hill and Wang.

Part 2

Reflections

Chapter 4

Testimony as Life Experience and Legacy

Dori Laub

INTRODUCTION

When trying to think of testimony, I realized that it has always been present with me as part of my life experience. I find its compelling presence in my childhood memories. I never just lived those memories; I always also observed them from the outside, in a way that I could see myself in them, thinking and understanding what was going on. This sense of enhanced presence, clarity, self-awareness, and even contemporaneity is true only for a select group of memories, mostly related to childhood traumatic experiences. Other memories do not possess this quality.

The first thing I did on entering the home I was born into after having been liberated from the Nazis in the spring of 1944 was to run to my toy cupboard. I opened it with excitement and with hope. What I saw was pitiful. It was mostly empty, and there were a few broken toys left on one of the shelves. Forty years later, when my mother gave testimony to the Fortunoff Video Archive, she took pride in describing the joy I experienced when I ran to the toy cupboard and found it full of toys, exactly the way I had left it. As I was sitting beside her at that moment, I had to correct her. My memory was totally different. She was crestfallen and said that perhaps I was right. She had so much wanted to bring me back home so that my childhood, which had been interrupted, could resume. Perhaps she remembered what she had wished for rather than what she had to face on our return.

Again, as she had done so many times before, she respected the integrity, the separateness of my voice—of my testimony. I realize now that I never resumed a normal childhood or a normal life on my return from the camp. Perhaps the rest of my childhood, and indeed of my life, was driven by the need to deal with what I had lived through in those early years.

Looking backward at my own life, I realize that the most precious possessions I have are my memories. They do not constitute a continuous, even flow over the years. They do not even feel to me as if they possess a temporal sequence. They are rather discrete experiences that stand out, powerfully etching their contours, their shape against a background that can feel rather amorphous. They are like islands that possess both clarity and force that create a field, a ripple effect around them, with wider waves of imagery and associations. Yet each island in itself contains very special realizations, as cornerstones of my own identity mosaic. I often marvel at what enabled me to experience such clear and precise knowledge of detail of the memory itself. Further, I am awed by the mechanism that allowed for reflection and self-reflection that exists underneath the power and radiance that the memories exert.

As I try to understand this, I have to think of my mother. Until the very last days of her life, she represented the same kind of clarity of vision, of absolute lack of compromise regarding what is true, as well as the total embrace of living, that I find in this testimonial dimension of my own life. She never changed in this respect as long as I remember her, in spite of a life fraught with a reality full of insurmountable dangers, massive losses, courageous acts, and difficult split-moment decisions. When in her old age, in her 80s, she had lapses of regression, I felt very afraid and deserted. I did not want to believe in her aging. My reactions most probably kept her both alive and younger for many, many years. I think I owe the brilliance of my memories to the sense of safety and trust she made me feel and that she literally provided for me. I owe the clarity of my memories to my mother, who once threw herself in front of a drawn pistol to prevent the bullets from hitting my father.

I was born in 1937 in the city of Czernovitz, in the district of Bukovina, in Romania. The country was run by a fascist anti-Semitic regime, which was militarily allied with Germany and participated in the invasion of the Soviet Union in the summer of 1941. It all began for me with a memory that dates to age 5. I was wearing a newly tailored suit and a photograph was taken in a studio. In it, I am standing smiling in front of a screen facing the camera with my right hand in the pocket of my new suit. I sensed the gravity of the moment—that this was going to be the last photo taken of an era, that things were going to change, and that it would never be the same; somehow, my childhood was at an end. I remember no particular sadness, only a certain determination, even excitement, about what was going to come mixed with a sense of fear. Incidentally, I still have that photograph.

The next memory is that of the deportation. It was a sunny, early summer afternoon, I think on June 22, 1942. We had a big, closed-in porch, a "veranda" as we called it. I was roaming around it on my tricycle. Uniformed men came in and spoke to my parents. The next thing I knew, we were packing to go to the train station. It felt that this was going to be something transitory; we were going to be back. We probably said good-bye to my maternal grandparents, with whom we lived, with the same expectation that we would be back very shortly. My father, after all, had a permit issued by the mayor that he was a much-needed municipal employee, except the color of the permit was red, and that proved to be the wrong color.

I remember the train station vaguely. I think we were searched, perhaps given a loaf of bread by representatives of the Jewish community, and ordered to the trains. I remember the journey into the night. People were standing quite crowded. Some were sitting on their luggage. People started crying. I did not know what possible reason there was to cry, but I started crying, too. My mother asked me why I was crying, and I answered that I missed my little brass bed in my bedroom. She responded that she had two coats in the luggage, and once we got to where we were going, she would sell one of them and would buy me another brass bed. I remember that promise clearly.

The journey continued. At some point, we left the train and crossed the river Dniester, the border between Romania proper and the newly occupied territories in the Soviet Union-Transnistria, to which Jews were being deported by boat. Eventually, we must have been picked up by another train, and our journey continued to an old abandoned stone quarry, which was ostensibly used by the Soviet regime as a penal colony. The name of the place was indeed in Romanian: the "Stone Quarry," Cariera de Piatra. There were barracks surrounding a square in which the "Appells" each day took place. Much later, I found out that this was the place where both parents of the poet Paul Celan perished. It was situated 300–400 feet from the River Bug, which was the demarcation line between the Romanian and the German-occupied territory in the Ukraine.

I think I was quite aware of what was going on but later refused to acknowledge and remember it. I looked a lot across the river Bug. I could see buildings and perhaps people moving on the other side of the river.

Years later, when I was 2 weeks into my psychoanalysis with a Swedish analyst while serving on the staff of a small psychiatric hospital in the Berkshires, I recounted a memory from my time in the camp. I was sitting with a little girl on the bank of the river looking into the German-occupied Ukraine. It was summertime, with a lovely view of a winding clear blue river and lush green meadows; she and I were having a lively debate about whether or not one could eat grass.

At this point, my analyst interrupted me with an anecdote of his own. "I was," he said, "a member of the Swedish Red Cross unit that was the first to enter Theresienstadt after its liberation. We took depositions under oath from many of the inmates. Several women declared that conditions had been so good that they received daily breakfast in bed, served by SS officers." My analyst said nothing more, but his remark was the most powerful commentary on my denial of what I had experienced in the Cariera de Piatra. It was his having been himself a historical witness that enabled him to see through my defensive position. His perceptiveness in turn helped to open the door that I had closed on my own story, which is part of a larger historical experience. I stopped talking about casual chats with little girls on beautiful summer days and started my own journey of recovering the gruesome events that I had lived through and witnessed. I continually felt a prevailing sense of dread and an urge to flee the camp. I often argued with my parents to let me go. They had lived, I said, and visited spas and vacation places. I had seen so little, lived so little in my life, and wanted to experience that, too. Being smaller, I thought, I could better hide, especially if I were on my own without grown-ups near me who would give me away. My mother argued with me, and I think they literally had to watch me and prevent me from running away. According to my mother, I once did escape, and they were able to locate me at night, freezing, under a bridge.

There are several scenes I very distinctly remember from the stone quarry camp. One of them was a public beating of an inmate, who was whipped over his naked upper back with the camp inmates forced to watch, standing in a circle. He was getting 25 lashes for a misdemeanor that I do not remember. I vaguely remember the whip hitting his body.

After the flogging ended, the onlookers were allowed to disperse. I did not move from my place. I was fascinated by what this man had gone through and wanted very much to find out what he thought and what he felt. I approached him and watched him in silence. I could see the bloody streaks the whip had left on his back. He was crouched over and smoking a cigarette, saying nothing. "How could he smoke a cigarette?" I thought to myself, but I did not dare to ask. I do not remember how this ended. Eventually, I also must have left, but I regard this moment as quite decisive in my life.

It was the moment in which I discovered that the urge to know and to bear witness to the experience of others was very compelling to me. It might have something to do with the ultimate choice of my profession as a psychiatrist and psychoanalyst and with the witnessing project I carry out in my professional life. I, for the first time, felt the inner compulsion to know and my own readiness to imagine what was going on in another person's mind.

I have an inner certainty that I must have watched other things, other scenes with much more brutality. While I can retrieve no clear memory of them, in some way I am certain that I watched a public hanging, and in dreams, this occasionally occurs. With all my efforts, however, I am not able to recapture a conscious memory of such events. It was only after my mother's death that it occurred to me that I could have asked her whether such public executions indeed took place. I never raised that question as long as she was alive, even though I had always wanted to know. Neither was I aware that I had failed to ask.

The most outstanding memory of the time spent in the stone quarry camp is the one regarding the day of its final liquidation. A list was being made of who could pay enough money. My family was not on that list. I remember myself as both understanding and experiencing the events with a clarity that exceeds the idea of a 5-year-old child's mind; events that had definitely not been explained or interpreted to me. I might have overheard grown-ups talking and gathered some of my information this way, but many memories are of actual moments that I lived through and visual experiences I had on my own. To this day, they are alive in front of my mind's eye.

What I remember is the gathering of all the inmates, numbering perhaps thousands, early one morning in the Appell place, the large open square that the barracks surrounded. We probably gathered there at dawn. Lots of soldiers were milling around, mostly Romanian, but some of them Germans. There was a certain disorganization everywhere. The inmates were in groups of 30, with a group leader keeping them under control. My father had that role with one of the groups.

Attorney Stoller, the maker of the list, was in the adjacent group to ours. I recall distinctly that all of a sudden, Stoller and his family, carrying their luggage, started moving out of the group. My mother turned to him and asked loudly where he was going. His answer was, "Where I go, you do not have a place; it is not for you." She promptly grabbed our luggage and took me by the hand, summoning my father to join us. He was hesitant, claiming that he had a responsibility to the group whose leader he was. Her answer to him was, "If you do not come, the child and I will go alone." He somewhat reluctantly joined us, following at some distance. We made our way between the inmates and the surrounding soldiers, who stood in some disarray. We followed Stoller and his family at a distance of probably several hundred feet. After some maybe 600–700 yards, we arrived at a house that was set aside from the larger complex of the barracks. All the doors were closed, and the windows were boarded. My mother knocked but did not gain admission. She pounded on the door forcefully, yelling, "If you do not open, I'll turn you over to the Germans." Finally, we were allowed inside.

The house was completely full, with room only for standing; perhaps 200 to 300 people were inside. We squeezed in, too, and everyone remained in complete silence. As hours passed, we could hear the sounds of trucks arriving. The inmates were loaded in the trucks to be carried across the River Bug, to the German side of the occupied Ukrainian territories. We heard screaming and crying. I also think that we heard shots. I have always imagined that some of the older, weaker people, perhaps even the children, were executed on the spot. There was an atmosphere of dread and of suspense. We all knew what was going on and tried to maintain complete silence. I had pertussis but stopped myself from coughing.

Sometime in the early afternoon, all of a sudden, there was shouting and banging on the door. A German patrol had discovered us and started shouting "Jews out" in German—"*Juden heraus.*" We were expecting the worst. I remember my father saying good-bye, embracing and taking leave from my mother, knowing that one of the first things that would happen was that men and women would be separated from each other. He gave her his watch so that she could sell it for food and perhaps be able to buy some time in this way. In the commotion, someone had the idea of calling the Romanian commandant, and a messenger slipped through. Luckily, the Romanian officer arrived and made his claim that the group of Jews in the house was indeed the specialists he needed to keep running the camp after the total evacuation.

As the afternoon wore on, things began to quiet down. I remember our return to the empty barracks. As we walked across the porches, there was an echo that resounded from our steps. I think it was early October, on a cloudless night bright with stars. I looked up into the infinity and asked my father how deep the sky was. Perhaps I even asked whether God was up there beyond all this. My father understood the real nature of my question, and his answer was, "Churchill and Roosevelt will not allow this to happen."

This was my last memory from the stone quarry camp. I know that we were advised not to be seen from across the Bug because the Germans might come again to fetch us. After some time, we were also told that from now on, we were nonexistent on any books. The camp population was no more. We dispersed in small groups with Romanian soldiers guarding us.

We eventually ended up in the Jewish ghetto of the town of Obodovka. We lived in a room with a window that looked out onto the main road. I spent endless hours watching this road. It was the route that the Romanian and German troops took to go to the front line. Infantry, artillery pieces, armored cars, and ambulances kept moving nonstop, day and night. Once, two German soldiers in gray-bluish uniforms came into our house. I was paralyzed with fear, but all they were looking for was a piece of rope. I remember seeing two youngish men, perhaps even boys, who were confused at our response. They definitely had no intent to harm.

One particular day, I noticed something strange. The movement on the road was now in the opposite direction: infantry, tanks, artillery pieces, armored vehicles, motorcycles, and most of all, ambulances, in an endless stream all day and night. I did not understand the reversal of direction. It lasted for about 7 days or longer, and then there were no more troops marching. The road was quiet for hours. In the distance, we could hear the rumbling sounds of artillery being fired. Then, all of a sudden, a group of motorcycles appeared. The soldiers wore different uniforms; something had totally changed. These were the first Soviet scouts who entered our town, and we were liberated. We joined the Soviet troops and began our way back home. We hitchhiked on trucks, buses, and trains. Jews came out from everywhere, ghettos, hiding places, and forests. No one knew who was still alive, but we were all heading home to Czernowitz.

When I review the pages that I have just written, what stands out glaringly to me is what I have left out. A pervasive experience I omitted from what I previously wrote was an almost continuous sense of dread. My days in the camp were times of sheer terror. I knew quite accurately what was happening. My so-called composure was both real and a façade—a thin exterior veil over an inner life flooded by dread. There were moments when it was obvious that something was imminent, that something new was going to happen. I could envision the gray-uniformed soldiers and their helmets. My vision was mostly of their legs, strutting by, raised high up with their knees unbent, marching. This is probably what I saw as a child; my gaze was focused on their shiny boots. When I looked up, I saw baby faces topped by steel helmets. I can remember their heavy belts, their shiny helmets tightly fitted on their heads, and their rifles loosely hanging on their shoulders. These soldiers were going to come and do something to us with the bayonets stuck on top of their rifles. I did not allow myself to feel any further. I could feel an overwhelming sense of terror piercing through my body, almost paralyzing me. I can almost feel it now when I merely think about it. It travels to my fingertips and is accompanied by a weird sense of numbness. I can hardly move. Some sounds are droning in my ears. I am almost outside myself. I am nauseated and start to retch. I may have screamed while retching. I was terrified that they were coming.

It is obvious to me that my leaving out these observations is an attempt to keep my childhood memories separate from my present life, as though belonging to a world of their own, which has ended and is no longer mine. It is a version of my father's refusal to know of the deadliness that permeated every corner of our lives. It is similar to his attempt to believe that by doing the right thing in following orders, he could keep the disasters at arm's length. The oversights I have mentioned put into question the integrity and the completeness of my testimony, the very testimony and reflection that is included in each one of the memories themselves. Like any other survivor, I therefore personify the conflict I mentioned, carried out explicitly between my father's denial and my mother's accurate perception and her capacity to respond and react consequentially to what she perceived.

After this detour to name the terror, but before returning to memories, I have to ask myself the question: How does testimony hold up when the reign of terror is complete, when its hold on life is total and all-encompassing? The answer to this question is shattering. It does not. When terror prevails, it eclipses everything else. It is like a hurricane that leaves only destruction in its path. But like a hurricane, it passes, and the sky clears up, and then a clearer vision is back. Any hurricane that just has gone by seems quite unreal, incomprehensible. Were it not for the destruction it left in its trail, one could almost deny its occurrence.

FURTHER REFLECTIONS ON TRAUMATIC TESTIMONY

There is another aspect to my memories, for which I would like to use the term *layering*. I shall begin with a personal communication from the psychoanalyst Marion Pritchard, from Vermont. This happened in the early 1990s at the meeting of the group Children and War in Boston, Massachusetts, which we both attended. During lunch break, I asked Marion how much children could understand situations that involved real danger. Marion Pritchard is of Dutch origin and participated in the resistance in World War II. She helped to hide a Jewish family and to protect them from deportation. On a particular day, perhaps because of an informant, the apartment was raided by the Gestapo and Dutch police. The Jewish family was able to reach the hideout and not be discovered. The search party left. Everybody came out from hiding, feeling that the danger was over. A Dutch policeman who was part of the search party who had a better understanding of the situation returned and discovered the fugitives. Marion Pritchard made a difficult choice in that moment. She was in possession of a gun and killed the Dutch policeman. She was able to dispose of his body without being detected.

When I posed my question, she responded by telling me a story. While the family was in hiding, one of the children was playing outside. A German uniformed man approached the child and started questioning him. Marion could overhear the conversation. "Where is your father?" the German asked. The child interrupted his play, looked at him with indignation and responded, "How dare you ask me such a question? One month ago, people in uniforms like you, came into our house and took him away. We haven't heard from him since." After his answer, the child, who was about 4, resumed his play. The German departed. No one had explained to the child what the situation had been or had prepared him for such an event. Somehow, he grasped it in a precocious manner and knew how to handle it, by misleading the German and sending him out on a false trail. He invented a story about a father who had been taken away by the Gestapo in order to prevent the German from asking more questions and even entering the house. He played before and continued playing after this exchange. He returned to being a child after responding in a most adult fashion in a situation of extreme danger.

What type of leaps into precocious understanding of reality, overlaid with age appropriate fantasies and play, did this 4-year-old boy undergo? Does this short vignette support our theorizing about multilayered memories? My own most vivid childhood memories stem from the ages of 5 and 7, the period of time spent in Transnistria. Developmentally, this is the Oedipal phase, the cradle, the paradigm of all future adventures in life. When I speak of memories of that time as layered, I want to emphasize that on the one hand they possessed all the clarity, comprehension, depth, and gravity of an adult experience—precociously out of step with what we assume a child of that age is capable of knowing—and on the other hand, they contained the excitement and the playfulness that imbue the experience of a child of that age. I shall further address the "adult layer" of my memories toward the end of this essay.

Let us return to the Oedipal phase and reiterate that it is a paradigm of adventure for the rest of life. Life events of the nature of atrocities occurring during the Oedipal phase of development acquire a particular "style of experience" and of "memory" and give adventurousness special valence and character. Adventurousness is marked for life by the occurrence of atrocity, and atrocity may acquire some properties of an adventure when experienced in the Oedipal phase.

First, a few words about the sense of adventure that permeates the Oedipal phase. Superman, space voyagers, knights, and dragons are abundant in stories that children read, tell, or make up during this phase. Curiosity about the secrets of the universe and those of sexuality abound, and exploratory activities are undertaken with a heightened sense of drama. Life dreams frequently originate in the vicissitudes of experience in this stage, and on a wider scale, diverse cultural mythologies flow from and come to reflect and immortalize these vicissitudes. Hence, there can be a sense of adventurousness with a conscious disregard of the starkness, deprivation, and dread when this experience occurs in a concentration camp.

It is also possible that when faced with the camp, the Oedipal child says to himself (and again I am speaking in third person, although I am talking about myself), "This is yet another adventure story or even a fairy tale of which I have heard so many and which always have a happy ending; happy enough at least so that I can go to sleep safely and dream of them." Contributing to that is what Erikson (personal communication, 1968) called the "absence of the sense of irreversibility," a development that comes with the establishment of the reality principle in one's internal representational world, at the closure of the Oedipal period. Up to that developmental point, dead people are able to get up and become alive again. Time is reversible, deeds can be undone, play dominates life, and the principle of play, in which stakes are not "truly" for real, governs. Therefore, the child can imagine that if he only so wishes, he can reverse the direction of the trains that leads him to the camps and give himself back the home, or that the lost parents will surely return.

The premature and unyielding confrontation with stark reality has an impact in how this Oedipal phase evolves and is resolved. The true state of affairs eventually dawns on the child, but much of his comprehension remains contained within pockets of "precocious thinking and understanding." Such precocious moments of understanding may come to be building blocks for the superego. A harsh, unyielding, nonresponsive, and brutal reality comes to take the place of one that is mitigated through parental love, in which the omnipotence of the child's aggression and the prohibitions against it are contained safely enough within the domain of thought and fantasy. Murder, abandonment, and castration are only imagined. The child knows full well that they do not happen in real life, and the dragons of his nightmares can be made to go away by wishful thinking. Adventurous fantasy can expand without limit under normal circumstances. When atrocity occurs—when life ends, when home vanishes, and the principle

of irreversibility mentioned prematurely forces its way into the child's perception—a split occurs between an experience and a memory of adventure
and the comprehension of an awesome reality, a reality that is most likely
confined to those layers of precocious memories that I mentioned. Those
layers of precocious memories really contain elements of cognitive and
emotional maturity that are not warranted by the mental state and age of
the child. I have already mentioned my amazement at the fact that I could
have thought of things as profoundly as I did, without having had any adult
input. At the same time, these memories have a certain playfulness; the
fantasy continues no matter how grim the reality is.

To give a few examples of how memories of a grim reality come to be
embedded into future "adventurous" life pursuits: Train rides become
excursions to mysterious lands, boat rides become the crossings of inviting and promising rivers, and embankments on the side of railroad tracks
become explorations of novel unchartered territories. While this "mode of
adventure" and perception of reality serves protective functions, it cannot
be seen as activated for the purpose of defense only. It is rather a phase-
specific and phase-appropriate way of experiencing and thus remembering
reality. It is not only denial.

In the long run, however, the curtailment of adventure, play, and accompanying fantasy because of an infringement of a harsh reality may create
a sense of loss and grief, as well as a lifelong search for adventure that is
allowed to take its natural course and *not* curtailed. The survivor thus
grieves the loss of his childhood play and of the Oedipal excitement; thus,
he or she might attempt to pursue a lifelong search for such Oedipal adventure in his career and in his love life instead. Momentous accomplishments
can be the result of such pursuits. New discoveries are made along with
new experiences; yet, as with any repetition compulsion, a sense of not
having quite arrived persists in spite of such achievements. The yearning
and pursuit of Oedipal adventure can persist, often with abandonment of
highly valued love objects, in search of new ones, which then become the
object of relentless grief.

FROM THE INTERNAL LANDSCAPE
OF THE EVER-PRESENT WITNESS
TO BEING A WITNESS TO OTHERS

Perhaps the most clear-cut memory fragment I have is of that man being
flogged in public. He silently smokes his cigarette, crouching afterward.
I want to know what his feelings are, what he is thinking about. This wish
from early on, to know what people think and feel, played a decisive role
in my becoming a psychiatrist and cofounder of the Yale Video Archive for
Holocaust Testimonies.

To take this event even further, I wanted to be someone who listens, joins the experience, and gets to the bottom of the secret, at the same time comforting and restoring. I wanted to acquire a language of thought, feeling, and speech that only few share and that creates a camaraderie of such intensity that it cannot be sustained for long. This is a camaraderie that allows for the realization that the lost ones are not coming back, the realization that what life is all about is precisely to live with an unfulfilled hope, only this time with the sense that you are not alone any longer—that someone can be there as your companion—knowing you, living with you through the unfulfilled hope, someone who physically accompanies you only until your testimonial journey comes to its end, saying: "I'll be with you in the very process of your losing me. I am your witness."

Let us return to my mother's promise—the little bed she was going to buy for me in the camp, the home to which she will bring me back. I took notice both of her omnipotence and of her limitations. Facing grim realities, I came to the realization that people cannot always keep their promises. Yet, it is terribly important that there *be* a promise, even though there has to be a simultaneous awareness that such promises sometimes cannot be kept. Still, the promise is the only thing we have to hold on to. I found in working with survivors that the human promise, the assurance of one's presence, is really the one that counts most and *can* be kept.

To return full circle to the initial question posed in this essay: What gave my memories the radiance, the clarity, and the mature comprehension that sets them so much apart from other childhood memories and from memories of other (nonsurvivor) children? What I have learned from the process of testimony, elaborated in the preceding pages, allows me to formulate my answer. Like the little urchin in the streets of Krakow in *Testimony: Crises of Witnessing in Literature, Psychoanalysis, and History* (Felman & Laub, 1992, ch. 3), who survived through his daily prayers to the photograph of his mother, I also felt completely protected and even safe by my mother's steadfast and daring battle for my life. Indeed, both my parents protected me, and as long as my father was alive in the camp, I slept between the two of them. Yet, it was through my mother that I created my ever-present, unwavering internal witness. She was the person with whom I was in continuous dialogue and to whom I could relate all that I experienced and felt. My inner landscape was therefore never a void, never an empty, abandoned space; because my mother was always there for me, I never faced terror and fragmentation alone. In times of massive trauma, I could therefore, at least momentarily, contain it and rise above my feelings of numbness and terror and look at and see and grasp what was happening. The memories I created during such experiences retain all their clarity, vividness, and comprehension and have come to be my "sparkling jewels" in the sea of terror I still inhabit.

When I came to Israel at age 13, I entered into a long stretch of my life during which testimony was absent. Rather than identifying myself as a refugee, it was important to assimilate into Israeli culture, into the image of a "sabra," a native-born (Jewish) Israeli citizen. The account of my camp experiences, which I had written up for the billboard newspaper of my school in Romania at around age 10 and posted in weekly installments, had been torn up by my mother before we left Romania. She was afraid that the search at the border would make us suspect if we carried such documents. I tried to live a new life and tried to become a new person, a person for whom the past camp experience had been replaced by what mattered in the present. This trend was all-pervasive in Israeli society at that time.

This attempt at erasure is best illustrated by the incidents involving one of my classmates in medical school, Levi Neufeld, who had also been my roommate several times over the 6 years in medical school. His parents placed him with a Polish couple before they were deported and murdered during the Holocaust; this is how he survived. He was an eccentric young man, apparently sociable but difficult to get along with. He was financially better off than most of the other medical students (because of restitution monies obtained from Germany), yet he would not share things he owned or food he bought. Such sharing was commonplace among medical students living in the same apartment. You were not supposed to touch what was "his" in the refrigerator. As we approached the final exams, Levi Neufeld felt increasingly terrified. I spent one day reviewing the material with him for his first exam, which was in dermatology. That was the only exam he took and passed with a good grade. He appeared at some of the other exams, but fled in terror before they began. Eventually, he gave up trying. He was said to be roaming the streets of Jerusalem on a motorcycle, then he totally disappeared.

Some months later, a series of murders occurred in various parts of the country. A man with an Uzi gun was shooting from behind bushes, killing people, one at a time. The police connected Levi Neufeld, who had vanished, with the serial killer. I was warned that my life was in danger because he had made threatening remarks about me. The biggest manhunt in the history of Israel took place, involving more than 4,000 police, who searched for Levi Neufeld and combed the country to no avail.

What was most striking about Neufeld's situation was the simultaneous generosity and the shortsightedness of the medical school. It was willing to allow this student many opportunities to take his exams, but to my knowledge, never considered him to be in need of psychiatric help. No one made the connection between his history as a child survivor and his present difficulties in facing life and taking his final exams. This simply was not an item on anybody's agenda at the time. Nor was it on my own. Conversely, he was seen not as a victim, but as the attacker from the dark of the night. Moreover, the year before those exams, the Eichmann trial was held in Jerusalem. Day after day, I could see the queues of people waiting in line to be let in to the proceedings. I listened to the proceedings with great interest but never set foot in the courtroom, which was on my way to my classes in medical school. I wanted to attend the proceedings myself, but never "got around to it." It really was not until much later, after I had started my analysis and my Swedish analyst interpreted my denial, as I have previously described, and after I experienced the omnipresence of the Holocaust during the Yom Kippur War, that I made the connection again and returned to my inner witnessing position.

Levi Neufeld's body was found, more than a year later. He had hanged himself in the attic of an abandoned house, months before the first Uzi murder occurred. There was a letter near his body in which he apologized to his friends. The Uzi murderer has not been found to this day.

THE WAKEUP CALL: AN UNEXPECTED ENCOUNTER WITH THE HORRORS OF THE PAST

When the Yom Kippur War started in October 1973, I was a junior faculty member in the department of psychiatry at Yale University. I flew to Israel and joined the IDF (Israeli Defense Forces) on the fourth day of the war. I was assigned to a treatment facility in the north of the country, which received casualties from the Syrian front. To everybody's surprise, the proportion of psychiatric casualties was staggering. Reservists had been called up from synagogues, thrown into makeshift units, and sent into the battlefield to stem the Syrian advance. The abruptness of the transition into combat; the absence of a familiar social support network that the comrades in arms (training and serving together) had formed within their regular units; the enormity of losses, dead, and wounded; and above all, the level of violence they were exposed to led to the psychological decompensation of many.

What I observed was that the most severe and least-treatable casualties were children of Holocaust survivors. One such case arrived in a deep depressive stupor. He had no name, family, or memory. After spending hours with him in a dimly lit tent and gently prodding him, I gradually learned that he had been a radio operator on the front line who saw tank crews stop on their way to the battlefield to refuel and restock their munitions. He heard their last messages before they went silent. They had knocked out many enemy tanks but had run out of ammunition and were surrounded by Syrian tanks. To him, those stranded tanks strongly resonated with the images of many family members who had been murdered in the Holocaust and whose names were mentioned but little more was said about them. They were, nevertheless, ubiquitously present to him in their very absence and in their silence. Gradually, as he was making this connection, he emerged from his stupor, remembered his name and recognized his wife, who was about to give birth to a baby. The baby, a son, was named after one of the fallen tank commanders.

Another example was a soldier who was brought in exhibiting a state of psychotic agitation. His utterances made no sense; his affect and his behavior were severely out of control. He was a military policeman whose duty it was to prevent civilians from reaching the front line. He had failed to stop a civilian car with two men in it—only to find it later destroyed with two mangled bodies inside. He proceeded to boot a Syrian POW (prisoner-of-war) officer in his head. In his ramblings, he told of his father's stories of SS men smashing the heads of Jewish children into a wall. The front-line brutalities triggered the memory of the tales of brutalities he grew up with, and that was more than he could contain. His mental state did not improve in spite of robust pharmaco- and psychotherapeutic interventions, and he had to be transferred to a facility for chronic illness.

The familial exposure to Holocaust violence in these two men increased their vulnerability to the violence of the battlefield. Whereas other soldiers could better insulate themselves from it by using the customary defenses against traumatic experiences, such as dissociation, derealization, depersonalization, and others, for these two men such defenses no longer worked. Extremes of violence had for them a personal–historical context that was continuously present and therefore could not remain unnoticed and be pushed aside.

THE BEGINNING OF THE HOLOCAUST VIDEO TESTIMONY PROJECT

After my return from the Yom Kippur War, I decided that my life's work was going to be with the emotional sequelae of the Holocaust. I applied to about 100 foundations for financial support, but the only positive response I received was from the Deutsche Forschnungs Gesellschaft (DFG), the German Governmental Research Foundation. The DFG supported the taping of survivor testimonies and publications that would ensue from this work. It took many years, but in 1982, there were 24 such testimonies audiotaped in Frankfurt (Main), Germany. When an Israeli psychoanalyst, Hillel Klein, and I arrived at the Sigmund Freud Institute (SFI) to begin the work, all we had were the survivors, who appeared for the scheduled appointments, and ourselves. No appropriate equipment, such as tape recorders, microphones, or audiotapes, had been prepared. The Institute's senior administrators questioned the German participation in the project. Their position was that this was a strictly Jewish study; therefore, a Jewish organization should carry it out. Luckily, I had brought with me all of the necessary equipment from the United States, and the work began right away. Within days, as secretaries were transcribing the interviews and staff members were reading them, the attitude at the Institute toward the work underwent a radical 180-degree shift. The SFI staff became mobilized and could not do enough in supplying us with the equipment and comforts that we needed to carry out our work.

Separately, I met a New Haven television producer, Laurel Vlock, in early 1979, who wanted to interview me for the Holocaust Memorial Day celebration. I suggested that we start a project on a much larger scope by interviewing many survivors so that it might lead to the making of a movie similar to *The Sorrow and the Pity* (1969), produced by Marcel Ophüls. This movie was based solely on interviews with protagonists from both sides of the conflict, military and civilian alike, who had lived through the experience of World War II. Some weeks later, Laurel Vlock called me to say that she had a camera crew that was ready that evening; if I could find survivors who would testify, we could start.

On May 2, 1979, the first interviewing session took place in my medical office in New Haven, Connecticut, with four survivors. We had to rearrange the furniture to accommodate the camera crew. The only person on the camera was the survivor, and we the interviewers were on each side of the camera, directing our questions to the survivor. No one, including myself, knew what to expect from the interview process. We thought we would be finished within 2 or 3 hours, but the sessions lasted into the early hours of the morning. Due to the limitations of the technology of the time, videotapes had to be changed every 20 minutes, and the interview had to be briefly interrupted.

To our surprise, once the gates had opened, the flow of the testimony was unstoppable. It was as though the survivors had been waiting for the opportunity to form a narrative that was ready to be told; it only needed an intimate trusted setting to begin. All we had to do was to keep a timeline, the sequence of events, perhaps ask for the completion of a particular episode, or insist on personal experience that was not a general accounting of events. It was as though survivors were driven by their internal memories that had already unconsciously taken shape. Those memories were accompanied by feelings, conflicts, and reflections that added depth and richness. They formed a containing context for the survivors' terror and dejection.

TESTIMONY TO AN INNER TRUTH

Testimony reveals an inner truth that is both deeply cherished and essential to survival.[1] In addition, testimony goes through an evolution over one's lifetime. It is at the same time textualized, nuanced, synthesized into an "inner Gestalt" and contextualized, so that it is put into its proper place in

---

[1] There are circumstances, however, and I think here specifically of perpetrators, when truth can be completely erased, with the possibility of its emergence delayed for generations. Davoine and Gaudilliere's *History Beyond Trauma* (2004) describes this in its detail and richness.

one's autobiography and in history. Most of all, as life proceeds, it becomes more and more integrated as part of one's life and less a split of part of the self. This mostly silent and unobtrusive work allows testimony to be both more contained and to gain fuller expression.

Eight of the survivors who were reinterviewed in 2005–2006 after a lapse of 25 years had a much clearer awareness of what had hurt them most and what had been most formative for their lives, even though their accounts left out some of the details of the brutalities to which they had been subjected. They could reflect on and tolerate their own silences, without being flooded by terror or by grief, without experiencing their own fragmentation.

Looking backward on my testimony work, what conclusions can I draw? One is that this process is ubiquitous and continuous. It is everywhere and goes on all the time. The more radical and the more extraordinary the experience, the more it will trigger the process of testimony, provided the self remains intact enough to remain present to such experience. At the same time, powerful defenses, both intrapsychic and societal, are set in motion. They range from dissociation to the forceful silencing of the inner voice. These blocks, whether they are from inside or from the outside, can severely compromise awareness, expression, and growth of the testimonial process. Such internal or external imposed silence can last for decades, if not generations.

For the testimonial process to emerge and to be set in motion communicatively, it requires a special holding space, a container, which has to be created. The Holocaust Video Testimonies have indeed created such space. The new holding space is found within oneself in the presence of an intimate, listening other. This other is able to be present internally, along with representations of family and community. In this space, the process evolves and progressively deepens. There is a subject who holds it and a direction in which to proceed; at the same time, it is directed to an "other"—a listener inside oneself and also in one's immediate proximity.

THE ROLE OF THEORY

My work is not guided by theory. What I find, what I hear, helps me to form a theory, although established theoretical models can help organize and understand experience. It is important for me to keep in mind concepts such as infantile development, attachment theory, the Oedipal complex, and anal struggle because these psychological templates facilitate my work, but theory is *not* what informs my listening. If I experience something and if theory fits, it helps me cover ground, but this is not the place from which I ask the questions. These questions instead come out from what I experience. What I observe in testimony, for example, exceeds by far and simply cannot be grasped through the classical paradigm of the power struggle, with its anal sadistic and phallic connotations. The paradigm that would most adequately capture the encounter with a Nazi perpetrator is that of the clash with an overwhelmingly destructive and malevolent authority that is not bound by human convention; like a tsunami, it destroys and fragments everything in its way.

ON THE MUTED WITNESSES OF STATES OF THE EXTREME

In listening to Holocaust survivors' testimonies, I became aware not only of the struggle to recapture memory in thought and imagination and to relate it in words within the unfolding narrative flow, but also of the many instances during which the struggle failed. The survivor would reach a certain point in relating his or her inner landscape, then perhaps stammer or fall silent, thus giving up. It was precisely at such moments that the interviewer could be of greatest help in keeping the process moving, but this did not always hold true. Occasionally, the blanks of memory prevailed, and the narrative had to be picked up at another point. It was these failed struggles that led me to approach a group of Holocaust survivors who had failed and given up their attempt to communicate their experience both to themselves and to those around them. They came to be the chronically hospitalized Holocaust survivors in psychiatric institutions in Israel who no longer had the ability to find the words through which they could represent and relate their traumatic experiences. Their "voids of memory" were given the names of familiar psychiatric illness, such as schizophrenia and manic-depressive illness, and they were sequestered in substandard institutions for decades, alone and abandoned, hidden away from public eye.

In 1993, the Ministry of Health of the State of Israel established a multidisciplinary psychiatric team to review the status of all inpatients who had been hospitalized within the mental health system for 1 year or longer. A survey of approximately 5,000 long-term patients identified about 900 Holocaust survivors (18% of the chronic hospital population) (Cahn, 1995; Vigoda, 1996).[1] Review of these cases has shown that these patients had not been treated as a unique group, but rather that their trauma-related illnesses had been neglected in decades-long treatment. At the Abarbanel Mental Health Center, Israel's largest mental health center, nearly 67% of their 74 psychogeriatric patients were Holocaust survivors (strikingly, almost all of them women). Of these survivors, 30% had experienced chronic hospitalization since the Holocaust. Most compelling was the finding that, in a large number of these patients, the medical chart contained no information on the patient's persecution experience, the trauma history

---

[1] A more recent study (Siegal, 1998) found Holocaust survivors to be in one in every six psychiatric hospital beds in Israel.

sustained during the Holocaust. Medical records, for instance, listed a patient as having been born in Poland in 1924, then as having *immigrated* to Israel in 1948, with no mention of the traumatic, wartime events sustained in between. This demographic information was subsequently followed in the chart by a diagnosis of schizophrenia in about 50% of the cases. Such patients were aggressively treated by traditional modalities specific to the treatment of schizophrenia, such as insulin shock, electroconvulsive treatment, and psychotropic medications. This miscategorization of survivors of a massive psychic trauma predictably led to both inefficient and inappropriate treatments for that population (Terno, Barak, Hadjez, Elizur, & Szor, 1998). It is for this very reason that the Holocaust Video Testimony study was designed to evaluate the clinical improvements and therapeutic effects of the testimonial process with this severely traumatized and psychologically affected group of patients.

Twenty-six of the chronically hospitalized patients from two institutions in Israel—Beer Yaakov and Lev Hasharon—agreed to give their video testimony. Extensive psychological testing conducted before and 5 months after the testimonial event demonstrated a 30% reduction in trauma-related symptoms, particularly in the withdrawal cluster of post-traumatic stress disorder (PTSD).

ON SELF-HEALING

After describing my own travel through the testimonial process and my encounter with the muted witnesses, I would like to entertain certain reflections this journey raises in me. I wonder if my work has come to be an essential element in my own self-healing from trauma. I have to break through the unknown continuously, and by breaking through to the unknown with others, I perhaps break through to my own. There are things I have not broken through yet. There are memories I cannot reach.

I was on a trip in Germany in 1994 to give a lecture on traumatic memories. All of my documents had been stolen in the Frankfurt (Main) railway station. I was without a passport, without a train ticket, and without a lecture text—"without papers"—on a train in Germany. I felt terribly alone, and my attempts to share what had just happened to me with fellow German travelers were met with a wall of silence. It was at that moment that I remembered my mother's death 3 months earlier and wondered why I did not ask my mother what I had seen while in the camp. I never remembered the lost memory, but I remembered the opportunity I had missed to retrieve it.

Is there, for me, a drive to open up the not knowing? Yes. The question I did not ask—what did I witness as a child in the concentration camp?—is pursuing me. Why did I not ask it and want to know? In a sublimatory way, I instead help other people ask the question. I do not get my own answer from that work, but I know that I can try to help them get their own, or at least realize the obstacles that impede their finding the answers they seek.

So, do I always want to find out what I do not know? I think so. I think this is also what makes me a better analyst, because there is an immediacy to my presence. My motive is not to gratify my own curiosity but rather to be fully present and totally immersed in the experience. Due to my experience, I personally know the absolute need for the inner other to face the trauma. Thus, I can join the search, understand the quest, and empathize with the yearning for what is missing. Sometimes, one cannot satisfy the yearning, but one can acknowledge it and can be present in it, and in that way one is already the inner other.

TESTIMONY AND OTHER HISTORICAL TRAUMATA

While Holocaust testimonies have become central to my life's work, I am fully aware of the fact that they are not the only testimony in existence. Through my psychoanalytic work and research experience, I have become acquainted with an array of testimonies, some with commonalities and some with discontinuities to Holocaust testimony. As I listen to other trauma testimonies and reflect on my own reactions to them, I further come to recognize the testimonial details that resonate with my testimony and those that signal to my unwillingness to be a witness.

On this topic, I want first to make reference to September 11, 2001, because for me these attacks lead in a straight line to Hitler. In my opinion, this extreme violence is related to the omnipotent narcissistic rage of mostly affluent Saudis, whose honor had been tainted and who resorted to violent religious extremism to rehabilitate it. It is a narcissistic rage that intends to destroy the world, very graphically and very literally, and it was enacted in the destruction of the World Trade Towers. The intended motivation to destroy the West is not much different from the desire of Hitler and Nazism to conquer and reshape the world. It is the enactment of narcissistic rage that I do not want to understand, but instead nip in the bud—literally put it to death. The danger is such that one has to deal with it in an extreme way. What is needed is a readiness and a resolve to go all the way when dealing with this phenomenon of extreme brutality, a phenomenon that rears its ugly head from time to time over the centuries and the millennia.

Is the tragedy of September 11 continuous with my own traumatic history? Yes, in some ways. But, September 11 is not a repetition of the Holocaust. I do not make it my story. It is a story that is different, and I do not want to appropriate it. Instead, I want to try to understand and grasp the contours, the Gestalt of this new onslaught on human life, at the same time acknowledging my personal traumatic commonalities with the Twin Towers' atrocity. One such commonality is that the perpetrators acted from narcissistic rage; another is that the casualties of the attack on the Twin Towers also have no graves. The differences, however, are even more important. The families of the September 11 casualties remained intact, waiting for their return, and mourning them. There was no disruption in the continuity of life. It has nothing in common with the concentration and death camps, where there was no family to return to. These are different narratives, both of which are equally important.

Let us turn now to another group I became somewhat familiar with—the East Timor refugees. They have their own narrative of what went on in 25 years under violent Indonesian oppression, which is a unique narrative. The East Timorese want the memory of the violence inflicted on them remembered: how they were bombed and driven into caves, exiled, and abused by their own people—the whole history of massacre and rape. They want to keep that memory alive so that a leadership and a tradition can emerge, to prevent the situation from becoming a continuous "ahistorical" presence, from turning into havoc and chaos with thugs and warlords determining the future. For leaders, who try to bring about change, it is important to keep such past memory preserved as a communal memory for the nation.

The Timorese narrative is, however, totally different from my own historical narrative. I have a narrative from my own people that comes from having been formed over thousands of years. So, yes, I go back to my own history while listening to other refugees, but the narratives are different. There are points at which the narratives touch, but there is also a need to allow the differences to evolve because I cannot and I do not want to make these other narratives my own. There is a temptation to compare narratives of suffering hierarchically, as if they were of the same nature. I refuse to do that. I cannot equate anything with Auschwitz; it is inequitable.

PROTECTING LIVING FROM THE NIGHTMARE

Societal resistance to face historical tragedy is paramount. Most genocides—the Armenian, the Cambodian, the Bosnian, the Rwandan—are not known. Even the Holocaust is not yet fully known. Addressing the resistance has a better chance than trying to break it, because when you try to break it, it only solidifies.

In trying to know trauma, I would like to separate out the blank space of what remains unknowable and unrepresentable. Persistent efforts for the trauma to be known will limit and delimit the space of the blank, but not eliminate it. Trauma, to some degree, will remain both blank and mute. The question is: How can one go about living life while circumventing and going around the nightmare and keeping the two separate to protect life from the nightmare? When working with psychotic patients, how can one delimit psychosis?

One could say to the patient, "You can have your psychotic episodes, and stay in the family, in the community ... until it passes I will be with you. ... You can keep your fears, but I will stay with you. You don't have to go it alone." Words do not always do it; sometimes touching is needed. At the end of a nightmare, the only possibility may be that of holding and of waiting for the emotions to rebalance themselves. It is a matter of tolerance and of persistence.

Over my lifetime of work and psychoanalytic inquiry, three distinct phases of experience resonated within me. Each phase, through accretion, has played an integral part in the development of both my identity and my work. First comes my own personal testimonial experience, the compassion awakened within me during my time in the camp, which laid the foundation for my testimony work. Second, the testimony from the soldiers I treated during the Yom Kippur War built on and solidified this foundation by forcing me to see the undeniable presence of the Holocaust in their lives. Finally, the culmination of my previous experience with testimony was my co-founding of the video archive and interviews with the psychotically hospitalized survivors. They highlighted for me the other, the far end of the spectrum—that of traumatic destruction of symbolization and narrative—wherein the process of testimony can no longer unfold. Each separate stage solidified within me an urge and a commitment to something I wanted and needed to pursue. These experiences combined and gelled within me to create a multilayer presence and a force that allows me to persist and proceed with my lifelong endeavor of testimonial work.

REFERENCES

Cahn, D. (1995, November 26). Holocaust survivors mistreated. Associated Press.

Davoine, F., & Gaudilliere, J. M. (2004). *History beyond trauma* (S. Fairfield, Trans.). New York: Other Press.

Laub, D. (1992). Bearing witness, or the vicissitudes of listening. In S. Felman & D. Laub (Eds.). *Testimony: Crises of witnessing in literature, psychoanalysis and history* (pp. 57–74). New York: Routledge.

Ophüls, M. (Director). (1969). *The sorrow and the pity* [Motion picture]. France: Télévision Recontre.

Siegel, J. (1998, August 11). Panel to probe plight of mentally ill Holocaust survivors. *The Jerusalem Post*. p. 4.

Terno, P., Barak, Y., Hadjez, J., Elizur, A., & Szor, H. (1998). Holocaust survivors hospitalized for life: The Israeli experience. *Comprehensive Psychiatry, 39,* 367–384.

Vigoda, R. (1996, January 28). American contingent to help Holocaust's haunted souls in Israel. A special focus: Those in mental institutions. *The Philadelphia Inquirer*. p. 6.

Chapter 5

A Note on the Testimony Event

Geoffrey Hartman

INTRODUCTION

Testimony about extreme events is a courageous effort to overcome silence. We are accustomed to think of interviews as a simple investigative tool, but interviewing Holocaust survivors as well as secondary witnesses (contemporary bystanders, or later affected persons, such as the sons and daughters of the survivors) calls for an exceptionally sensitive and nonpressured approach. The taping project of Yale's Fortunoff Video Archive for Holocaust Testimonies assigned no time limit to its interviews. Also effective was fostering a sense in the witnesses that they were being listened to, that there was a possibility of social sharing.

THE SURVIVORS AS PART OF THE AUDIENCE

In this area, then, communication is never free from questions about the actual communicability of traumatic suffering. Yet, what helped motivate the testimony givers was the need to converse with themselves as well as others. With themselves, because there had been no adequate conversation partner, or because something still all too present, all too oppressive, remained separated off, shunted from consciousness. Not only the narrative-enabling "I" but also a recipient "You" had been injured. "When one cannot turn to a 'you'," Dori Laub, a founder of the Yale project remarks justly, "one cannot say 'you' even to oneself. The Holocaust created in this way a world in which one could not bear witness even to oneself" (Felman & Laub, 1992, p. 80). Research into the interpersonal effect of testimony giving has underestimated, in my opinion, this intrapersonal feedback.

TESTIMONY AND TRAUMA

Aleida Assmann (2006) made a challenging remark in defining the video testimony as a new genre. She pointed out that while in autobiography "memories are collected and selected in such a way that they can be integrated to construct and support a biography; in the case of these Video Testimonies, memories do the very opposite: they shatter the biographical frame" (p. 264).

I agree with that; many books and filmings containing testimony excerpts make use of narrative extenders that produce a merely wishful integration of what remains unintegrated. Yet, we should not deny that the very process of interviewing, which allows the shattering to be depicted, may also be restorative. Some such belief has always attended storytelling, however difficult its content. The survivors strengthen through the testimonial act a reconstructed identity—reinforce it by a sense of inner control, of coping with their memories and drawing from these a more than purely negative legacy.

THE TESTIMONIAL ALLIANCE

Maurice Halbwachs, in his classic work *On Collective Memory* (1992), posited an "affective community" as essential for the very genesis of memory as well as its transmission. A good interview, moreover, frees the witnesses to speak in their own voice rather than through the proxy of impersonal narrators; the witnesses address, via such self-representation, a maieutic listener rather than a phantom audience. They speak with the interviewers as delegates of a larger audience finally willing to listen without a reaction often encountered in the early years: "Yes, yes, but now leave all that behind, get on with your life." Hence, while the link between a breakthrough narrative and trauma relief needs to be explored beyond any easy assumption of a permanently rehabilitative effect, there is hope for a healing aspect insofar as the interview stimulates the possibility of dialogue, of "sharing" a traumatic experience not only with others but also (however paradoxical this sounds) with oneself.

This dialogue of self with self does not always occur on the spot, during the interview. Sometimes silence persists, and sometimes the release felt by witnesses is such that, in talking more openly than before, they turn their testimony into a barely interrupted series of monologues. At the same time, as I have said, the very presence of interlocutors who represent the contrary of a world that was indifferent or silent during the Holocaust conveys a new era of civic responsibility.

Indeed, the Yale videotaping project started as a civic initiative in 1979. The wisdom and persistence of a group of citizens in New Haven ensured the initiative's adoption and preservation by Yale 2 years later. The university guaranteed this local Holocaust Survivors' Film Project an archive with an educational and research mission. Continuing to transmit the spirit of the original founders, the Yale archive encouraged a testimonial alliance between interviewer and interviewee, one that aimed at recognizing the importance of oral history as well as making public awareness of the genocide more of a reality.

Because of the victim's trauma and the perpetrators' attempt to hide all traces of the genocide, the concept of a testimonial alliance seems more adequate than the tacit "autobiographical pact" that, Philippe Lejeune (1975) speculated, supports the relation of author and reader in more conventional memoirs. The concept of a testimonial alliance, equally focused on what was personally experienced, offers more than a relatively inexpensive promise to tell the truth. For these life stories, being life-in-the-midst-of-death stories, enlist the interviewer as a helpmeet on a precarious journey toward realities that often seem so inhuman they verge on the improbable or incommunicable.

MAIN FEATURES OF THE TESTIMONY INTERVIEW

Holocaust testimony remains personal and "subjective" even when a great number of converging accounts have been recorded. Objectivity is not its exclusive aim. There is a performative as well as informative dimension to the witness accounts. Despite well-known types of subjective error, such as the conflation of incidents or the retroactive blending of what was revealed in print or movie afterward, each witness account places us in the presence of an individual; conveys something of the original impact of what was experienced; retrieves in the spontaneous flow of the interview forgotten episodes; retains the colloquial force, or broken eloquence, of the witnesses' speech; and is generally unafraid of the emotional demand on listener and viewer.

The spirit in which the testimony interview is conducted plays a crucial role in achieving this result. It respects the witnesses by not taking away their initiative for the sake of pursuing a research agenda. Ideally, the open-ended interview still used at Yale (we remain ready to this day to record the survivors, refugees, and other witnesses) tries not to interrupt trains of thought by following a rigid sequence of questions. The aim of the interviews is to release memories, including repressed or dissociated ones.

To this end, the interview's support structure fosters an atmosphere that is the opposite of an interrogation. It recruits sympathetic questioners who are not an on-screen presence, so that the testimony giver stays at the center. (This is very different, of course, from the not-always-admirable example of

Lanzmann's 1985 highly visible, domineering presence in the film *Shoah*.[1])
Moreover, as I have already suggested, each testimony addresses itself to a
double recipient: not only directly to the interviewer but also—by a reflex-
iveness that usually remains implicit—to the person testifying, to narrators
whose sense of identity has been shaken, sometimes so radically that cor-
roboration and self-acceptance are still needed.

An urgent and related motive for testifying often mentioned by the persecuted is their concern for the passing of the eyewitness generation and
consequent attrition of the collective memory of the Holocaust. Every survivor becomes, at some level of consciousness, the last—the only remaining—witness. Each is, as in Job, the "I alone have escaped to tell thee."
Sporadic moments of despair arise, expressed by admonitory variants of
"Has the world learnt anything?" I surmise, then, like Dori Laub, that the
testimonies extend the hands of speech beyond the interviewer toward a
less-defined but necessary other, akin to Paul Celan's intimate yet ghostly
"Du" ("Thou") that evokes a listener who might remove the solitariness of
those not-listened-to.

INTERPRETERS AND TEACHERS

I have suggested that the survivor's still-beleaguered self re-enters, through
the interviewing process, albeit provisionally, a social bonding, necessary
for both the retrieval and the transmission of memories. That process continues when historians not only find and interpret sources but also sift and
explore rather than dismiss sparsely documented or unique evidence.[2] It
also benefits from the attentiveness of teachers, researchers, museum professionals, and filmmakers trained to add context and the nuance of literary
and psychological interpretation.

From a pedagogical point of view, moreover, to show videotaped testimonies lessens the risk of "secondary trauma" in young people, despite the
terrible scenes often described; the testimonies are not photos or simulacra
that burn themselves into the mind. Presented in the form of stories told by
persons with whom we can try to identify, the ferocity, shame, and terror
of what happened become somewhat more bearable. Interest shifts from

---

[1] It is not the interviewer's conspicuous self-presence as such, especially in a film with a
strong cinematic function, that is questionable, but its combination with the pressure put
on the survivor by the interviewer. Yet Lanzmann's insistence, accompanied by subtlety
and irony, is necessary and effective when he questions Nazi bureaucrats or bystanders who
disclaim knowledge of the perpetration.

[2] When the persecution has been vast and vicious enough, a single voice may have to break
the silence. As Jan Gross (2006) has written: The "fate of several hundred Jews murdered
in the Belzec extermination camp must be unpacked from the one and only line that its
victims have left" (p. 428). Even in less-disastrous instances, there is much interpretive
unpacking to be done.

the mystery of evil that shrouds the perpetrator to the humanity of the victim. Instead of a cinematic or other type of sensationalism—always self-defeating in the long run, for it eventually turns people off or becomes so routine that heightened doses of stimuli are needed—the testimonies keep to the human face and voice, without dramatic additives.[1]

REFERENCES

Assmann, A. (2006). History, memory, and the genre of testimony. *Poetics Today*, *27*, 261–275.

Felman, S., & Laub, D. (1992). *Testimony: Crises of witnessing in literature, psycho-analysis, and history*. New York: Routledge.

Gross, J. (2006). One line at a time. *Poetics Today*, *27*, 425–431.

Halbwachs, M. (1992). *On collective memory* (L. A. Coser, Trans.). Chicago: University of Chicago Press.

Hartman, G. (2004). Audio and video testimony and Holocaust studies. In M. Hirsch & I. Kacandes (Eds.), *Teaching the representation of the Holocaust* (pp. 209–212). New York: Modern Language Association of America.

Lanzmann, C. (Director). (1985). *Shoah* [Motion picture]. France: Historia.

Lejeune, P. (1975). *Le pacte autobiographique*. Paris: Seuil.

---

[1] For an extended discussion of pedagogical issues, see the work of Hartman (2004). The present chapter is part of a larger essay that has been published in German by the Federal Memorial Foundation in Berlin in charge of the Monument for the Murdered Jews of Europe.

Chapter 6

A Holocaust Survivor's Bearing Witness

Henri Parens

THE DECISION TO WRITE MY HOLOCAUST MEMOIRS

I had long known that one day I would have to write about my Holocaust experience. I would have to tell what happened to us, my mother and me and many others who had followed, or rather had been led down a similar path during those miserable years. I had to bear witness.

I was not aware that I actually was resisting writing my memoirs of what happened to us. I hid behind the principle that a psychoanalyst should remain anonymous about very personal matters—that making personal experiences public, as would writing papers and a book about my memoirs, would violate that principle, a principle with which I am in accord. Of course it makes sense; we want to know what drives the patient as little influenced as possible by what drives us. In my Institute, the principle was held to so vigorously that when in 1979 I was invited by CBS to do a television series on parenting (Parens, Scattergood, Hernit, & Duff, 1979)—I was then well into our parenting optimizing prevention work and had been talking about it for several years (Parens, Currie, & Scattergood, 1979; Parens, Pollock, & Prall, 1974)—I consulted with the director of our Institute[1] to seek his advice on whether I should accept such an invitation, which would require exposing my views on parenting and all that goes with it, including myself, on television three times a week for 3 months. Would that not go counter to the principle of self-disclosure? He did not hesitate: "Of course you should do it! Do it for psychoanalysis!"

In addition, facilitating my resistance, I felt justified not to reveal this part of my past, knowing that once I made this tortured part public, one that draws much sympathy from many in our communities, some of my patients would in turn experience yet another resistance-inducing factor in them. As one patient eventually said to me after she had read my memoirs, "You shouldn't have written that book," and went on to tell me that she found it too painful. She had felt compelled to read it and empathized

---

[1] I am indebted to the late O. Eugene Baum, MD, for his wise counsel.

painfully with my experience. Another patient, long after analysis, told me she had read my book; automatically—and wrongly—I asked her, "Any thoughts?" She smiled, I think incredulous that I would ask, and turned away. More than one has said to me, "After what you've been through, how can I tell you about my problems?!" This one is not so difficult to handle. Since a number of these patients have been traumatized within their own families, I tell them that having been traumatized by their own mother or father, from whom one expects love and protection, is much more hurtful than having been traumatized by one's enemy, who in our case—given the long history of discrimination and pogroms against the Jews in Europe and, specifically, the Third Reich's human rights denying, anti-Semitic 1935 Nuremberg Laws—we knew was determined to demean and harass, and even destroy, us. These concerns, genuine as they are, however, served my resistance. It was a fortuitous falling into place of three factors that led to my finally writing.

First, when I turned 70—decade anniversaries especially do this—time seemed now to become a reality that, while I have and continue to be in good health, I can no longer take for granted. There is ample evidence in everyday life that personal catastrophes happen, and it became more difficult then to deny that such may happen to me. While I have long advocated facing the fact that someday something sudden or predictive of the end of my life will happen to me, or to those in my vintage who I love, even as I readied myself to start writing, I delayed. Now, urgency set in.

Second, when I was 71, I had been reading several of Primo Levi's books. The poem with which he opens *Survival in Auschwitz* (1959/1996)—the unfortunately revised title of the English edition of his book about his year in Auschwitz, which originally carried the title of the poem, "If This Is a Man"—struck me deeply and activated in me what had long been waiting to happen. Here is that poem:

> You who live safe
> In your warm houses,
> You who find, returning in the evening,
> Hot food and friendly faces:
>> Consider if this is a man
>> Who works in the mud
>> Who does not know peace
>> Who fights for a scrap of bread
>> Who dies because of a yes or a no.
>> Consider if this is a woman,
>> Without hair and without name
>> With no more strength to remember,
>> Her eyes empty and her womb cold
>> Like a frog in winter.

Meditate that this came about:
I commend these words to you.
Carve them in your hearts
At home, in the street,
Going to bed, rising; [and Levi concludes:]
Repeat them to your children,
   Or may your house fall apart,
   May illness impede you,
   May your children turn their faces from you. (p. 11, emphasis
   added)[1]

Levi's admonition, especially the last line, really hit me, and heightened my resolve to act.

The third factor was the upcoming 60th anniversary—another decade anniversary—of my mother's having been sent to Auschwitz: August 14, 1942. On that anniversary, August 14, 2002, I started to write my Holocaust memoirs. It started a flooding of memory, of wide-ranging emotion, sadness and quiet rage, miserable itching and scratching, rumination for the 16 months it took me to write this three-part work. The first published copies of the book came out 21 months after I started to write.

THE EXPERIENCE OF WRITING
MY HOLOCAUST MEMOIRS

I did not ask: "Why should I write about what happened to us?" I felt that the Holocaust had an impact on those who were victimized very differently, and that bearing witness meant to tell of the particular things that happened to us, in their various malicious forms. We need to tell not only those who want to know but also and especially the many who do not want to know but should not be let free from making it part of their reality. We must counter those who deny it—to add just one more voice to challenge their denial. In addition, the Holocaust had an impact on us along various distinguishing parameters: one's age, family circumstance, losses, camp incarceration—which included significant levels of harshness from detention and its consequences, to slave labor, and to death camp brutality and murder—or whether one was a hidden child or a child in a protected group home or even experienced a sequential combination of these. Sure, there were experiences we all had in common, such as malignant prejudice against us, loss of house and home, incarceration in camps or ghettos or

---

[1] "If This Is a Man," from *Survival in Auschwitz* by Primo Levi (translated by Stuart Woolf). © 1959 Orion Press, Inc. Used by permission of Viking Penguin, a division of Penguin Group (USA) Inc.

compelled emigration, humiliation, starvation and miserably unsanitary conditions, and so on. To bear witness, individual accounts would be the only way to fill out in detail just what large numbers of *Homo sapiens* of this era did to others, to us. What was our Holocaust experience, my mother and me? If I spoke about what happened to us, I would also be telling what some others among us experienced.

Nor did I ask: "How should I write about what happened to us?" It was August 14, 2002, the 60th anniversary of my mother's having been sent from Rivesaltes[1] (one of four concentration camps[2] in the southeast corner of France's frontier with Spain) to Drancy (outside of Paris) and from there, on August 14, 1942, to Auschwitz. In 1945, according to Serge Klarsfeld (1978), only one person of her convoy was alive. Having told my family I wanted to start to write on this day worked well with their plans to be off somewhere with their children. I just started to write. But, I quickly realized that in wanting to speak of what we experienced, that I would speak mostly of my mother and me. I therefore had to account for the fact that I could not include my father and my brother in what I started to say since by then we had not been together for years. I had to start with a brief chapter about our family history. But once I started to tell what happened, feelings, memories took over and drove the narrative. I let it happen.

It was not my intention to write a history of what happened. I am not a historian like Nora Levin, William Shire, Marrus and Paxton, Saul Friedlander, or Denis Peschanski.[3] How else could I share what happened, what a child survivor, and therefore many like this child survivor, experienced? There are great Holocaust writers, foremost Primo Levi and Eli Wiesel; I am not a writer, not a good historical storyteller like Irene Nemirovsky (*Suite Française*, 2006), and not a serious news carrier like Rudi Vrba (*I Escaped from Auschwitz*, 2002). There are many serious Holocaust autobiographies told by teachers, commercial designers, and others like Anna Ornstein and Saul Friedlander. I did not think of, nor

---

[1] I later learned that this was the first convoy to be sent by the Vichy France government to the death camps east on Nazi-German requisition. This was while the unoccupied zone was still "Free France"; the Germans invaded this heretofore-unoccupied zone 3 months later in reaction to the Anglo-American forces landing in North Africa. It is well established that the Vichy government of the unoccupied zone of France was collaborationist with Hitler's plans for Europe, including its anti-Semitic laws abolishing human rights and French citizenship for Jews (Bailey, 2008).

[2] In the Pyrénées Orientales Department (a "province" where France has a frontier with Spain and Perpignan is its principal city), there were four concentration camps: Rivesaltes (the most infamous), Argelès, St. Cyprien, and Barcarès. At the time, the Vichy government spoke of them as "camps de concentration"; so did Marrus and Paxton (1983). Currently, historians and others speak of them as "detention camps." Rivesaltes became the hub in the Free Zone from where the Jews in that Free Zone were deported to Auschwitz starting on August 9, 1942.

[3] See Friedlander (2007), Levin (1968), Marrus and Paxton (1983), Peschanski (2002), and Shirer (1959).

did I take, any models. I just needed to speak with my own voice—which has characterologically become that of a psychoanalyst. As I said, "feelings, memories took over and drove the narrative." I since have said that I wrote self-analytically. It turned out to be, as my wife, Rachel, said it would be, a self-analysis. She was right; I was doing what I ask my patients to do: to say whatever comes to their mind, whatever they feel. And I value having done it that way—with its repetitions, self-preoccupations, perhaps even self-indulgences. And as I wrote in *Renewal of Life: Healing from the Holocaust* (2004), the emotional experience of writing it brought with it a fulminating nummullar eczema, traces of which continue to this day. I believe I developed this skin reaction as a somatic manifestation of emotions long repressed as well as that of reliving in a self-analytic process the turmoil this trauma wrought. I take some comfort in my dermatologist's observation that there may have been wisdom in my soma selecting the outer layer of my body for reactivity rather than some more vital interior system. Perhaps a greater degree of sublimation and distancing from inner turmoil might have spared me such a psychosomatic symptom. But then, I would not have borne witness to the experience of at least some Holocaust survivors. Friends who are also child survivors do not want to think about what they went through; several do not read or watch programs about the Holocaust. Several others I know in our field write about their experience indirectly, some in the third person, even while a key theme of their professional writing can be linked to their Holocaust experience.

THE PROBLEM OF NOT KNOWING

A factor that I felt heavily at the time of the writing is the knowledge that has long been part of my life, that there is so much I do not know about my roots, about my family, my prehistory. In the writing, I came face to face repeatedly with the problem of "not knowing." This is part of a multifactorial dilemma: "knowing/not knowing." There is (a) not knowing, ever, and (b) having known but not remembering with certainty. On the other hand, there is knowing with certainty, even when what is historically reported is at variance with it. A good example of the last is a discussion I had with Denis Peschanski (2002), professor of social history at the University of Paris, who wrote a history of the French "internment camps." Peschanski questioned my report of the sequence of the camps Savic[1] and I were in. According to the documents he studied, Récébédou was not opened to foreign Jews until into 1941. But Savic and I are unequivocal that we were in Récébédou (outside Toulouse) from late September or very early October 1940 and were then transferred to Rivesaltes (near Perpignan) in very

[1] Savic, now Sam Chirman, MD, was in both Récébédou and Rivesaltes at the same time as I.

early January 1941. The point I stress here is that many documents were destroyed, I believe to hide what many French did not want to remember or reveal to the world about their collaboration with the German Nazis, which many French have decried—much has been said, and there is more to be said about this, but this is not the place for it.[1] Peschanski is open to my insistence on this point.[2]

More nagging is "not knowing." "Not knowing, ever," is the most troubling. Had I known I would never see my mother again when we said goodbye in 1942, I would have asked a thousand questions about everything, from more than the little I know about my father and my brother, why my parents divorced, who and where my grandparents were, my uncles and aunts, my cousins, about so many things I do not know, as I said, my roots, my prehistory. I have two photos of my mother and two of my father and my brother. Where exactly did I come from? Knowing it was Lodz (Poland) is not enough. Because I do not know where my father was born, where he and my brother lived, exactly what work he did (other than that he merchandised in furs), my brother's birth date, the names or addresses of where my grandparents lived, I have been unable to trace what became of them. Many agencies want to help us find, but to find, one has to have sufficient information at the beginning. Just a name and a large city are not enough.

And then, there is knowing, but not remembering with certainty. Of course, none of us remembers all important things with certainty. But when one needs to know, and not remembering enough is troubling, it is distressing to have no one to turn to, to fill in the details. Not knowing leaves a vacuum in one's life, in addition to all the losses of family, home, and the like. As I said in *Renewal of Life*, "No ... this life, as of June 1942, was not the life I was living before the war. ... My original life ... had been shattered" (p. 92). This is a sentiment experienced by many child survivors.[3]

---

[1] Pertinent is that Bailey (2008) learned that when the Germans retreated from the Pyrénées Orientales Department, they destroyed bridges, gas reserves, and food reserves, but they made sure to leave intact their files on those French who had collaborated with them. My guess is that they left it to the French to take their wrath out on one another.

[2] Another example of knowing with certainty is that Germaine Masour, directrice of the home I was in in St. Raphael (Southern France), confounded it with another home she directed, in which she encountered a degree of difficulty with some challenging teenagers; she did not in St. Raphael. This fact interested the French historian of the OSE (*Oeuvres de Secours au Enfants*), Katy Hazan, who is currently reconstructing a history of the OSE homes during the era 1940–1945. Germaine Masour was a wonderful human being who devoted herself to saving children.

[3] Yehuda Nir, a New York psychiatrist, is a teenage survivor of the Warsaw uprising. His memoir is *The Lost Childhood* (2002). See also Isabelle Choko, Frances Irwin, Lotti Kahana-Aufleger, Margit Raab Kalina, and Jane Lipski (2005), whose book is *Stolen Youth* (2005). It is one of the series sponsored and published by Yad Vashem and the Holocaust Survivors' Memoirs Project and printed in Jerusalem, Israel.

Not knowing enough of my origins may have played a part in my wanting to write about what happened to us for my sons, their wives, and my grandchildren so they may know as much of their origins as I can tell them. This, attached to the paradox as I noted in *Renewal of Life*, is that I want them to know and at the same time I want them to forget about it.

HOW DOES IT FEEL TO HAVE MY MEMOIRS READ?

It is important for me to have my memoirs read. The book does not arise from my work but from my experience, an experience that has universal implications. In addition, I must have readers because without them I cannot bear witness. I cannot fulfill my responsibility to my people and to all who are subjected to genocide. Primo Levi has emboldened in my brain the admonition *Zachor*[1] and "You must bear witness … or … may your children turn their faces from you!"

But what of the reader? While concerned for and with the reader, once I committed myself to tell my story, I could not think of what the reader would feel or think. A self-analysis is very private; I could not have written some of the things I did if I was hampered by what the reader would think of it. I think that at a preconscious level our patients, and we, worry about privacy all the time. But I felt that to bear witness, I had to tell about my experience, not just facts already told many times. And, I know that some readers want to know, not just the history of it, but, "What was it really like to be there?" Some are wise enough to know that empathy may not carry them close enough to the experience; approximate, they can, but really experience it? Of course, many do not want to experience it.

It would have been a mistake to try to write my bearing witness in a voice other than my own. Is it bearing witness if it is not in your own voice? I am grateful to my readers. I have gotten many meaningful notes of appreciation, verbal and in writing. I treasure the ones in writing because they are hard proof of my bearing witness. Many readers have told me how difficult it was to read my work even as it fulfilled their need to listen to witnesses to work through some of their share of the experience of being affected human beings, Jew and non-Jew. But I have also been dismayed by a couple who felt that I was repetitious, one even suggested that I complain too much. I think many readers recognized that I was unconsciously driven in the writing. Should I have prefaced the book with the statement that it was a self-analysis? I am considering this for the French edition due to come out soon. It is simply difficult. If you were silent, that created problems; if you spoke up, this created problems. Boris Cyrulnik, the renowned French psychiatrist and author of many books, spoke indirectly about his

---

[1] "Remember" in Hebrew.

experience by having made resilience to trauma one of his major areas of research; he told me that in France it was just too difficult to write directly about what happened to him. Many survivors have encountered disbelief, countersilence, even laughter—as if to a fabrication told by an overzealous raconteur. Many French do not want to know, I believe, because they are then unavoidably confronted with, "What did the French do during 1940–1945?" Rosemary Bailey (2008) spoke extensively about this. Even to this day, many in France distort what happened there. Some Poles say that more Poles died in Auschwitz than Jews. Interestingly, after a generation of silence, while many continue to deny it, many Germans more readily than others acknowledge what their Third Reich did—some experiencing profound shame about it (Bar-On, 1989, 1990, 1995; Goschalk, 1995).

SPEAKING TO OTHERS: BEING LISTENED TO WHEN TELLING

How I speak to others, as would anyone, is determined by the audience: speaking to adults, to children, to my family, especially to my own children.

Most adults know about the Shoah. Medium-size audiences (less than 50) give me a comfortable sense of connection with my listeners. A smaller group, say 10–25, works best; I can look at individuals. Audiences of 100–300+, while rewarding that so many would come to listen to yet another survivor, tend to challenge the feel of direct connection—I am not sure whether it is that seeming distractibility on the part of some listeners is more likely or whether I am just unable to feel intimacy with that large a number of people. So many, flatters, but it lessens the connection I want with the listener for this topic. Speaking to about 100 at a Barnes & Noble book signing, people strung out in clusters amid shelves of books, seemed to work better than such a number in an auditorium. It is clear that when I see responsiveness contingent with what I am saying, I feel that the audience wants to hear my tale, and I then let myself go more easily. I am surprised at times with the strong level of attentiveness the audiences bring.

I confess that I like talking to kids better than to adults. There are two reasons: First, I am very comfortable with kids—sure, with many adults, too. But I especially like kids; I love their responsiveness. They invariably amaze me; even to this day, after years of working with them, I find their questions at times so moving, so bright. I know that is why I became a child psychiatrist and analyst, and I can easily talk to their level of experiencing. I think most child clinicians can do that. Second, to most, what I am telling them is new; many have only barely or not even heard about the Holocaust. Invariably, the teachers, usually of social studies or history, prepare them for my lecture. In one school, the teachers introduced me before I came through a YouTube piece of an interview we did for Thanksgiving. It is visible that it makes history real for them; I am a witness that it happened; some have said this to me. I like both, the younger ones, say 10 to 14, and the high school kids.

Interestingly, larger groups of kids, like the 500 high school students at the Germantown Academy, do not feel inaccessible to a connection. I sense that I am telling them something they have not yet heard (much) about. But in addition, I tell them that the kind of thing that happened to me when I was about their age or even younger than they are now (the high school students) is something that they all know something about, prejudice and bullying. I try to personalize it with them, and I explain to them my thoughts about how prejudice gets started, what some of the basic dynamics are—for example, that it includes the displacement or projection of loads of hostility we cannot discharge against those who hurt us; that we then take it out on less-threatening individuals. I tell them that something can be done to prevent it, and that they are the next generation on whom society is going to depend to deal with it. I tell them that they are needed by society; that they need to think about prejudice and bullying and even begin to act to prevent it among themselves. Invariably, in all schools there are kids of different ethnic groups, and some nod when I say that I know some of them know exactly what I am talking about. I have had some priceless questions from them. One that stands out is when a tall African American high schooler asked me what he and his friends could do when, as they walk down the street, whites come toward them, see them, and cross the street. I sympathized with his feeling offended, acknowledged how insulted he and his friends must feel, and told him this is exactly the kind of thing we all need to do something about, that they have to be part of the solution. Obviously, I cannot answer all their questions; I just give them the best I have.

If several kids in a hundred hear me and take me seriously, I feel it was worth my coming to their school to talk with them. I want more, but I am glad of the few who do more than just listen to what I am telling them. It brings to mind Margaret Mead's well-known remark that, paraphrasing, "one person can change the world," paralleling the well-known Jewish saying that, again paraphrasing, "a person who saves one life saves a universe." One high school girl from a Philadelphia suburb communicated with me months after I talked there and asked if I would read a 10-page paper she wrote responding to an assignment, with a topic of the student's choosing. She talked about the Holocaust with surprising sophistication, a very moving experience for me—which I know it also was for her. In fact, she subsequently played Anne Frank in the play by that name. But there is an aspect of telling and being listened to that is much more challenging—it is troubling.

SPEAKING TO THOSE NEAR-DIRECTLY
AFFLICTED BY THE HOLOCAUST

As I said, it was difficult to write knowing that, while many want to know, to read, to see documentaries and movies—all toward achieving a degree of mastery over the challenges of life—there are many who do not want to know. They will not read, or watch documentaries, or the like. Some want to deny it happened for varied reasons.

But, there are those who want to know while they also do not want to "know." They do not want to know to protect themselves against the pain of identification. The pain may be too large; they cannot listen. This is nowhere more pertinent than within families of survivors. I have lamented for years, and always will, the burden my Holocaust experience has caused those most important to me. As I wrote:

> One of the largest torments I continue to experience following from what happened to me is the pain and the burden this past has caused my wife and our three sons. No survivor has escaped this; we can't prevent it; *wives and kids cannot not be burdened by it.* Now my grandchildren have begun to ask me, with a note of seriousness and caution, "Zaida, were you in the war?" Their fathers know that I have long wanted them to know, and now that I want their children to know, that they can say to me, ask me, anything at all about what happened to me, to all of us. In the hope of helping them deal with this burden with the least possible injury, I have tried to facilitate our talking about what happened over there. I sense that my sons have tried to protect me and themselves by taking up the past with me, mostly only on specified occasions like the Jewish Holidays. ...
> The sins of the father will be visited on the child. ... I understand how it happens. ... But what sins did I commit in all this? *The pains of the father will be visited on the child.* That's what applies to us; and it makes me weep. A father cannot have better sons than I have. And, I am hung in a paradox: I want my sons and my wife to put it all to rest; but I want us all to remember it, and I want to remind others of it, hoping they will not let it happen again, nor wish to perpetrate it again. (2004, pp. 169–170; italics in the original)

To talk about it at home has been and still is a challenge. How much is too much? How much too little? With a wife and three sons, they do not all have the same measure of tolerance for hearing about what happened; each has her or his own psychic strengths, conflicts and burdens, and more. And it has been a challenge for me: Can I talk about it when I want? Of course not; I must heed each of them, where they are at a given moment with regard to their life and this question. Of course, much has been said about this specific problem. And most critical, it applies to the families of both the victims and the perpetrators (see Bar-On, 1989, 1995; Goschalk, 1995). Boris Cyrulnik, himself a child survivor in France, put it essentially this way:[1] It is a polar problem: Those survivors who never or rarely talk to their mates or children may subject them to the *trauma of silence* (see Bar-On, 1989); those survivors who talk too much—overly listener dependent, struggling to gain some mastery over their tragic experiencing—may subject their mates or children to the *trauma of engorgement* (French, meaning "saturation to the point of congestion"). Finding one's way between this Scylla and Charybdis is rendered more difficult the more family members there are. Individual prescriptions are warranted: One child may want to know more, another less. Each wants to know more or less at different ages and at different times. Family talks and individual dialogue are often warranted. Foremost, a reciprocal entente is needed. In addition, as with all pain-inducing topics, it is likely that not all details of the conversation will be absorbed. The parameters are many. "You never talked about it" has been leveled at me, when I did from when I felt my children were of age to hear about it, especially during the Jewish High Holidays and at Passover and Thanksgiving, holidays that lend themselves to such talk and thought.

The topic is preoccupying for the survivor and those with who the survivor is in a primary relationship.[2] I believe it is permanently emotionally invested and recorded in both *implicit* and *explicit memory*, by means of those factors and pathways that account for generational transmission of highly emotionally invested experiences that not only parents bring to their children, mates to their mates (which may be what Karl Abraham meant when he observed that couples who have long been married begin to resemble one another), but also children over the years bring to their parents.

I believe that *traumatism* (Cyrulnik, 2008) caused the individual by the genocidal extermination of his or her family, be it of one or several of the family, can never be totally metabolized. Its inscription in the amygdala and forged pathways to the frontal cortex I believe cannot be totally metabolized (i.e., totally suppressed and overridden by new neural pathways)

---

[1] In a colloquium in Perpignan, near the Rivesaltes concentration camp, June 6–7, 2008.

[2] "I have written that *primary, secondary* and *tertiary relationships* depend on the level of emotional investment we make in them and that a measure of that emotional investment is the degree to which we mourn when such a relationship is lost" (Parens et al., 1997). "The loss is largest when it occurs within the nuclear family which consists of *primary relationships*, that is, relationships between parent and child, siblings, mates, grandparents, and grandchildren, whatever the state of ambivalence in these relationships. *Secondary relationships* occur in wider family relationships where emotional investment is less and contact is occasional but meaningful; so are good friendships, strong student-teacher, patient-doctor relationships and the like. The loss of one of these is felt, but the work of mourning is not so large. *Tertiary relationships* have some meaning for us but their loss will not engender mourning" (Parens, 2008, p. 3).

by in-depth analytic working through. It bears on Freud's (1939) conviction that "[we] bear the indelible stamp of [our] origin" (p. 199) rendered by massive psychic trauma (Brenner, 2004; Krystal, 1968). The degree to which traumatic losses that arise from genocide can be mourned is, I believe, limited. In this lies my questioning Kogan's observation arising from her clinical work with survivors and their children that they defend against mourning. Perhaps some do. But I think that in most cases, the explanation may have more to do with the indelibility of massive psychic trauma. Kandell's important findings and theorizing on synaptic formation and the possibility of overriding old neural pathways by new ones is limited—while I do believe that we should not abandon trying to do so until long-term analytic efforts seem to hit the brick wall of indelibility.

Once our children (of survivors) internalize to a given degree and organize an emotional context of their parent's traumatism, they are likely to identify with what their parent went through and are left for life—it is hoped less and less as they grow—to cope with these identifications and their parent's unavoidable occasional episodes of what Primo Levi (1947/1959) spoke of as "the pain of remembering": "the comrade of all my peaceful moments ... the pain of remembering ... attacks me like a dog the moment my conscience comes out of the gloom" (p. 142).

This is why, at the 2007 International Psychoanalytic Association meetings in Berlin, I felt compelled to make a comment that seemed to have struck some listeners, some with appreciation, some with skeptical surprise, but also one, a Holocaust survivor herself, who—hearing about my comment indirectly—misunderstood what I meant. What happened is that in the course of an eloquent and sensitively done presentation by a well-regarded colleague, the adult daughter of a Holocaust survivor, several other children of survivors verbalized painful difficulties they experienced in their homes because their parents manifested behavioral symptoms and troubling reactivity that caused their children much distress over the years. There was an edge of anger in the tone of one child of survivors, a man very pained by his life with his traumatized parents, with which I empathized, that touched directly my pain as a parent-survivor. He also seemed to me to imply that his parents could have been more aware of their growing child's experience. There are many instances when this is known to be the case. Facilitated by the fact that I felt the audience as sympathetic and accepting, and troubled by the younger man's years of pain, I welcomed the chance to address him. I wanted him to know that I am a parent-survivor, that while I know that many parents have been so emotionally handicapped by their Holocaust experience that they transmit blatantly, sometimes disturbingly, their suffering; and that even those among us who have struggled to protect our mate and children are aware that by virtue of the trauma that was inflicted on us, we have burdened our children and our mates with that past. And that I weep about it. It cannot be avoided, I said, and I fear that children cannot, not be burdened by it. We cannot make our ever-present-near-the-surface pain go away.

I do not mean that Holocaust survivors, their mates, or their children are constantly experiencing that pain. It is an old, ever-to-be-sensitive scar that cannot fully heal. But, many of us and our mates and children, and the evidence is ample, are gratified, even highly so, emotionally rich, human beings. Many among us have effected very good, useful lives professionally, familially, socially, and individually. And our children are well on their way to such kind of life. But they will, from time to time, feel pain, and perhaps realize that one of the roots of this pain lies in their parents' past. But I believe that the good times may and can, as they have, far outweigh the bad.

ON HEARING OTHERS TALK
ABOUT THE HOLOCAUST

Ahmadinejad says the Holocaust did not happen. He is not the first; he will not be the last.

Some hold that the Holocaust is unique, that it cannot be compared with, or talked about with, other genocides. In many ways, the Holocaust is unique; but if we think ahead, I feel that we must think of genocide—"How do we stop genocide?"—among which the Holocaust was unique.

First, it was unique in that, unlike the other 20th century genocides, the Holocaust was law abiding. The government of the Third Reich opened the way to it with its infamous Nuremberg Laws of 1935. This was the springboard for what eventuated not only in Kristallnacht on November 9–10, 1938, but also in the Wannsee Conference on January 24, 1942, where the "Final Solution" was decided in a meeting that lasted 90 minutes. The infamous Nuremberg Laws set up by the government of the Third Reich were also adopted on October 4, 1940, by the government of Vichy France several months after France's armistice with Germany. It should be noted that Vichy France was not directly governed by the Third Reich; it was governed by France. Laws degrading citizenship and human rights such as these, while a step backward in both Germany and France, are, however, not unique to what happened in the Holocaust era. Such laws disallowing citizenship for Jews long existed in Europe prior to the 1800s. But, Europe is not alone in its shameful history; legal denial of such human rights long existed in the United States with regard to Blacks. In the face of this fact, it is not easy to hold that the 1935 Nuremberg Laws made the Holocaust unique.

The second step taken by the Third Reich is more likely to lead to consensus that the Holocaust is unique: It is that the then-German government sponsored the Final Solution. But, it would never have reached its known dimensions had not France, Poland, Russia, Hungary, and a number of other

European countries collaborated handsomely in its execution. The Third Reich instituted it to render Europe, and especially Germany, *Judenrein* ("clean of Jews") in the service of making the Aryan people the "master race." I find it incredible that the leaders of the Vichy French government (Marshall Petain and Pierre Laval) were convinced that the Third Reich duly represented and was to be the future of Europe (see Bailey, 2008).

A third distinction the Holocaust holds as compared to other genocides is the number of human beings destroyed by it. The figures are staggering: 11 million were murdered in the Third Reich's camps, of which 6 million were Jews; among the others, 3 million were Russian prisoners of war, and the remaining 2 million were Romas, Seventh Day Adventists, political prisoners, and others. The total murdered in the four other genocides of the 20th century: in Armenia (1.5 million) in 1915; in Cambodia (about 2 million) between 1975 and 1979; in Rwanda (800,000) starting April 1994 in 100 days; in Bosnia (8,000) July 11–12, 1995; come to about 4,308,000. Yes, in this also the Holocaust is unique.

This distinction of the government mandate with regard to the Holocaust and the staggering numbers murdered as compared to the other genocides of the 20th century, however, is felt by many among us as well as by institutions, including the U.S. Holocaust Memorial Museum, to not warrant separating out the Holocaust from the other genocides. Of course, for each ethnic population victimized by the genocide of its people, that genocide will become part of that ethnic culture and history, that people's "chosen trauma" Volkan (1988). But, if our wish is to prevent genocide, then genocide as a human phenomenon has to be addressed. It is to the advantage of all the murdered, of whatever race, religion, ethnicity, political denomination to focus our collective concern on genocide wherever it takes place. And, it also has a bearing on the worldwide abuse—even if not murder—of masses of humans on the basis of malignant prejudice (Parens, 2007) against them, as has happened in all corners of the globe.

But, there are other challenges on hearing people talk about the Holocaust, challenges of greater and lesser dimensions. During the 2007 meetings of the International Psychoanalytic Association (IPA) held in Berlin, I was moved by the number of sessions in which our German colleagues talked about the Holocaust, about Germany's responsibility for it. For years soon after the end of World War II, the challenge of "reparation" for the terrible losses wrought by the Holocaust continued to bring Germany's role in it out in the open, to world view. Germany's heads of state acknowledged it. But, it took the French 50 years before Jacques Chirac, then president of France, spoke out about the shame of the French Vichy government's collaboration with the Third Reich's Final Solution. On July 16, 1995, he said:

These instances, it is difficult to bring them to mind because these black hours sully forever our History and have damaged our past and our tradition. Yes, the crazed criminality of the occupant was seconded by Frenchmen, by the French State. France, land of light and asylum, France that day achieved what is irreparable: she delivered those who sought asylum there to their murderers.[1] (my translation)

I was grateful, but I was furious. It took the French 50 years before their president could formally admit what they did. And according to Rosemary Bailey, who rather recently interviewed a number of them, many French to this day claim that they were in the Resistance, which is highly improbable. What do you do when you love a country and its people do to you and those you love what the French did to us, and they cannot face up to what they did? My experience is that more Germans, who I know and do not know, acknowledge what they and their parents did than do the French. I feel that of course the blame lies most with the Germans and their forebears, but the French, Austrians, Hungarians, Poles, and Russians, among others, were eager collaborators. As I wrote:

Transports from France to Auschwitz started on March 27, 1942. According to Marrus and Paxton (1983), at the outset of their odious collaboration, the Vichy-French plan executors worked with such alacrity and efficiency that they sent their first train convoy before the Germans were ready to receive and temporarily house them, causing an embarrassment for the poor German Nazis! But by August, the time convoy #19 was shipped out, the dispatching to the Death Camps in Poland of Jews who had sought refuge in France seems to have proceeded smoothly. And since the "Final Solution" once set in motion in January 1942 called for expeditiousness, no doubt the transfer of my mother and others from Rivesaltes via Drancy to Auschwitz probably took no more than [five] days. Once there, extermination was efficiently expedited. (2004, pp. 116–117)

We all know that after years of silence, many Germans, especially challenged by their third-generation offsprings' questions, began to openly acknowledge their role in the Holocaust and the shame that comes with it. Again, given the blame ascribed to them, the Germans could not tell their

[1] "Ces moments, il est difficile de les évoquer parce que ces heures noires souillent à jamais notre Histoire et sont une injure à notre passé et à notre tradition. Oui, la folie criminelle de l'occupant a été secondée par des Français, par l'Etat Français. La France, patrie des lumières et d'asile, la France ce jour-là accomplissait l'irréparable, elle livrait ses protéges à leurs bourreaux." From the address given by then French President Jacques Chirac on the occasion of the 55th anniversary of the "Raffle du Vel d'Hiv" at which Jews from Paris and the environs were arrested by the French Milice (Gestapo equivalent French police) and within days were deported to death camps in Poland. Part of the commemorative ceremony is recorded at http://www.ina.fr/economie-et-societe/vie-sociale/video/CAB95040420/vel-d-hiv-chirac.fr.html

children, "We didn't do anything wrong." The world had pointed it out to them, and many people the world over still ascribe the Holocaust only to the Germans. Our own universe, the psychoanalytic world, held such an opinion as well, and it was not until 1983, nearly 40 years after the massive genocide, that the IPA met in Germany, in Hamburg, for the first time since the war. This is why there is cause to celebrate the fact that even within our own psychoanalytic world the acknowledgment by the Germans is so welcome.

But, comments about the Holocaust, even benign ones, trigger in me an alert, and the negative ones create a ripple in my sensitized threshold of Holocaust-attached pain and rage. This past summer, shopping in a small resort town, standing in line ready to pay for the few items I bought, the customer in front of me registered a minor complaint, even with some humor, to which the young woman at the cash register responded: "Oh my God, it's okay, let's not start a Holocaust over this." I was shocked. Without thinking, with a serious tone, I said to her, "Please choose your words more carefully!" She looked at me a bit surprised—perhaps she thought I was making too much of her naïve comment. The customer behind me added a brief comment of agreement with me. But simultaneously I felt compelled to add: "I was there!" The young woman turned serious and embarrassed, apologized. For those of us who were there, we will always be acutely sensitive to any comment about the Holocaust.

REFERENCES

Bailey, R. (2008). *Love and war in the Pyrenees: A story of courage, fear and hope, 1939–1944*. London: Weidenfeld & Nicolson.

Bar-On, D. (1989). *Legacy of silence: Encounters with children of the Third Reich*. Boston: Harvard University Press.

Bar-On, D. (1990). Children of perpetrators of the Holocaust: Working through one's moral self. *Psychiatry*, 53, 229–245.

Bar-On, D. (1995). Encounters between descendants of Nazi perpetrators and descendants of Holocaust survivors. *Psychiatry*, 58, 225–245.

Brenner, I. (2004). *Psychic trauma*. Lanham, MD: Aronson.

Choko, I., Irwin, F., Kahana-Aufleger, L., Kaliha, M., & Lipsi, J. (2005). *Stolen youth*. New York and Jerusalem: Yad Vashem and The Holocaust Survivors' Memoirs Project.

Cyrulnik, B. (2008). Children in war and their resiliences. In *The unbroken soul: Tragedy, trauma, and human resilience* (pp. 21–36). New York: Rowman & Littlefield.

Freud, S. (1939). An outline of psycho-analysis. In J. Strachey (Ed. & Trans.), *The standard edition of the complete psychological works of Sigmund Freud* (Vol. 23, pp. 211–253). London: Hogarth Press.

Friedlander, S. (2007). *Nazi Germany and the Jews, 1939–1945: The years of extermination*. New York: HarperCollins.

Goschalk, J. (1995). A second meeting between children of Holocaust survivors and Nazi perpetrators: Obstacles and growth. In H. Adam, P. Riedesser, H. Riqueline, A. Verderber, & J. Walter (Eds.), *Children: War and persecution* (pp. 191–196). Osnabrueck, Germany: Secolo Verlag.

Klarsfeld, S. (1978). *Le Memorial de la Deportation des Juifs de France.* Paris.

Krystal, H. (1968). *Massive psychic trauma.* New York: International Universities Press.

Levi, P. (1996). *Survival in Auschwitz* (S. Woolf, Trans.). New York: Simon and Schuster. (Original work published 1959)

Levin, N. (1968). *The Holocaust: The destruction of European Jewry, 1933–1945.* New York: Cromwell.

Marrus, M. R., & Paxton, R. O. (1983). *Vichy France and the Jews.* New York: Schocken Books.

Nemirovsky, I. (2006). *Suite Française.* New York: Knopf.

Nir, Y. (2002). *The lost childhood.* New York: Scholastic Press.

Parens, H. (2004). *Renewal of life: Healing from the Holocaust.* Rockville, MD: Schreiber.

Parens, H. (2007). Malignant prejudice: Guidelines toward its prevention. In H. Parens, A. Mahfouz, S. Twemlow, & D. Scharff (Eds.), *The future of prejudice: Psychoanalysis and the prevention of prejudice* (pp. 269–289). New York: Rowman & Littlefield.

Parens, H. (2008, June 5). How does the proximal environment impact resilience? Presented to Séminaire sur la Résilience, Boris Cyrulnik, Chair. Paris, France.

Parens, H., Currie, J., & Scattergood, S. (1979, March 3). Education for responsible parenting: The Germantown Friends School Pilot Project Tape Cassette of Presentation and Discussion, Chairperson, J. Currie. National Conference of the National Association of Independent Schools, Washington, DC.

Parens, H., Pollock, L., & Prall, R. C. (1974). *Film #3: Prevention/early intervention mother-infant groups.* Philadelphia: Audio-Visual Media Section, Eastern Pennsylvania Psychiatric Institute.

Parens, H., Scattergood, E., Duff, A., & Singletary, W. (1997). *Parenting for emotional growth: The textbook.* Philadelphia: Parenting for Emotional Growth.

Parens, H., Scattergood, E., Hernit, R. C., & Duff, S. (1979). *Parenting: Love and much more* [Television series]. Philadephia, PA: CBS Broadcasting.

Peschanski, D. (2002). *La France des Camps: L'internement 1938–1946.* Paris: Gallimard.

Shirer, W. (1959). *The rise and fall of the Third Reich.* New York: Simon and Schuster.

Volkan, V. D. (1988). *The need to have enemies and allies: From clinical practice to international relationships.* Northvale, NJ: Aronson.

Vrba, Rudi. (2002). *I escaped from Auschwitz.* New York: Barricade Books.

Chapter 7

"Too Young to Remember"

Recovering and Integrating the Unacknowledged Known

Sophia Richman

LIES AND SECRETS

My earliest memory is the lie my mother told me. It was shortly before my second birthday, and she warned me to stay away from the attic because she said, "A dangerous wolf lives there." Unbeknownst to me, the wolf was a fabrication meant to keep me away from the attic space adjacent to our apartment where my father was hidden after his escape from a concentration camp. My parents feared that I could not yet be entrusted with such a secret, but shortly thereafter I discovered the man I came to know as *tatush* (daddy). Then, I was warned again, this time never to reveal his presence to anyone. Even as a toddler, I seemed to understand that heeding Mother's words was a matter of life and death.

And so, we three survived World War II in hiding; Mother and I out in the open with a Christian identity and Father hidden out of sight in the little garret used for storage. We had found shelter in Zimna Woda, the small village on the outskirts of Lwow, the city in southeastern Poland where I was born. After my father's imprisonment in the Janowska concentration camp, my mother obtained papers that enabled her to assume the identity of a deceased Catholic woman, and with the help of a childhood friend she found us a place to live where no one knew our true identity. Eight months later, my father miraculously escaped from the camp, located our whereabouts with the help of gentile friends, and under cover of night, Mother brought him to our attic. Our unsuspecting landlords had no idea that they were harboring a Jewish family in the upstairs apartment of their two-family house.

Fortunately for the three of us, Mother was a courageous woman and very good at dissembling. Having come from an assimilated Jewish family, she spoke flawless Polish and had many devoted Catholic friends. With their help, she was able to obtain shelter and assume a Polish Catholic identity. She created a believable story to explain the absence of a husband, telling people that he had joined the Polish army at the start of the war and was missing in action, presumed to be dead. She had come to this little village with her baby because she had a friend who resided there. It was he who had helped her find this place to live. No one in the village knew that this friend was himself a Jew who had converted many years before the Second World War. It was also our good fortune that with my blond hair, fair skin, and blue-green eyes I did not look Jewish. Such a baby was a great cover to help Mother with her disguise.

In those early formative years, I learned to be cautious, unobtrusive, and compliant. By the age of 3, I was well schooled in deception as I proved one day when confronted with the ultimate test. Mother had left the apartment to do some chores, and I sat at the kitchen table across from *tatush*, who would come out of the attic from time to time to stretch his legs. The landlady must have heard voices inside the apartment, and she had seen my mother go out. Through the door she asked "Zosia, whom are you talking to? Is someone there with you?" I saw the panic in my father's eyes as he raised his finger to his lips and gave me the sign that I was to keep the Secret—so I lied to the landlady and said, "No one is here *Pani Donikowska*, I'm alone."

This traumatic experience indelibly imprinted on my memory was validated years later when my father wrote a memoir about his wartime experiences. Our versions of the incident are almost identical. I believe that this event and the circumstances around it influenced what I came to regard as my lifelong speaking inhibition. During those early years, when I was learning to talk, the act of speaking was associated with grave danger. Spontaneous expression of any kind was risky, and words uttered out loud had to be most carefully chosen. Faced with the chilling possibility of letting something forbidden slip out of my mouth, it was better to be silent and not give voice to thoughts or feelings.

The impact of the hiding experience was far reaching and continued well beyond the war years. In time, I learned that my reaction was fairly typical of children who had survived in similar conditions (Kestenberg & Brenner, 1996). Hiding becomes a way of being; its reverberations continue without intention or awareness. It influenced many of my life choices and shaped my character and identity. Mitchell (1988) wrote about certain evocative metaphors, like the "damaged self," which come to serve as the centerpiece of an elaborate psychodynamic configuration. In a previous article (Richman, 2004), I proposed that the "hidden self" is another such self-defining metaphor that organizes experience and provides continuity and connectedness with one's internal and interpersonal world. Born of early traumatic experience, it comes to be a way of experiencing oneself, a part of one's identity, and tends to be reenacted throughout life.

Certain cultural and historical circumstances reinforce such personal metaphors. In postwar America, a curtain of silence seemed to descend in the aftermath of the Holocaust. After liberation, intense and collective defense mechanisms operated to keep memories and awareness of Nazi horrors from surfacing (Bergmann & Jucovy, 1982). With few exceptions, survivors did not want to talk about what had happened to them during the war years, and society did not want to know the details; it was a perfect collusion.

Even mental health professionals were subject to the general atmosphere of denial (Danieli, 1984; Kuriloff, 2010). In the 1960s when I first entered psychoanalysis, few psychotherapists were sensitive to issues brought in by survivors, and many imposed their theories of development on to us. Some overestimated the impact of the Holocaust, seeing only damage in their patients, but most were inclined to minimize or ignore the powerful and pervasive effects of the Holocaust trauma. My first therapy was a case in point. Although I spoke about my wartime experience, it did not seem to lead anywhere. As I remember it, the analyst was more interested in the way that the Oedipal complex played out in my family than in the long-term effects of having spent my early years living in terror and in hiding. He never encouraged me to explore the meaning or implications of what had happened to me or help me understand the relationship between some of the symptoms troubling me at the time and my early trauma.

Like my parents before him, the analyst minimized the impact of my early traumatic experiences. In the case of my parents, however, the intentions were protective of me as well as of themselves. They were eager to believe that because of my young age, I would not remember or understand what had happened, and therefore, they reasoned, I would not be affected by it. In her video testimony, my mother said: "I was thanking God that she is so young that she didn't know much about what was happening" (T-291). The naïve conclusion that a lack of understanding protects one from trauma was a common belief in those days. Even today, some individuals still do not understand that confusion and mystification can in fact compound trauma rather than attenuate its effects.

THE UNACKNOWLEDGED KNOWN

The phrase I heard many times, "You were too young to remember," has always felt like a denial of my reality. I had my memories; though they were few, they were precious to me like old faded, fragile photographs tucked away for safekeeping. Without validation or a context to give them meaning, the memories were robbed of their significance and therefore could not be integrated into the rest of my life. My parents' injunction was to leave the past behind and begin life anew. I complied and behaved as if my life really began at the age of five when we arrived in Paris, the year after the war had ended. Since I was especially good at knowing what was expected of me, I quickly adjusted to my new surroundings. My past seemed irrelevant, so I kept it to myself. If I was asked directly about the early years, I answered matter of factly, without emotion as if I was talking about someone else's life.

Many years later, I came to understand that in those days I was largely functioning in a state of dissociation in which my emotions were disconnected from the events. This state of both knowing and not knowing was a way out of the impossible situation in which I found myself. Those I loved and trusted said that nothing of any significance had happened to me, yet I had my memories to prove otherwise. The only way out of this dilemma was to hold on to my memories but behave as if the past had nothing to do with my life. It took a long time to recognize that what had happened to me was traumatic. For a child to be able to put words to feelings, the child needs the adults to be witnesses and help him or her to make sense of the world. Because of their own trauma, the significant adults in my life were unable to function as witnesses for me. They imposed a construction on my world that did not fit my experience, but I never took issue with it or questioned it.

I adopted their narrative of my life and eventually took on their view of me—a lucky, well-adjusted, happy child. I felt pretty good about myself; I had many friends and enjoyed much success at school. Perhaps there were glimmers of another state—a sense of numbness when it came to certain feelings, some awareness of inhibition and a seeming lack of capacity for spontaneity, a quality I admired in others. While the compromise worked pretty well for me, I was not aware of the price I paid for my "good adjustment." The consequence of living out someone else's narrative is that certain aspects of self remain outside awareness, split off and dissociated and unavailable to experience life fully. As I wrote in my memoir, "One can't mourn what one doesn't acknowledge and one can't heal if one does not mourn" (Richman, 2002, p. xiv).

FROM HIDING TO AUTHENTICITY

The road to recovery was a long one. My first therapy experience had been a lost opportunity to create a meaningful narrative that would be different from the one my parents had created for me. Besides the limitations of the analyst and the *zeitgeist* of the times, another significant factor was my own lack of readiness to deal with the past. It took many years before I could face my history and come to know aspects of myself that had been denied. Much of the work went on without awareness, and most of it took place outside therapy. It was understood only in retrospect and coalesced in my middle years when I reflected on the choices that I had made in my life.

Middle age is a developmental phase that gets short shrift in psychology. While the literature on child and adolescent development is extensive, few theorists or researchers have focused on midlife as a developmental stage. For me, one of the most significant aspects of this life stage is the shifting perspective that it can bring. It is a time of reflection and review of life. One is more aware of the finiteness of life, which intensifies the present and can lead to a sense of urgency about fulfilling what has heretofore existed only in the realm of possibility. A sense of "now or never" can lead to action. In that context, some refer to the midlife crisis, but I believe that midlife is an opportunity for repair, restitution, and the development of earlier unrealized potential. For many, it is also an opportunity to mourn, to face past losses, and to come to terms with limitations. Those who can use these opportunities are the fortunate ones for the alternative is a sense of despair and emotional paralysis.

One of the factors that determines whether midlife becomes an opportunity for new growth or leads to a sense of despair seems to me to be the capacity to cope with life's disappointments and hurts that has developed over time and through earlier life stages. In my own case, the choices that I made along the way were motivated by a drive to repair what had been damaged by early trauma.

The drive to express myself was powerful. Since speaking remained problematic, other forms of self-expression drew me—painting, writing, singing, dancing all became opportunities to express feelings and to connect with others. Drawing in particular was an art form that connected me with both parents. My father appreciated art and eventually in retirement turned to painting as a hobby. My mother encouraged drawing and engaged me in a drawing game in early childhood; she would draw a picture of an object and I would guess what it was, and then I would draw something and it was her turn to guess. Pencil and paper were more accessible and affordable than toys. In fact, the first present that I remember was the one left for me on Christmas morning by Papa Noel shortly after we arrived in Paris—it was two large colored pencils, one red, the other blue.

The forms of expression that took root were those arts for which I was fortunate to have some talent—writing and painting. I decided that when I grew up, I would be a writer and an illustrator. Those creative activities that were admired by my parents brought me great pleasure and, unbeknownst to me, were opportunities to work though some of the early trauma. Writing in particular lent itself to the expression of themes and feelings that could not safely be expressed in other ways. One of the first stories that I ever wrote was about a little boy who had survived the war separated from his parents. I titled it, "The Boy With No Name." To my recollection, this short story was my first attempt to deal with the experience of childhood survival and its aftermath. One of the most fascinating aspects of this short story was the fact that I wrote it under the pseudonym Dorothy S. White. I do not recollect if at the time I was aware of the significance of my choice of pseudonym. "Dorothy White" was the English translation of my mother's maiden name—Dorota Weiss. The middle initial S represented my own name. I had apparently given my mother the authorship of this story—was this my way of approaching a subject that I was not supposed to address? Did the disguise allow me to express what I needed to say? Was it an attempt to communicate something to my mother?

By the time I reached adulthood, I abandoned my goal of being a writer and illustrator and instead turned to psychology as my profession; once again, at the time I did not realize the potential for self-healing that it could provide. My early experience of massive confusion had led to a powerful need to understand and to make sense of the incomprehensible—a state of mind that is perfectly compatible with the goals of the profession.

Strange things had gone on when I was little. The adults whom I relied on to help me understand the world failed to clarify anything; in fact, they created the confusion. According to my mother, first there was a wolf, then there wasn't; who was this strange man who came out of the attic and went back there to hide? And, why did I have to keep his presence a secret from the people Mother seemed so friendly with? She smiled when we were outside of the apartment yet looked so sad and frightened when we were alone—why? None of it made sense to me, and I was not supposed to question it. The need to understand became a driving force and pervasive theme in my life, which found fulfillment in a profession dedicated to making sense of puzzling behavior and troublesome feelings.

A healing profession is not only healing for the patient but also for the therapist. Helping others to express their suffering and deal with it puts us in touch with our own struggle and mastery around similar issues. Sharing innermost thoughts and feelings facilitates connection and counteracts the sense of alienation that attends trauma. The analyst is a witness to one's suffering, and having a witness is an important component of the healing process (Poland, 2000).

The desire to be known along with a fear of it, expressed in terms of how much to reveal versus how much to conceal, is universal. But, this struggle is heightened for trauma survivors, who are caught between the need to expose what they have endured and to hide it because of the shame about having been victimized.

While creative activities and professional choices provide opportunities to make up for what has been missing, the greatest potential for repair comes from meaningful relationships with a spouse, a therapist, and friends and through the chance to parent. After some initial failed efforts, I was able to create a good marriage, to have a child, and to find a therapist whom I could trust.

Relationships with friends have always sustained me. After the war, the few family members who had managed to survive were scattered all over the globe. So, my parents and I consisted of the only family unit I knew. In the aftermath of trauma, the atmosphere at home was permeated with loss and tragedy. In addition, my parents were preoccupied with the struggle of refugees/immigrants to adjust to a new country. It was in school and among friends that I found relief from the oppressive atmosphere at home. Friendship was such an important part of my life, that in addition to the playmates in school and in my neighborhood, I created imaginary companions. When I lived in Paris, I created a character, a little girl named Françoise, who was exactly my age and who shared identical interests to mine. The way that we were different was that while I was a foreigner trying to fit in, she was truly French (as the veiled reference to France in her name would indicate). I aspired to be a little French girl just like her. Françoise was my witness; I conjured her up when I was alone and wanted to share something with someone who knew me intimately and who accepted me unconditionally. My desire to share the joys of my life with her was as strong as my need to share my frustrations.

One of the most common places where Françoise would make her appearance was the bathroom located outside our apartment and shared with other families, a small room with a toilet consisting of a hole in the ground with footholds on either side, requiring that one squatted and carefully aimed. Those toilets in postwar France were the bane of my existence; I always feared falling in. Françoise's presence helped me cope by distracting me from my fear and giving me comfort. We had conversations about things that were important to me. Once when I received a doll for my birthday—a very special present—I brought the doll into the bathroom to show to her so that she could appreciate its beauty.

My imaginary friendships were a solution to my loneliness, but I think more importantly they were a way of dealing with my need to be recognized. A hidden child who had to be on guard much of the time could not readily trust others to be witnesses. Through these fantasy relationships my powerful need to be known could be met without jeopardizing my security needs. Only in imagination does one have full control over the response of the other; there is no risk of disappointment or danger of having one's perception tampered with, as had been the case for me in my early years. A witness of one's creation is totally safe because it is an aspect of oneself. I believe that the imaginary witness is a dissociated self-state serving the crucial function of mirroring, affirming, and validating our experience. It is a healthy and positive coping strategy, a way of using a self-state for therapeutic purposes. As such, the creation of an imaginary witness is an achievement particularly when it is not a substitute for real relationships but merely a transitional space providing a bridge to connection with significant others.

Eventually and gradually, imaginary friends disappeared from my life. It is difficult to say just when they made their final exit, but I am inclined to think it was when the need to be known became stronger than the propensity to hide and the pleasure of mutuality in real relationships outweighed safety considerations. It coincided with the capacity to be more authentic in my relationships with others. The shift from hiding to authenticity was a crucial part of the healing process. The witnessing function continued, but its nature was transformed.

TESTIMONY AND MEMOIR: TELLING AND WRITING THE NARRATIVE

Slowly, steadily, and with increasing momentum, there was a significant shift in America with regard to the Nazi Holocaust. It took about 30 years after the Second World War for the general public to acknowledge its significance as one of the greatest tragedies of the 20th century and to recognize the plight of survivors. The silence that had followed the war was gradually broken and replaced by an ever-increasing din to expose and examine what had taken place in Europe. As the number of survivors dwindled, the impetus to record their stories grew, and increasing numbers of survivors began to talk about their wartime experiences. Archives were established to collect these stories, and a plethora of creative activities and products emerged around the theme of the Shoah. My father's memoir was one of those. In the mid-1970s, he published the account of his year in the Janowska concentration camp (Richman, 1975); the manuscript he had written in hiding in the attic was translated from Polish and self-published. For me, this act of going public represented a kind of permission to deal with a subject that had been off limits. I identify that event as the beginning of my long journey out of hiding.

As society was recognizing the impact of Holocaust trauma, a parallel process seemed to be taking place in my own life. In an atmosphere that welcomed exploration of wartime trauma, I was encouraged to examine my own experience. With the passing of older survivors, the torch of memory was being passed on to us. We, the children who had not even been considered survivors, were encouraged to tell our stories. One of the significant events that took place in the early 1990s was the formation of an international organization by and for child survivors. The Hidden Child Foundation gave child survivors from all over the world an opportunity to meet and share stories about our common past and its effects on our current life. The term *hidden child*, coined at that point in time, gave us an identity—something that had been missing for so many of us.

With all these factors converging—a climate receptive to survivor accounts, an acknowledgment of the long-term effects of trauma, the maturity of survivors reaching a stage of life that lends itself to reflection, and my personal striving for self-expression—all came together to influence my decision to write a memoir. In that endeavor, I joined countless survivors who were turning to creative expression as a means to healing.

Now that I had overcome the injunction against facing my past, the legacy of my childhood, there was still another injunction to manage. This one was specific to my profession. Since the early days of psychoanalysis, the taboo against therapist self-disclosure had influenced most therapists to keep their private lives from entering the consulting room. Initially, my clinical education and my early experiences with a classical analyst reinforced this idea, but during my psychoanalytic training in the early 1970s, a different attitude toward analyst self-disclosure began to emerge. By the time I wrote my memoir, a dramatic shift had taken place in the field with regard to this concept, and most contemporary analysts whom I respected no longer held these traditionally narrow views about disclosure. Elsewhere, I have written extensively about the impact of the memoir on my practice (Richman, 2006a).

The healing potential of narrative is at the heart of our therapeutic enterprise and a subject of growing interest in our field (Richman, 2009; Schafer, 1994; Spence, 1982; Stern, 2010). With an empathic and trusted listener, we examine our life and coconstruct our story. But, written narrative undertaken alone is a different kind of experience; it is a form of self-analysis. While both have been immensely beneficial in my life, it is through writing that I have found my voice. Despite my belief in the analyst's well-meaning intentions, a vestige of the fear of coconstruction always remained. No doubt my childhood experience with parents who structured my world in a way that fit their needs has continued to affect me deeply. Exploring my inner life through writing felt safer than doing so in the presence of another where my emerging narrative could be revised, edited, or influenced by someone else, even someone whom I respected, admired, and trusted (Richman, 2009).

The way that the writing experience evolved is a testament to its incredible power. The process of self-analysis unfolded with an energy and enthusiasm that I could not have predicted; words seemed to flow effortlessly as if they had been waiting a lifetime for this moment. The emotions blocked by years of numbness now burst forth, and a creative flow of ideas spilled onto the page. Suddenly, things began to make sense, some that I had forgotten, but most that had always been available yet existed as separate entities without pattern or meaning until the moment that they appeared on paper. Writing about my life enabled me to examine it in its entirety and in sequential order. My early years had been so unstable that it was even difficult to put the pieces into a clear timeline, let alone organize them into a meaningful thread. By the time I was 11, I had lived in four different countries and changed addresses at least nine times, not counting a couple of months in Paris hotels before we found an apartment and a period of detention at Ellis Island waiting anxiously to learn whether we would be deported back to Europe. Telling the story chronologically provided me with a sense of order to counteract the chaos of my early childhood.

Writing was an organizing experience, and it fostered a sense of continuity and sameness over time, a welcome state for a person whose life had been disrupted by historical circumstances. It was also an immensely empowering experience. To be able to face what had been outside my control, in an active way but from a safe distance, fostered a feeling of mastery. For me, dissociation had come in the form of a split between my knowledge and my feelings, and now I found myself moving toward an integration of my emotional and cognitive self. As a result, I experienced a sense of vitality and wholeness that felt entirely new.

Although writing is a solitary activity, I have come to believe that in some respects it is relational as well. As I wrote my autobiographical narrative, I found myself in dialogue with a projected reader, an amorphous presence without distinguishing characteristics, an interested observer, a witness, someone who wanted to know more about me and my life. Recently, I have come to recognize this imaginary entity as another version of my imaginary childhood friends. My need for witness to my trauma was now expressed in this new way. Perhaps again the imaginary other gave me an opportunity to enter a transitional space that would make it safer eventually to reveal myself to the world.

INTERGENERATIONAL TRANSMISSION OF TRAUMA AND RESILIENCE

The need to memorialize tragic events and their victims, and the responsibility to transmit knowledge of them to future generations so that they will not be forgotten, takes various forms. Museums, archives, the memoirs of survivors, all give names and identities to those who lived and died without leaving traces of themselves. On a smaller scale, another way to remember those who were lost is to pass on their names to the next generation. Through those "memorial candles," the dead are kept in memory.

Memorials to the Holocaust are the product of conscious decisions to perpetuate the memory of what transpired, but there are other, less-deliberate ways in which the legacy of the Shoah lives on. The concept of *intergenerational transmission of trauma* refers to the continuation and perpetuation of trauma-related themes that are passed on from one generation to the next, usually without conscious intention. The term has increasingly found its way into the Holocaust literature since its identification in the late 1970s, and for the most part, it has been conceptualized as a negative legacy. While I agree that trauma undoubtedly has a ripple effect felt for generations, I believe that this effect has been conceptualized too narrowly.

Intergenerational influence is a complex phenomenon; sometimes, it takes unpredictable twists and turns. Some years ago, I heard the following story from a friend, a child survivor, like myself. During the war, a Polish

Catholic man had saved both her and her parents from the Nazis. He had found a hiding place for her with a family and hid her parents and several of their relatives underground in his cellar. For 2 years, he took care of them, brought them food, and protected them from the Nazis. Until the end of the war, he kept this heroic act a secret from his wife and his children. Although heroic and uncommon, this is not the remarkable part of the story. We know that there were some gentiles willing to risk their own lives and those of their families to protect Jews. What makes this story especially curious is that many years, and several generations, later, the rescuer's grandson relocated to Israel, converted to Judaism, and became highly religious. He married an Israeli, changed his name from Miloslaw to Meir, and raised his children as Orthodox Jews. When he was interviewed about his unconventional decision, he said that he had been inspired by his grandfather's courageous undertaking to save a Jewish family during the Holocaust (Bensoussan, 2010). The traumatic events that had taken place long before this man's birth had a profound impact on him; they shaped his life and the lives of his children.

For me, this is an example of the complexity of traumatic events, their long-term effects, and their echoes in the lives of future generations. It is regrettable that the concept of intergenerational transmission has been almost exclusively associated with the inevitable transmission of pathology rather than more broadly as an influence that can have both negative and positive consequences.

Recently, there has been much interest and research into the phenomenon of resilience to trauma. Many survivors have endured great adversity both during their wartime ordeal and in its aftermath, and yet they have been able to create meaningful lives for themselves and their families. Survivors can communicate and model astounding strength, courage, and resilience for their children and grandchildren.

Anna Ornstein, a psychoanalyst who survived Auschwitz, shares my views about the irresponsible generalizations of professionals that focus on the automatic transmission of pathology (see Ornstein, 2006). She has said wryly, "We need to be alert to the transmission of unfortunate generalizations from one generation of psychoanalysts to the next."

While psychologists and psychoanalysts have tended to focus on the pathological and dysfunctional aspects of trauma and its aftermath, there has been a recent movement highlighting the fact that devastating life events can actually present opportunities for growth and positive personal change. Recovery from trauma can be a springboard to further individual development. The term *posttraumatic growth* (Tedeschi, Park, & Calhoun, 1998) has been used to describe this phenomenon.

The growth-enhancing properties of creative expression were discussed previously. Creativity provides the ultimate possibility for transformation and transcendence of traumatic experience, and it is in this area that familial transmission is most evident. Talent runs in families; children inherit their talents from their parents; parents are likely to recognize, appreciate, and nurture areas of achievement that are familiar to them. Not only are children exposed to works of art but also they can turn to parents as role models for ways of coping with adversity through the creative process.

In my own family, there are three generations of trauma survivors who have turned to the creative arts to deal with trauma—my father before me and my daughter after me. My father, Leon Richman, was drawn to painting and writing as a means for self-healing; I have chosen the same artistic modalities as my own, and my daughter, Lina Orfanos, who survived trauma in her own right, turned to music for self-expression and recovery.

Leon Richman was not introspective, but he had a powerful desire to record his experiences and document what he saw. Before he escaped from the Janowska concentration camp, where he was imprisoned for a year of his life, he kept notes on the horrors that he witnessed, including the names of perpetrators and victims. After his escape from Janowska and during the years when he was hidden in the tiny attic attached to our apartment, he turned those notes into a manuscript with the intention of creating a document, an objective record for posterity. But, it was not until 30 years later that he had the manuscript translated and published. This work was a testimonial to what he had seen and suffered. He was proud of it; it gave his life meaning and purpose.

In his middle years, after he retired, my father turned to painting as a source of pleasure. Leon had few pleasures in his life. He was a bitter, angry man deeply wounded by his wartime trauma. He did not enjoy relationships with people and always seemed angry with my mother and me for one reason or another. Only his creative and intellectual activities seemed to bring him satisfaction. This was his source of self-esteem; he could gaze on his artwork or immerse himself in his memoir and shut the world out.

His paintings, rendered in a childlike primitive style, had a quality of innocence about them. They depicted pretty bucolic scenes of places where he had traveled, and they seemed to capture another side of the man who was so disillusioned with humanity. Perhaps these scenes featuring the beauty of nature were meant as a counterbalance to the ugliness of human nature that he had witnessed. Only one painting stood in stark contrast to these pretty landscapes—a self-portrait of a man with a tortured expression on his face. This painting that seemed to capture the inner self in its utter despair and terror was never framed or displayed along with the others. Instead, it was hidden away in a closet for me to find after his death.

I never felt like my father's child. This taciturn, distant, rageful man was not anyone I could easily identify with. Yet, as I look back on my life, I must acknowledge that in some ways we are alike, and I have been influenced by him. Like him, I love learning and intellectually stretching, and like him, I derive great pleasure from creative expression. Even the modalities, writing and painting, are the ones that he and I share. It cannot be a coincidence that we both have written a memoir and that we are drawn to landscape painting in our artwork.

My daughter Lina's talents lie in another direction. She was born with a remarkable gift, a hauntingly beautiful soprano voice that has been described by some as "unearthly." Lina inherited her talent from my mother's sister Jadwega, who was murdered during the Holocaust. It is a triumph to know that this beautiful voice, silenced by the Nazis, continues to live on in Lina.

In addition to being a "second-generation" survivor, Lina has suffered her own tragedy. As a young girl of 14, she was diagnosed with a brain tumor and subsequently underwent a series of harrowing surgeries. Robbed of her adolescence, she now lives with the emotional and physical scars of her illness. Yet, Lina has shown amazing resilience. Her positive attitude and her engagement in life are inspirational.

It is in music that her pain has found its expression. Her voice is the vehicle through which she expresses her emotions about the tragedies that have happened to her and to her people. The mournful art songs that are her specialty bring up images of loss, longing, and an awareness of the fragility of life. They also communicate a sense of hope and inner strength to overcome adversity. When she performs, she evokes similar emotions in her listeners, giving shape and form to their own unarticulated feelings. Lina is a living example of the capacity of creative expression to transform traumatic experience.

The paths we take in life are influenced by numerous forces, our talents, our history, and the way we have defined ourselves through verbal and nonverbal narrative. Our story defines us; it helps us make sense of the past, integrate it into our present, and move into the future with greater wisdom. Our hope is that ultimately our life story will be rich in texture and meaningful and will feel authentic to ourselves.

REFERENCES

Bensoussan, B. (2010). The savior's grandson. *Mishpacha Magazine, 301*(17), 54–61.

Bergmann, M., & Jucovy, M. (Eds.). (1982). *Generations of the Holocaust*. New York: Basic Books.

Danieli, Y. (1984). Psychotherapists' participation in the conspiracy of silence about the Holocaust. *Psychoanalytic Psychology, 1*, 23–42.

Kestenberg, J., & Brenner, I. (1996). *The last witness: The child survivor of the Holocaust*. Washington, DC: American Psychiatric Press.

Kuriloff, E. (2010). The Holocaust and psychoanalytic theory and praxis. *Contemporary Psychoanalysis, 46*, 395–422.

Mitchell, S. A. (1988). *Relational concepts in psychoanalysis: An integration.* Cambridge, MA: Harvard University Press.

Ornstein, A. (2006). Memory, history, autobiography. *Contemporary Psychoanalysis, 42,* 657–669.

Poland, W. S. (2000). The analyst's witnessing and otherness. *Journal of the American Psychoanalytic Association, 48,* 17–34.

Richman, L. (1975). *Why: Extermination Camp Lwow (Lemberg), 134 Janowska Street, Poland.* New York: Vantage Press.

Richman, S. (2002). *A wolf in the attic: The legacy of a hidden child of the Holocaust.* New York: Routledge.

Richman, S. (2004). From hiding to healing: A psychoanalyst's narrative of personal trauma. *NYS Psychologist, 16,* 2–7.

Richman, S. (2006a). Finding one's voice: Transforming trauma into autobiographical narrative. *Contemporary Psychoanalysis, 42,* 639–650.

Richman, S. (2006b). When the analyst writes a memoir: Clinical implications of biographic disclosure. *Contemporary Psychoanalysis, 42,* 367–392.

Richman, S. (2009). Secrets and mystifications: Finding meaning through memoir. *Psychoanalytic Perspectives, 6,* 67–75.

Schafer, R. (1994). *Retelling a life: Narration and dialogue in psychoanalysis.* New York: Basic Books.

Spence, D. (1982). *Narrative truth and historical truth: Meaning and interpretation in psycho-analysis.* New York: Norton.

Stern, D. B. (2010). *Partners in thought: Working with unformulated experience, dissociation, and enactment.* New York: Routledge.

Tedeschi, R., Park, C., & Calhoun, L. (Eds.). (1998). *Posttraumatic growth: Positive changes in the aftermath of crisis.* Mahwah, NJ: Erlbaum.

T-291. Richman, Dorothy R. Fortunoff Video Archive for Holocaust Testimonies, Yale University Library, New Haven, CT.

Part 3

Reverberations

Chapter 8

Leiser's Song

Myra Sklarew

INTRODUCTION

On June 15, 1940, the Soviet Union occupied Lithuania. A year later, on June 22, 1941, Nazi Germany broke its pact with the Soviets and invaded Lithuania. The Red Army fled. A killing rampage against Jews took place in over two hundred villages. In my journeys there over nineteen years, I have yet to visit a village that has no massacre pit, although some are hidden in deep forest. The Jews of Kaunas, some 30,000, were ordered to move into the Kovno Ghetto in August 1941, an area that contained approximately 7,000 people in what is called Slobodka or Vilijampole, across the river from Kaunas. It was here, in August 1941, that my cousin Leiser Wolpe, then a teenager, moved with his pregnant mother into a stable used to feed pigs. His father had been killed earlier by Lithuanians in the cellar of their apartment house in Kaunas.

In recent years, I discovered, thanks to a physician friend who had known Leiser many years earlier, that he was alive and living in Zurich, Switzerland. And thus a correspondence began that took place over 9 years until his death. For the most part, our conversations were by telephone, almost on a daily basis and often several times a day. His wife, Ada, a painter, would write lengthy and beautiful letters. The drawings and paintings reproduced here are by Ada (see Plates 1 and 2).

What follows here are bits and scraps of our conversations, in no particular order, in the same way that his thoughts followed no logical order but were often interrupted by intrusive images, memories, avoidances, repetitions. Although I often had to hurry to keep up with his sudden shifts of thought, I had one distinct advantage—I had walked the places of his suffering many times. And, by one of those strange coincidences that life can offer, during my very first visit to Lithuania in 1993, a survivor of Keidan—the very town of Leiser's birth—walked with me, describing every family who had once lived there. I did not know at the time that it was Leiser's birthplace or that many others of my family had lived there as well. As Simon Schama has written, I knew Leiser Wolpe's territory and landscape through "the archives of the feet." I had, with survivors, walked the perimeter of the burial pit where many of Leiser's family had been murdered. I had walked through Slobodka, site of the former Kovno Ghetto where he and his mother managed to survive, in the company of those who had been imprisoned there as well. And, I had walked those places alone, touching the buildings and the earth where so many perished. I talked to witnesses, rescuers, survivors, and collaborators in those places. I did not go to Dachau, or walk in the steps of his forced march, or to Stutthof concentration camp, where his mother died. But, perhaps it helped that he knew that what he told me was not abstract, but was palpable because I had embodied the physical places and presences of the world he was sharing with me. I will always be grateful for his friendship and trust.

LEISER'S SONG

Friday fell off the calendar. Just at the moment when an old man was crossing Bahnhofstrasse in Zurich. The day fled the calm progression of days. He was carrying his parcel of food from Kaufmann's. He had only to reach Bahnhofplatz to find his tram stop and go home. Did he hear the approaching tram? He could not see it, his eyesight nearly gone. What did he think as he stood there, in the path of the speeding tram? Did he imagine his small brother burning alive in a hospital in Slobodka? Did he remember then the tiny newborn infant brother born in the ghetto who he had to bury when he was himself little more than a child? Did he see the face of his mother in Stutthof concentration camp? Or his father dying in his arms in the cellar at 78 Laisves Aleja? Did he remember at that moment how he rose up from that cellar of death and tried to get help? How no one would open their doors to him? That?

Or did death cover him like a blanket, muffling thought, extinguishing memory? Was it like that? Or did he send a final message to the one who had been so kind to him? To Stephen? *Help me again.* Did he say that? Is that why Stephen noticed a small message on a local television station about an old man hit by a tram? Why he called the hospital, dreading what he might find out?

*   *   *

He calls. Three in the morning, his time. Nine in the evening, mine. He calls back. He's dressed. He's having tea. Soon he will leave his apartment. I, on the other hand, will go to sleep. My night is beginning. *Have a good morning,* I tell him. *Have a good rest,* he tells me. And then, *Cheerio!* And then a few more quietly told goodbyes. It is hard for him to hang up.

He seldom sleeps. Sometimes he lies down for an hour or two. *Did you sleep when you were a little boy?* I ask him. *Oh, it wasn't like that,* he answers. I've made him go there again. I hadn't meant to do that. I must be more careful next time. *After the war, I would have terrible nightmares. Ada was afraid the neighbors would complain. I would call out. I would scream. In St. Ottilien I was too sick to cry out. They put ice on my chest to stop the bleeding. In Gautien, when the nun named Innocent took care of me, I was too sick to cry out. But later.*

I thought I would go to the police station. So I would have somebody to talk to, he tells me. He has changed the subject again. *I don't think that's a good idea,* I tell him, concerned that a visit to the police in the early morning hours might result in a longer stay than he intends. Now he calls me two times a day.

* * *

On this day, the ninth day of July, he will be buried. The man who never slept will have eternal sleep. There, in the cemetery with his beloved Ada. Companion artist who painted the shadows out of his life. *I painted him in the garden at Tessin, there among the flowers and trees. But there was only the sun, brightness and color,* she wrote to me once. He told me that he could not have lived had he not met her. *She was a veil between me and the Holocaust.* That's how he put it.

But perhaps the man who never slept will wander through the nights of the afterlife as he wandered through them in life. At first, I thought it was the nightmares he was afraid of. That all the details of his past, so critically intact, would suck him back into that mire of pain, torture's innovations imposed on him. But later I found out it was something altogether different.

I begged them not to sedate me, he told me, *when I was in the hospital. And why was that?* I asked him. *If one is in pain and cannot sleep, medication is usually given in hospitals. I did not know what I might do, what I was capable of. I could hurt someone. I might kill someone,* he told me.

* * *

He called me nine times yesterday. And left messages. They all ended with *Cheerio!* The last call was in the middle of the night his time. When Ada was alive, he would go into the kitchen and make jam at 3 in the morning.

Today I call him. *Leiser,* I begin. *What ... what do you say?* He can't hear me. Sometimes I think he is listening so hard to what is going on inside his head that it is hard for anything from outside to penetrate. But maybe today he has forgotten to put his hearing aid in. Or perhaps it needs a new battery.

I need you to help me, I say. *What, what?* he asks. And in German: *Wie bitte? Bitte? I want to know how we are related,* I say, my voice getting louder and louder, sailing across the state of Maryland, rushing over the Chesapeake Bay, going east, all the time east, all the way to Zurich.

He hears me. At last. I can feel him listening. He begins slowly. He would rather tell me about how he ordered Joel Elkes's books from London, the book Elkes wrote about his father, Elchanan Elkes, who was head of the Altestenrat in Kovno during the Nazi occupation. Elkes who attempted to stop the murders of 10,000 Jews and was beaten nearly to death. Elkes who died in Dachau and wrote to his children: "Remember, both of you, what Amalek has done to us. Remember and never forget it all your days; and pass this memory as a sacred testament to future generations."

And now he remembers my question. *Do you think*, he begins, *that when we lived in Keidan we thought about family trees, about genealogy? About making a map of all the families? We thought about Shabbos. We thought about how will we be able to get a chicken for Shabbos. I was a little boy. I don't know.* We burst out laughing. We laugh and we laugh, the distance is swallowed up. We are in each other's arms laughing.

* * *

I've made a decision, he tells me, changing the subject again. *Adrian told me to get rid of everything. I look at all the things—paintings, drawings, jewelry, vases and carvings and Ada's brushes and paints.* I know before he goes on what he will say. *I will learn to paint,* he announces. Before Ada vanishes from inside him, he will take all those years when he watched her work, when he cooked for her, and stretched canvases, and carried her paintings and drawings from place to place, and he will turn into her. He will become a painter and she will be inside him, and his arms will move as she moved them. He will see the world through her eyes. And he will paint.

But a moment later, he proclaims he must work: He has too much to do. He must prepare the exhibition of Ada's work. Not for December, but for spring.

Another subject, quite suddenly. I am not quite prepared for the next words. *Did you read the Joseph Roth book yet?* he asks me. He wants very badly for me to read that book. I ordered it from Canada because it is out of print in America. And because he told me to. I think I will find Leiser inside that book. That the poor beggar on the cover will turn into Leiser. I am saving the reading of it. I think I will find out something about Leiser that may frighten me. But there is nothing that can frighten me more than what I already know about him. Lying in the cellar of the apartment building among the dying men, lying in their bleeding. Lying in his father's blood. His younger brother burned alive in the hospital.

* * *

I came up from the cellar. There was a window you could look through into the yard. To see if the Lithuanians came back. The caretaker of the building said in Polish when he caught sight of me: "What! You are still alive! Go back to the cellar." He called the Lithuanians to get me. But I escaped.

On the 22nd of June 1941 the Germans came to Lithuania. The murders of my father and the other men took place on June 27. I was wounded. On the first floor lived a family taken away. One man who was paralyzed remained with some small children. He didn't let me in. On the second floor, the family Kacerginski. They were too frightened to let me in. I ran to the third floor, the family Zacherkhan from Klaipeda with two girls, two nurses. Mr. Zacherkhan didn't take me. I walked back down, came to the first floor where the sick man lived, gave him a push, came in and locked the door. In the bathroom I took a towel to wipe up the blood on the floor and steps. They had some suitcases. I hid in a corner where they could not find me, took one coat from the cabinet. My coat had blood on it. Later I walked up to the Jewish Hospital. I could see the German soldiers taking groups of people away, but I was able to get to the hospital. Moshe Braun and another professor operated on me. After the War when the professor returned to Lithuania, he was arrested by the Russians. I left the hospital. My mother came back to Laisves Aleja. On the 28th day of August, 1941, we were closed into the Kovno Ghetto.

* * *

He is spelling again. *"T" as in "torture," "A" as in "Aktion," "R" as in "round-up," "H" as in "Hitler."* He laughs. He is still there, in the concentration camp, in the roundup, in the ghetto, still lying in the dark basement of his building among the dead and dying men, among them his own father. He has never come home, not really.

* * *

He is sitting in a restaurant having breakfast. He doesn't know what to do. He has a dilemma he cannot solve. A boy, an American boy, for some reason, is photographing his food at the next table and inadvertently includes Leiser in the picture. When the boy realizes this, he steps over to Leiser's table to apologize. Leiser invites him to sit down with him. The boy is traveling, on a vacation. Somewhere, back a while, he has had a breakdown, but now he seems to have recovered enough to make this journey.

They end up spending the day together. Leiser, despite his age, walks the boy around Zurich. Joseph knows nothing about the Holocaust. He is about to get a complete lesson from the old man who takes him to the synagogue and to the cemetery where his wife was recently buried. He takes him to see art, the Chagall windows, to share a meal, and to the studio where Ada's paintings are stacked by the hundreds on the floor in every conceivable inch of space.

By the end of the day, they have become friends, the old man and this young boy. *I need you like a bodyguard,* Leiser tells Joseph.

* * *

Since Leiser died, I cannot sleep. I have taken his habit. No more than an hour or two at a time. I am become him. That shall be my way of mourning this time. Each death is different. So, will I dream of his mother? Or his brother enveloped in flames? Or the small infant wrapped in a man's undershirt and buried? I do dream. Of a purse. With identity papers. A missing purse. Perhaps it is to death we go. Without identity. No need then.

* * *

In the cemetery where Ada is buried, he brings small stones to place on the *matzevah. Now it piles up like a little mountain,* he tells me. At first, he could not find stones in the graveyard to place on Ada's gravestone, for remembrance. So, he bought stones at the market, twelve Swiss francs for three stones. It seemed strange to me that he had to buy stones, so I sent him a beautiful stone my son had given me a long while back. I wrapped it carefully and mailed it. I wanted Ada to have something from me. When it arrived in Zurich, Leiser was afraid to open the package. *I will take it to the rabbi,* he told me. *Leiser,* I said, *please get the package and open it while we talk together on the phone. Wait a moment,* he says, putting the phone down and dropping it. Now he is back. *I have your picture here. When I talk to you on the telephone, I see your face,* he tells me. He is always saying we must meet again face to face. *Panim el panim,* I tell him. *Like Moses on Mount Sinai, face to face.* The only place in the entire Bible where God appears to a human being. But not like that, I think. Only a poor old man and an old woman attempting to be of help from a great distance.

Now he has the package. *Open it, Leiser!* I say. He opens it slowly as if it might go off, like a bomb. Inside the tissue paper, he takes out the beautiful tiny stone. The next day he takes it to the cemetery and puts it on Ada's grave. He tells me that some days later there was a terrible storm and all the little stones flew off. Only my stone remained.

I imagine Ada's grave with all the stones he has brought. He goes there nearly every day to talk with her, to receive her messages. But he need not do that. He has only to open any of the hundreds of pages she has left for him in her journals and diaries and between the pages of their books. He could receive messages from Ada for a thousand years, and they would not be depleted.

* * *

Today he has called seven times. Like seven lean years and seven plentiful ones, in Pharaoh's dream. The dream that Joseph interpreted. I call him this time. *Are you comfortable?* he asks. I don't know if he means if I am sitting down, if he has something terrible to tell me. *Your home, I mean,* he says. *Did you buy oil? I'm wearing a thin pullover and a tee-shirt,* he tells me. *Like a sauna! Don't stint to save money by not ordering oil,* he says. *I always kept it warm in the studio in Tessin for Ada. If she wasn't happy, she couldn't paint. Sometimes it would get so hot in the winter, she'd have to open the window. I would tell her—you see all the mountains; the beautiful landscape will always be there but we are going away.* I think of the ghetto stable where he helped his mother to give birth. I think of him in Dachau in winter.

* * *

The conversation the next day begins without preamble. It takes a moment for me to realize that Leiser is talking about Joseph. *I started to write to him. I didn't like to take any food. I made jam. I had a lot of plums. We had eaten plums. I had to rest. It is like homemade. I filled two glasses. You see what I wrote to him is in Yiddish. He will have to go to the rabbi.* Leiser bursts out laughing, trying to imagine how this kind young man will manage with this letter from him in Yiddish. The irony is that the rabbi in the main synagogue where this young man lives is also a cousin to Leiser. Leiser does not know about this.

Here is what he has written in the letter to Joseph: "*My dear Yossel, Yosele, Yoshke, ...*" We both laugh. Leiser has given this lovely young man the most affectionate of Jewish names, all the diminutive versions of Joseph in Yiddish. *Now I like that you can laugh,* he tells me. *I have a very bad conscience to tell you about the Holocaust.*

"*In 1940,*" the letter continues, "*the Russians came into Lithuania and Jews were not allowed to write in Yiddish. You are like a star come from the heavens. Your whole life is before you. You are young. Your photograph is standing before me on the table. You have a nice expression on your face, ein Schmakel. Like the rays of the sun. That's the photo what you made. I hope you had a nice time in Rome and came home to your mama, sister, granny, girlfriend.*"

"*I went through fire. All is exploded in flames. I can shout. I can't pray because my life during the war got mixed up. A lot of members of my family are lying in a grave in Keidan, 2700 lying in the grave. Nineteen meters long, nine meters deep, nine meters wide. My brother Chaim was burned alive in the hospital in the small ghetto. Benjamin, my baby brother, lived only a few days after my mother gave birth. I brought him to the cemetery with an old man and wrapped him in an old shirt and buried him. My mama was killed in Stutthof Concentration Camp. My father was shot in front of me. I was lying under the dead people. I was the only one wounded and I could run away. The sadness is in me. And this is part of my life.*" Now Leiser stops reading and comments: *The rabbi will have a difficult time.* He laughs. *How will he translate this letter for Joseph?* They say that anger is the last defense before tears, but perhaps with Leiser it is laughter.

Now he has suddenly switched subjects again. *They couldn't digest it.* I hurry to catch up with his thought. Twenty-five-page letters he wrote after liberation. He was suffering from tuberculosis and was in a sanatorium in Davos, Switzerland, and had time to write down his experiences and thoughts. But his family in South Africa threw all the letters away, according to Leiser. (However, copies of letters written in 1947 and 1948 in Yiddish and German have survived.)

* * *

The next day, Leiser continues reading his letter to Joseph: *"Monday, when you sat opposite me, your sunshine face was a miracle. Now it is getting cold. Soon will come snow. The snow makes the air clear and dry and very beautiful. When you came to Zurich. ..."* What does the rabbi do when he puts his two hands together? he asks me. A blessing, I answer. *"I bless you for that. What can I tell you more? It was so good to be with you. I have to be very strong. To remember you."* Here Leiser begins to cry. He is remembering Ada who has died. Perhaps he is remembering his little brother. And perhaps he is afraid he will never see this boy again. Perhaps this boy is the one he might have become in another life. *"And now,"* he continues, *"you came on my road and maybe we can something do. It is great you are a born photographer."* She—he speaks of his wife suddenly—*was a very great believer in being a nice person and she had a good heart and she said to me: You have to believe in the good of people. I couldn't. The letter is not finished,* he tells me. *I made my bed every day,* he says. *I don't like the meal we had together in the restaurant. It is a mass production. I said to Joseph, Come on into this shop. I took him to a shop to buy a little meat and vegetables to take away the bad taste of the other food.*

* * *

And so another day is coming to an end. I am only afraid that Leiser will never see Joseph again. He will be very disappointed. But for now, he will send a shawl to Joseph's granny, a lemon-colored one. And in a little while, around two in the morning, he will take a bath and lie down for an hour or two, the most he ever sleeps. And by four in the morning he will be wandering around again, receiving messages from his wife Ada, sorting through her papers, taking the washing down to the washing place where it has been accumulating for several weeks. And if he is lucky, a boy name Joseph from America will remember him and will one day return to Zurich. And if he is really lucky, this old man will be there to receive the boy.

* * *

What do I know about Leiser so far? I know that he takes a bath twice daily. Once in the morning—whatever his morning means. And once in the evening. I know that he goes to Germany to have his hair cut, even though he has hardly any hair. He tells me he does not like it to get long in the back, that it is not clean. Perhaps in the ghetto and in the concentration camp first the hair was long and then it was shaved because of lice and to dehumanize, to make them anonymous. He often talks about money, about how much things cost, how much it would be to have a haircut in Zurich, how much in Germany, even though it means traveling to Germany. It does not seem to concern him that he goes to the place that caused him so much suffering. He does not seem to blame the younger generations of Germans. He often switches subjects, as if the fire he has come on in memory will burn him and he must be spared for the moment until it overtakes him once more. He can be in the midst of describing the murder of his brother when he suddenly shifts to a detail he has told me about many times—how he went to Manon to have a cup of coffee, how he never eats all the food he has ordered but brings it home so he will have another meal of it later. Like Minnie in the nursing home in America whom I visit each week. At lunch, she drops part of the chicken covered with gravy into her large black leather purse. Never mind that whatever else is in the purse is now covered with thick gravy. But for Leiser, saving for later may have saved his life.

I know that Joseph should have returned home to America by now, and that Leiser is waiting to hear from him, to see if what had happened, what he experienced was real, if Joseph will come back. I know that Leiser does not sleep in a regular bed. He keeps trying to tell me, *Like in the army*, he says. *A sleeping bag?* I ask. He does not know what that means. We are talking through the veil of language—his German, Yiddish, Hebrew. My English, poor German, scant Yiddish and Hebrew. His difficulty with hearing in the first place. And when he is manic, his wish not to hear at all, but only to speak, to speak without stopping. Sometimes I have to hold the phone away from my ear. I feel so overwhelmed by his energy, his frenetic, powerful energy. I know that Ada has left hundreds of journals, and that they are all over the floor. He tells me that if he cleans out the sleeping room and removes some sort of bed that she used, he will have a place for the journals. And he is trying to clear a place for Joseph, when and if Joseph returns. He does not forget to ask me if I am warm, if I have ordered oil. He does not remember that he has already asked me that many times, and that I have answered him. I know that he is named the same name as my grandfather's father. I know that the name is repeated throughout the generations of our family. Eliezer.

* * *

Leiser is in the hospital having lost total vision in his left eye. The nurse saw him walking in the corridor during the night and gave him a sleeping tablet. *I told her that I should not be given sleeping medication. I can even kill somebody. I can do something very bad. I would even ... once I went into the kitchen and turned everything ... tore everything into pieces. I could kill even Ada.*

* * *

Family Tree

Frieda Rabinovitch: great-grandmother
Heshel and Simche Damerecki-Rabinovitch: maternal grandparents
Rubin and Esther Packer-Damerecki and their children, Meril, Leibka, Mendke Packer: sister of Leiser's mother
Israel and Yentka Donski-Damerecki and their children, Sorela, Chanala, and two babies: sister of Leiser's mother
Moshe Eliyahu and Chaye Libe Wolpe-Oppenheim: paternal grandparents
Susmann and Esther Musikant-Wolpe and their children, Itke, Berele, Daniel Musikant: sister of Leiser's father Abraham
Simon and Fruma Graz-Oppenheim and their daughter Sara Graz: Fruma, sister of Leiser's grandmother Chaye Libe Wolpe Oeppenheim
Chaim Oppenheim, his wife Dora, and their three children: Chaim, brother of Fruma Graz Oppenheim and Chaye Libe Wolpe Oppenheim

Murdered in Keidan, Lithuania on August 28, 1941 in the pit dug on the banks of the Smilga stream.

* * *

Message from A. J. [a relative]: Leiser survived the German onslaught while hiding in a bunker. There was no particular evasive action on his behalf that secured his survival from the event. During the liquidation of the Kovno Ghetto (July 1944), all identified bunkers were bombed to the best of the Germans' ability. Those in the houses or caught fleeing from bunkers were murdered. Where Leiser was, there was a two-level bunker. He and his mother were in the upper-level bunker and Rabbi Ephraim Oshry and others in a bunker below. This lower bunker was well constructed, and when the Germans bombed the top bunker, the bottom bunker remained concealed and intact.

Leiser and his mother survived the upper-level bunker explosion and were—with a luck Leiser does not understand—rounded up with other bunker survivors and taken to Waneustrasse, a collection point. There they were kept for a day or two before being loaded onto cattle cars and railed to Stutthof, Germany.

As for Rabbi Oshry, he and approximately eighteen others survived the liquidation explosions as well as the onslaught of the Germans and were liberated by the Russians in 1944 in Kovno.

* * *

Leiser is in Sant' Agnese recuperating from surgery. He washes his socks and hangs them on the balcony outside his room to dry. He is told by the nurse that it is forbidden to do that. He asks: *What is this? Auschwitz?*

He looks out at Lago Maggiore and says, *All six million could fit into that lake. On this day*, he says, *it is the anniversary of the Kinder Aktion in the Kovno Ghetto. The Germans made me collect the children to be murdered. They were put on a bus with windows darkened so no one could see in and the children couldn't see out. They were gassed on the bus. By the time they arrived at the Ninth Fort, nearly all were dead. They were thrown into pits there.*[1] On this night he calls at 3 a.m., and again at 4 a.m., and an hour later, again.

* * *

Leiser has spent from eight in the morning until five in the evening at a printer's copying drawings of Ada's. All went well except for the drawing of Rabbi Kosofsky. *Rabbi Kosofsky was geshnippened, circumcised by the printer. From the left side and the right side. And the Rabbi can't take Ada to court!* The printer has taken away too much of the drawing. Leiser thinks better of this joke as he says it, as if to say that Ada is in the ground, and it would be disrespectful. Leiser took her last words on March 23, 2003, where she has written: *"Without Jews, the Christians would not have Jesus,"* and has attached them to the drawing of the circumcised Rabbi Kosofsky. It is for this that Ada might be taken before a jury, but she is nowhere to be found. Leiser wishes to tell the lady in the print shop: *"What you did to the rabbi, from the right and from the left, he would be very cross."*

---

[1] There is no consensus about what happened to the children who were taken from the Kovno Ghetto during the two-day Children's Action when German troops and Ukrainian auxiliaries rounded up those who remained. Shalom Eilati, a child survivor in hiding, recalls hearing cursing in German and Ukrainian as children are pulled crying from their mothers and speaks of buses for transport. "So it seems that the Aktion against children—the Kinder Aktion—encoded and prefigured the manner of the ghetto's destruction," he writes in *Crossing the River* (2008, p. 130), Tuscaloosa: University of Alabama Press. According to Leib Garfunkel, the vice-chairman of the Jewish Council of the Kovno Ghetto, 1000 children and elderly were taken on March 27, 1944 on buses with windows covered and driven in the direction of the city of Kovno, 300 on the next day. According to researchers at the USHMM, it is still unclear the manner in which the children were killed. According to other accounts, the children were taken in trucks/lorries to the 9th Fort and killed.

* * *

We suddenly shift to Tessin, the house that he and Ada bought with some of the money she received for her paintings. It was her inspiring studio, and Leiser gardened there. She often painted him in the garden. The house was stables when they bought it—unlike the stables in the ghetto where he helped his mother to give birth. *I saw the lake and the mountains in the morning and the evening. You see the mountains and the snow.*

Now, he speaks of the man who built a great synagogue in Jerusalem, a non-Jew. And about subscriptions he buys for others. And now the subject of *sheitels*, the marriage wigs worn by orthodox women. *They need five sheitels*, he says. *Each one costs close to three hundred francs.* The shifts are so rapid, I can barely keep up.

* * *

I come just now in. We spent the whole morning in the hospital. She had to stay there. They give her something in the vein. And then I brought her back. Time-table for her tablets. And then I left for the apothecary. Post office. She knows it. It is something unexpected. Ada felt already pain in her right side. Thought it was rheumatism. And she was given a massage. More pain. And it was like this—everything started in December. And at night Ada said the pain was moving around like in a tram station. This is not normal. After the x-ray she was sent to the emergency room. Since the chemotherapy she vomited only twice. Doctors are very nice. She made a drawing: Der Schmertz, the pain. It was very sad. Like Edvard Munch's "The Cry." She made it on paper, like she saw it before. The tree without leaves. I pass by it every day. The tree like a crucifixion. The tree that had the image of a devil in it. My interpretation: She felt all of these things before. She didn't know what comes but she felt it. Everybody has cells but no one knows when they will wake up.

* * *

Last night something happened to me. For the first time I heard Ada calling me. I got up. Did you ever have that happen? Did you hear of that?

* * *

I have sent Leiser information from a number of galleries and Holocaust museums about how to have Ada's paintings considered for their collections. For a Holocaust collection, the artist must have been in a concentration camp. He comments: *She was not in a concentration camp. For 44 years she was in a concentration camp with me. I cannot go back and change myself. Let them come and see for themselves. Did I show you my concentration camp number and the photograph in the ghetto with my star and documents from then? And the original war speech of Hitler? In Yad Vashem they sit there in an office like collection managers. They can do nothing for me. It is a pity. Even when one is 60 or 62, one has to be in good health. When I was in America in 1981, perhaps then. Now, I am Basha the Blinder, Fishko the Lame from Keidan. I get only 3 hours' sleep. By me it is quarter to 2 in the morning. I think I will go to the police station. I need someone to talk to at 2 in the morning. You know we have open phones with a little table to put your things. Yesterday, I see a big red purse. No one is there. I open it, a whole collection of cards, but I don't look. I see cards, a passport and a lot of money. What am I going to do? I ask myself. I think of a finding place* [lost and found]. *But when I come there the office is closed. It is a holiday for young men in Zurich. I take it to the police station. Now I am going the same way I came. I see a young woman. She is crying terribly. Are you the one who lost a wallet? But she couldn't speak German or English, only French and Portuguese. Come, I say, and I take her to the police station. The police had phoned a doctor in Portugal from the cards in her purse. They wanted to know if I took anything from the purse, but she looked and nothing was missing. She gave me an envelope and inside were a hundred Euros. I took the purse not to my own police station but to the center of Zurich. Now you go, I said to myself, the same way back. And that is how I found her. Sheherazade,* he tells me. As if he is Sheherazade, telling stories to stay alive. As if by telling stories he can prevent a calamity.

* * *

A thousand drawings and three thousand or more altogether. I have nobody to talk to. When will you go to sleep? Now I will have a glass of tea and sleep for a little. And then Stephen will come to the studio. I didn't want to schlep Ada's paintings hin and her. Her bouquet of paintings to the left and to the right [here he refers to the selections during the Holocaust]. *But I can't do it by myself. After I am gone, someone else will have to do it.*

* * *

Leiser wants to visit Dachau for the first time in fifty-eight years since his incarceration there. I am concerned that the visit there and his attempt to walk the miles of the forced march they were taken on by the Germans might be too much for an elderly man. I remembered that he had been taken to St. Ottilien, a monastery, after his release. He was emaciated, ill with tuberculosis, and in need of care. I thought that if I contacted the fathers at St. Ottilien, it might soften the pain of going back to Dachau.

Leiser did go to St. Ottilien, where he was kindly greeted by the fathers. On his return, he told me the following: *Dachau. Forced March to Bavaria—8–10 days, 30 miles, no food or water. The Germans forced us into a pit. The pit was shaped like a bottle—the neck of the bottle was the route by which we entered the pit, the rest of the pit widened out like the body of the bottle. Likely the Germans would have killed us there, but the Americans arrived, and a battle ensued. Some Germans fled, others were killed. Approximately half of those in the pit died of exhaustion and illness. Despite the fact that I had TB and was spitting up clots of blood, I saw something beautiful along the way, Waakirchen. We were the last group to leave Dachau in May 1945. At St. Ottilien, when they took off the lice-ridden, filthy clothing, I asked that they save my number. I didn't know that my uncle David Wolpe was there. David was in a transport train from Dachau. He jumped from the train and hid in the forest and eventually came to St. Otillien near Bad Worishoffen. I was locked on a certain floor, quarantined. Nuns looked after me there. David was in a part that was not quarantined. I asked why I couldn't go outside, and I was told that I had TB. I didn't know what it was. I underwent pneumothorax.*

* * *

Two years after that first visit back to Dachau, Leiser talks of going again, this time with a German historian. We talk about St. Ottilien, the monastery where he stayed after liberation and which he visited after his first return to Dachau. *Yes,* he says, *St. Ottilien was one of the worst experiences of the war.* I was dumbfounded. I had thought that at last he and the others were comforted there, were cared for. Perhaps it is an American fantasy that once the doors of the concentration camps opened, the survivors—gravely ill, starving—were welcomed back into the world with care, that the horror was over. But it was nothing like that. Many who had managed to survive unimaginable horror could not survive what happened next. *I can't talk about it,* he says. *Read a certain book. It is called* Surviving the Americans. *You will find out everything you need to know.*

* * *

I located the book by Robert Hilliard (1996) and read it at once. The "Introduction" begins this way:

> "What's the difference between you Americans and the Nazis," a concentration camp survivor said to me, a U.S. soldier in U.S.-occupied Germany a few months after World War II had ended in Europe, "except that you don't have gas chambers!" The war was over and the survivors of the camps had been freed. But the Genocide that the

Germans had begun did not end. ... Genocide by neglect, some called it. Deliberate neglect, others suggested. ... In the months following the end of the war, many of those who thought the defeat of the Nazis would release them from the living hell they had come to know under the German regime found themselves starved, raped and even shot by the same American forces that had freed them.

If ever there was testimony and witness to what each individual is capable of in righting the world, *Surviving the Americans* is such an example. Two young army privates—Robert Hilliard and Edward Herman—in the American occupation forces stationed near St. Ottilien found a way, by writing letters and secretly getting food as well as medical supplies into the monastery, eventually to claim the attention of President Truman and the American public about the horrendous conditions that survivors had to contend with. After some months, help began to arrive, and though many were lost, some including Leiser Wolpe and his uncle David Wolpe did manage to survive and to live their full span of life.

* * *

Did you know the men who killed your father and the others in the cellar of your apartment house on Laisves Aleja? Two Lithuanians. Nazi sympathizers. I was the youngest in that cellar. I was the only survivor. Did you have any memories because of your visit to Dachau? I remember everything, like in a computer. Until I pass away. There was a village within eyesight of the concentration camp. They could see when we came and what was going on. But they couldn't help. They would be shot. Even if they wanted to help.

* * *

Leiser talks about other towns where Wolpe family members lived: *I was a child then. I went on a school trip to Vilnius and to Palanga, but not to Dotnuva, Josvainai, not to Ariogala, Babtai. Girtigola, Ponevezh, Krok, Rasein, Shavl, Vilkomir, Utian, Vendzhigola, Yanova, Yosvine, Ruseiniai, Utian.*

* * *

The cellar—it was dark and full of blood.

* * *

On Ada's painting of Leiser attempting to help his father after he had been shot in the cellar: *I don't yet understand her painting. The whole picture is like an x-ray, a shining light, like something white, a light that came from somewhere else. A light that covered me. I was the only one alive. A light from somewhere, a strange licht, as if from outer space. I don't understand Ada's painting. The artist doesn't always understand his own work. It comes from the unconscious. A light from God, a light from heaven, if you were a believer.*

* * *

When I ask Leiser how he and Ada first met, he says a German word I cannot make out. I ask him if he means in Yiddish *bashert*, fated. *No*, he says, *his guardian angel helped him to meet her.*

* * *

Don't go there alone, he tells me carefully. This is before I met him. But I know his voice. We talk on the phone quite often. He has given me a sacred task. But now he cannot sleep at night, even his small share of sleep, thinking about it, about what I might uncover. But was not I the one who told him to stop going back to Dachau?

Don't go there alone. Take someone with you, he insists. Who does he think would be willing to go with me? To the cellar where all the men and boys who lived in his apartment house had been taken at four in the morning and shot. The place where his father died. Where he, only a boy himself, crawled out from among the dying men, wounded and bleeding, and climbed the steps to knock on the door of a family too frightened to open the door.

How many times have I walked past that very place—78 Laisves Aleja—Freedom Way—in Kaunas. It is always the same. Not a word about what happened there. Like when I was in Keidan where he was born, at the Zhirgunai barns, and the others looked at one another knowingly. But they would not say a word to me. Yet, I knew something terrible had happened there. Just a stable. Where the horses were kept. Only later, reading a relative's account of the murders, is my sense of it confirmed. They were taken there, women and children, men, locked up with no food, no place to urinate or defecate, no place to sit or lie down, and after some days, taken to the massacre place in small groups, the young, healthy men first, then the women and children, murdered. Not all. Some were still alive when they were thrown into the pit. They tell that the earth heaved for days over that pit.

* * *

Reenacting the Holocaust: He is never in one place for long. In the apartment in Zurich, in the house in Tessin, in the atelier, in the basement, the attic, the flea market, on the tram. As if to create alternatives in the event of catastrophe.

He keeps possessions in all of these places, always packing and unpacking, moving items from place to place, carrying them up and down many flights of stairs. The atelier is not used at all for painting but is completely filled with boxes and items for the flea market. Only Leiser seems to know the pathways through the large space in order to get to Ada's paintings, which he brings out, one by one, as in a ceremony. One feels that he must not be disrupted in this ritual, or helped, although many of the paintings are very large and heavy, and boxes must be moved to get to them and he is elderly.

* * *

Ada's painting of Leiser holding his father who is shot in the cellar of 78 Laisves Aleja. *Did it happen that way?* I ask him. No. *I was kneeling and when I held him, he was already dead.* He shows me his scar on his left arm and on his chest from the bullets. *In Dachau we were awakened brutally every morning at 4 a.m.*

It is always with me. I cannot put it in a cupboard. It is good that you did not come in 1981. This is the right time. Ada's painting is a curtain *between the Holocaust and me. They killed something in me. Without Ada I would not have lived.* I ask why I did survive. *Why did I not go to the Ninth Fort* [the Czarist fortress where tens of thousands were killed] *with the others?*

* * *

I have brought to him from the Kaunas archives a number of documents that he does not seem to be able to concentrate on—a picture of his mother on an internal passport, a list of eligible voters with his family names, photographs of Laisves Aleja. I tell him that 78 Laisves Aleja is gone now and in its place a natural history museum. But I have taken pictures in the alley behind it, which has some of the original buildings and even portions of the earlier buildings, including the cellars. I have a picture of the pedestrian walkway, the post office, school, by which he might be able to identify the place where he had once lived. But he barely notices.

Though prior to my visit, he and Ada had asked that I record our conversations, once there, he does not wish me to do so. The conversation is intensely painful, not because of its content but because of feeling fixed at the point of a knife. News that I brought from a fellow survivor, Solly Ganor, that a group of Dachau survivors from Lithuania meets every July at Dachau—since Leiser has returned to Dachau twice and hopes to do so again—did not seem to register for him.

* * *

At the airport: He stands there, a small, compact, solitary figure, wearing a cap, and waves to me. And I turn around, and he is still standing there. I wave again. And he waves. And I walk further and turn, and he is still standing there. I wave and walk away. I have the thought that he is like a small child who stands there and does not move from the spot and waves and waves until I am far out of sight. And I am filled with a terrible sadness.

* * *

Leiser worries about what will happen to Ada's paintings and to all the objects in his various domains after his death. *After all*, he says, *I am not Tutankhamen. I can't take anything with me.*

He calls again. He asks me how those survivors who stayed in Lithuania after the war can bear to pass each day by the places where their families were murdered. I have wondered the same thing. Usually they say they had no choice. They were not able to leave. Not to leave their families. Not enough money. Not under communism. No place to go.

He will tell me about Dr. Elkes (head of the Kaunas Ghetto Altestenrat). But not on the phone. Only in person. About how Elkes tried to save Dr. Nabrisky in the ghetto. About how he could not. About how Elkes tried to stop the Aktion that took 10,000 of them to their deaths in 1 day. How Dr. Elkes was beaten and had to be carried back to the ghetto.

He will tell me about how his mother was pregnant and was due very soon to have her child, his small brother. How his own living brother was burned to death in the hospital—when the doctors and nurses and patients were locked inside, and the hospital was set on fire. He did not understand why his brother was there in the first place. His mother gave birth, but after 8 days the infant died. Two sons lost. He will tell me when I am there, with him, in the same room. But not on the phone.

How many times he circles these losses.

His wife Ada tells me she has made a painting of Leiser in the garden. He stands there among the tall flowers, among butterflies and birds. She paints him into the light. She leaves no shadow in her paintings that he might fall into. And when he is in her paintings, he does not dream about the killing.

* * *

In the end, I do not know if I am a conduit for them. Or an imposter.

* * *

I don't wish even my enemies to be blind, Leiser begins. *I will tell you something very nice. I always like elephants. Because elephants—people think they are big monsters—they can think. They can talk. Not like human beings. To their keeper, ein Warter, in German. He talks to the elephant and the elephant gets to know his voice. He knows he is not an elephant. You can teach him to say, "Thank you," and "Please," and now you have something and don't be afraid. You are not allowed to touch the body, only the ears and trunk and feet. Their skin is very sensitive and when you touch them on the body they get afraid. Ada also loved the elephant because they brought flowers to the graves of dead elephants. Like a big matzevah, put flowers and grasses. And one day the elephant saw not breathing flowers but paper flowers. He didn't know they were paper. I was always interested in katzen and dogs, but mostly elephants. The keeper tells him to say "Thank you," and when the elephant is happy, he takes his foot and stamps it and says, "Danke," and if he is very happy, he stamps his foot two times and says, "Danke, danke," and if he is very very happy, he says "Danke schoen," and then stamps his foot three times.*

Now you have a phone call from a blind man. And he makes you laugh. I saw elephants in Africa. And in India they put us on the top of a big elephant, and we went to the Taj Mahal. Ada would have a school holiday and she would say, "If you like you can come with me." So I went with her to China, to Bulgaria, to Yugoslavia, to Uzbekistan. Forty years ago. Ada was the youngest child. She wanted to study art with Diego Rivera in Mexico. She taught herself Spanish and went to the Mexican Consulate but she couldn't get a visa because Africa was an apartheid country in those times. So she went to England in 1948.

* * *

Ada's siblings were born in Plunge, Lithuania. Her brother, 4 years her senior, Lippy Lipschitz—her father wanted him to be a doctor. But he went to Paris to study to be a sculptor. When he was 4 years old in Plunge, they set out. It took them 3 months to make the journey to South Africa. Ada and I were married in the 1950s. I met Lippy first and a friend of Ada's in London where she studied for 10 years. Sometimes I think it would be better to be an elephant. He has a guardian, a shomer, a keeper. When the keeper says: "You now stay here until I am back," and he will stay the whole night. If the keeper told him a lie, then the elephant would kill him. The elephant knows exactly when the keeper is sleeping. I could hear the shooting. Leiser has abruptly changed the subject. The past has intruded without warning. We are back in the Kovno Ghetto during the Great Aktion once again, where nearly 10,000 Jews are taken from the Ghetto to the Ninth Fort and killed over a period of 48 hours. *Nothing to do about it,* he goes on. I hurry to follow him. *Your book is like a mosaic, like weaving a carpet. You can make it a very good carpet or one with mistakes. It doesn't matter. To see what humans can do.* Now he switches to the fact that he is nearing his 80th birthday. And he talks about how, in Switzerland, when a person turns 80, they have a big celebration.

* * *

Each day, I try to take hold of the fine thread that connected Leiser to me. I want to say this in the present tense—the thread that connects Leiser to me. Sometimes, I imagine that I am holding one end of the thread and the other end is caught by the wind and is far away, and there is no one holding the other end. Even for those who are near us, who live in this world with us, the thread of knowing them, knowing each other, can be broken. So, I hold to Leiser's words as a living presence. What is this compelling power that drives us to need the connection to the past, our past. Through Leiser, I am able to recover my own past, one that would have been invisible otherwise. Yet, it is more than that. I think that through me Leiser was able to travel a little further into the present. The gentle titration of movement—not holding too firmly, but holding on nonetheless while we are both in motion. The way Rilke[1] said it in his poem "Herbst" ("Autumn")—

> The leaves are falling, falling as from way off,
> as though far gardens withered in the skies;
> And in the nights the heavy earth is falling
> from all the stars down into loneliness.
> We all are falling. This hand falls.
> And still there is one who holds this falling
> endlessly gently in his hands.

* * *

When I went into the sea, I saw a sea of blood. In Spain. I wanted to paint. I would paint only blood. Is something wrong with me? No. I was in Spain. In Palanga. In school. I was with the school in Palanga. An excursion. A few days. I was never to the seaside. Only Palanga. Then to Spain. I was so dirty. I have a feeling I have to wash myself 300 times. It was not normal. In the first flat, no warm water, no shower, no real bed, a camping bed. First time I had a feeling, a sea of blood with dead people. Then it went away. Then I enjoyed it. A holiday in Spain and Italy. Mostly, I kept everything in order.

* * *

---

[1] "Autumn" by Ranier Maria Rilke. I was unable to find the precise translation source. The closest I could come is a Rilke collection published in 1962.

A blind man comes into the bank and asks for 50,000 Swiss francs. The bank manager takes me into a room. I am old and blind, I tell him. And I can use the money.

* * *

Opened now a secret German archives after 65 years. Marchers from Dachau. Dead men walking. April 29, 1945. Dachau to Waakirchen. Star Paper from Johannesburg. 74 dead marchers.

* * *

Though Leiser has told me parts of this memory a number of times, on this night he tells it in more detail. It is as if there are concentric circles around an inner core, and he must start with the outermost circle, which contains the barest details, and with each telling he moves to an orbit closer to the fiery inner core of memory. For instance, this:

My mother and I are living in a stable for animals that adjoins a block house in Slobodka, Kovno Ghetto, after my father is murdered at 78 Laisves Aleja, with all the men and boys in the apartment house and all those up and down Laisves Aleja. I was wounded but I crawled out of that basement to look for help. My younger brother, Chaim, was burned alive in the hospital in Slobodka along with all the patients, doctors, and nurses. My mother is 8 months pregnant and delivers a baby on the earthen floor of the stable whom she names Benjamin after the biblical Joseph and his brothers, Benjamin the youngest son. Though I am 16, it is my duty to bury the placenta, and a few days later when the infant dies, I, along with an older man, must bury the infant. My mother, Luba Damarecki Wolpe, ended up in Stutthof concentration camp.

* * *

Here is another telling of the infant brother's birth. New details are added. Does it mean that he can remember more with each subsequent telling? That part of the memory awakens another? And another? Or is it that he cannot bear to tell it whole? To put the whole image into his view at once? That he could be overwhelmed by doing so? Paul Russell, in *Trauma, Repetition and Affect Regulation* (1999), speaks of repetition occurring "in lieu of something we cannot yet feel, a kind of affective incompetence" (p. 4). The eventual goal is a gathering of the forces of earlier competence before the trauma occurred, in an effort toward emotional wholeness. But, it was my sense that Leiser's use of repetition was as though to build an impermeable wall against what might burst through at any moment and take him under.

Or, is there something else at work here? What is the nature of this continuous further elaboration? Repetition can sometimes bring the image before one sufficiently to confront it fully, to discover its truth or its meaning, to remove its potency. But here, somehow, the function seems different. It seems as if the repetition is a kind of infinite regress, that it might go on forever, like images in a mirror.

1941. My mother was pregnant, eighth month. Stable. Earthen floor. One window. Clay hearth. My mother said to me: "Put on hot water. Call for Dr. Nabrisky." He came late in the evening. The baby was already born. The doctor gave me the placenta. "Put it into the earth." The baby lived only a few days. Came an elderly man, wrapped the baby in an old shirt. We took the infant to the Jewish cemetery and buried it.

Was it difficult for you?

Yes and no. I didn't understand all these things. My brother, Chaim, was burned in the hospital in Slobodka on October 4, 1941. Friday. The stable was where they cooked food for the pigs. It was attached to the only block house in the ghetto. It was made of moss and wood. Inside the block house lived other Jewish people.

* * *

October 28: The Great Aktion. We were required to gather at Democratu Square. All would be killed who did not come. They were taken away to the Ninth Fort. The kleine ghetto, bridge. My mother and I were standing by the bridge to see what was happening in the small ghetto.

The block house next to the stable where we stayed had a cellar. When bad things happened, we went to the cellar. It had a small kitchen and fireplace. I could hide myself in the fireplace, behind the chimney in a small place behind a wall. When the Germans came, I could hide. My mother was a very interesting woman. The block house was on Majeo Gatve? Or Marjo Gatve? It had one room, one bed. I could see it through a window. I am "The Blind Witness." I am 82.

In 1944 I was sent from Stutthof to Dachau. We were liberated by the Ninth American Army. I spent 1 year in Germany and in 1946 went to Davos, Switzerland, to a TB sanatorium.

* * *

Last night I could not find Leiser. The sky was a soft dark velvet patch, and it was empty. I seemed to be looking up. He had backed off, like God's angel that Rilke writes about who refuses to take the last breath of Moses so that God himself must claim Moses's soul. Leiser is beyond me. Missing.

* * *

Aftermath: What we imagined was the opening of the metal gates and the revived souls rushing through into the air of spring, suddenly restored to the living, years of privation washed from their torn bodies, years of humiliation and torment and loss vanished in the light of freedom. But it was not to be. To get rid of the evidence, even the dead bodies were brought to the surface and arranged in stacks like firewood and set to burning. And for those few who had survived, some were taken on forced marches by the Nazis in a frantic attempt for their American liberators to find the death cages emptied. Most, already malnourished and weak, died along the way. Some were put on ships, starved for days and thrown into the sea, like my cousin, whose sister drowned moments before reaching the shore. Of those who survived, some were taken to a monastery, or hospital, or left to fend for themselves. And some were kept in the very places where they had been imprisoned for so long under conditions not much better than before.

* * *

The tram driver suddenly caught sight of an elderly man with a white cane. He automatically pushed on the brake with all his might, but nothing could halt the power of speed once attained; no inertia or breaking force was enough.

As Leiser fell into his new state of being, he was set aflame with the last of his energy, as his small brother had been set aflame in the locked hospital all those years ago. He knew at last what the boy had felt as he and his mother witnessed the burning, as his mother felt the first of her labor pains, as if at the moment of the death of 12-year-old Chaim, Benjamin announced his wish to enter this world. That he also would last no more than a few days was beside the point.

The police did not mention what specifically had been Leiser's damage, thought by Stephen to be an act of kindness. But there was one more such act—a young mother who had sometimes stopped by to give Leiser his eye-drops lest he not lose all sight in the remaining eye heard the police knocking on Leiser's door and went to learn what the commotion was all about.

Just as it was that Leiser, no longer himself, but with a heart that refused to stop beating, lay in a hospital bed for 8 more hours.

When they told the young woman of the accident, she and a neighbor went to the hospital and stayed by Leiser's side until he took his last breath at exactly 1:15 in the morning—the time this sleepless man would likely have been in the kitchen preparing tea for the start of his long day.

* * *

Postscript: *On September 25, 2011 in the woods next to the massacre pit where twenty-nine of Leiser's family were murdered seventy years ago, in*

the town of Kedainiai, Lithuania, I kept my promise to Leiser not to for-
get the names of our family. Rimantas Zirgulis, director of the Kedainiai
Regional Museum, worked for months to orchestrate a ceremony that
included an artist's rendering of a steel wall with the engraved names of
those who lay in the massacre pit. We lighted a menorah, and spoke of
what happened in this place, and placed stones of remembrance. The chil-
dren had embedded a golden menorah of flowers in the earth at the head
of the burial place. A woman sang and two musicians—a drummer and
trumpeter—opened and closed the ceremony. Leiser never dreamed that
this remembrance would take place in the town of his birth.

REFERENCES

Eilati, S. (2008). *Crossing the river*. Tuscaloosa: University of Alabama Press.
Ganor, S. (1995). *Light one candle: A survivor's tale from Lithuania to Jerusalem*.
    New York: Kodansha America.
Hilliard, R. L. (1996). *Surviving the Americans: The continued struggle of the Jews*
    after Liberation. Seven Stories Press.
Oshry, E. (1989). *Responsa from the Holocaust*. New York: The Judaica Press.
Oshry, E. (1995). *The Annihilation of Lithuanian Jewry*. New York: The Judaica
    Press.
Rilke, R. M. (1962). *Translations from the poetry of Rainer Maria Rilke by M. D.*
    Herter Norton. New York: W.W. Norton & Company, pp. 74–75.
Russell, P. (1999). *Trauma, repetition and affect regulation: The work of Paul Russell*.
    London: Rebus Press.

Chapter 9

Psychological Witnessing of My Mother's Holocaust Testimony

George Halasz

If you have listened (repeatedly) to old lessons, you will listen to new ones.

Berachos, 40a

Trauma—and its impact on the hearer—leaves, indeed, no hiding place. As one comes to know the survivor, one generally comes to know one-self; and that is not a simple task. (p. 72) … Silence is for them a fated exile, yet also a home, a destination, and a binding oath. To *not* return from this silence is rule rather than exception. (p. 58)

Dori Laub (1992, italics in original)

After the Black Saturday bushfires in Victoria, Australia in February 2009, I was asked how to manage traumatized children. Having struggled for years to come to terms with my own family's history of Holocaust trauma, I offered two principles: first, to do no harm; second, to normalize children's traumatic experiences. When one person asked if I meant that children should be encouraged to forget their losses or that parents should distract them when they spoke of trauma, it became clear that I must explain normalization.

The priority for children's physical safety is a given. Next, children should resume daily routines as soon as possible: school, their favorite hobbies and sports, family and social relationships. However, it is my experience that while this approach is necessary for all children, it is not sufficient for some. Should a child not return to health after some weeks or show disruptive behavior or withdrawal, this may signal that masked emotional responses to the trauma are "stored" in the body. The body remembers trauma even if the mind cannot and expresses it either as over- or underactivity of the nervous system.

Traumatized children need their experience of trauma to be coaxed from them. The psychological witness to their trauma should be prepared to be overwhelmed by disorientation, numbness or "compassion fatigue," which are symptoms reflecting vicarious trauma. If a child's caregivers are unable or unprepared to take on the demanding role of witnesses to trauma, then I recommend specialist intervention.

The task of the psychological witness—to remain receptive to what for lack of a more specific term we call *trauma*[1]—is not for the faint-hearted. Often, I have found myself, as a child psychiatrist, overwhelmed during or after meeting with trauma survivors. Over the years, I have learned to pay special attention during such encounters, to recognize the onset of vicarious trauma in even a vague sense of uneasiness, before it progresses to a feeling of becoming "unreal." This lesson I keep on relearning.

* * *

I have a particular need to be mindful of trauma because of my own experience as a child of Holocaust survivors. In retrospect, I have realized that the traumatic experiences I was witnessing as a psychiatrist were unknown yet strangely familiar. I came to understand this part of my personality through my professional focus on how children and infants cope with their traumatized parents, and they with their children. Indeed, this focus on the simultaneous operation of psychological coping mechanisms, by infants with their parents and between traumatized parents, is at the heart of my research into psychological witnessing of 'relational trauma,' the term introduced by Schore (2001).

Children, being emotionally dependent on parents, are naturally receptive to their parents' emotions. According to current research, the children of parents who are reenacting past trauma both receive parental trauma directly and may also experience vicarious trauma. In other words, infants and children may be said to be immersed in an environment of subtle or overt traumatic enactments.

If children can experience their parents' trauma both directly and vicariously, how is such trauma, I wondered, passed from parents to children? Is trauma transmitted between the generations? If so, how is such trauma repaired?

At a personal level, I wondered how I had dealt with my experience of my parents' Holocaust trauma. In midlife, I reflected on my family relationships from infancy to early adulthood and saw that I have lived in a state of denial about the deep impact of my parents' trauma on my personality. To overcome my deepest level of denial, I decided to research the subtle communications with my mother and to explore the paths and processes that trauma might follow between parent and child.

* * *

---

[1] Trauma victims who lack the cognitive and emotional structures to assimilate the experience immediately use the state of consciousness known as dissociation to escape from the full psychological impact of the event (Classen, Koopman, & Spiegel, 1993).

In 1998, the year after my father, Laci Halasz, of blessed memory, passed away, my mother was interviewed at length by the interviewer from the Visual History Foundation. I was present through the interview and asked to join my mother near the end of her Holocaust testimony. The question posed to my mother, while I was sitting next to her, confronted the impact of the Holocaust on her parenting of me:

INTERVIEWER: Do you think your experiences affected the way that you brought up George?

GEORGE HALASZ: This is the question.

MRS. HALASZ: I want to know, you know, we were really very protective parents but I'm not so sure that our bring up or from the war, that I'm not so sure. Maybe it's both of them.

INTERVIEWER: Do you think much about that time, or do you have dreams about the Holocaust and the experiences?

MRS. HALASZ: No. Never, never. I never. I had the dreams soon after the war about the ... but not anymore, no.

This transcript has a fragmented quality. This is my mother's normal style.

I had repeatedly asked myself such questions and had addressed them in therapy during my 20s and 30s and in ongoing self-therapy. For me to explore such questions meant breaking the then-taboo of silence and secrecy. A few years later, I would come to realize that I needed to focus more systematically to uncover what really happened between my mother and father "after" (some claim it never finishes for survivors) the Holocaust, before I was born and years later between my parents and me. But here, in my midlife, an interviewer openly and directly confronted my mother. Next, the interviewer questioned me:

INTERVIEWER: George, I was ... speaking of your mother with respect to your own reflections as a child and adolescent of survivors. You study in a clinical manner the effects war has on children, your mother was a child at the outbreak of the war. ... She was 12 years old. From your own, your professional view, how do you think that her war experiences have affected her?

GEORGE HALASZ: I understand the question very clearly, but it's probably beyond the limit of one's imagination to respond to such a question. If you were to ask me how a third party is affected, I could give you chapter and verse I think, very easily. I think because of the emotional bonds and the history that we share, personally I'm not very comfortable to let my imagination just freely roam in this setting.

Also, I think, because after we've finished [this interview] there's still a relationship that we have. Having said that I actually feel that my mother would probably have been affected more at the ages of 15 and 16 when Budapest was actually invaded, and from the accounts that I've heard, the first few years whilst their lives in Budapest was constricted, there was nothing very dramatic.

Nearly 2 years after this VHF interview with my mother (Halasz, 1998), I returned to view that video. My hope was to observe and to capture some fleeting moments seen on my mother's face as her reactions to her narrative, and juxtapose my reactions to her. Then, so I thought, I might become a more reliable witness to what was transmitted between us, to qualify for evidence for the "transmission of trauma" between the generations.

This review of my mother's testimony video resulted in my decision to produce a split-screen video, *Many Faces of Trauma* (see Plate 3). The split-screen technique is a research approach used in mother–infant studies that focus on the fine interaction between mothers and their babies. I thought that I could adapt that approach to capture my mother's facial expressions during her narrative of her Holocaust experiences while showing my own facial reactions while I was filmed watching her. The two video films were then synchronized into split screen. I then viewed this split screen in my subsequent research in which I became a "witness," witnessing her at the same time as my own reactions to her.

During the filming of my reactions to viewing my mother's video, the filmmaker asked about my reaction to viewing my mother's testimony:

INTERVIEWER: All right George, what was happening to you when you were watching your Mum's video?
GEORGE HALASZ: Yes, I, I think at different times the overall happening I think was times of quite a lot of headache, of tension, and in a surprising way what happened was when I myself became emotional, I felt a lot of the headachy tension state relieved and then I'd be in a much more relieved state until the next sort of wave of tension, headache started. Then again it would be relieved by either laughter or if there's an emotional reaction.

* * *

Now, as I look back over the last decade, it is clear to me that my motive for seeking visible evidence for transmitted trauma had its provenance in my experience as a silent child witness to many fleeting, recurrent moments of invisible experiences. I wanted validation if not vindication. I wanted to understand more precisely what I had witnessed. I had decided to become my own psychological witness. Were those "fleeting moments" of intense switching between my face "matching" and then becoming "detached" markers of my internal emotional state in which I was attuned up to a point and then had to dissociate? Could my facial expressions be equated to a psychological process of attunement and dissociation, markers of relational trauma? If so, what made these moments "traumatic"?

Others who knew me as a child have suggested that I was an excessively sensitive child. Might that mean that I experienced ordinary parenting as traumatic due possibly to a heightened sense of empathy with my mother and father? Could that account for my excessive absorbing of my parents' unspoken traumatic experiences?

Some writers have observed and written of the double life of survivors— the manifest coping life that masks the hidden trauma. It seemed at least possible that I also lived a kind of double life, my chosen profession as a child psychiatrist masking the silent child witness of parental trauma. I likened this child witness to a participant in a self-imposed witness protection program who was anxiously waiting to give evidence in a case of transmitted trauma.

I will try to describe how I arrived at giving my "testimony" from an infant's perspective. An infant obviously cannot speak of his experience being "traumatic." The split-screen images afforded me the opportunity to study closely my facial expressions, as I witnessed my mother, and to capture fleeting moments of detachment as seen on my face. These occurred as a response to my mother experiencing overwhelming emotional states, in either intensity or prolonged time.

When I say that I came to "testify" from an infant's perspective to my mother's extreme trauma by studying our facial images on the split screen, I suggest that I found a way to speak of the silent moments, to tell my story in images, beyond words, with the images testifying of my detached states of mind (dissociations). I made the assumption that such moments represented an outer marker of my inner dissociation, the fleeting moments of relational trauma.

Here, I need to update the impact of my increased awareness of my dissociations on my relationship with my mother. After these years of exploring the subtle cues that triggered my adult reactions to my mother's Holocaust video testimony, a major change has been occurring in our "lived" relationship. I found that I was more and more able to relate with her, and others, in authentic ways. This occurred as I learned to track our social interactions, to register new levels of my awareness to subtle triggers from my mother, as fleeting moments that previously had passed below my radar.

It is precisely those moments that in the past would have rendered me numb that I now nip in the bud. For example, when I start to register my own discomfort in response to my mother's intensity reflected in her breathing rate, which I have learned as a trigger, I now tend to speak up, to ask her if she is aware that she is getting tense or nervous. This is a slow but profound change in the way that we are relating. Thus, over time, incrementally changing each time, the accumulated reshaping of our relating has resulted in our ability to sustain longer and more meaningful conversations before our inevitable disconnection sets in.

This emerging capacity, to recognize and thus regulate the onset of potential relational trauma in our relationship, prevents me succumbing to dissociation, depersonalization, or derealization—marked by my detached face. I make an effort to prepare myself before I see her, to remain mindful during our time together, and to leave some time to debrief myself following potentially traumatic meetings.

* * *

Those of us who are trained professionally to look unflinchingly into the faces and meet the eyes of trauma survivors see fleeting instances of frozen faces or averted or blank gazes. Less frequently are we taught to pay careful attention to the patterns of breathing, theirs and ours.

I have discovered that paying special attention to the face, gaze, voice, and breathing patterns of my mother is critically important if I am to avoid a reenactment, becoming yet again the traumatized child of a survivor. I have learned to confront, by making visible and audible, those invisible and silent barriers that now I increasingly respect as the gateway to my becoming mindless in the past. For once those barriers have been breached, the trauma stored in the body has the power to trigger processes below our threshold of awareness. Vicarious trauma sets in.

These frozen moments beyond our ordinary awareness are measured in microseconds, but they can be captured on video and then analyzed using freeze-frames. During these fleeting moments of reenactment, an animated face becomes still; a musical and rhythmic voice becomes robotic or silent and is perhaps accompanied by a critical look; or a familiar gentle touch is withdrawn, as responses become erratic or unpredictable.

I have become aware that I am entitled, indeed that I need, to claim such moments as my own experiences of trauma, direct or vicarious, even as they parallel my mother's reliving of her own moments of trauma. And this understanding opens up new questions. How do the symptoms of traumatized children affect their carers? It seems to me that the responses of witnesses to trauma depend on the balance between their capacity to allow themselves to empathize with—to let in emotionally—the other's experience and their need to keep such powerful identifications at arm's length.

Each traumatized person, whether infant, child, or adult, is entitled to have his or her experience witnessed and validated. Yet, the playing out of these competing entitlements between family members is fraught with problems, as are definitions of the nature of those traumatic and fleeting experiences. For example, when a child feels a sense of shame, humiliation, or embarrassment on learning that a survivor parent had witnessed members of his or her family being murdered, can that child be said to be traumatized? Or, likewise, is the child traumatized when the child learns that a parent lives with the scars of torture and starvation or has been treated as subhuman? That moment of learning extends beyond the "facts."

For the child, the emotional undercurrent that accompanied that fact may reverberate for decades, each time that fact is recalled. This undercurrent, the Gestalt of sensations and emotions; subtle changes in facial expressions, breathing patterns, and skin tones; alteration of the tone and rhythms in speech is my focus when I try to testify as a psychological witness to transmitted trauma.

As parents, carers, and professionals we need to be aware that trauma, both direct and vicarious, produces similar effects—it disrupts awareness, alters levels of consciousness, and in the extreme we literally faint. We should also be mindful that changes in awareness, including dissociation, depersonalization, and derealization, differ markedly in adults and children.

Such differences arise in part from the immaturity of children's brains. For example, clinical and research experience highlights that children's symptoms may be so fleeting they are easily overlooked by busy or untrained adults. This partly explains why we perpetuate the mistaken notions that "children will get over it," that "they are resilient," or that "they're just children." The fact is that the younger the child when he or she experiences trauma, the greater the risk that the child will face long-term developmental consequences.

* * *

My personal experience of relational trauma has deepened my understanding, informed by my 30 years as a psychiatrist, that subtle, intimate moments when the infant's or child's attachments are disrupted can be as traumatic as earthquakes, tsunamis, floods, or fires or as wars, torture, or deliberate terror attacks.

It may seem inappropriate for relational disruptions in otherwise loving and caring homes to be labeled *traumatic*. Yet, sleeper effects experienced later in life, such as "anniversary reactions" that recall losses of significant others, sometimes decades after the event, are evidence of such relational trauma.

I learned as a 7-year-old child, when we escaped during the Hungarian revolution in 1956, that even my devoted parents were unable to shield me from experiences of loss of some of my most intimate attachments: family and school friends, my pet dog, toys, my bedroom, in fact home and country. These were my known, visible losses. Later, I learned about the less-visible ones. My memory of those events, as reconstructed during a lengthy and intensive personal analysis in my late 20s to mid-30s, included the smells associated with seeing my parents digging up our kitchen floor, the damp earth hiding buried valuables that they needed to retrieve before we escaped.

I have no memory of what my mother's and father's face might have looked like in this childhood scene, but I do know their instruction to me—this incident was to be our secret. This was one of many secrets, part and parcel of our family plans to prepare for our eventual escape to Austria and Australia. Later in life, I learned that family friends who had also tried to escape were captured, mother, father, and daughter, detained by the police in Hungary. I can only wonder how many times an anxious small boy's gaze was met in return, or mirrored, by his parents equally anxious, silent, frozen faces.

In my video, I try to elicit how suppression of these seemingly invisible experiences that leave the traces of trauma in the body may trigger mental events, undercurrents, more subtle than those visible losses that I could recall.

To start a new life often demands a necessary forgetting of the old life in order both to survive and to free up the energy that grief and mourning consume. Such was my parents' fate after they survived the Holocaust. Just over a decade later, they started all over again in Australia, and on this second beginning of a new life, I also was there. But, neither they nor I had psychological witnesses to our less-visible losses to whom we could articulate our feelings of loss of safety and security, of the need for regular and predictable mealtimes, and so on.

As I child, I had some sense that my parents' worded worries on arrival in Australia took priority over anything that I might have been experiencing. For example, it was self-evident that while my uncle and aunt temporarily took us in to their small home on our arrival, my parents' priority was clearly to find a new home, to find work to earn some money, and to send me to school, as soon as possible. My worries on being unable to speak English, starting school after the disruption of leaving my home, escaping and being unable to speak even in my mother tongue with my parents about what had happened to my world, or was happening to me each day, seemed to be low on the list of priorities in the chaos that was my experience of the grown-up world.

It was to try to find and, if possible, to identify these invisible and inaudible transformations and to learn how to read the many faces of stress and trauma—frozen faces, whispered voices, stilted gestures—that I began to explore the potential of split-screen video.

My approach may offend some people. Some may rightly say that my parents faced "real" threat to their lives during times of capture, imprisonment, starvation. As evidence, they may cite that my family members were murdered by gas, bullets, or drowning. There is admissible, visible evidence for my parents' trauma. How could I compare that trauma with my focus on the "soft" evidence of losses experienced by an infant or child—as I suggest that follows from changes from a familiar soft, reactive face to a frozen one; or a gentle musical voice to a robotic one; a warm lingering hug to a quick pat on the head; a fleeting but constant eye gaze to an aversion of that gaze? Critics may claim that to label these experiences as "traumatic" is absurd or obscene. How dare I compare or even juxtapose these events with my parent's real traumatic experiences?

It is certainly not my intention to set up competition between experiences of suffering due to trauma, for that would miss the point. Rather, my point is to highlight that children can and do experience trauma, and that they are entitled to that experience, even if it is their parents' view that they are not, for many survivor parents find it impossible to be psychological witnesses of their children's traumas. I understand that one of the barriers to this understanding arises from the fact that it is precisely the legacy of the parents' trauma that is the source of the relational trauma for the infant.

Many people who have had no parental witnesses to validate their experiences of childhood trauma have turned to therapy groups or workshops to find that validation or authentication. Over the years, I have learned in such workshops that there are some survivors who keep reminding others of their own traumas while seeming incapable of understanding or empathizing with their own children's experience of similar events that may also be traumatic.

In other settings, during my intensive psychoanalysis, I began to discover how my parents' Holocaust experiences had shaped my life. However, in that phase of my life as a young adult I could tolerate only a limited understanding of the power of trauma. So, along with many children of survivors, a great part of my life's quest continues to center on restoring missing and vanished narratives and associated visceral experiences that derive from the losses in my family's past.

As I restore more and more of my past, I gradually see how much of that unresolved family trauma was connected to my family's tendency to catastrophize even relatively minor everyday mishaps *as if* they were occurring during the Holocaust.

One outcome from my work on psychological witnessing has been to claim permission to include as legitimate my own trauma experiences as part of my family history of trauma. To do so demanded that I apply a double construct of family trauma: my parents' alongside mine—not in competition, but insisting that both needed to be acknowledged. To this day, my insistence sits uncomfortably with me. My struggle is to transform my sense of identity that professionals label as a "parentified child," one whose role is to parent the parent, to now assume an identity as an "ordinary" person with personal needs and desires separate from looking after my parent's feelings.

* * *

It is now a decade since the making of the video *Many Faces of Trauma*. In the years immediately afterward, I reviewed segments of my mother's

Holocaust testimony many times. I spoke professionally at conferences and personally with my mother, family, and friends. I continued to research and write about my experiences. Now, I have returned to those moments, to continue my exploration at a deeper level.

Heeding the warning of Dori Laub, that the speakers of trauma on some level prefer silence as a means of protecting themselves, I asked myself if I dared to disturb my survivor mother's "fated exile"—to use Laub's term. In asking that question, I realized that if there was exile to be disturbed, it would not be hers, as she had already recorded her testimony. Could it be mine? In observing my own reactions on the split screen, I considered the possibility that ours was a double exile.

To explore this thesis, I reviewed many times the split screen, to analyze my moment-by-moment facial expressions. I made the assumption that my facial expression would serve as a marker of microreactions to verbal and nonverbal triggers in my mother's testimony. Through freeze-frame analysis, I found that many fleeting moments and vanishing facial reactions, hers and mine, had indeed been captured. As psychological witness, I could then analyze these moments as a sort of afterimage, much like pressing on an eyeball can create images not actually seen.

A core theory of psychological trauma posits that people's reactions to trauma are instinctive and physiological, using the mechanisms of fight, flight, or freeze, and that dissociation is part of this stress and shock reaction. This process, it is claimed, limits memory and recall of events, leaving the person with "traumatic amnesia." Their access to these memories is limited, but under special conditions like hypnosis, flashbacks (as in the flashbulb memories of posttraumatic stress syndrome), or dreams, recall may be possible.

The split-screen video enabled me to explore the impact on her adult child of the adult survivor's narrative and facial expressions when relating events of personal trauma. I was curious to see my reactions to my mother's traumatized face and to track the alterations in my facial patterns. For example, would I find a synchronicity between our facial reactions when my mother was relating to her most traumatic autobiographical memories? Would I be dissociated if she was dissociated? (And here I stress that such moments are not to be confused with facial expressions that accompany states of depression.)

The details of my findings have been published in "Can Trauma Be Transmitted Across the Generations?" (Halasz, 2002). I offered four explanations to account for the periods on the split-screen video that I labeled "absence of resonance," both in my mother's facial expressions and in the absence of facial responsiveness on my part. I interpreted these as habituation, dissociation, moments of psychic retreat, and finally as expression of the "exiled self."

I concluded that article with Laub's observation that the survivor's plight of silence is a "fated exile, yet also a home, a destination, and a binding oath," and ventured some trajectories for how such silence may affect the second generation—the infant who was "the bystander, an intimate witness to the survivor's fated exile." For that infant was also "a participant witness, precisely to those exiled moments when he, the infant, was hungering for relatedness. Instead he met the survivor parent's 'fated exile,' a wall of silence." I asked whether exile can be transmitted: "Can those predictable, intolerable moments, when the wall of silence between survivor parent and child seems impenetrable, be breached?" (Halasz, 2002, p. 218).

In the most recent years, I feel blessed to have shared experiences with my mother that offer a possible response to these questions. Based on our experiences, I am starting to believe that it is possible to breach what seems to have been an impenetrable wall of silence between us. For me, this breaching of the ever-deeper layers of that wall continues. I am mindful that my curiosity has been paralleled by and entwined with my mother's own committed explorations.

I am left to conclude that we both needed to be willing partners in this journey, to return from our respective exiled selves. Some suggest that this requires courage on both our parts. That may be so. I would suggest it arises from a familiar sense of desperation that all families experience when they feel unable to make connections with loved ones. In our case, we have been fortunate to find a creative approach as we continue to try to bridge the well-known abyss of Holocaust trauma's generational legacy.

POSTSCRIPT

Since starting my research with the *Many Faces of Trauma*, during the last decade my mother and I have shared the following Holocaust-related experiences: first, the intergenerational dialogue workshop organized by Tania Nahum; second, the Adult March of the Living (AMotL) organized by Pauline Rockman; third, this chapter, invited by Marilyn and Nancy. Finally, all this research I apply to my real daily relationship with my mother, Alice.

Tania Nahum's intergenerational workshops provided an ongoing annual forum (2000–2006) with six to eight weekly sessions of regular group work that provided safe, ongoing professional settings to "normalize" the struggles in communication faced by survivors. They attended knowing that the agenda would be personal—hurdles in the "simple" daily tasks of talking with their families and children. In the later years of the group, we turned to the third generation—grandchildren. For my mother, the added agenda was a meeting place with her son, as I was a facilitator in these annual workshops.

Pauline Rockman, director of AMotL, provided a once-in-a-lifetime shared experience for my mother and I. Based on the success of the March of the Living program (initiated by Sue Hampel), to coincide with the 60th anniversary of the liberation of Auschwitz, 1945–2005, my mother returned to the site where she "witnessed" the disappearance of Esther and Zsuzsi, her mother and sister—murdered in the gas chambers. Before our pilgrimage, I asked her why she wanted to return with me. She answered in Hungarian that she wanted to return to that place so that we could breathe the same air, and that on this occasion she could walk out of the camp with a living relative.

The invitation to write this chapter on witnessing arose unexpectedly when I received an e-mail from Marilyn, in which she referred to my work on trauma transmission in the video *Many Faces of Trauma*. She asked to view the video as she was then writing a chapter for a book dealing with Holocaust trauma. I sent her a copy. A year or so later, she sent me a copy of her published chapter.

Another year later, as I was preparing a trip to the United States, I e-mailed Marilyn to arrange a catch-up meeting in person during my visit to Washington. It turned out Marilyn and Nancy were about to start writing a book on witnessing the Holocaust. The rest, as they say, is history.

One example of my mother's keen interest in all my Holocaust research work was her eagerness to understand and to make sense of her experiences. At the same time as she gained deeper insights, I also clarified many areas of confusion. One such moment centered on my use of the word *overwhelmed* in an earlier draft of this chapter.

For some reason, she read the word phonetically, which ended up with her misreading it as *overhelmeted*. So convinced was she of this word that she asked friends for its meaning. Of course, no one had heard of the word. A little time later, during a visit, she asked me for its meaning. Naturally, I also had not heard of the word, so I asked her to show it me. We eventually found the word in the text as *overwhelmed*, found it in her English-Hungarian dictionary, and here perhaps pictures explain the joy of discovery better than words (see Plate 4).

ACKNOWLEDGMENTS

I give thanks to my father, Laci Halasz, 1923–1997; my mother, Alice Halasz, for her continued support, encouragement, and inspiration to keep on being a witness to Zsuzsi and Esther Klein and Giza Halasz and others.

For their ongoing support in more ways than they know, I thank Anne Handelsmann-Braun; Peter Handelsmann; Rabbi Shimshon Yurkowicz; Drs. Vicki Gordon, David Toffler, Paul Valent, and Chili Napastek; Professors Frances Thomson Salo, Maurice Preter, Allan and Judy Schore; Mr. John

Ziltzer; Otto Gunsberger; Ethel Tillinger; Pauline Rockman and staff, Adult
March of the Living (2005); Tania Nahum, Dr. Paul Valent, and staff,
Intergenerational Dialogue Group (2000–2006); third-generation con-
tributions: Dr. Amelia Klein, Natalie Krasnostein's Third Generation
Workshop series (2006); Denise Same's Holocaust support group mem-
bers (1990–current); VHF for permission to use images from Alice Halasz
Testimony, and staff at the VHF: Daisy Miller, Michael Engel, Janet Keller,
Kim Simon, Neil Sokol, Stryk Thomas, Jessica Wiederhorn, Ari Zev; survi-
vors of the Shoah, Visual History Foundation.

REFERENCES

Classen, C., Koopman, C., & Spiegel, D. (1993). Trauma and dissociation. *Bulletin of the Menninger Clinic, 57*(2), 178–194.
Gorldwurm, H. (1997). *Talmud Bavli, Tractate Berachos*, volume II. 40a(3). New York: Mesorah Publications.
Halasz, A. (1998, February). *Testimony. Survivors of the Shoah*. Visual History Foundation, Interview 40521. Melbourne.
Halasz, G. (2002). Can trauma be transmitted across the generations? In Z. Mazur, F. H. König, A. Krammer, H. Brod, & W. Witalisz (Eds.). *The legacy of the Holocaust: Children and the Holocaust* (pp. 210–223). Cracow: Jagiellonian University.
Laub, D. (1992). Bearing witness, or the vicissitudes of listening. In S. Felman & D. Laub, *Testimony: Crisis of witnessing in literature, psychoanalysis, and history* (pp. 57–74). New York: Routledge.
The Many Faces of Trauma. (2000, December). Video by G. Halasz, produced by S. Gery. Melbourne.
Schore, A. N. (2001). The effects of early relational trauma on the right brain development, affect regulation, and infant mental health. *Infant Mental Health Journal, 22*, 201–269.

Chapter 10

Bergen-Belsen 2009

Renée Hartman

For my sister Herta

PLACE AND AURA

In a dismal forest of spindly tree trunks, several kilometers from the nearest villages, stands the newly built Bergen-Belsen memorial museum. It is a long, narrow building of concrete, steel, and glass. At the far end is one large glass window that marks the border of what was the concentration camp. The placement of this window wall seems to have been influenced by the Yad Vashem Holocaust museum in Jerusalem.

The Jerusalem window points to the golden light of the panoramic hills beyond. In Bergen-Belsen, the view is toward an absence, something that was once there but no longer is except in memory. And yet, not many yards beyond, there is a clearing with large rectangular mounds.

Each mound has a brass plate indicating that under it are thousands of bodies. Those mounds mark graves formed by the English liberators, so the precise number of the anonymous dead buried there is, while massive, unknown. There are also symbolic gravestones placed after the war by family members to commemorate relatives who perished in the camp. Among these is a stone with Anne and Margot Frank's name, dedicated by their father, who found Anne's diary. Another is dedicated to a member of the deNoailles family (a family that survived the French Revolution). A large monument built by the Russian government honors its dead soldiers, who were the first prisoners when Bergen-Belsen was a Stalag. In 1943, it became a concentration camp with Jews as the majority of inmates.

In January 2009, my husband was invited to an international conference (which had been delayed for 2 years) to celebrate, along with several other scholars of the Holocaust, the completion of the museum's documentation center.

The organizers at the museum wanted me to accompany my husband. The museum had my testimony for some time, as well as my correspondence with Thomas Rahe, a former director of the memorial site, whom I now met again. It turned out that I was the only Bergen-Belsen concentration camp survivor at the conference. I had been reluctant for years to return to the place of my sister's and my childhood horror, but this time I agreed to come since I did not want my husband to travel alone in the depth of winter. My reluctance was compounded by previous experiences of Holocaust conferences.

We were picked up at the Hanover airport and driven to Celle, the town nearest the camp, where we were staying. The young woman who drove us pointed to a bridge that was a replacement of the one bombed by the British because next to it was a munitions factory. The workers there were forced laborers, *Zwangsarbeiter*, many of them killed in the bombing; those who survived fled into the woods. The soldiers and townspeople chased them. "*Es war eine Hasenjagd*," she said: "It was a rabbit hunt." As we passed through Celle, the town looked as normal in the wintry afternoon sun as it must have looked in 1944–1945 when Bergen-Belsen was crammed with the dead and the half-dead by the thousands.

Joanne Rudof, the archivist at Yale's Video Archive for Holocaust Testimony, confirmed my impression of the deeply dismal feel of the site, which felt as if it were in nature and yet with a deadness that even sunlight did not lessen. Joanne had been there at the height of summer, and she found it no less dreary than in January. The trees looked sickly and stunted, and I could not get the song of camp laborers out of my mind, especially the line from "The Peat Bog Soldiers": "*Die Eichen stehen kahl und krumm*"— "the oaks are standing bare and crooked."

When my sister and I arrived in Bergen-Belsen from the transit camp Sered, I lost all sense of time about the length of the trip in a cattle car filled with a mass of people, to me total strangers, many of them crying and moaning. The car had straw on the floor on which we had to sit since there were too many of us to lie down, and only the very old and sick were given extra space. In the middle of the car were two huge containers, one filled with water to drink and, next to it, an empty one for toileting. There was no privacy and eventually all of us filled it despite our shame. During the trip, we had no food, and the water disappeared quickly and was refilled before we reached, after what seemed a very long time, our destination.

At the stop, we were made to wait until nighttime. We had heard the rain all day, its sound loud and relentless on the roof of the wagon, and when the doors were unlatched, we saw with consternation how heavy the rain was. We were told to jump down quickly, form into three rows, and march straight into the dark.

My sister and I had one small valise and a rolled-up quilt given to us by a very nice office worker in Sered. I knew that the quilt would be soaked, but it astonished me how heavy it became with the rain. I held on to it with my right hand, the left one holding the valise. My sister also held on to the quilt, and I asked her to let go and rather help with the suitcase. Eventually, as the march seemed never to end, out of exhaustion or confusion my sister let go and wandered to the other row. Within a minute, I lost sight of her, and in a panic rushed to the other row. It was useless to call her, as my sister was deaf. Holding on to the suitcase and quilt, I ran and finally spotted her, and rushing to be beside her and with my arms weighed down, I bit her on her cheek to get her attention. She burst out crying, but she held on tight. Only then did my panic turn to anger, which kept us both going. Finally, we went through a gate and were directed to a barrack.

Exhausted and soaking wet, we sat on a bunk, the lowest one, as there were two above us. We then saw our shoes, ankle high, with the mud we had slogged through. None of us had the strength to remove the shoes, and we just collapsed with our wet clothes on the straw pallets. My sister reproached me for the bite, the mark of my teeth visible on her cheek, but I explained how terrified I was at the thought of losing her. She was then 8½, and I was 18 months older, but I was also her ears.

In 2009, one of the staff of the museum mentioned that the distance between the train stop and the entrance of the camp was almost 6 kilometers (about 4 miles). I still cannot get over the shock. To be weighed down after days in a train, hungry and exhausted, marching in pouring rain through thick mud—how did we manage? In the black night with only the soldiers' flashlights pointing the way, we could not tell if the elderly and sick made it through the gate or even if all in the cattle wagons survived the trip. I did not then have the strength to consider anyone except my sister and myself. Today, I am fully aware of what the condition of that first night and all subsequent ones meant. The end of the line was annihilation.

THE GAPS

The conference title was "Witnessing: Sites of Destruction and Representation of the Holocaust." After a long hiatus, the state of Lower Saxony supported the building of this significant documentation center next to the site of the concentration camp. The conference dealt (though not exclusively) with how experiencing the very sites on which the Nazi atrocities occurred affects our memorial thinking. Since the conference was in cooperation with the Fortunoff Holocaust Video Archive at Yale, it also dealt with issues of survivor testimonies on video and how this new genre is useful to history and memory. Such video testimonies are one of the strongest educational media in the documentation center.

The interior of the museum is remarkably simple. The long lower floor has on the left side, in front of the bare cement wall, a stretch of video monitors at 5-foot intervals. The first videos show Russian solders giving testimonies in Russian with German translation in subscript. To the right are glass cases with photos and other objects and artifacts of the Stalag. As one keeps walking, the videos and exhibits advance in chronological fashion and cover the main aspects of the concentration camp period and its aftereffects. It is interesting that the oral testimonies are confirmed by showcases of photos and written documents, so that as one walks along the exhibits to the large border window one realizes that what one has heard and seen really did exist in the place just outside that window.

Historically speaking, it is incredible that this small museum has such a considerable amount of material. On the second floor are the main archives, registers, books, and photographs, most from German sources and liberators, others from inmates and survivors, and some from the Swedish Red Cross (which facilitated the placement of my sister and myself in Sweden). The most significant collections are photos and films taken by the English, and the originals are in the British War Museum.

Even so, there are gaps. In looking over the pictures of imprisoned children, too many have no names attached. Some of the children I could identify, but many who died remain nameless, buried quickly, also for sanitary reasons (typhus had raged in the camp) in the collective graves I have already mentioned.

Most difficult for me is the abyssal gap between the historical evidence of what happened and my inability to understand why. Neither religious nor philosophical explanations make sense, and the psychological ones are inaccurate. And with every attempt to understand, our collective memory seems even more orphaned, and no museum or memorial can ever repair the deep losses.

THE OVERFULLNESS OF REMEMBRANCE

As I pored over the pictures in the archives, I came upon those of Otto Klein and Lusia Wolkowicz with their tragic eyes. Both of them were in the same children's barrack in Bergen-Belsen and then in Sweden with my sister and me. How they looked in the photos is exactly how I remembered them, faces like theirs being the true site of memory for me. Events, which in ordinary times have deep associations, are for me ambiguous if merged with wartime experiences. On the one hand, I retain the impression they make on me, sometimes with upwellings of love. On the other hand, there is much distress to be overcome. But, much as I suffered in Bergen-Belsen, I cannot forget the one joyful day, when, sometime after liberation, a group of us were taken outside the camp, and I saw a field of lupines of all colors growing in the distance—as far as I could see. I felt a profound gratitude that nature remained and that flowers could grow next to a site that had not even a blade of grass. In short, I feel myself at home everywhere and nowhere.

I revisited Bratislava, my hometown, twice, the first time after 45 years of retaining in my mind the image and history of the apartment house (once the summer palace of a Viennese nobleman) where we used to live. On this first visit, the place was already gutted; only the outside walls were left and a few of the inside ones. My sister and I managed to get into the courtyard and look up at our windows. Gone were the iron railings where we let the tendrils curl up from peas we planted in wet cotton balls and from which we peered to see our father returning from work. Gone also was the apartment with sand on the floor, which a gypsy family was able to rent. The Old City, as our neighborhood was called, was in fact a ghetto for the poor, where most Jews had to live. The main artery of Jewish Bratislava, the Judengasse, had been totally demolished after the war and transformed into a highway and bridge across the Danube. Also, after the war, all around the town ugly Soviet-style apartment blocks were erected on sites that I remembered as landscapes.

A couple of years later, I again quickly revisited my old home, also my grandparents' apartment. Our gutted apartment house was finished, but the courtyard architecture was reversed. Our side of the courtyard had no balconies; they ringed the opposite side. The rebuilt side had balconies on our side and none on the other. And the new tenants were multinationals. Gone was the slightly dilapidated charm that existed before, gone also the impoverished feel of the whole neighborhood. The Old City had become the "in" place, the most sought-after quarter.

What has not been renewed is the trilingual ability of most of the populace. In my childhood, everyone I knew spoke German, Slovak, and Hungarian, a legacy of the Austro-Hungarian Empire. I still miss the ability to speak Slovak and Hungarian, which over the years I have forgotten. Though I have learned other languages, the memory of their sounds remains in my memory like oft-heard music. German, the language we spoke at home, my father being Viennese and my mother educated there, remained with me despite the determination not to speak it for 5 years except with my sister. I never went to a German-speaking school; in fact, I did not go to any school until after liberation, so that at almost 12 I had to catch up for the 5 lost years in all subjects except for reading, which I had begun before my fifth birthday—the joyous year when I got several books as birthday presents. This was also the year my mother began to be annoyed with me, for I never heard her call when my nose was stuck in books or anything printed.

All these memories rushed at me once again as I looked at the Bergen-Belsen landscape. Nothing there hints at what happened, yet the illusory image of innocence of place had disappeared; instead, the bareness, the lowering sky, the horizon asked for interpretation. I and other survivors know of the blood and bones in the ground, but once we are gone, what would the landscape tell? Can hunger and pain and trauma ever be historicized? Alas, they remain a burden on memory that is already overfull.

DISTANCE AND DISTORTION

Around the age of 16, a little over a year after arriving in the United States after a 3-year stay in Sweden, I wrote a story based on my experience in Bergen-Belsen. It was my first attempt at writing in English other than high school homework. My relatives found the story interesting enough to send it to the *Ladies' Home Journal* and other women's magazines. All of them returned the story with the notation that it was "not appropriate for the magazine." I had to agree with them since the magazines dealt with beauty tips, cooking, pleasing husbands, and raising children. It took another generation for these magazines to deal with the darker side of human experience.

During my high school years, I began to collect books on the Holocaust. My first one was Thomas Geve's *Youth in Chains*, about his concentration camp experience and meant to be a textual accompaniment to his drawings. I never saw the drawings, but the text was marvelously accurate. I picked up whatever books I could get my hands on and was deeply moved by books like John Hersey's *The Wall*, about the last days of the Warsaw Ghetto. In the 1960s, Ilona Karmel wrote *An Estate of Memory* and *Stephania*. *Estate of Memory* I thought was one of the best novels about concentration camps I had read, and still think it outstanding; that it is not better known has to do with the fact that it came out long before Holocaust writing was popular. The remarkable work by Charlotte Delbo appeared long after my school years, as did translations of Primo Levi's astonishing books. During those early years, I already heard complaints that too many books on the Holocaust were being written. In college, studying history, I saw that the Holocaust was rarely mentioned and was relegated to Jewish history rather than being viewed as a central part of modern European history. I am still not certain that this has been righted. And no amount of documentation lessens the persistence of Holocaust deniers. What do the deniers gain by their distortions? Do they refuse to acknowledge the dark side of societies? Do they enjoy the new pain they inflict? Are they distancing themselves from reality or think they can control it? Since every country has these deniers, I wonder what they have to say about the presence of slavery and prostitution even in our times.

CATASTROPHE AND ARCHIVE

In 1979, after being part of the first group of interviewees in the Fortunoff Video Archive, I became an attendee at many conferences, met numerous scholars, and began to be acquainted with their work. I have not, however, attempted to be a scholar in the field. Over the years, I have listened to them, read their books or papers, and learned a great deal, yet for me it has always been a strange experience to listen to people who knew so much more than I ever did.

Sometimes, it felt surreal when I sensed that the scholar "owned" the subject. I felt they did not own it in the way I owned my experience, and the scholars who did not exhibit that trait were the ones I admired the most, such as Saul Friedlander and Lawrence Langer. But the two writers who gave me the feeling that they were most with me in spirit were Arthur Cohen, who called the Holocaust a "tremendum," and Terrence Des Pres in *The Survivor: An Anatomy of Life in the Death Camps.*

Why are some books more influential than others? Time will eventually do the sifting, but alas many fall by the wayside undeservedly. It is not always possible for a group of people to "read" their own experiences, but I am pleased when I can say to myself, "Yes, this is how it exactly was." Yet, this recognition is almost always accompanied in my mind with, "I can't believe that it really happened."

Even now, in my old age, I keep being amazed that we survived against such odds. As a parent and grandparent, I often wonder: Our children, when they are my sister's and my age, could they survive? I hope that our love and caring has strengthened them, yet I am aware of how imponderable and chancy all wars and catastrophes are. There is no predicting the first and subsequent reactions.

I thought I would have a difficult time in Bergen-Belsen, remembering the first zombie days after our arrival. But now, in my seventh decade, I find myself inured to a small extent by my sense of irony and pessimism, though not sufficiently, as I realized after hearing Father Dubois, the French priest who has been instrumental in recently locating hundreds of unknown mass graves in the Ukraine. The film he showed at the conference gave the testimony of peasants who after all these years described the slaughter and revealed the location of the pits. Irony and pessimism, moreover, cannot suppress sorrow and pain; they simply quietly indicate how low human beings can sink, how the world's catastrophes are mostly humanmade, and that our modernity is a myth. The 20th century was the most efficient killing machine devised.

THE LYING CIVILIZATION

On my return home, I was once again bothered by the many dissonances between our conception of what civilized life is and what happens in it. The contrast between the comforts of today and the distresses of the past was not made easier by even a small fact revealed during my talk with the Bergen-Belsen archivists, who changed my perception of space (my new awareness of the distance my sister and I had to march on that terrible first night), and I realized again how difficult it is for a child to estimate things without objective aids.

In the camp, without a calendar, I had no idea what day of the week it was, and the seasons impinged as seasons only by heat or snow. There do exist means for clarity, exactitude, and truth telling, yet there is also a panoply of constant and intrinsic lies fostered by civilization itself. It is well known that the Nazis and their followers, in one of the most civilized countries, lied about the Jews in their midst—lied about their power, their danger, their wealth—and they did not perceive the poor among the Jews or the centuries of their oppression.

This unease resulted in a dream about 10 days after my return to the United States. In the dream, I am on the top floor of an apartment house. Suddenly, I see a man falling from somewhere above who lands on the pavement outside, but leaves nothing of his body except the puddle of his blood, which dissolves his clothes. I am frightened and move away from the window. I enter a very large apartment of a woman psychiatrist, whose husband is a musician and who is talking to a male psychiatrist who is German. I am being shown around by the three of them, and the apartment is filled with musical instruments and hundreds of fascinating artifacts that I cannot immediately identify except for a small kouros. Then, they bring me to an empty room. "You can take it and fill the room with anything you want," the woman says, and turning to the men, they begin to speak together in German. I am surprised, as we had spoken English. "I understand you," I say to them in German, "you want me to furnish this room and move in, too." I am more than reluctant because looking back through the open door I see the shadow of the falling man in the furnished section of the apartment, and something in me likes the emptiness of the room offered. I am uneasy, moreover, with the German psychiatrist and suspicious of all three with their extreme politesse and smiling demeanor. I then discover that in the empty room there are no windows behind the curtains, just a peephole that points to a space from which the falling man came. And just then I hear wild knocks behind a door. We all open the door and see a group of wild pigs attacking each other. I quickly close the door, but then notice the door next to it, which looks as if it had been mauled as well. Opening that door, I see lying wrapped in a sheet my dead mother. I lift her tenderly and in English say to her, "Mama beloved, Mama Love." Suddenly, she opens one eye, in a slit, looks at me, then closes her lid again. I keep holding her like a baby. I wake up instantly, unable to breathe, until I repeat "Mama Love."

I realize then that the dream had an element of posttraumatic shock. The rest of the day, I am haunted by the dream, the empty room, all the artifacts of civilization; haunted by the remembrance of loss, which is all that civilization, at that moment, had to offer.

Chapter 11

Miklós

A Memoir of My Father

Katalin Roth

For Michael Roth 1914–2008

INTRODUCTION

"The migration of my parents has not subsided in me" wrote the poet Yehuda Amichai, and the migration of my parents is something I can never forget.

This chapter is not humorous, but I will start with a joke. A few years ago, our family was gathered at my home for Thanksgiving, and before dinner I chanced on my sons and their cousins rolling with laughter. "What's so funny," I asked, hoping to share the joke, but they would not meet my eye and gave each other guilty looks. After a pause, my niece spoke up: "We are taking bets," she said, "on dinner, and exactly how many minutes after we sit down before someone"—someone meaning me, or my sister or brother—"mentions the word *Holocaust*." Later, I learned that there is a variant on this, called the Holocaust drinking game.

And so the experience is felt not only by me and by my sister and brother, the second generation, we who are the children of the Holocaust, but also by our children. But this story is not about me, and my worries for my children; it is about my father and how I have come to understand him.

Miklós Roth was a very special person, responsible and honest, a man of faith. There was always a twinkle in his eye, and his children adored him. But he was also, in some ways, typical of the Hungarian Jews of his time. His story shows how a good man survived and moved on to build a new life.

EARLY YEARS

My father was born, at the start of the Great War, in Abaújszántó, a town of some 5,000 people, which lies in a valley between the rolling terraced hills of the Tokay wine district, not far from the chalky caves and hot springs of Lillafüred, a spa favored by the kaiser and Hungarian noblemen.

He was given the Hungarian name Miklós and the Hebrew name Moshe. The Hungarian name Miklós is usually translated into English as Nicholas, but when he came to the United States, he took the name of Michael and was called Mike. His father Hermann had a shoe store and a few properties in the Hungarian town, and the family enjoyed a two-story house with a porch and courtyard. He was the oldest of six children, and all of his life he felt responsible for his younger brothers and sisters.

Hermann was a distant and somewhat mysterious figure to his children. He came from a small town near Bratislava (then called Presburg), only about 100 kilometers from Abaújszántó, but he was emotionally distant from his family. After World War I, the Austro-Hungarian Empire was fragmented, and it was difficult to cross the border into Czechoslovakia. Hermann rarely visited his parents and sisters, and my father never met his Roth grandparents. My grandmother Gisela Frankfurter, known to all as Gittel or "Goody," was a countrywoman who wore long black dresses and high boots, and in the old photos there is always a kerchief over her hair. Gittel's parents lived in Felsőcéce, a tiny one-street village in a broad farming valley, where her father, Abraham, was the tavern keeper. The Frankfurters were the only Jews in the village, and Abraham was a pious and learned man. Every summer when school was out, my father Miklós spent the summer with his grandparents, and these summer vacations were the happiest times of his childhood. He loved and revered his grandfather.

Miklós was the best student in his class, winning the mathematics and recitation prizes, and often chosen to lead the students. He would have liked to study medicine or engineering, but Hermann forbade it, telling his son that he would not remain an observant Jew if he attended university. So Miklós was sent instead to Poland to study in a famous yeshiva. He often told us this story, as if it explained everything about how his life had turned out. But we, his American children, could not understand how our independent, strong—and indulgent—father could have been so obedient that he followed his stern father's instructions. When I was 5 years old, a visiting relative asked me what I wanted to be when I grew up. I said I wanted to be a doctor, and this aunt replied, "You can't be a doctor, you are a girl, you will be a nurse." I burst into tears, and my father defended me, saying, "She can be whatever she wants." And he took great pride in the educational accomplishments of all of his children.

At age 18, my father left home and set out for Miskolc, the provincial seat, at that time the second-largest city in Hungary. He apprenticed and learned the wholesale wine merchant's trade and soon built his own business, buying wine from the rural farmers and selling wholesale to taverns and stores. His business required him to work with non-Jewish Hungarians in the countryside and city; he had to get along with the government bureaucrats who controlled the licenses to sell alcohol and raw spirits that were used to fortify the wines and liquors. Although Miklós was Sabbath observant, he was clean shaven and wore no head cover, and he tasted the wine and drank with his sellers and buyers. It was essential to his business. Later, in the United States, as an Orthodox Jew, he was disdainful of the idea of kosher wine; he never thought that wines needed to be rabbinically blessed, although in deference to guests he observed the local customs and bought only kosher wine for his own home. Miklós was very proud that he had friends among the gentiles, and in fact his good relations with everyday Hungarians, and his partial assimilation, may well have helped save his life during World War II.

In his early 20s, my father married a woman named Ilse, in an arranged marriage that produced a son, my brother, Paul (Pál) (see Plate 5). He bought a house in Miskolc, down the lane from the large hill that contained the limestone cave he used as a wine cellar. But in 1943, my father was drafted into the Hungarian forced labor brigades, or Munkaszolgálat.

MARCHING

Recently, when I read *The Radetzky March*, written in 1932 by Joseph Roth (no relation, as far as I know), a satirical novel about Austro-Hungarians before World War I, much of my father's early history became clearer to me. At first, I was exasperated by the obedience of the characters: In each generation, the fathers directed their sons into unsuitable careers, yet the sons would not contradict their fathers. The first father was a soldier, who, hating war, forbade his son a military career and directed him to be a civil servant; the civil servant father, in turn, frustrated in his own ambition, insisted that his gentle son choose a soldier's life. In this picaresque novel, there are Poles and Bulgars, Hungarians and Slovenians, all the mess of the Austro-Hungarian Empire, and of course, there are Jews of every type, assimilated and not, merchants and doctors and even soldiers. There is a recurring figure of a Jewish tavern keeper in the village, a patriarch with a long white beard, who sells the soldier plum brandy and beer and lends him money. That tavern keeper could have been modeled on my own great-grandfather Abraham, a Jew among the rural gentiles. And Hermann treated my father the way these characters treated their sons, neither asking their opinions nor heeding their preferences.

Like the characters in *The Radetzky March*, Hungarian Jews like my father's family loved the Austro-Hungarian kaiser (emperor), who had given them civil rights and the opportunity to take pride in their country. (Miklós's two favorite maternal uncles, Simon and Martin, had fought for the kaiser in the Great War.) Later, these Hungarian Jews loved their Hungarian government, which they saw as the last bastion of the kaiser's empire. Their loyalty persisted despite the humbling and shrinking of Hungary after World War I, when Hungary became a landlocked country with an admiral at its helm. And when Admiral Horthy drafted these Jewish men like my father into the forced labor brigades, Munkaszolgálat, they followed orders as they had been taught to do, just like then gentiles and Jews who marched to the tune of the *Radetzky March* in Joseph Roth's novel.

MIKLÓS AND THE TYPEWRITER

My father often told this story about his time in the forced labor brigades during World War II. He told it in great detail during his Holocaust testimony at Yale, and I am still trying to puzzle out its importance to him. During his time in Munkaszolgálat, my father had, among his belongings, a typewriter.

It became known that the company commander needed a typewriter. My father heard this and proposed to his troop captain a trade, the typewriter for a furlough to buy shoes and shoelaces for the platoon. He did not tell his captain that he had a typewriter, only that "he knew where one could be found." The captain relayed this proposition, and the commander agreed, provided that Miklós be accompanied by two regular soldiers on the furlough. So, Miklós exchanged the typewriter for a short leave, and the three men left the Ukrainian front and went back to Miskolc for supplies. Miklós went to his bank to withdraw funds from his personal account for shoes and shoelaces for his comrades in the forced labor brigade, but the bank manager at first refused to release my father's funds. My father leaned over and whispered in the banker's ear, and the money was then paid out without further trouble; the men made their purchases and returned to the camp. Miklós would not tell the soldiers what he had whispered to the banker, but 50 years later, he told his children. Roughly translated from the Hungarian, what my father said was: "When the war is over, I am coming back, and if you don't give me my money now, I promise I will cut off your balls."

WAR AND LIBERATION

Two of my father's brothers died in the Munkaszolgálat during the war, Simon of appendicitis and Manuel of a gunshot wound; they had served in different brigades than my father. When his two younger brothers, Béla (Bill) and Jenő (Eugene) were drafted, Miklós arranged for them to join him, and he protected them as best he could. All three of them survived the war. Eugene and my father were very close: For almost 50 years, they were business partners, and Eugene and his wife, Shirley, lived next door to us in Connecticut. When my parents moved to Florida, the two men spoke every day on the phone. Eugene told me that during the war Miklós protected them: My father found them food, and he would not let them fall during the terrible marches. They believed that they would not have survived without Miklós's encouragement and protection.

Miklós was wounded by Russian shrapnel near Kiev. He never hid the coin-shaped scar at the base of his neck, right between the collarbones. The Hungarian Jews in the labor brigades were not supposed to carry weapons; their work was to carry and dig trenches and latrines, but my father told me that when the going got rough, they took guns and fought side by side with the Hungarians, who were also their jailors. Although his military service was forced, he was proud of his bravery under fire.

When the Germans withdrew from the Russian front, the Hungarian soldiers also marched west, and my father spent the last 8 months of the war in Austria, first in the concentration camp called Mauthausen and then in a nearby munitions work camp, Gesen. He was the leader of his work detail and took pride in how he looked after his men. He told tales of outsmarting the guards and cheating the Germans of a piece of potato and recalled celebrating Passover with a crust of bread and a slice of bacon.

A stocky man of medium height, my father weighed less than 50 kilos at liberation. When he arrived home, he learned that his wife Ilse and his son Paul were killed at Auschwitz, along with his mother Gittel; apparently the women refused to make "Sophie's choice" and would not be separated from Paul, then age 4. Young and strong, Ilse would otherwise have been sent into the work details and might have survived. Hermann was also at Auschwitz, and he died of typhus 2 days after the camp was liberated; he was only 55 years old. The only one of my father's family to survive Auschwitz was his younger sister Elaine.

LEAVING HUNGARY

After the war, Miklós rebuilt his business, and the Jewish community of Miskolc rebuilt their lives. His friend Andrew introduced Miklós to his niece Anci, or Anna, my mother. Recently, I learned that Anci and Miklós were married not once but twice. It seems that the Hungarian civil authorities would not declare Ilse dead for 2 years, so they were married first under Jewish law, and only a year later was there a civil ceremony. My mother's first pregnancy ended in a stillbirth at 7 months, and so had that boy baby lived, he would have been illegitimate under Hungarian law. My mother says she lost that baby because of famine after the war; she told us that she had no choice but to eat rotten and sprouted green potatoes. Once I thought her explanation foolish, but now scientific research has established that folic acid deficiency contributes to neural tube defects. Folic acid probably would have prevented that child's spina bifida and death. So in a way, I lost not one but two brothers because of the war and its aftermath.

In Miskolc, Anci and Miklós lived in the same house on Lonovics Utca that Miklós had shared with Ilse and Paul. I was born in September 1948. In December 1948, my father's friend in the local police warned him that he would soon be arrested; at that time, businessmen were targeted for "reeducation" by the new communist government. He quickly went to Budapest and hid with friends while my mother packed a few suitcases. In Budapest, they found a truck driver to smuggle them, and me, into Austria. The first escape attempt went wrong; the driver was shot in no-man's-land, we fled into the night, and my parents actually walked back into Hungary. A few nights later, another truck made the trip successfully, and our family found safety in Austria. My father's American cousin, our much-beloved Uncle Sidney, a colonel in the U.S. Army, sponsored us. After 5 months of waiting, first in Vienna and then in Paris, my parents and I arrived in New York City aboard the S.S. America on May 9, 1949. Of course, I do not remember that voyage—when I was 7 months old—but I heard the tale retold often. In the 1950s a favorite family excursion was a drive to New York harbor to watch the great ocean liners dock and depart, and these outings were always occasions to relive that journey.

In the two suitcases they smuggled out of Hungary during their dramatic escape, my parents managed to pack many treasures, including Anci's leather-bound prayer book, family photos, the silver tea set that Miklós bought for my mother to celebrate my birth, and even a Hungarian typewriter.

SECRETS

For most of my childhood, no one in my family spoke of the horror of what had happened, and the term *Holocaust* came later—in our family we referred to "The War." In the 1950s and 1960s, what had happened was rarely discussed at home, never in school. We were not exactly shielded; we saw the tattooed numbers on Aunt Elaine's arm. But my parents and relatives did not tell stories in those decades; they were busy building new lives.

New lives in America meant business, family, synagogue, stability (see Plate 6). My parents started with a small chicken farm in northern New Jersey, and then my father learned the retail carpet business from Andrew, the uncle who had introduced them in Miskolc. My father opened his own store in New Haven, Connecticut, in 1954, and there the family settled. Life revolved around work, a growing family—my sister, Martha, was born in 1952, my brother, Jeffrey, in 1959—and the rhythms of Jewish observance and the Sabbath. Weekly gatherings of aunts, uncles, and cousins were the norm, and my memories are of happy times. My parents, my uncles Eugene and Bill, and my aunt Elaine rarely spoke of the war years or their own privations; they were too busy with the everyday demands and pleasures of their young families.

My father loved America and the freedom it represented. The first television I remember seeing was the Army-McCarthy hearings. My father was no friend to communism, which was the Hungarian regime he fled, yet I remember my father's anxiety about the anticommunist witch hunt of the 1950s. I was a child of 4 or 5 when he said to me, "Do you see that, that is fascism, that is how it all started in Germany." Later, his children's opposition to the Vietnam War pained him greatly.

As in all émigré families, the older generation switched to the mother tongue when the adults did not want the children to understand. But we understood that there were secrets that they did not want us to know. The biggest secret was about my brother Paul. There is a small photo of Paul on the wall of my study, and his family resemblance to my own baby photos is very strong. When, as a child, I asked about that photo, I was told he was "just someone" who died in the war.

I did not learn about Paul, or about my father's first marriage, until I was 16 and then only by accident, when correct information had to be entered into my citizenship application. Fearful of bringing up the past, my parents forbade me from telling my younger sister and brother about Paul, and for several years I obeyed. Later, my father did not want me to say Kaddish for Paul; he said it was up to him to "give permission." Maybe he said this because of an old world Ashkenazi superstition that only parents can say Yizkor (the memorial service for the dead); anyway, it took me more than a decade to disregard his advice. But over time, the secret became more open, so that by the time my younger son, Adam, spoke of Paul during his Bar Mitzvah, my father was clearly pleased.

CHILDREN OF THE HOLOCAUST

My first few years in the United States were spent on a farm, and I had few playmates. Like many lonely children, I had rich fantasies and wonderful daydreams. In my daydreams I sought adventure, but I was also always running away from pursuers. I was a cowgirl, or a pioneer, or a resistance fighter fighting alien invaders, but there was always fighting and always a need for hiding places. I had weapons; I needed survival skills. I lived in forests or among strangers. I was always blond; I was never Jewish. I always had a hiding place.

Later, when I read Helen Epstein's *Children of the Holocaust* (1979), I learned that in the substance of my daydreams I was not alone, and that my fantasies were actually stereotypical of many of the second-generation Holocaust survivor children. In my fantasies, I reenacted and also romanticized and made heroic my parents' struggles to survive.

GOING BACK

One amazing thing about my father was that he could always see the other fellow's point of view. He had an amazing ability to put himself in another person's shoes, a quality of empathy. It gave him gravitas as synagogue president and as family patriarch. He was excellent at calm debate and discussion. In his Holocaust archive testimony at Yale, he even spoke kindly about his commander in forced labor.

In 1994, I visited Hungary with my parents. This was their second trip back. They had gone there with my brother in 1982, and they had returned unsettled and distressed. Nothing was the same as when they had left. Still, they decided to go back in 1994 because commemorative ceremonies were being held, to remember the 50th anniversary of the deportation of the Hungarian Jews to the death camps in 1944. There was a ceremony at the great Dohány Street Synagogue of Budapest, with notables from all over the world gathering to memorialize the devastation of Hungarian Jewry. More important, the names of my father's parents, brothers, and wife and child were read aloud at a ceremony in my father's hometown. My father was pleased to show me around Abaújszántó. My father shook the hands of townspeople whose parents had not protested when my grandparents were carted away to their deaths.

Later, we drove to Cece and found the Jewish corner of the town cemetery, where for 50 years our family had been sending money to maintain the Jewish graves. My great-grandfather Abraham lies in a cemetery surrounded by fields of golden sunflowers.

THE THINGS THEY LEFT BEHIND

My parents loved beautiful things, and they worked hard to buy silver and other ornaments for their home. Always prominently displayed on the sideboard was a simple silver vase, marred by a deep vertical gash. This vase was one of the objects buried under the dirt floor of my father's cellar during the war; when he went to retrieve it, the shovel struck the soft silver and cut into it deeply. They did not repair it, but rather kept the damaged vase as a remembrance of how much had been lost and how much had been saved.

RELIGION

I tried to be a dutiful orthodox daughter, but my skepticism about religion started at a very young age. When I was 6, my best friend dared me to take a bite of her ham sandwich. I ate, and nothing happened. My parents never suspected. So I learned early that God did not care if I ate ham and that my parents were not omniscient. As a teenager I struggled to find my faith, but I could not understand how a divine God could allow terrible things to happen—like the Holocaust. At 14, I decided I had to announce my agnosticism to my father. I picked a weekday morning for my proclamation, while he was in his bathroom, shaving, concentrating on his image in the mirror. He used a razor in those days, and I remember that his face was half shaved, half lathered when I told him, "Daddy, I do not believe in God." I was expecting a terrible response; I expected to be disowned or sent away. My father did not look at me directly but rather looked straight at me in the mirror. Without missing a stroke of the razor, he said, "Well, some people do, and some people don't. It is up to you."

Later, he told me that he saw many Jews lose their faith during the war. His beloved brother Mano was a nonbeliever, a Socialist, and a Zionist—all reasons that Mano became estranged from their father, Hermann. My father told me that while he had many doubts during the war, he had never ceased observance. During the long march to Mauthausen (one of the so-called death marches), he found God again. One day, exhausted, he began to falter, and he knew that if he fell, he would be shot by the Germans. "But then God picked me up and gave me the strength to keep walking."

LAST YEARS

My father lived to the age of 94. His last few years were marred by illness—but his spirits and his mind were strong up to the end. Even when he was no longer able to drive, and relied on a cane and then a walker, he still maintained his cheerful outlook. He loved his view of the Miami beach and would sit on his balcony for hours watching the ocean tides and the ship traffic. For a man who had grown up in a landlocked country and who had never seen the sea until he crossed the Atlantic Ocean at age 35, living in a beachfront condo in Miami Beach was a triumph over adversity and brought him great joy.

At the end, the legs that had carried him on those long European death marches turned black with gangrene, and he fell into a coma on the eve of Yom Kippur, the aweful Day of Atonement. He died a few hours after the holiday ended. In Jewish tradition, on the day of Yom Kippur a Jew is cleansed of all of his sins. When a man dies right after the holy day, without having had the opportunity to make any mistakes, he dies pure and without sin, so he ascends more quickly to heaven.

WHAT HE CARRIED IN THE WAR

The night my father died, my mother went to a chest of drawers and pulled out a kittel, the white garment of purity that Jewish men wear on holy days.

"He wore this kittel when we married," she said, "and he will be buried in it along with his oldest tallis." And then she brought out a creased and stained yellowed prayer shawl, and she said, "He carried this from Miskolc into the labor brigades, to the Russian front, on the march to Mauthausen, and he brought it with him when we escaped Hungary in 1948." My brother and I gasped. We had no idea that this fragment had survived or that they had cherished it all these years.

CHEATING DEATH

In 2009, I visited the concentration camp where my father spent the last 8 months of the war. My husband Phillip and I visited Mauthausen on a sweltering day at the end of July. The camp is located at the top of a high hill, commanding a view of the whole valley. The concrete and wooden buildings have been preserved, but the tent cities that housed additional Jewish and Russian prisoners at the end of the war are gone. Mauthausen was built in 1939 as a camp for prisoners of war; the Jews came much later. First came Communists and homosexuals, Spanish Republicans, Italian resistance fighters, British prisoners of war. It was a brutal place, famous for the "stairs of death," where prisoners carried huge heavy stones up steep steps from a deep quarry pit. If one slipped, he might knock down all of the other workers behind him, and many died in the excavation of those hard gray stones. The steel gates, barracks, common latrines, and high fences topped with barbed wire made me shiver. Fortunately, Miklós did not stay long; he was soon marched off to Gesen, one of the satellite camps of the Mauthausen complex. There he and his brothers loaded ammunition into shells until the end of the war.

When the camp was liberated, Miklós went directly back to Miskolc; his brothers were too weak to make the journey back and stayed on for weeks to recuperate. But they had survived, together. Maybe the twinkle in his eye was from that secret knowledge, that he had tricked fate and could still savor life.

A DREAM OF MY BROTHER

Last week, I dreamed I was at my niece's wedding, and there met a relation of the groom, a man about my age, a Jew from South Africa. We felt a strange and strong attraction to each other and talked for a long time. Slowly, we told each other our life stories. He told of being a blond toddler, rescued from the gas chambers at Auschwitz by a German officer's wife who longed for a blond baby. Later, he came to know that he was Jewish, but he never learned who his parents were. In my dream, I recognized him from old photographs and knew that he was my brother Paul. I awoke in tears.

MY WORK WITH REFUGEES

For more than 10 years, I have volunteered to do medical evaluations of refugees who are seeking asylum in the United States. Giving up a few hours a month, I act as a witness to human rights abuses all over the world. From these refugees, I hear amazing stories about political unrest, personal tragedies, destroyed dreams. I do my best to document their scars, physical and emotional, evidence of the suffering that impelled these people to leave their homelands to seek safety in a strange new place. Helping these refugees is a way for me to reach out a hand to my own past. My own parents kept most of their stories from us, shielding us from what they went through. But now I must probe: To support these refugees' claims for political asylum, I need to know the harshest details.

And the final determination is a concrete benefit: To help a refugee achieve legal status in this country is really to save a life.

MY MOTHER

I have not spoken much of my mother in this essay. Hers is another story, equally interesting. Anna's experience of the war was different, yet she also suffered. She grew up affluent, on a large farm, schooled in a Catholic gymnasium in Nyíregyháza; later, she studied textile design in Budapest. Her first boyfriend was killed in the labor brigades, and her whole world of privilege and safety was shattered by the Nazis. Most of her own family survived, saved by visas from Raoul Wallenberg and by hiding in cellars and warehouses during the last chaotic weeks of the war in Hungary. Like my father, she suffered the trauma of leaving a familiar home to seek a better life in a strange new country.

In the taped testimony my father gave to the Yale archive, my father said that when he proposed to her, he told my mother, "I am a broken man." She replied, "I will heal you." And for 62 years, she shared Miklós's life.

As the poet Yehuda Amichai wrote (1988):

> The memory of my father is wrapped up in
> White paper, like sandwiches taken for a day at work.
> Just as a magician takes towers and rabbits
> Out of his hat, he drew love from his small body,
> And the rivers of his hands
> Overflowed with good deeds. (p. 82)[1]

---

[1] "My Father" from Amichai, Y., *Israeli Poetry: A Contemporary Anthology* (W. Bargad & S. Shyet, Eds.). © 1988 Indiana University Press. Reprinted with permission.

REFERENCES

Amichai, Y. (1988). The memory of my father. In W. Bargad & S. Shyet (Eds.), *Israeli poetry: A contemporary anthology* (p. 82). Bloomington, IN: Indiana University Press.

Amichai, Y. (1994). And the migration of my parents. In *Yehuda Amichai, a life of poetry: 1948–1994* (p. 51). New York: HarperCollins.

Epstein, H. (1979). *Children of the Holocaust*. New York: Penguin.

Roth, J. (1932/1996). *The Radetzky march*. New York: Everyman's Library.

Chapter 12

The Power of Memorable Moments

Margit Meissner

When I think back on the memorable moments of my life, they are always associated with strong feelings: love, fear, success, failure, loss. Assimilating and remembering these moments help me explain how I became who I now am. These memories continue influencing my life.

I am a survivor of the Holocaust, of the persecution of Jews in Europe during World War II. I had not dwelt on my wartime experiences for many, many years. For most of my life, I was too busy to take time to explore my past. I had other things on my plate that demanded my attention: adapting to new situations, supporting myself, marriage, children, work, and then retirement. I was catapulted into the past when, in response to relentless urging from my children, I started writing my autobiography, *Margit's Story* (2003), when I was 81 years old. When writing my book, I was faced with a difficult decision. Should I recount my experiences the way I remembered them, or should I look at documents and letters that I had written that presented the story very differently. After much soul searching, I decided to go with my memory because that was real to me even if it was not factual. I was not writing a PhD thesis that had to have footnotes for every claim. The book starts with my grandparents and describes my life from childhood to age 80. I spent 2 years—on and off—looking through old documents and letters before starting to write, but primarily I rummaged around in my memory. I was amazed at all that I had experienced. What had been buried for so many years now suddenly assumed importance.

By the time the book was completed, I had lost interest in the volunteer activities in education about which I been passionate since retiring from public education in Montgomery County, Maryland, at age 70. It seemed to me that the proper place for me was to become a volunteer at the U.S. Holocaust Memorial Museum. I wanted to share my story with visitors to personalize their understanding of this terrible history. I was eager to emphasize that the Holocaust could have been avoided if the world had paid attention and had intervened at the right time. More than anything else, I wanted visitors, especially the young ones, the future leaders, to recognize that genocide was still occurring around the world, and that we all had a responsibility in trying to prevent it. "Never again" was not to remain an empty slogan.

As I repeated my own story in the Museum, I became aware of how fragile memory is. I found that my story was influenced by new knowledge that I had not considered. Expectations of listeners and questions often shaped how I presented my narrative. My understanding of memory keeps evolving. I realize that the more often I repeat my story, the more it is subject to the group to which I am speaking. I was recently invited to speak to a group of students in Puerto Rico who had studied the Holocaust from the point of view of Jehovah's Witnesses, a severely persecuted group by the Nazis in World War II. I was greatly impressed by their questions, which tried to probe how persons became rescuers. They wanted to know what personal qualifications were needed for a person to resist the Nazis and remain true to his or her own ethical convictions. It is a question that I reflect on frequently when I tour groups through the Holocaust Museum. I have no answers beyond that of the historians, who are still debating the question. Fortunately, in my own experience I found helpers who were not threatened with arrest or death for helping me. However, I am thrilled that my own experience elicits this kind of incisive question. It strengthens my resolve to use my memories as tools to alert the public to the lessons of the Holocaust.

In reflecting on my experiences, I started to consider the wartime experiences of my family. I often talked about the past with my mother after she came to live with us at age 80. We also talked about the past with my three brothers when they came to visit. My immediate family, three brothers and my mother, had been able to leave Czechoslovakia before Hitler's onslaught. We survived World War II in different parts of the world: my eldest brother Paul in Australia, Felix in the United States and then Spain, and Bruno in Canada. Each one of us had a different survival story. Each one of us had a personal memory that was surprisingly different from what we thought we knew about each other. Secondhand memory is another kind of memory that is unreliable. Sometimes, it seems as real as if you had lived it. Although my brothers and I were well adjusted in our new surroundings, the past always mingled with the present, and we never examined what it meant for each of us to have been uprooted and transplanted. Somehow, we did not dwell on our memories and instead emphasized the present and the future.

When I was asked to write about my wartime memories, I was perplexed. Should I mention my arrival in Paris, alone at the age of 16? The bicycle ride out of Paris before the advancing German Army? Accidentally finding my mother when I had no idea where she was imprisoned? Being led by police into a medieval Spanish building that turned out to be a jail? Or arriving in America in 1941—in the land of the free?

I finally turned to a half hour after midnight in Paris on June 13, 1940, when I expected to be arrested for violating the curfew but instead lost my virginity. As you continue reading you will understand how this brief encounter made a crucial difference in my life. I felt entitled to take my life in my own hands.

Let me set the stage.

I was born in 1922 into a wealthy Jewish family in Innsbruck, Austria, the fourth child and only girl. When I was a baby, my family moved to Prague, where I lived until 1938. In March 1938, Hitler annexed Austria. Believing that Hitler was serious when he said he would annihilate all Jews in Europe and aware of the persecution of Jews in Germany, my mother thought it would be wise for me, an Austrian citizen, to leave Prague and go to Paris, where she thought I would be safe. I was to live with a suburban French family that took in paying guests. I was to spend the first few months perfecting my French and in the fall enlist in a dressmaking school. Since no one knew what the future held for us, and since in Germany most Jews had been deprived of all their assets, it seemed wise to assume that we would lose all our money. In that case, I should learn a trade with which I could make a living anywhere, whether or not I knew the language of the land. Remember that in 1938 ready-to-wear apparel was almost nonexistent; dresses were made by dressmakers, and dressmaking was a respected and profitable profession. I had been an expert maker of doll dresses for a number of years. The idea appealed to me. I was pleased to leave school in the middle of 10th grade. I was a very good student because I knew how to take tests, but I was by no means an interested student. I was more interested in the opposite sex, who did not seem very interested in me. Thus, at age 16 I flew by myself from Prague to Paris. Flying was very glamorous then. In the nonpressurized plane, the pain in my ears was so intense that I could hardly greet the host family who came to pick me up.

Impoverished aristocrats, my French hosts lived in a suburb of Paris in a rundown château, surrounded by a moat that must have been impressive in former times. The teenage children of the house were friendly and tried to make me feel welcome and at home. Their mother, who had been a French teacher, suggested I study with her 3 hours every morning and then do 2 hours of homework by myself. I agreed. As a result, in 3 months I learned enough French to speak it without a recognizable foreign accent. We got along well, but relations were formal. As a matter of fact, I did not have a single good friend for many years to come after leaving Prague. If I was homesick, I do not remember. I was very busy because I also attended courses in French civilization at the Sorbonne. I was an enthusiastic learner, and that enthusiasm eclipsed any feeling of loneliness I might have experienced. I did not miss the protected environment of Prague. It never occurred to me that I would not be back in a few years. After a few months, a newcomer arrived. Sophie Freud, the granddaughter of Sigmund Freud, came to the château. She was a few years younger than I, and I felt quite protective. We used to cut out paper dolls together. We are close friends now.

Meanwhile, the political situation in Europe worsened for the Jews. Every day, new restrictions appeared in Austria, now part of the Reich. In France, there was palpable fear that there would be a war for which France was not prepared. Nevertheless, my life continued without major worries. Mother and I exchanged weekly letters; telephoning was very expensive and often not possible: no cell phones, no texting, no e-mails.

At the beginning of the summer, Mother came to visit me to help me select a dressmaking school and a place to live in the city so that I would not have to commute. She left Prague during a time of great upset. The German-speaking regions of Czechoslovakia were agitating for annexation to Germany, which the Czech government adamantly opposed. The situation was very tense. In addition, in Austria, any Jew who had the opportunity was trying to emigrate. Jews in Austria were leaving in droves. Although Mother had contemplated emigrating, she still believed that Czechoslovakia, a democratic country, would shield all its citizens. When she came to Paris in August 1938, she had left everything behind, just as if she had gone on vacation.

A few weeks after her arrival, Hitler ended the stalemate by invading the German-speaking Sudeten border regions. When the Czechoslovak government objected, Hitler threatened war. But before going to war, he invited the French and British prime ministers to a meeting in Munich. There, he persuaded the French and the British to accept the takeover, promising that he had no further territorial ambitions. Without consulting the Czechoslovak government, France and Great Britain signed the Munich agreement on September 30, 1938, abandoning Czechoslovakia to the Nazis. Neither the British nor the French were willing to go to war for an obscure bit of borderland that nobody could even find on the map.

It now seemed certain that Mother would have to return to Prague, close down her apartment, and prepare for emigration. Where to? How? There were no solutions in sight. At that time, brother Paul was in India, sent there on assignment by a large Czech munitions factory, Felix had already gone to the United States, and Bruno was still in Prague, certain that the crisis would blow over.

I started dressmaking school in Paris in September. I found room and board with a distinguished, impoverished elderly French lady who was happy to increase her income. Instead of going back to Prague, Mother went to the south of France to be with her brother, my uncle Robert, where life was cheaper than in Paris. She procrastinated because the idea of returning to Prague and preparing for emigration to who-knows-where seemed too overwhelming. She did eventually return to Prague in late 1938.

At my landlady's, I met Jean Pierre, her grandson. He seemed interested in me although he was 11 years older than I. He was very handsome, and I was quite flattered by his attentions. We used to go walking hand in hand along the Seine, and although we talked about the threatening political situation, I was only focusing on how good it felt to be with him. I did not dare think that I could be in love with him.

As an Austrian citizen, I was very much aware of my inferior status in France. I was considered an enemy alien who had to go to the *prefecture de police* once a week to prove that I had not escaped or done anything forbidden. There, I was kept waiting for long hours until my number was called. The officials made sure that I understood that I, as a refugee, was inferior and unwanted. These visits eroded my self-esteem. When I first arrived from Prague, I did not have any feelings of inferiority. I was proud that I had come to Paris by myself and that my mother had enough confidence in me to send me into the big wide world alone. I felt good about learning French so quickly.

However, I was not so sure about my standing vis-à-vis the other sex. My brother Bruno had always said that no man would ever look at a girl with such an ugly nose as mine. I believed him. Yet, shortly before my departure from Prague, I had met Karel, one of Bruno's friends. I had a real crush on him, and he liked me. His caring helped diffuse some of my insecurities. Until that time, my experiences with boys were very limited. Karel and I spent a lot of time necking in the movies; he was several years older than I and had been to the Soviet Union, which he admired. When we didn't neck, he explained the advantages of communism to me. I was easy prey. Of course, I was upset to leave Karel, but I agreed that it was in my best interest to leave Prague. I was sure I would return soon.

So now I was in Paris, infatuated with Jean Pierre. My feelings for Jean Pierre added to the confusion in which I was living. Mother was in Prague, preparing to ship her belongings abroad. Bruno was in Prague still refusing to believe that Czechoslovakia was vulnerable. They were totally unprepared when, on March 15, 1939—6 months after Hitler had promised that he had no further territorial ambition—the Nazis invaded all of Czechoslovakia. Again, the West stood by and let the Germans annex Czechoslovakia without a fight.

With courage and ingenuity, Mother and Bruno were able to leave Prague immediately after the German occupation. They had one suitcase each, leaving everything behind. With my Uncle Robert's help, Bruno was able to enter England the last day before the borders were closed. Mother had a French return visa, which enabled her to come to Paris. With all means of communication disrupted, I had no news and no idea whether or how she would come. I went to the train station every day to meet the Prague express train. There I waited until all the passengers had come and gone. She had not arrived. Dejected, I went home fearing that mother had not been permitted to leave. I thought I would never see her again. She finally arrived a few days later. The waiting and the uncertainty were a most unsettling experience for me.

I have no idea how much money Mother was able to take along, certainly not much because the banks were closed almost at once after the occupation began. The days of waiting and fear had been so intense that once Mother arrived I dealt with being upset by denying it. I just could not deal with the fear and the uncertainty. I continued dressmaking school, I saw Jean Pierre once a week, and life seemed to assume a certain familiar routine. With me well looked after by the old lady's crotchety housekeeper, Mother went back to the south of France. In August 1939, Mother and I were returning from a short vacation in the French Alps when the bus on which we were traveling suddenly stopped midway. Terrible confusion ensued. What was happening? Eventually, we were told that war had broken out. Germany had invaded Poland and France, and Great Britain had declared war on Germany. We barely managed to get back to Paris. The question of "What now?" was no longer rhetorical. The French did not want us there, but nobody else wanted us either. The world had closed its doors to Jewish refugees.

Uncle Robert, a British citizen, left immediately for the United States. Without him, we felt completely abandoned. I was envious: He could travel freely, whereas we were trapped without any prospect for escape. Back in Paris, we found a sublet in a very elegant district in Paris. It was a mansard apartment of an American painter who had returned to America when war broke out. He was willing to let us rent the apartment provided we would keep Maria, his trusted housekeeper.

In the eyes of the French, with our now-invalid Austrian passports, we were even less welcome than before. Mother and I were in a peculiar situation in Paris. Most of our friends were Czechs. The Czechs were considered friendly aliens—the French had a bad conscience because they had not honored their mutual assistance treaty with Czechoslovakia and had abandoned the country in the moment of greatest need. Mother and I felt completely isolated. The only people we knew who shared our fate were Sophie Freud and her mother, Esti. The entire Freud family had gone to England from Austria, leaving Sophie and her mother to their own fate in France. Sophie's father, Martin, was not fond of his wife. For them and for us, entry into the United States was out of the question. The Austrian quota for immigration to the United States was oversubscribed for the next 10 years. There were endless discussions about the best course of action, but we never reached a decision. We did not have many options, and we had no money. We were in touch with my brothers, hoping they could help. They could not.

As the war progressed, Mother's permission to live in Paris was revoked: She had to go live in a neighboring community, a move by the chaotic French government ostensibly to rid Paris of potential spies. She found a room in nearby Versailles, where she established legal residence. Trying to approximate a normal life, she came to Paris by train every morning and returned to Versailles every night. I came home from school every day so that we could at least have lunch together.

Although France was now at war, there were not many actual signs of warfare, except for propaganda posters and war broadcasts. Germany was fighting on the eastern front, and Paris was lulled into a kind of stupor. The press dubbed the situation *drole de guerre*, the strange war. So I, too, settled in and continued my dressmaking course. I also started taking art classes. A dress designer needed to be able to sketch.

My outings with Jean Pierre were the highlights of my life. Our weekly walks became a peaceful oasis in the dangerous turmoil in which we were living. At the same time, they left me confused. He was very respectful and hardly ever touched me. Of course, I really did not know what normal courting behavior was. I grew up in a world where sex was taboo. Many years later, when I confronted Mother, she said it was a husband's job to initiate his wife in the world of sex, and that she would have never considered talking to me about it. At the time, there were no magazines or books that I knew of that could have enlightened me. I probably would have been too embarrassed to look at them if I had found any. Interested though I was in my sexuality, I accepted my ignorance. I had no close friends in Paris with whom I could discuss my anxieties. Again many years later, after my relationship with Jean Pierre resumed after the war, he told me that he had been very much in love with me, but that he did not dare corrupt a minor. So, he limited our togetherness to hugging and kissing on isolated benches on the quays of the Seine.

I lived in a state of suspension: I knew that the situation was extremely dangerous, yet I was able to deny the reality and live as normally as possible. I read *Gone With the Wind* during that period (*Autant En Emporte le Vent* in French). I was fascinated by Scarlett and her love affairs. I knew nothing about the United States at that time, I had never heard of the Civil War, and I only remembered the emotions described in the book; the war part escaped me. This book was my first introduction to the United States, which would eventually become my home.

And then in the spring of 1940, the real war started. Germany had now achieved all of its goals in the east and was ready to attack the west. The German army bypassed the supposedly impenetrable Maginot Line and attacked France through Belgium and Holland. Jean Pierre cancelled one of our outings and told me that he had been called up to join his regiment. I was crestfallen. It seemed that my last beacon of support would evaporate. I accompanied him in a taxi to the railroad station. In the cab, he held me and sang a lilting love song that I have never forgotten. We said a heart-rending good-bye, certain we would never see each other again.

I never talked to Mother about Jean Pierre. I was not sure whether it was proper to be so smitten by him or whether I was being promiscuous after having just left Karel in Prague a few months earlier. How could I reconcile my very strong feelings for him with my equally strong apprehensions of what was proper behavior for a young woman of my station? A few weeks later, I heard from Bruno that Karel had been a member of the underground. He was captured by the Nazis and shot on the spot. When I heard this news, an unforgettable sense of despair engulfed me. But again, my coping behavior was to deny it to myself. It could not possibly be true; it must have been a rumor.

A few days after Jean Pierre left—after I kept hearing the lilting love song from the taxi ride in my mind's ear at the most improbable moments—Mother found a notice from the police in her room in Versailles ordering her to report to a certain assembly point in 3 days. She was told to bring whatever belongings she could carry, a blanket, and enough food for 3 days. She was going to be jailed and evacuated to the south. Of course, she was going to comply with the order; it never occurred to either of us that she could go into hiding.

Intent on leaving me with as many resources as possible, Mother came to Paris the day before she had to report to the police and gave me 10,000 francs. I had no idea from where she had that much money. It was enough to last for several months. She also gave me the address of a Monsieur Weil. I had never heard the name of Monsieur Weil before. Mother had apparently gotten the name from German friends who left Paris to return to their home in Spain when the shooting war in the west started. These friends had promised to help us get into Spain and reassured us that they would try to help us from Spain.

The last thing mother said before leaving was that it was now up to me to get us out of there. I have never found out what she meant by this remark. These events happened so quickly that I hardly comprehended what was going on. Too stunned to be frightened, I had no idea where she would be taken or how to contact her. Now, it was clearly up to me to find a way to get out of France.

My own situation rapidly grew more frightening. I was now supposed to go to the police every day to prove that I had not escaped. Because they were unable to stem the advance of the German army, the French authorities increased their monitoring of aliens. The police categorically denied my request for permission to leave Paris. They threatened me with detention if I ever tried to leave without permission. The French authorities could not have been more belligerent.

In the first days of June, the war came closer, and the noises of the guns became louder. The fires created by burned documents in the courtyards of the French government offices created a haze over the sky of Paris. The war was now here, and for the first time I realized that I was personally in danger. With Mother gone, I felt totally abandoned. I heard from Sophie and her mother that they were going to try to get to Brest in Brittany and from there find a way to England, where the rest of the Freud family was. I decided to join them.

I finally went to see Monsieur Weil. He promised to get me a travel permit if I came back the next day. In the meantime, not waiting for Monsieur Weil, I went to the railroad station to try to obtain a ticket to Brest in case the police relented. The train station was closed. There were big signs: "No more trains until the end of hostilities." Paris was completely blacked out, and the streets were deserted. The eerie silence and the lack of activity were frightening. I was scared, and I felt caught. In sleepless nights, I imagined one scenario more frightening than the other, always ending up alone, stranded somewhere, with nobody ever hearing of me again. I was not sure whom I should fear more: the advancing Germans or the hostile French.

On June 14, Italy joined Germany and declared war on France. It was a warm summer evening, the city was blacked out, the Metro was running until midnight, and there was a midnight curfew. In great agitation, I went back to Monsieur Weil. The room was crowded with others who apparently had come for his advice and help. When he saw me, he strode across the room, put his arms around my shoulder and said that he had not been able to get me any permit to leave. He simply could not help me or find out where Mother was kept or get her released. I should not come back.

In the crowded room, I noticed a handsome lieutenant who turned out to be Monsieur Weil's son, Albertito. His mother was from Argentina. In uniform, he was on his way to the train station to rejoin his regiment. Despite my anxiety, I noticed that he was tall, dark haired, dark complexioned, and dashing in his neatly pressed officer's uniform. As I was leaving, feeling totally dejected, with all hope lost, he offered to accompany me home.

We waited for the Metro. I was impatient because it was getting late. I was afraid I would not be at home before the midnight curfew. In the almost-empty train, Albertito sat next to me on the bench and started embracing me. His arms felt good. He asked me in a sort of muffled voice: *"Tu veux faire l'amour?"* ("Do you want to make love?") I did not understand what he meant, but body language must have seemed positive.

When we left the station, the large and normally bustling Place de la Concorde was completely deserted. We had to cross the entire square to get to my street. As I had feared, a gendarme approached us and asked for identity papers. I thought this was it: I would now be arrested. When my escort showed the gendarme his officer's orders and winked, saying: "And this lady is my friend!" the gendarme understood and went away. The relief and gratitude that I felt were overwhelming.

When we reached my building, Albertito said he wanted to come up. Because in Paris at that time no one had a house key, I had to ring the bell for the concierge. She would peek out of her window and buzz the door open. I knew it was totally improper for me to come home at that hour of the night with a strange man. I knew I could explain if anybody asked. Luckily, nobody asked.

Upstairs, in my apartment, we were alone. Maria, like all housekeepers, slept on the floor above in the maids' room. I was keenly aware of how unseemly it was to be with this young man by myself at this late hour. To overcome my embarrassment, I offered to make him tea. But before I had time to put the water on the stove, he embraced me and led me to the bedroom. I was startled but did not resist. I was not sure what was happening until I realized later that I had just lost my virginity. He kept saying: "Why didn't you tell me that you were a virgin?" I had no idea how to respond.

After a few moments, I became totally lucid. I was overwhelmed by shame. How could this have happened? I had felt protected and safe in this stranger's arms, but the elation that I thought I was supposed to feel eluded me.

After I regained my composure, I asked him to leave at once. He was stunned. I did not care that it was 2 in the morning, that his troop train would not depart until 6 a.m., and there was no Metro and the buses were no longer running; I knew he would be out on the street during curfew, but I felt no pity for him. I was not angry at him, only confused. I never saw or heard from him again. I have often wondered what he must have thought about my behavior. I also agonized over how he spent 4 hours on the street, but at the time I really did not care.

Unbelievably, at age 18, I did not know the facts of life! Although I did not fully understand what sexual intercourse was, the impact of this short encounter was profound. I suddenly felt that my situation had changed; I was no longer this "proper" young lady who had obeyed all the restrictions of middle-class society. I was now a woman. Unsure of the meaning of this sudden and so unexpected transformation, it liberated me. Unburdened by conventions that I did not believe in but had taken for granted, I now felt capable of battling with the French police and, above all, escaping from the Germans. In the early morning, I went to the police to get permission to leave. The police station was open but empty. The gendarmes had joined the crowds fleeing before the advancing Germans. I was going to leave without permission.

The streets were now filled with moving humanity. People were pushing baby carriages, loaded with belongings, some with a canary cage on top. Others had overloaded wheelbarrows. The mass of cars was all going in the same direction—south—and the roads were completely clogged. People who did not know how to drive tried anyway, with disastrous results. Others ran out of gas in the middle of the road and contributed to the monumental traffic jam.

Hurrying home, I found Maria in the kitchen. I told her that I was leaving Paris by myself. She looked at me incredulously but did not comment. I was not about to tell her what had happened during the night and what had prompted me to take my fate into my own hands. I explained that I wanted to buy a bicycle so that I would not have to join the crowds who were streaming out of Paris on foot. I was hoping to meet the Freuds in Brittany.

Maria went with me in search of a bicycle. We could not find one any-where. Either shops were closed or they were out of bicycles. Finally, quite far from our house, we spotted a bicycle store that seemed open. The store had only one men's racing bike that was reserved for someone. I was des-perate enough to want the bike, unsuitable as it was. Maria was able to con-vince the store to sell it to me. With part of the 10,000 francs that Mother had left me, I also bought an inexpensive watch and a map of France.

Anxious to leave as quickly as possible, I had taken a little case with me when we went in search of the bicycle. The case fit on the rear parcel carrier of the bike. I had a change of underwear, two *pains au chocolat* (chocolate rolls), and notes from my pattern-making course. For some unexplainable reason, I also took along my box of oil paints. As I prepared to go in search of a bike, I remember very clearly reminding myself that I was now a dif-ferent person. The taboos that governed a girl's behavior did not apply to me anymore. On one hand, I felt quite liberated; on the other, I was deeply ashamed of what I had done. How could I ever tell my mother what had transformed me—or anybody else for that matter. The truth is that I never did tell anybody. Only when I started writing my autobiography, 63 years later, was I finally able to describe this incident in my book.

To summarize the rest of my journey quickly, I rode my bicycle for 2 days until I found a train that I thought would take me to Brest, as I had intended. I had no idea where Mother was, although I had received a notice that she was in a concentration camp near the Spanish border. Serendipitously, the train went southwest, and I ended up 10 miles from where Mother was interned. Miraculously, we found each other. With many more miracles and lucky coincidences, we managed to leave France, survive a Fascist jail in Spain, and wait for 9 months in Portugal until we were able to get a pre-viously unobtainable immigration visa to the United States.

Who knows what my life's trajectory would have been without that half hour after midnight on June 13, 1940? As I now contemplate how events of the past continue to inform the present, I marvel at how clearly some events have remained etched in my consciousness and how they foreshadowed the essence of my life: an independent woman, a risk taker, and a survivor who learned from wartime experiences to trust herself sufficiently to live life fully.

I am now 89 years old. I am thrilled that I am able to interact with visi-tors in the U.S. Holocaust Memorial Museum in Washington, D.C., either as a guide or as a speaker. It almost feels as though I had acquired a new persona: the survivor. I am frequently asked to speak to special groups, judges, foreign journalists, social workers, university professors, about my own experiences. When I am a guide, the universal comment from the visi-tors is: "What a difference it makes to see this Museum with a survivor as a guide. It makes the whole experience unforgettable." When I am a speaker, I can almost feel the palpable emotions engendered in the listener by hearing a story firsthand rather than reading it. These reactions emphasize the power of witnessing and make it worthwhile for me to get out of bed early to meet groups and to repeat my story again and again. When sharing memorable moments leads to increased understanding and active involvement by the public, I feel that I am making a valuable contribution to make "never again" more than a hollow slogan.

REFERENCE

Meissner, M. (2003). *Margit's story: An autobiography*. Rockville, MD: Schreiber Publishing Company.

Chapter 13

The *Defiant Requiem*
Acts of Witnessing

Marilyn B. Meyers

INTRODUCTION

We will sing to the Nazis what we cannot say to them.[1]

In the fall of 1941, the Germans turned the town of Terezín (60 kilometers outside Prague, Czechoslovakia) into a ghetto for Jews and renamed it Theresienstadt, as it had been originally called. The orders for the deportations to the ghetto were issued directly from *SS-Obersturmbannführer* Adolf Eichmann.

The Jews who were sent to the ghetto included many prominent artists and musicians. The prisoners were housed in barracks, where they were crowded into three rows of triple-decker wooden beds. The living conditions were extreme: A single toilet room with several commodes was shared by 300 to 400 people, food was scarce, starvation and disease were rampant. The highest number of prisoners at any one time was 58,497; the final death toll in Terezín was 33,419. Of the 140,000 inmates in Theresienstadt, there were 17,000 children, most of whom did not survive.

The presence of the many distinguished artists, scholars, composers, poets, intellectuals, and writers led to a unique atmosphere within the ghetto. The creative efforts and gifts of the people in the ghetto served as powerful forms of witnessing and kept spirits alive in the context of inhuman conditions of starvation, death, disease, and threats of annihilation. It was a surreal combination of death and creativity. The historian of Terezín, Joza Karas (1985), has said, "Where there was not food for the body there was food for the soul." Norbert Fryd said, "If Terezín was not hell itself, like Auschwitz, it was the anteroom to hell. ... Culture was still possible, and for many this frenetic clinging to an almost hypertrophy of culture was the final assurance. We are human beings and we remain human beings ... despite everything" (http://www.Lexhamarts.org/theater/200906/backgroundinfo.htm).

---

[1] As reportedly said by Rafael Schaechter in Terezín.

There were numerous performances of opera, theater, orchestral music, choral music, chamber music, jazz, and cabaret. The musicians and composers who were deported to Terezín quickly came together to present music to the people in the ghetto. Concert programs were created, announcing the works to be performed; tickets were printed, and reviews were written. In a review of Dvorak's *Serenade*, conducted by Karel Ancerl, Viktor Ullmann wrote, "Anton Dvorak's famous *Serenade* took ... the hearts of the listeners by storm. ... The technically easier and joyful work suits our orchestra, and in its rendition was at its best" (Karas, 1985, p. 67). Edgar Krasa, in an interview discussed further in this chapter, reported:

> Many of the composers were deported from Terezín to extinguish the "degenerate" music, and the painters were deported for having some real life drawings smuggled out. They all had jobs during the day. Some worked in the technical bureau making blueprints for the infrastructure of Terezín ... and at night they were drawing real life stories, the hearse carrying all the dead bodies in the morning, taking them to the morgue, and on the way back the kids were pushing the hearse loaded up with bread because on the return as they went by the bakery and loaded up the bread without disinfection right onto the same hearse.

In April 2006, I went to Prague to hear a performance of the Verdi *Requiem* in the Terezín Ghetto; the last time the *Requiem* had been performed in Terezín was in 1944. In this chapter, I show the power of witnessing as it affected me and all those involved in this experience. I write about the rediscovery of Verdi's *Requiem* and my witnessing the performance of it in the Terezín Ghetto, where it had been previously performed under the direction of the conductor Rafael Schaechter during the horrors of the Nazi regime. The story of the rediscovery of the performances of the Verdi *Requiem* in the ghetto and its homecoming to Terezín captures the essence of the vitality and creativity in the midst of unspeakable terror addressed in this book. The people in Terezín were determined to maintain their sense of self and aliveness despite their ordeal. There were daily threats of deportation, along with constant brutal conditions. My witnessing the performance of the *Requiem* and meeting Edgar and Hana Krasa left an indelible mark on me. They bore witness to their own experiences and continue to do so today. Through them, I was witness to what had happened, to what was being revisited and to their story.

PERFORMING VERDI'S *REQUIEM* IN TEREZÍN: DEFIANT WITNESSING

Among the creative artists transported to Terezín was the pianist and conductor Rafael Schaechter. In July 1943, he organized a chorus of 150 Jews to perform Verdi's *Requiem* (Mass for the Dead) in Terezín. He became obsessed with the performances of this music despite the fact that deportations to Auschwitz drastically depleted the chorus many times. Schaechter possessed one copy of the Verdi score and, of course, no orchestra; he had access to a single legless upright piano. One survivor described Schaechter as a "crazed man on a mission." The fact that he chose the Verdi *Requiem* was challenged and greatly disputed within the ghetto. The Catholic liturgical music led some of the members of the Council of Jewish Elders to feel that it might be viewed as an apology for being Jewish. The arguments were intense, but Schaechter insisted that, "We will sing to them what we cannot say to them." In his mind, Schaechter transformed the Mass for the Dead into a Mass for the Dead Nazis (as told by Schaechter to Edgar Krasa, with whom he shared an attic room in Terezín). The head of the council, Rabbi Jakob Edelstein, reportedly said to Schaechter, "If the Nazis find out that you are interested in this, it will create controversy in the camp, and the way the Nazis will resolve the controversy will be to shoot you, deport your chorus, and stop all free-time activity." Despite these dire predictions, the members of the chorus chose to remain and sing the *Requiem* 16 times. In 1945, Schaechter was transported to Auschwitz, where he was killed in the gas chambers.

The text of the Requiem includes the following:

Liber scriptus:
A written book will be brought forth,
In which everything is contained,
For which the world shall be judged.
And so when the Judge takes his seat,
And whatever is hidden shall be made manifest,
Nothing shall remain unavenged.

These words speak to the intent of the performances by the Jews of this monumental work in the Theresienstadt Ghetto: "We will sing what we cannot say."

Rediscovery of the *Requiem*

Murry Sidlin, a conductor and former dean of the Rome School of Music at Catholic University in Washington, D.C., discovered a book, *Music at Terezin* (Karas, 1985), while working in Minneapolis, Minnesota. In that book, he saw the words "Rafael Schaecter, choral conductor, opera coach, pianist, piano teacher … organized performances of the Verdi *Requiem* in the camp." This discovery led Sidlin to go on a quest to find survivors who had sung in the chorus at Terezín. Among those he contacted was Edgar Krasa. Edgar not only had sung in the performance, he also had lived with Rafael Schaechter in the ghetto. When Sidlin called Edgar and asked if the name Rafael Schaechter meant anything to him, Edgar replied: "My son is named Rafael—does that tell you that you have the right guy?" Subsequently, Sidlin created the concert drama titled the *Defiant Requiem*. The premier performance was held in Portland, Oregon, in April 2003. Since then, the *Defiant Requiem* concert drama has been performed a dozen times at other venues. Among these performances was one in the fall of 2010 at the Kennedy Center in Washington, D.C., as well as a performance in the massive train station in Budapest.

The Homecoming in 2006

In May 2006, the *Defiant Requiem* was performed in Terezín for the first time since June 1944. The performance was held in stables that dated back to the 1700s. The building had fallen into disrepair and was cleaned up in preparation for the performance. The concert drama consists of the entire Verdi *Requiem* performed by chorus, orchestra, and soloists; portions of the infamous Nazi propaganda film showing the ruse for the benefit of the International Red Cross; filmed testimony given by survivors (Edgar and others); and three actors portraying key figures in the ghetto. One of these portrayals is of Schaechter. The performance concludes with the chorus and orchestra soundlessly leaving the stage. Film of the freight trains taking prisoners to be deported to Auschwitz plays on the large screen behind them while a solo violinist plays the mournful Oseh Shalom—music drawn from the Kaddish prayer for the dead: "May he who makes peace on high make peace for us below." Many of the prisoners, both in Terezín and other camps, sang that song as they were led to the gas chambers in various concentration camps.

Present at this event in 2006 were several survivors who had sung in the performances at Terezín. Murry Sidlin had been told by the survivors that thousands of Jews were able to maintain their sanity in the midst of the insanity of life in Terezín because of these performances.

Edgar Krasa, a man of immense vitality in his 80s, was there in the front row with his wife, Hana, also a survivor of Terezín. Their sons, Daniel and Rafael, were there to sing in the chorus. Their grandchildren were sitting in the audience with them. In my mind, this brought the witnessing to a profound depth of emotion. I felt it in my body. There was a palpable anticipation and anxiety as the performance was about to begin.

The quality of light in the space was strangely mysterious. It had a high vaulted ceiling in which the light that came through the windows was absorbed. Pigeons flew in and out of a window behind the chorus. The singers assembled silently. The sound of their shoes on the wooden planks erected for the chorus echoed in this vast building; this was the only sound before the performance began. Members of the audience greeted each other in whispers, aware of the solemn mood. This was unlike any musical performance I had ever witnessed or heard before. It went beyond music—the music came from a place deep inside the performers and resonated in the audience profoundly. The depth of feeling, the vitality, defiance, and desperation of the prisoners and survivors was communicated bodily.

After the performance, one member of the audience wrote:

> I listened to the *Requiem* with desperation, as though I never heard music before. What a rejuvenating and hopeful experience it was. I can't clearly describe the actual physical effect it had on us. People have asked me so often, how did the chorus sound? But I can only respond with words about what the music meant to me. I don't think I can describe the sound of the chorus. I just know that I listened and heard desperately. It's not as though they weren't singing, of course they were, but what I heard was the music coming from them; the music, not just the sounds of the music, but a clear, enveloping of all that this music was created to mean! I achieved a relationship with music I never knew as possible. For the first time in my life—maybe the only time—I listened with the same focus and intensity with which I would have run to grab a piece of bread that someone had dropped. But this music was not merely nourishing, but consuming. Listening was not the normal and usual option, but no option, an absolute necessity.

In a conversation with Edith Steiner-Kraus, then in her 90s, Sidlin asked: "How would you describe the quality of the chorus?" She responded curtly:

> The superficial nature of your question troubles me terribly—as if any of that mattered. We had returned to the source of the music. ... We were at Verdi's table. ... You'll never understand or get close, to what music truly meant to each of us as a sustaining power ... beyond any superficial evaluation—we were music.

EDGAR AND HANA KRASA: WITNESSING AND PREVAILING[1]

What follows are portions of the conversations Nancy Goodman and I had with Edgar and Hana Krasa. I see them as symbolizing much of what we

[1] We are deeply grateful to Edgar and Hana Krasa for their generosity in allowing us to spend many hours sharing their memories and providing detailed editing. They also permitted us to photograph the works of art they have in their home. Alan Meyers took the pictures with great care. Bruce Zimmerman helped enormously in cropping and improving the photographs for publication. Kathy Quackenbush transcribed the tapes with patience and sensitivity. When we approached Edgar and Hana with the idea of interviewing them for the book, we had no idea that we were forging a friendship with two amazing people who, in their lives, testify to the strength of the human spirit.

emphasize in this book. They are witnesses to their own experiences; they keep the memories alive and are full of vitality. They keep acts of witnessing and their meaning intact. The trauma is neither denied nor does it rule their lives. They are determined to remember and bear witness without remaining frozen in the past. Their children and grandchildren keep the stories in their minds as well.

Edgar performed in all 16 performances of the *Requiem* in Terezín and had lived with Schaechter in the ghetto. He was a cook in the camp. Hana survived Terezín, largely by working in the fields and thus having a somewhat reliable source of food. She told us that she owed her survival to the fact that her supervisor in the fields, a German civilian, did not permit any of his workers to join their families as they were deported. Her parents died in Auschwitz.

Although we were essentially strangers, we were greeted warmly by them. Their home was filled with family pictures—parents, children, grandchildren. One room in the house is reserved almost exclusively for artwork from Terezín and other memorabilia from that time. It is a room that stands as a symbolic representation of the deprivation and terror as well as the creativity and resilience of their lives. There are bookshelves filled with books about Terezín—some quite old and rare. (We include here photographs of some of the artwork and commentary by Edgar and Hana; see Plates 7–12.) Immediately adjacent to the living room is the dining room. The table was set for the four of us on our arrival. Nancy and I were hungry and had brought some meager food both for ourselves and our host and hostess. We quickly realized that we need not worry about being fed. Edgar invited us into the kitchen, which was abuzz with activity. In fact, the entire time that we were with them, we ate. Edgar had been a cook, both in Prague and in Terezín and elsewhere after the war—Israel, Switzerland, and Tanganyika. Edgar speaks German and Czech, both of which he learned in school; he learned Yiddish from Polish prisoners in Auschwitz, Russian from Russian soldiers at liberation, Italian and French while working in Switzerland, Romanian and Arabic while working in Israeli hotels, and Swahili while teaching cooking in Tanganyika. Our meal began with homemade hummus (a "secret recipe"), followed by cauliflower soup, omelets, bread, salad, and homemade cranberry nut cake. We felt completely at home, as if we were family. We talked as we ate, pretty much nonstop. Our eating together served as both a backdrop and a diversion. It was notable that in listening to the recordings and reading the transcript afterward, serving, eating, and commenting on food distracted us and provided some relief from the trauma in the conversation.

We began by explaining why we were there:

NANCY: Marilyn and I have this long-standing determination to remember the Holocaust and to help people talk about it. ... We are working out this idea of demonstrating the power of witnessing ... to highlight the idea that being a witness, whether it's through testimony or artwork or speaking at schools, this act of giving testimony and being a witness to this unspeakable horror. ... We want to articulate more about what it means to be a witness. And so we thought, let's start talking to people. ... We want to hear your story ... but we also want you to reflect on what it has meant to you to reveal your story over time. ... The returning to Terezín for the enactment of the *Requiem* is such a remarkable occurrence, and we want to know what brought you to that, what that meant to you. ...

EDGAR: I never had time to think about it. ... I had to work. ... I came from Auschwitz with absolutely nothing.

MARILYN: You were in Auschwitz after Terezín?

EDGAR: Yes and my parents came with almost nothing back from Terezín, so I had to work. I had two jobs and then having been a cook there was not much to cook with in postwar Czechoslovakia. I lived in Switzerland for 2 years. ... I was determined not to live a second time under a dictatorship. ...

NANCY: How did you get the sense to be silent? What was it that let you know, don't talk about it?

HANA: People told us straightaway when we came back.

NANCY: They told you?

HANA: Straightaway when we came back. Don't talk about it.

NANCY: Who told you? Friends? Relatives?

HANA: Anybody. ... We didn't have any relatives left, but the people we met, the friends of my parents. They didn't even want to know what happened to our family. "Forget it, that happened, now it's a different time." It was the first thing we heard.

NANCY: So you would just talk to each other.

HANA: We wouldn't even talk to each other. ... In Czechoslovakia it was silent through the whole community.

Auschwitz: "Nothing Like That Is Possible"

HANA: Nobody had the idea that Auschwitz was a death camp, but even if there was something that was very bad, people were allowed to write postcards ... 30 words in 1 month, and a few people wrote from Auschwitz. ... They wrote, "I saw Uncle M"—this was a code. I saw Uncle M was code for being in the same concentration camp. The person writing the card knew that he had died in the concentration camp. ... They turned it backwards. The recipients thought that it meant that Uncle M was alive. Nobody wanted to believe.

EDGAR: They deceived beautifully. At one time they said we need a thousand men, age 18–50, who are going to build a labor camp, and with the next transport, they said to the wives of those men that they can volunteer to be with their husbands. ...

HANA: They never saw them again.

EDGAR: There was one guy who escaped from Auschwitz ... an SS man who had been his schoolmate gave this guy a uniform and took him out on a motorcycle. He came to Terezín. ... He told the Council of Elders about Auschwitz and they dismissed it because nothing like that is possible. ... They wouldn't let him talk about it. ... They didn't let him mention it to anyone else. ... There was a work detail group who was helping the people to disembark, those who came and loading them when they were deported. ... One of them told his friend who was deported in his wagon there is a loose frame on a small window at the top. Put under that frame the name of where you are going ... he put Auschwitz ... but it didn't mean anything because he put it there before he got off and found out what Auschwitz was ... just the name Auschwitz didn't help.

A Cruel Deception: The Red Cross "Visit"

On June 23, 1944, the International Red Cross came to Terezín to "inspect" the ghetto. The intent on the part of the Nazis was to demonstrate that Terezín was a "model" ghetto in order to quell rumors about the concentration camps. In advance of the visit, approximately 7,500 elderly and sick people were sent to the gas chambers in Auschwitz. Others who looked ill or emaciated were hidden from view. Young, well-dressed girls sang "happily," a soccer game was played in the newly constructed soccer field, and an orchestra played in a gazebo on the "town square." No detail was overlooked. The inspectors never asked a probing question and never looked beyond what they were shown. At the direct order of Josef Goebbels, the Nazis filmed the whole charade and titled the film *Der Fuehrer gab den Juden eine Stadt* (*The Leader Gave a Town to the Jews*). Portions of that film are included in the *Defiant Requiem* performance.

Hana and Edgar shared their memories of that day:

HANA: There was a bank opened on the street and there were two stores, a clothing store and a shoe store. Those were supplied from two sources, one when someone died in Terezín and didn't have family or the family didn't want the clothing or the shoes, or the Nazis went in for the purpose to send it to Germany for their people. ... When the transports arrived, the Germans came to welcome them and went through their luggage and confiscated from that little bit the better pieces of clothing and shoes, also to be sent to Germany. There was never any footage of the Red Cross visit without being staged.

MARILYN: Were you there when the Red Cross came?

HANA: Sure we were. We planted all the grass and flowers in the town square. There was never [laughing] there was never grass in Terezín until the summer of '44. We planted it; I worked in the field, so we had to plant the grass. And a gazebo for the music was built in the town square. When the visitors came some prisoners were promenading to the sound of the music. That was done in '44 and when the commission left, there was nothing. It was not used any more.

MARILYN: You knew what was going on when you were getting the grass?

HANA: We knew what it was, but we were told to stay in our rooms.

MARILYN: The Red Cross—they didn't think this was weird?

HANA: The Red Cross was not asking questions.

Edgar's Survival After Liberation

NANCY: You were in Terezín and then Auschwitz and then a labor camp?

HANA: Gleiwitz and Blechhammer.

NANCY: You were liberated from the labor camp?

EDGAR: After the Death march ... I was liberated in January by the Russians ... near Auschwitz in another labor camp. ... Those labor camps were subsidiaries of the mother camp. Auschwitz, Majdanek, Treblinka ... and they squeezed out the last piece of juice from you and then they gassed the unable body. We worked 6 days a week and on Sunday, they took us to the stone quarry, loaded us up with boulders, and we carried them to the other end of the quarry, and next Sunday we were bringing them back. ... I thought if they treated us better, we could produce more. But it wasn't the program. ... They had enough prisoners to replace us, when somebody's capacity diminished ... they were shipped back to Auschwitz and went up through the chimney.

HANA: They didn't consider us human, but they didn't see it.

EDGAR: You want more of the salad?

NANCY: It's good to have a break to think about food.

EDGAR: After 3 days of marching, suddenly we were free ... and on the third day I knew I couldn't continue. ... We were running because the Russians were coming near and we heard the artillery. I had these Dutch wooden clogs, no pleasure running in those. ... On the third night I slipped into the ditch next to the road face down. There was a zealous guard who shot me. But maybe because of the dark, the bullet went under my arm and got stuck in the rib, and the blood spread all over the snow, which was good because nobody attempted to make another shot. Such a big bloody puddle. When the column of Russians passed I ran into the forest and found other prisoners who had the same idea. Luckily they had not been shot. There was a camp doctor among us who operated on me in the camp. ... He was there in the woods ... and one of the benefits of being a doctor, he could keep a pocket knife ... and with the pocket knife and some snow to numb the area, in the dark, he couldn't see a thing, just with one hand he was touching and with the knife in the other hand he was taking out the bullet. ... In the morning we went to the edge of the forest. ... On the top of the hill was another camp. The gate was open, and prisoners walked out, and no guard in the watchtower. So yesterday I couldn't walk, but suddenly I could run toward the camp. ... The Russian soldiers came to eat with us because our food was better than what they were getting. One day they said to us there is a nearby pig farm and the pigs were screaming because no one was feeding them. ... I said we are going to get ourselves a pig. It wasn't kosher, but anyway we had a sled, we can transport a pig. So I found a small hammer ... and a piece of rope ... and we went there and tied one pig's hind leg to a column and hit it with that hammer, and nothing happened other than everything swelled up no matter how hard I hit it. I was too weak. Suddenly we hear machine gun fire outside. I said, "Oh my God the Germans are back." I look outside and there at the top of the road a Russian convoy was going and they were shooting the pigs and throwing them onto the trucks. So one saw me with the knife and they took me to eviscerate the pigs. So about 20 pigs I did for him, and after I finished I said now you can come with me and shoot my pig. He came and shot it. One of them didn't want the whole pig; he only wanted the hind legs, the ham. So we had a pig and a half and about 20 livers and kidneys and we were cooking till past midnight, rendering the lard and taking it apart. There was no problem with refrigeration because it was cold enough. ... The one who was helping me got a job in Israel on the Dead Sea as a cook, just what he learned in those 6 weeks.

The *Defiant Requiem* Performance in 2006

In this part of the interview, we asked Edgar and Hana to reflect on the experience of the performance in Terezín in 2006.

HANA: Our sons wanted to do the *Requiem*. We didn't ask them. We didn't even ask them to come with us to Prague.

EDGAR: They wanted to sing ... in the same place I sang 60 years ago.

At this point, their son Daniel arrives unexpectedly. We think, afterward, that perhaps he was checking up on us as he did not know who these strange women were who came to speak with his parents.

HANA: Somebody's knocking. I think it's Danny.

DANNY: Who are these ladies?

HANA: This lady [pointing to Marilyn] was in Terezín at the *Requiem* when you were singing and she remembers you.

NANCY: Was it the first time you sang in it?

DANNY: My only time.

MARILYN: What was it like for you?

DANNY: It had a lot of dimensions ... bringing the kids there. ... Our kids have been in Prague ... but I don't think they had been in Terezín before. ... It's in their genes. ... They hear about it a lot. My father's talked in their schools and things like that and here they were in the actual place. ... The first rehearsal was Friday night. ... We were all pretty jetlagged. ... During the rehearsal there was a thunderstorm. ... Windows blew in, shutters were banging around. ...

EDGAR: Birds were flying in. ...

DANNY: And that was just before we were singing the song about the wrath of God ... and the singing was over quickly. It seemed that we came to the end really quickly ... and then the walking afterwards. ... It was difficult. ... We practiced that we would walk out and go to the railroad station.

EDGAR: Where people were deported from Terezín to Auschwitz.

DANNY: It wasn't planned to go there the way, we were to go out the door, take a right, take a left, and then go back ... but there was no place to stop, so we went all the way, and still singing Oseh Shalom, the song that's at the end of this. ...

EDGAR: Kaddish.

HANA: The prayer for the dead.

DANNY: So it was really eerie. ... Rafael and I led the whole thing out. ... It was really strange, walking all the way there.

HANA: And past the windows of my room ... where I lived in the barracks.

DANNY: I don't remember the singing so much anymore. ... The walking felt like I was part of the group going to the railroad tracks.

EDGAR: The first half Hana was pretty well together, but then she saw her two sons going to the place where she had accompanied her parents when they went to Auschwitz.

HANA: It was too much.

DANNY: Her window was right over that spot.

HANA: Well at that time I wasn't living there anymore, but it was before that. We watched them build the railroad. ... I was on the second floor. ...

DANNY: At some point you were in that window, in that room.

THE "TEREZÍN ANTHEM"

I would like to conclude with the words to the "Terezín Anthem," which was written in 1942 by Karel Svenk. It is a simple work for chorus and piano. The lyrics and the tempo progress from a somber mood, reflecting the harsh conditions in Terezín, then are followed by hopefulness. This song is often sung at reunions of survivors of the ghetto. I think that it captures the depth of the pain and the spirit of resilience in the face of such deprivation. Here is an excerpt from the song (Karas, 1985, p. 14):

Who is longing for the town on the Vltava (Moldau)
Who is not happy (satisfied) with turnips and coffee,
Whose soul gets around with a Czech song.
Who toils as a slave,
Everybody of this or that kind,
In short who does not like it here,
Will surely find a reason
To sing with us.
Days will come, days will go,
Always moving restless crowd,
We can't write with only thirty words allowed.
Wait for we will see a newer dawn
Must rise to lift the heart,
The time will come to pack our bags
And home we'll joyfully depart.
We will conquer and survive
All the cruelty in our land,
We will laugh on the ghetto ruins
Hand in hand!!

MEMORY AND HOPE FOR THE FUTURE

A 1991 performance in Terezín of the Czech opera *Brundibar*, which Hana attended with a group of friends who had been with her in Terezín, closed with the Czech national anthem, "Hatikva," and then the "Terezín Anthem."

HANA: I didn't know, hadn't heard or sang it or remembered the words since the 1940s, and this was in 1991. It all came back. We girls all started and we all, everybody that was at Terezín who survived was there singing the anthem. Next to me was a Czech woman who asked, "You were there?"

EDGAR: It was pretty defiant to sing the anthem in Terezín, but it was sung in Czech, so the possibility that the SS would understand was minimal ... "in the ruins."

HANA: "Holding our hands in the ruins of the ghetto, we will laugh."

EDGAR: "Dance!"

HANA: "And dance."

MARILYN: "Anything goes, with good will, we will join hands and at the ruins of the ghetto we will laugh."

HANA: "Tomorrow a new life is starting, and that is coming near the day we will be free again."

REFERENCE

Karas, J. (1985). *Music in Terezin, 1941–1945.* New York: Pendragon Press.

Chapter 14

One Thousand Days
in Auschwitz

Joseph Neumann and the Will to Live

Elaine Neuman Kulp Shabad

THE STORY OF JOSEPH NEUMANN

The last time my mother Boruska (Barbara Blau) saw her mother (Ilona Blau) was on November 4, 1938, in Michalovce, Czechoslovakia. I, my parents' only child, am named Elaine after my grandmother, Ilona. My mother, the oldest of eight children, reluctantly boarded a train toward an unknown and unwanted destination, America. She was 22 at the time. My mother separated from her mother and father, watching her mother holding her hand over her heart (something I have done all of my life). She never saw her mother, father, or seven younger brothers and sisters ever again. Ilona and Adolph (her father, my unknown grandfather), Helen Fucho Blau, Anna Blauova Blau, Sarolta Markovits, Zoltan Blau, Ruzena Blau, and Moritz Blau all perished in concentration camps. Ilona died in Buchenwald.

My father, Ervin Neuman, was the second oldest of 14 children. He left Snina, Czechoslovakia, at the age of 17 for America, where his older brother, Armin, worked in a lighting fixture store. My father left home to ease the financial burdens of his very large family. He never saw nine of his siblings again. They, like my mother's parents and siblings, were murdered in unknown ways in the Holocaust.

Three of my father's siblings survived Auschwitz. His younger brother, Joseph Neumann, was my father's hero, his guiding light and his source of strength. When speaking of Joe, my father often said: "You just don't know the horrors he went through."

It was hard for both of my parents to express and experience pure conscious joy and pleasure—too much survivor guilt. My father was self-denying and sacrificial. My mother was often like a lonely little girl, scared and confused and often unable to smile.

My husband, my sons, and some of my dearest friends have read the testimony that Joseph Neumann gave to a non-family member about 10 years before he died. I have not been able to take more than a darting glance at this document, still terrified and haunted by what I frequently imagine happened to him in Auschwitz. These images haunt me in vivid, excruciating detail.

In the following poem, which I wrote several years ago, I am referring to an incident when apparently Joe, having escaped from Auschwitz, was with a group of Russian prisoners. They were all assigned to a work detail, possibly in a warehouse (the exact details are not known). At some point, the Nazis were hunting for a Jew (specifically Joe) who they would identify by the number branded on his arm. In the life and death split second of that moment, he stood up to offer the Nazis a "hand" in looking for the person with that number, his own number—to save some precious time. The Nazis left without Uncle Joe.

This poem was written to express the oscillation between passion and torment of a survivor. My own frantic dance between aliveness and despair has been a steady companion in my own life journey.

My greatest meaning comes from my loving family and dearest friends. My children, Jeff and Josh, saved my emotional life and lifted the loneliness that came from my childhood mission to heal the sadness and sometimes deadness that I saw in my parents' eyes.

1000 Days in Auschwitz: Joseph Neumann and the Will to Live

What names the fiery passion
That dwelled within your eyes
You searched for your own number
While Nazis searched for you

What lightning quick decisions,
Saved your and others' lives
From what inner sources
Came your will to fight

All those awful headaches
Eyes that burned with pain
Scenes of such brutalities
Dancing in your brain

What names the fiery passion that swells within your eyes
How my heart would light with your every word
One loud angry outburst
Withering my soul
One strong vote of confidence
I soared away with hope

All those awful headaches
Eyes that burned with pain
Scenes of such brutalities
Dancing in your brain

Give away your bread
Flirt away your loss
Dare to live life passionately
Never mind the cost.

THE PAINTING: INSPIRED BY THE ART
OF MIRA HERMONI-LEVINE

> The palette knife becomes a surgical knife by which I dig and befriend
> what I find underneath. ... It exposes innermost contamination.
>
> Mira Hermoni-Levine

The painting of my mother was inspired by an experience I had over 10 years
ago (see Plate 13). I was in a shopping mall in Chicago and looked through
the window of the Josef Glimer Gallery. I was moved to tears by Mira's
paintings. The gallery owner called the artist, Mira Hermoni-Levine, in
Jerusalem while I was sitting there to tell her about my strong emotional
reaction to her paintings. The paintings communicated to me the capture
of the souls of young girls who carried a familiar, haunting, and lonely
pain. I trusted that the pain depicted in the painting was connected to the
Holocaust. Mira's story is that her father survived the Holocaust but lost
his wife and daughter, who was named Mira. He remarried, and his second
wife gave birth to my now very dear friend, Mira Hermoni-Levine. Mira is
an incredible artist and human spirit. She currently lives in Jerusalem and
lives passionately as wife, mother, grandmother, and extraordinary artist.
She also carries the haunting, compelling internal burden of living her own
life as well as expressing the unlived life of an unknown sister after whom
she was named.

Chapter 15

My Lost Father

Clemens Loew

Several years ago, I sculpted from clay the full body of my father (see Plate 14). In making my father's sculpture, *I could not have anticipated the experiences that would evolve from that creation.*

Since I have no memory of my father—he was killed when I was about 4—I used the wedding picture of my mother and father taken in 1936 as the model for his head and my son, then 23 years old, as the model for his body, purposely trying to establish a continuity from grandfather to grandson.

I carved his torso and put on a double-breasted suit that he might have been wearing in 1941—the last time I had any contact with him. But, sculpting his head is what engrossed me. That is when the most depth and intensity of emotion emerged.

With my fingers, I carved my father's eyes, nose, ears, and cheeks. I looked closely at the photo to see the shape of his mouth; his lips were thin, but his cheeks were high, with eyes set open. I molded, twisted, and rubbed his face. With my forefinger, I pressed a hole for his inner ear. I felt a sensation stirring in my fingers. Touching his mouth aroused images of my children when they were babies in bed with me, poking their fingers in my mouth, ears, or nose, into any opening they could find to express their exploration. I remembered those times as warm and loving experiences, a close and joyful attachment to my children. Now, sculpting my father, I began to experience myself as a child exploring his face *for the very first time.*

The more time I spent touching my father's face, the more surprised I felt by the surge of a warm, childlike feeling, but also the deep sadness and pain of *not* having him in my life.

In June 1941, when I was 4, my family and other Jews were rounded up at gunpoint and corralled into the ghetto. My father was caught in a roundup (*Aktion*) and herded onto a train to Belzec concentration camp.

In the sculpture class, as I shaped my father's earlobes, I became tearful. For the first time in my adult life, I could feel his presence, as if I were conducting a séance. I knew that I was experiencing something unique and profound, and I did not want to let it go. So, I stayed long after class and into the evening to be alone with him. I was by myself, in the empty studio that smelled of clay, glue, and dust, surrounded by sculptures draped with white cloth. They reminded me of birdcages covered to fool the bird into thinking it was night or a morgue full of covered cadavers.

I felt as if I were with a living person, exploring his face with my hands. I sensed in my body that I was with my father.

When I left the studio, late in the evening, I was saddened, but I also felt a sense of security and stability, as if my center of gravity dropped below my knees, making me more physically and psychologically stable and more difficult to tip over.

An artist, knowing my history, looked at the statue and asked me, "You know, I wonder what was behind his eyes when he knew he might not see you again? I was thinking, what were his thoughts?" I felt jarred. The question surprised me. He was encouraging me to fill out my father's emotional presence, something I had not thought of before.

I was always focused on *my* loss and *my* abandonment. Here was someone asking me to consider feelings of my father.

As I molded my father's face and its features, pulling his cheeks, enlarging his ears, thickening his eyebrows, I felt my perspective shift abruptly from my own to his. I now found myself inside him, 32 years old, younger than either of my children, about to lose his only child of 4 years—me—not knowing if he would ever see his son or his wife again.

And, what was going on for him during that cattle-packed train ride to the concentration camp? I could not imagine the fears he felt about his losses and knowing what was about to happen to him, that he was doomed. My eyes teared up, and I was filled with a compassion that I never had before. Belzec was the death camp. There were no inmates. He thought he might be a prisoner, I imagine, but instead the Germans took him to a hotel with no rooms.

That day of sculpting was extraordinary because I felt soothed, and most importantly, for the very first time, I was able to empathize with my father about the loss of his son and the ending of his own life, a compassion that strengthened my closeness to him, despite the fact that I have almost no personal memory of him.

Chapter 16

The Shadow of Shira

Marilyn B. Meyers

There was always the family-whispered story of Shira, which I have only come to know recently. My knowledge is incomplete. I feel bewildered, I go numb, I turn away, yet I keep returning. This is the story as I have known it: Shira was born the same year I was (1942) in Lithuania. I think that the family spent some time in the Kovno Ghetto. Under the coming threat of the Nazis, her parents left her with a family in Italy. There was a baby sister who died (or was she killed?) with her parents. I overheard whispers of Shira when I was a child—mysterious, fascinating, frightening. When the war was over in 1945, Shira's uncle (my grandfather's brother) went to find her. Her parents had been murdered in Auschwitz—the exact circumstances remain unknown. Her uncle felt compelled to take her into his family of survivors, then living in South Africa. I know this story through fragments that I overheard as a child—in whispers. Clearly, it registered in my mind in some unformulated way. I have a letter in my possession, which is a communication to the uncle written by a person from a Jewish social service agency. (I feel uncomfortable as I write this section—guilty as if I am taking her story away.)

The letter is dated December 1, 1947 from Rome and signed by I. Lipschitz (Shira was just 2 years and 4 months old).

> On Tuesday, 7th inst., I went south to the Lecce area in the heel of Italy, to see the Birger family and investigate the position of the child [Shira] then named Sara Tarshis. ... They live, like most families in these "Camps," in the township of Lecce which has been requisitioned almost in toto by the Allied authorities for the refugees. ... I presented your case [to the Birgers] as it was told to me ... and as it appears in the documents. ... Regarding the child, Sara, they told me a thrilling story of her rescue by both Birgers, the father and the son. At the risk of life, she was taken out of the extermination camp by Birger junior and subsequently carried, literally carried, across countries and borders until they arrived in Italy. Mr. Birger was a wealthy man in Kovno and he staked every thing he had left to get this child, as well as one

other one out of the clutches of death and bring them to safety. [I still don't understand the relationship of the Birgers to my family.] ... [Sara] is an extremely beautiful child, vivacious and talentful [sic]. ... She is obviously very attached to both Senior Birgers whom she calls "Papa" and "Mama." ... When asked whether she would go "with the uncle to South Africa, she just laughed saying she would remain only with her 'papa un mama'." ... The nett [sic] result [from my visit] is this. 1. The Birgers are attached to Sara as parents would, perhaps even more, and will not part with her. 2. Sara is given all the care and attention a child requires and regards the Birgers as her parents 3. Your brother ... has agreed that she remains in their hands. 4. Their intention is to go to Palestine where the child will grow up [They were killed in Auschwitz]. Under these circumstances I advise you not to pursue the matter of demanding her transfer to South Africa.

As I read this letter, my thoughts and feelings ebb and flow from the good feeling of knowing the detail and making some of this come to life. I also am confronted with horrifying images—all too real.

Ultimately, over these clear and empathic objections, the child was taken to South Africa, where her uncle and other members of the family had fled. Into adulthood, she refused to talk about her experiences. Actually, she went mute for a year after the abduction. This letter poignantly evokes images of a child ripped from the only family she had known—by an uncle who had his own motivation for the abduction. I have images of a child screaming—like those TV images of the surrogate mother handing over her child to the birth mother. Shira died without ever talking about her trauma. Perhaps it was her way of maintaining ownership of her life story, of protecting her children, of "moving on." Nonetheless, she stands for the unknown and untold story of the losses and trauma of the Holocaust in my extended family—and countless others. It remains an untold story without witness. Or, perhaps I serve as a witness, far removed, but nonetheless identified with her story. With regard to my reaction to revisiting this letter, my images became much more disturbingly clear, less vague, less obscured. I allow myself to "know."

Recently, as I have been working on this book, I had a thought. Whatever became of my mother's family? I am shocked and embarrassed that I had never thought about this. I was very close to my maternal grandfather, and it did not occur to me until that moment that he had no family that I knew of. My image of him instantly shifted. The warm, kind man who I knew as a child became shrouded in loss. I think that then the sadness that he carried and wordlessly communicated registered for me. Is it also this recognition that drives me to this project? A trace, a reverberation?

I now have an image of him as untethered, a man alone, and I think that I now have a deeper understanding of the intensity of his love for my mother,

her sister, and me. I always felt that there was a kind of tragic air about him. Now, I am keenly aware of the absence for me of knowing. Perhaps this project is part of that sense of wanting to make connections and to know. Like many therapists, I am compelled to know the "unknowable" and ask questions, to put the pieces of the puzzle together, with the knowledge that there will always be gaps and absences.

For the moment, my personal search ends here. I write out of a need to write—to bear witness. My motivation is still not entirely clear to me, but I feel compelled to do so.

Plate 1 (Chapter 8) "Leiser in the Garden" by Ada Wolpe.

Plate 2 (Chapter 8) "Leiser in Ländli," by Ada Wolpe.

Plate 3 (Chapter 9) Split-screen of George Halasz and his mother, Alice, from *Many Faces of Trauma*. (Courtesy of the Visual History Foundation [VHF].)

Plate 4 (Chapter 9) George's mother, Alice Halasz. (Courtesy of the Visual History Foundation [VHF].)

Plate 5 (Chapter 11) Paul Roth at age 2. Born in Miskolc, Hungary 1940; died in Auschwitz 1944.

Plate 6 (Chapter 11) In the United States: Miklós, Anci, and 2-year-old Katalin in 1950.

Plate 7 (Chapter 13) *Hana:* That picture is a caricature of my father made in Terezín in 1943, that hangs in Yad Vashem. They wouldn't give me the original, but they gave me a negative. The original is different. We were there this year to see the original. My son wanted to see it. ... My mother died at age 50 [in Auschwitz]. ... The artist, Leo Haas, was a friend of my father ... [He was] a famous painter from Terezín. *Edgar:* Hana's father was the head of the economy police, internal police, watching the cooks and the storekeepers in Berlin, they shouldn't steal too much. That's what this is about here. This is in German. It says "report" and this hand reaching out ... behind the running cook. *Hana:* When Leo Haas died his friend sent all his drawings to Yad Vashem. I mean I never knew about it, and my father never told us that he did this drawing. Both signatures are here, this is my father's and this is Leo Haas. ... a friend of mine, the only one from my childhood, who lives in Brazil sent me a card—"I saw a caricature of your father." I went to see it in Yad Vashem. They [the museum] had no idea about the caricature, the history.

Plate 8 (Chapter 13) *Hana:* That's a picture that Edgar got from the artist; it shows the imprisonment, the bars on the window; it shows the violin, the music that Edgar loved, and it shows the ray of freedom in the window. ... The artist is Fritta, his name was Fritz Taussig and his artistic name was Fritta, and he made that in Terezín.

Plate 9 (Chapter 13) *Edgar:* This is a very rare picture of Prague. Most pictures show the Castle, but this one is the view from the Castle. He made it in Terezín; it is so perfect that he must have done it from a postcard. ... He smuggled it out of Czechoslovakia, and it's on wrapping paper.

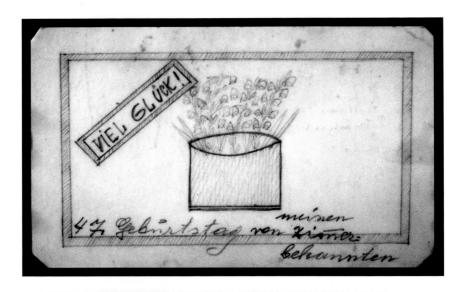

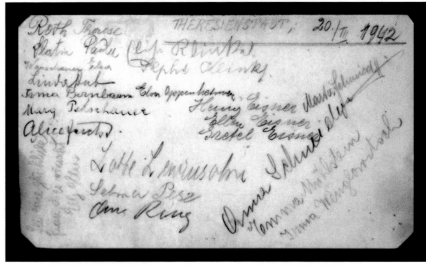

Plates 10 and 11 (Chapter 13) *Marilyn:* This is the birthday card. *Hana:* The 47th birthday of my mother-in-law. She lived in Terezín until liberation. She lived in Prague until she was 90 years old. She then came to live with us in Boston. *Hana:* The women in the barracks gave it to her as a present. It's all in German and all handmade. *Marilyn:* What is *viel gluck*? *Hana: Viel* is lots, lots of luck.

Plate 12 (Chapter 13) *Hana:* This is in Terezín, done by Zadikova, that's the women's washroom. That's how we were washing ourselves in the barracks. *Marilyn:* When you see this picture do you remember the scene? *Hana:* Oh, sure, every day we had to wash ourselves ... only cold water, no hot water.

Plate 13 (Chapter 14) A painting of Boruska (Barbara Blau), mother of Elaine Neuman Kulp Shabad.

Plate 14 (Chapter 15) Sculpture of Clemens Loew's father.

Plate 15 (Chapter 18) "September 1942: After the morning raid the Gestapo were returning. We fled across the fields to the woods, my mother directing me to separate." (Reproduced with permission of Art and Remembrance.)

Plate 16 (Chapter 18) "This was my family on the morning of October 15, 1942. We were ordered by the Gestapo to leave our homes by 10 a.m. to join all the other Jews on the road to KraÅLsnik railroad station and then to their deaths." (Reproduced with permission of Art and Remembrance.)

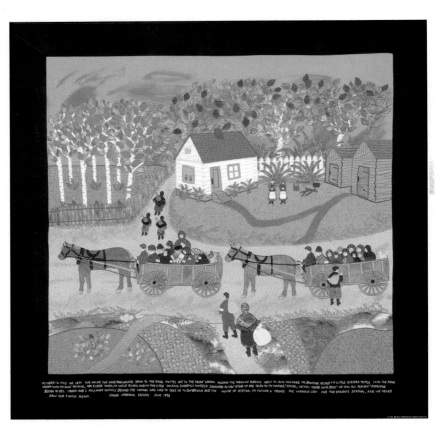

Plate 17 (Chapter 18) "October 15, 1942: We left our house for good and walked down to the road. Mottel sat in the front wagon, holding the Torah. My parents went to join him while my brother helped my little sisters settle into the rear wagon with my Aunt Trushel, her sister Golda, my uncle Ruven, and my five little cousins. Suddenly Mottel's daughter-in-law stood up and cried to my mother, 'Rachel, we will never come back! We will all perish!' Everyone began to cry. Mania and I followed quickly behind the woman who was to take us to Dombrowa and the house of Stefan, my father's friend. The wagons left for the KraÅLsnik station, and we never saw our family again." (Reproduced with permission of Art and Remembrance.)

Plate 18 (Chapter 18) "On Friday, October 15, 1942, it was the beginning of the end—the somber march of the Rachow Jews to their deaths." (Reproduced with permission of Art and Remembrance.)

Plate 19 (Chapter 18) "October 15, 1942: After being abandoned by a neighbor whom my mother had paid to take us to Dombrowa, Mania and I met our cousin Dina, on her way to KraÅLsnik with her baby and the other Rachow Jews. As the road began to curve around the mountain, I realized how close we were to KraÅLsnik, and I was suddenly terrified. I pleaded with Mania to come with me to Stefan; she finally agreed after Dina told her, 'Go Mania, go with Esther.'" (Reproduced with permission of Art and Remembrance.)

Plate 20 (Chapter 18) "October 15, 1942: My sister and I arrived in the village of Dombrowa and went to the house of Stefan, our father's friend. We begged him to help us. He embraced us and promised to help. But after two days, he sent us out into the rain, with no place to go but the forest." (Reproduced with permission of Art and Remembrance.)

Part 4

Traces

Chapter 17

Blood

Reading the Holocaust

Arlene Kramer Richards

Picking up brilliant shards of a glass table spread across the winter
  going turf
cuts my fingertips; specks and thin lines of red liven my pale
  wrinkled flesh.
The hurt slices into the pain of reading poems of those who died and
those who did not die and those who killed and did not die and those
who died so they would not kill and those who killed when they
  had no
need and those who thought they needed to do it and those
  who wanted
to kill but could not and those who did not want to do it, but did,
and those who could not stop when their danger was past and
  those who
kill now for what happened then.

Arlene Kramer Richards

As a young child—I was 4 in 1939—I already heard of the terrible things
going on in Europe. While the terrible things were happening there, my
family was frantically trying to get enough money together to bring relatives to the United States. One came: cousin Aaron, who had walked across
Poland into Italy and gotten to a boat coming to America. This pink-cheeked
18-year-old immediately enlisted in the army and soon went back, first to
Africa, then to Italy, and eventually to Germany. He sent me a treasure
from Egypt. It was a camel skin bag decorated with green palm trees and
improbably red camels tattooed onto the soft white leather. He was my
hero, but he came back from the war with stories even more horrible than
the ones he told when he first came to us.

The worst was the present someone brought us later. It was called *The
Black Book of Polish Jewry* (Apenszlak, 1943). At the time, I did not know
that it had been written by several Jewish journalists and scholars. It had
stories of the horrors that people perpetrated against people. They were the

German soldiers and their Ukrainian and Polish accomplices; they were the Christians. We were the Jews. They killed us. They maimed, tortured, and degraded us. We were hated, hunted, killed. How could I make sense of this? It has taken my whole lifetime so far, and I am sure that I am not done yet.

Thinking about this past and how it intrudes on my present and the present of the larger world grew some weeks ago when a patient had a strange reaction to a local event. The patient had seen notices of a police hunt for a man who had killed an 85-year-old woman while attempting to rob her. Her analyst, who had seen the same notices, remarked about the rape that had been part of that crime. Amazingly, the patient reacted violently, crying and telling the analyst that she had hurt her horribly. Why would rape be so much more traumatic than murder? Suddenly, it became clear. The rape victim lives on, having the horrible event echoing in her head for the rest of her life. Haunted by images of the pain, images of the perpetrator, images of helplessness, of hopeless hatred, the survivor of rape is tortured forever. By contrast, the murder victim loses everything at once. No longer sentient, she cannot feel pain. Under extremely painful and hopeless conditions, people prefer death. The survivor feels the pain but can work on answering the questions of whether it is better to live or die, be the victim or the perpetrator, whom to love and whom to hate, how to feel hope for humanity, and how to love.

I think it is this what Adorno meant when he said: "After the Holocaust there can be no poetry." The horrific images are unbearable in themselves. If the function of poetry is to express and convey feelings, these bruising traumatic feelings cannot and should not be conveyed. To convey them is to pass along the trauma. But conveying feelings somehow strengthens the possibility of coping with them. It makes possible a context that is not horrible, which contains the horror even as it evokes the most pain in the listener or reader. One way to soften the impact of horror is to set it in the context of love as Fanya Heller (1993) has in her memoir of being a hidden teenager sheltered by her lover.

So, who can speak the pain of those who died? The poem that speaks best to my own feelings and my understanding of the feelings of those deported is this fragment from Dan Pagis:

Written in Pencil in the Sealed Railway Car

here in this carload
i am eve with abel my son
if you see my other son
cain son of man
tell him that i (1996, p. 29)[1]

---

[1] From Pagis, D. (1996), *Selected Poetry of Dan Pagis* (S. Mitchell, Trans.). © University of California Press. Reprinted with permission.

Having read this poem in a book of essays about the Holocaust, I misremembered it as having actually been written by a woman in a cattle car on the way to Auschwitz rather than as it really was written, by a man after the war to speak for those who had been murdered. This parapraxis attests to the power of that poem to make me believe. It also leaves the bitterest message to the world. In this poem, the dead are Abel. All the others are Cain. To survive is to bear the burden of guilt forever.

Are we all guilty? Are the guilty bad through and through? The paradox of the cultured people who committed the most detestable crimes fuels this poem by Paul Celan:

Death Fugue

Black milk of daybreak we drink it at sundown
we drink it at noon in the morning we drink it at night
we drink and we drink it
we dig a grave in the breezes there lies one unconfined
A man lives in the house he plays with the serpents he writes
he writes when dusk falls to Germany your golden hair Margarete
he writes it and steps out of doors and the stars are flashing he
whistles his pack out
he whistles his Jews out in the earth has them dig for a grave
he commands us to strike up for the dance

Black milk of daybreak we drink you at night
we drink in the morning at noon we drink you at sundown
we drink and we drink you
A man lives in the house he plays with the serpents he writes
he writes when dusk falls to Germany your golden hair Margarete
your ashen hair Shulamith we dig a grave in the breezes there one lies
  unconfined

He calls out jab deeper into the earth you lot you others sing now
  and play
he grabs at the iron in his belt he waves it his eyes are blue
jab deeper you lot with your spades you others play on for the dance

Black milk of daybreak we drink you at night
we drink in the morning at noon we drink you at sundown
we drink and we drink you
A man lives in the house your golden hair Margarete
your ashen hair Shulamith he plays with the serpents
He calls out more sweetly play death death is a master from
  Germany

he calls out more darkly now stroke your strings then as smoke you
  will rise into air
then a grave you will have in the clouds there one lies unconfined

Black milk of daybreak we drink you at night
we drink you at noon death is a master from Germany his eyes
  are blue
he strikes you with leaden bullets his aim is true
a man lives in the house your golden hair Margarete
he sets his pack onto us he grants us a grave in the air
he plays with the serpents and daydreams death is a master
  from Germany

your golden hair Margarete
your ashen hair Shulamith (1980, pp. 50–53)[1]

The contrast between the golden hair of the beloved and the ashen hair
of the Jewish woman, gleam of gold alongside the ashes, somehow makes a
beautiful image, and it is all the more horrible for its beauty. How can such
beauty describe such hatred, such cruelty, and such inhuman preening?
It was only on later readings that I noticed that Margarete is the name of
Faust's beloved, that he has her only by making a contract with the devil.
So, the master from Germany is a Faust, a man who has his Margarete
only because he is willing to pay for her by selling his soul to the devil.
And it was later still that I understood the name Shulamith as quintes-
sentially Jewish. Unlike the biblical names that many Protestants give their
daughters, Shulamith is never used for Christian children. It has the further
ironic connotation of shalom: peace. The black milk is the smoke black air
filled with the ashes of humans. And the sweetness and playfulness of the
master from Germany as he calls for music, for his serpents and his dogs, is
the very essence of the fallen angel: the devil. The black milk smoke theme
plays out musically as a fugue, swirling through the lines of the poem,
enlarging the horror with the repetition and furthering the story with the
variations as the theme is played over and over again.

How to answer the evil? One survivor, Renée Hartmann, wrote of her
experience in the spirit of resistance; she wrote long after that spirit con-
gealed over time into the spirit of revenge:

Lice

The wooden pegs
and empty shelves

---

[1] From Celan, P. (1980), *Poems of Paul Celan* (M. Hamburger, Trans.). © Persea Books.
Reprinted with permission.

they stare at us—
emptied even of sleep.

What we have we carry,
every shred of coat or flap of string—
whatever covers and holds.

On my legs shoes hang
I shiver in them.
The leather is cracked like the skin

Over which a louse
crawls with a slowness
that mimics eternity.
Every louse I kill I christen Hans.

I hunt my enemies in seams
I shiver, in terror unclothed,
for the lice outnumber
the stars in heaven.

I beg forgiveness
that I cannot share my blood
but turn savage in my itch.
The hungry hours pass.

Whatever in me is warm
comforts only those beasts
who are larger than visions—
I see how fat my enemies grow.

Today all ten plagues descend. (2007, p. 80)[1]

The reality of the days in the camp was only clear to the poet when it had turned into memory. The large enemies and the small are the same; both are out of scale, neither can really be killed. Yet, even in the camp she pitied the small, apologized for having to kill them while the large beasts are killing her. It is the scale of the evil that cannot be believed. She recalls that when she was killing those lice, she did not know that they spread the deadly disease called typhus. She called them her enemy in an attempt to kill the larger, visibly armed for harm enemy that she knew wanted to kill her.

---

[1] From Hartman, R. (2007), *Wounded Angels*. © Renée Hartman. Reprinted with permission.

Abraham Sutzkever, the author of the next poem, compared the agony of the experience with the release from the nightmarish reality. Unable to experience joy, the person who remembers the horror will try to understand the memory that cannot be erased, cannot be cleansed of horror, the memory that forces the person to look deeper and deeper into the horror in the search for cause.

How?

How and with what will you fill
your cup on the day of release?
In your joy, are you ready to listen still
to your yesterday's black shrieks
where shards of days shudder in spasm
in a bottomless, roofless chasm?

You will seek a key instead,
to fit your shattered locks.
You will bite the streets like bread
and think: Earlier was better.
And the time will quietly persist
like a cricket enclosed in your fist.

And your memory will be compared
to an old and buried town,
and your outward vision like a mole
will burrow, dig down ... (1987, p. 676)[1]

The memory poisoned the earth for Sutzkever, but it poisoned the air for Nelly Sachs:

O the Chimneys

And though after my skin worms destroy this
body, yet in my flesh shall I see God—Job, 19:26

O the chimneys
On the ingeniously devised habitations of death
When Israel's body drifted as smoke
Through the air—
Was welcomed by a star, a chimney sweep.

[1] From Sutzkever, A. (1987), *Penguin Book of Modern Yiddish Verse* (I. Howe & R. W. K. Shmeruk, Eds.). © Viking Press. Reprinted with permission.

A star that turned black
Or was it a ray of sun?

O the chimneys!
Freedomway for Jeremiah and Job's dust—
Who devised you and laid stone upon stone
The road for refugees of smoke?

O the habitations of death,
Invitingly appointed
For the host who used to be a guest—
O you fingers
Laying the threshold
Like a knife between life and death—

O you chimneys,
O you fingers
And Israel's body as smoke through the air! (1967a, p. 3)[1]

Sachs remembered that it was not just those on site who did the killing;
she asked who prepared the site, who built the chimneys, who participated
in the building of the road that led to such camps? Was it the responsibility of the church that taught that the Jews were responsible for the killing
of Christ? The journalists, poets, intellectuals who decried Jewish "pushi-
ness," "crassness," "money grubbing"? Was it the politicians who singled
out an external enemy to blame for national disasters?

Sachs went on to talk for those who were not sent up in smoke but lived
to bear witness, to bear pain and sorrow and images of death:

Chorus of the Rescued

We, the rescued,
From whose hollow bones death had begun to whittle his flutes,
And on whose sinews he had already stroked his bow—
Our bodies continue to lament
With their mutilated music.
We, the rescued,
The nooses wound for our necks still dangle
before us in the blue air—
Hourglasses still fill with our dripping blood.
We, the rescued,

---

[1] From Sachs, N. (1967a), *O THE CHIMNEYS: Selected Poems, Including Eli, a Verse
Play.* © Farrar, Strauss, and Giroux. Reprinted with permission.

The worms of fear still feed on us.
Our constellation is buried in dust.
We, the rescued,
Beg you:
Show us your sun, but gradually,
Lead us from star to star, step by step.
Be gentle when you teach us to live again,
Lest the song of a bird,
Or a pail being filled at the well
Let our badly sealed pain burst forth again
and carry us away—
We beg you:
Do not show us the angry dog, not yet—
It could be, it could be
That we will dissolve into dust—
Dissolve into dust before your eyes.
For what binds our fabric together?

We whose breath vacated us,
Whose soul fled to him out of that midnight
Long before our bodies were rescued
Into the ark of the moment.
We, the rescued,
We press your hand
We look into your eye—
But all that binds us together now is leave-taking,
The leave-taking in the dust
Binds us together with you. (1967b, p. 25)[1]

Sachs spoke to the final horror, that the persecuted may in turn become the monsters they survived:

That the Persecuted May Not Become Persecutors

Footsteps—
In which of Echo's grottos
are you preserved,
you who once prophesied aloud
the coming of death?

---

[1] From Sachs, N. (1967b), *O THE CHIMNEYS: Selected Poems, Including Eli, a Verse Play.* © Farrar, Strauss, and Giroux. Reprinted with permission.

Footsteps—
Neither bird-flight, inspection of entrails,
nor Mars sweating blood
confirmed the oracle's message of death—
only footsteps—

Footsteps—
An age old game of hangman and victim,
Persecutor and persecuted,
Hunter and hunted—

Footsteps
which turn time ravenous
emblazoning the hour with wolves
extinguishing the flight in the fugitive's blood.

Footsteps
measuring time with screams, groans,
the seeping of blood until it congeals,
heaping up hours of sweaty death—

Steps of hangmen
over the steps of victims,
what black moon pulled with such terror
the sweep-hand in earth's orbit?

Where does your note shrill
in the music of the spheres? (1967c, p. 55)[1]

And even worse, a poem from a man who became the killer of his own child, Abraham Sutzkever lamented:

To My Child

Because of hunger
or because of great love—
your mother will bear witness—
I wanted to swallow you, child,
when I felt your tiny body
cool in my hands

[1] From Sachs, N. (1967c), O THE CHIMNEYS: Selected Poems, Including Eli, a Verse Play. © Farrar, Strauss, and Giroux. Reprinted with permission.

like a glass
of warm tea.

Neither stranger were you, nor guest.
On our earth, one births
only oneself, one links
oneself into rings and the rings into chains.

Child, the word for you would be love
but without words you are love,
the seed of the dream,
unbidden third,
who from the limits of the world,
swept two of us into consummate pleasure.

How can you shut your eyes,
leaving me here
in the dark world of snow
you've shrugged off?

You never even had your own cradle
to learn the dances
of the stars.
The shameful sun who never shone
on you, should shatter like glass.
Your faith burned away
in the drop of poison
you drank down as simply
as milk.

I wanted to swallow you, child,
to taste
the future waiting for me.
Maybe you will blossom again in my veins.

I'm not worthy of you, though.
I can't be your grave.
I leave you to the summoning snow,
this first respite.
You'll descend now
like a splinter of dusk
into the stillness,
bringing greetings from me

to the slim shoots
under the cold. (1989a, pp. 494–495)[1]

Was the Holocaust so terrible that it even killed any chance of poetry, any chance of putting feelings into words without being trivial? One Jewish woman, Malke Heifetz Tussman, said:

In Spite

You say:
"You are a Jew and a poet
And you've written no poems
On the destruction.
How can a Yiddish poet not,
When the destruction is enormous,
So enormous?"

Simple:
In spite of the destroyers,
To spite them I will not cry openly,
I will not write down my sorrow
On paper.
(A degradation to write
"Sorrow" on paper.)
To spite them
I'll walk the world
As if the world were mine.
Of course it's mine!
If they hindered me
Fenced in my roads,
The world would still be mine.

To spite them I will not wail
Even if (God forbid) my world becomes
As big as where my sole stands—
The world will still be mine!

To spite them
I'll marry off my children
That they shall have children—

[1] From Sutzkever, A. (1989a), *The Literature of Destruction: Jewish Responses to Catastrophe* (D. G. Roskies, Ed.). © Jewish Publication Society. Reprinted with permission.

To spite the villains who breed
In my world
And make it narrow
For me. (1986, p. 617)[1]

Decades after the events, the irony of power still resonates in this poem by Abraham Sutzkever, translated from the Yiddish by Ruth Whitman:

Prayer for a Sick Friend

The wicked have too much power,
It would be enough for them to have the strength of rabbits.
Fed the weak one with mercy,
for here he lies: half man; half bedsheet.

I'm his prayer. His lips
have already lost the words.
They're despoiled sea shells
without echo, without salt, without pearls.

He still needs to light up a sentence
in the temple of his dark burrow.
He must accompany the young
queen of the bees to her be-starred dawn.

I've seen a fish leap
from the sea-heart to the clouds
and carry the clouds with him—
is my friend less than a fish?

Instead of little red circles
in his veins, red fiddles
are swimming, mastered by you—
no one else can play them.

He must still hear how his pulse
is spring-rain running in his body.
He must still sip dreams, keep faith,
and—in late fall—putty the windows. (1989b, p. 40)[2]

---

[1] In Tussman, M. H. (1986), *American Yiddish Poetry* (B. Harshav, Ed. & Trans.). © University of California Press. Reprinted with permission.
[2] From Sutzkever, A. (1989b), Prayer for a Sick Friend. © *The New Yorker Magazine.* Reprinted with permission.

In this poem written long after the Holocaust by a Lodz ghetto fighter who now lives in Israel, the embers of the Shoah still burn in everyday injustices. The stern beginning reproaches the one to whom the prayer is addressed. The sickness of the friend contrasts with the strength of the wicked. Who would arrange things this badly? But the poem is funny; puns and playful images start with the rabbits, continue with the "half man, half bedsheet." Nature images lighten the story. The poet says of a man with cancer of the red blood cells, "red fiddles are swimming." And the poem ends with a most mundane image: puttying windows. This conjunction of the horrible death by cancer, the young queen of bees, the dawn, and the fish speaks of a reverence for all life, a hopefulness for a future, and a return to the mundane that is the best, and perhaps the only, retort to the evil.

Do we need to know evil and guilt in some abstract way or only as it meets the present? Abba Kovner has written elsewhere about the day he refused his own mother entry into the safe house in the Warsaw Ghetto where he and a group of strong young partisans fought and survived the ghetto battle while she did not.

On the Way

Mother and father are beginning to die inside me
Thirty years after their deaths in the storm
they withdraw quietly from my rooms,
from my moments of grace.

I'm sure about it. Voices and words have stopped,
they're free now. They no longer visit
my house, but not because they are angry.
A living man must be on his own.

Somewhere father is getting up early,
walking around in his sandals, pretending
as usual he doesn't see how mother cries
as she knits a warm sweater for her son,
camped on the way, in the night. (1986, p. 102)[1]

Standing against all the pious calls to remember this poem celebrates forgetting the dead and attaching oneself to life. Kovner continues to be a hero in poetry as he was in war. He was as unafraid to shatter pieties as he was to cross gender boundaries when he hid in a convent as a young man

---

[1] From Kovner, A. (1986), *My Little Sister and Selected Poems* (S. Kaufman, Trans.). © Oberlin College Press. Reprinted with permission.

posing as a nun or as he was as a fighter in the Warsaw Ghetto—or as a son refusing his mother shelter to protect his comrades in arms.

But, the poet whose work about the Shoah is closest to my heart is Irena Klepfisz. Here are a pair of poems that try to make sense of the incomprehensible:

Bashert: These words are dedicated to those who died.

These words are dedicated to those who died
because they had no love and felt alone in the world
because they were afraid to be alone and tried to stick it out
because they could not ask
because they were shunned
because they were sick and their bodies could not resist the
     disease
because they played it safe
because they had no connections
because they had no faith
because they felt they did not belong and wanted to die

These words are dedicated to those who died
because they were loners and liked it
because they acquired friends and drew others to them
because they took risks
because they were stubborn and refused to give up
because they asked for too much

These words are dedicated to those who died
because a card was lost and a number was skipped
because a bed was denied
because a place was filled and no other place was left

These words are dedicated to those who died
because someone did not follow through
because someone was overworked and forgot
because someone left everything to God
because someone was late
because someone did not arrive at all
because someone told them to wait and they just couldn't wait
     any longer

These words are dedicated to those who died
because death is a punishment
because death is a reward

because death is the final rest
because death is eternal rage

These words are dedicated to those who died

Bashert (1990a, pp. 181–183)[1]

and:

Bashert: These Words Are Dedicated to Those Who Survived

These words are dedicated to those who survived
because their second grade teacher gave them books
because they did not draw attention to themselves and got lost in
  the shuffle
because they knew someone who knew someone else who could
help them and bumped into them on a corner on a Thursday
  afternoon
because they played it safe
because they were lucky

These words are dedicated to those who survived
because they knew how to cut corners
because they drew attention to themselves and always got picked
because they took risks
because they had no principles and were hard

These words are dedicated to those who survived
because they refused to give up and defied statistics
because they had faith and trusted in God
because they expected the worst and were always prepared
because they were angry
because they could ask
because they mooched off others and saved their strength
because they endured humiliation
because they turned the other cheek
because they looked the other way

These words are dedicated to those who survived
because life is a wilderness and they were savage
because life is an awakening and they were alert

[1] From Klepfisz, I. (1990a), *A Few Words in the Mother Tongue: Poems Selected and New (1971–1990)*. © Eighth Mountain Press. Reprinted with permission.

because life is a flowering and they blossomed
because life is a struggle and they struggled
because life is a gift and they were free to accept it

These words are dedicated to those who survived. (1990b,
    pp. 183–186)[1]

The effect of this poetry on me has been to disturb my sense of having reached some resolution of my pain about losing many members of my family to the Shoah. Each poem reawakened the memories of listening to survivors' stories immediately after the war when I was sent to bed so I did not hear what they were telling my parents. I was 10 years old and curious; I stayed close to my bedroom door and listened. The stories were horrendous. My parents wanted to hear them to find out what happened to the relatives. They wanted to help any of them who had survived to come to the United States. Only the women in the part of my father's family who had lived in Paris had actually survived. No one had seen any of the Polish relatives, and the men of the French family had been recorded among the dead at Auschwitz. The stories the survivors told went far beyond the questions my parents asked. The survivors clearly needed to unburden themselves of the nightmares they were still having about the horrors they had experienced. It was amazing to me how many stories there were; it is amazing to me now that I listened and understood and somehow tolerated the awful knowing.

Maybe it was the awareness that my parents wanted to shield me from the horrors that made those stories bearable. I was an accidental witness, yet they left the door open to accident, both literally and metaphorically. The conflict between wanting me to be American, healthy and unscarred, and wanting to share their experience, their pain and their loyalties, emerged in this way as in many others. They wanted me to assimilate, be an American, enjoy my life, but they also wanted me to be their daughter, like them, willing and able to understand them in ways that no American could. I tried. I tried to learn their culture, but I did that mostly in secret, staying the healthy, athletic American girl in the daytime, reading about and listening to the horror at night. Only as I write this do I understand how I became an insomniac.

My own interest in poetry began with cradle songs my grandmother sang to me in Yiddish. She was a recent immigrant from Poland; she spoke no English. My mother worked making hats to support my out-of-work father, herself, and me and help support her parents and three brothers. So, my grandmother brought me up in Yiddish until I was 5 and went to kindergarten. Learning English in school was difficult because no one else in my

---

[1] From Klepfisz, I. (1990b), *A Few Words in the Mother Tongue: Poems Selected and New (1971–1990)*. © Eighth Mountain Press. Reprinted with permission.

class knew any Yiddish, and the teacher conveyed her disapproval of my inability to follow directions and my inability to ask when I needed to use the toilet. I learned the power of poetry when we played "farmer in the dell" in the schoolyard, and I wound up as the cheese who stands alone. Now, I knew how poems can hurt. When I was 6, my father got his first job, and my mother stayed home to have another baby. I was sent to live with my parents. Used to my grandmother's old world cooking, I refused to eat my mother's more American plain food. To get me to eat, my mother read Mother Goose rhymes to me at mealtimes. I eagerly learned the rhymes, their rhythms, and from them got a serviceable, if quaint, English vocabulary and became hooked on poetry for life. Her reading was an act of reconciliation. It was intended to give me a focus on pleasure and humor to mitigate the longing for my spicy Yiddish-speaking grandmother and her spicy food. It was meant to allay the longing for a past that had itself been marked by longing for my own mother. The poetry of longing for a vanished Yiddish past resonates now with my own childhood longings and fills me with the food of love. It reconciles me to what cannot be even as it gives me hope for what can be now.

The problems with Holocaust poetry are many. Does the Holocaust experience give the survivors and their children the right to defend themselves against those who threaten them? Does the Shoah make anything written about it sacred? Or good poetry? Does it justify the establishment of a Jewish state? Is the establishment of such a state defensible if it requires expelling Palestinians from their homes? Did those Palestinians who left when Israel was established choose their own exile? Is Gaza a revenant of the Warsaw Ghetto with Israelis acting like Germans toward Palestinians, who are treated as the Jews were in the Holocaust? Such questions haunt the poetry and those who read it now.

REFERENCES

Apenszlak, J. (Ed.). (1943). *The black book of Polish Jewry.* New York: American Federation for Polish Jews.

Bergmann, M. S., & Jucovy, M. (1982). *Generations of the Holocaust.* New York: Basic Books.

Celan, P. (2002). Death fugue. In *Poems of Paul Celan: A bilingual German/English edition, revised edition* (M. Hamburger, Trans.) (pp. 50–53). New York: Persea Books.

Hartman, R. (2007). Lice. In *Wounded angels* (p. 80). Hamden, CT: Porlock Press.

Heller, F. (1993). *Strange and unexpected love.* Hoboken, NJ: KTAV.

Kestenberg, J., & Fogelman, E. (1994). *Children during the Nazi reign.* Westport, CT: Prager.

Klepfisz, I. (1990a). Bashert: These words are dedicated to those who died. In *A few words in the mother tongue* (pp. 181–183). Portland, OR: Eighth Mountain Press.

Klepfisz, I. (1990b). Bashert: These words are dedicated to those who survived. In *A few words in the mother tongue* (pp. 183–186). Portland, OR: Eighth Mountain Press.

Kovner, A. (1986). On the way. In *My little sister and selected poems* (S. Kaufman, Trans.) (p. 102). Oberlin, OH: Oberlin College Press.

Pagis, D. (1996). Written in pencil in a sealed railway car. In *Selected poetry of Dan Pagis* (S. Mitchell, Trans.) (p. 29). Berkeley: University of California Press.

Sachs, N. (1967a). Oh the chimneys. In *O THE CHIMNEYS: Selected poems, including Eli, a verse play* (p. 3). New York: Farrar, Strauss, and Giroux.

Sachs, N. (1967b). Chorus of the rescued. In *O THE CHIMNEYS: Selected poems, including Eli, a verse play* (p. 25). New York: Farrar, Strauss, and Giroux.

Sachs, N. (1967c). That the persecuted may not become persecutors. In *O THE CHIMNEYS: Selected poems, including Eli, a verse play* (p. 55). New York: Farrar, Strauss, and Giroux.

Schiff, H. (Ed.) (1995). *Holocaust poetry*. New York: Saint Martin's.

Sutzkever, A. (1987). How? In I. Howe & R. W. K. Shmeruk (Eds.), *Penguin book of modern Yiddish verse* (p. 676). New York: Viking Press.

Sutzkever, A. (1989a). To my child. In D. G. Roskies (Ed.), *The literature of destruction: Jewish responses to catastrophe* (pp. 494–495). Philadelphia: Jewish Publication Society.

Sutzkever, A. (1989b). Prayer for a sick friend. *The New Yorker Magazine, 65*(8), p. 40.

Tussman, M. H. (1986). In spite. In B. Harshav (Ed. & Trans.), *American Yiddish poetry* (p. 617). Berkeley: University of California Press.

Chapter 18

Through the Eye of the Needle: The Art of Esther Nisenthal Krinitz

Witnessing the Witness Through Filmmaking

Nina Shapiro-Perl

In preparing recently for a lecture in a course I am teaching in documentary storytelling at American University, I read about how artists and survivors of political torture in Chile came together in New York to explore dramatic ways to use testimony. Inspired by the use of testimony in Latin America called Theatre of Witness, the group *Theatre Arts Against Political Violence* captured the stories:

> [O]ral histories *were conducted* [emphasis added] with torture survivors as a way for others to enter into the experience of remembered torture, but in a broader landscape than one-on-one therapy (or oral history) could provide. The actors modeled the experience of torture through their bodies, symbolically transferring the words into a lived experience that would be witnessed by the public to break down the conspiracy of silence that often confines the survivor in a world of isolation. ... The goal of the production was to give torture survivors the ability to stand outside their experience and witness the transformation of their suffering, on stage in the company of friends and fellow survivors. The survivors became the critics and ultimately the *authors*, of the transformation. (Clark, 2002, p. 102)

The story hit very close to home. For the past three years, I have been producing a documentary film about the art and story of Esther Nisenthal Krinitz. It is an account of the Holocaust through the eyes of a 50-year-old woman, looking back to the day in October 1942 when the Jews of her tiny village of Mniszek in central Poland were marched out of their homes to the death camps. She remembers herself as a strong-willed, pigtailed girl of 15 refusing to go, running away with her 12-year-old sister, Mania, never to see her mother, father, older brother, and two small sisters again. She remembers the new identities and names she created for herself and her sister—now Polish Catholic farm girls—as they hid in plain sight from the Nazis and narrowly escaped death.

Esther's story of survival is remarkable on its own, but it is all the more extraordinary because of her method of storytelling: *through the eye of the needle*—sewing, stitching, and embroidering, Esther created a series of 36 wall-sized fabric collages in exquisite color and minute detail that tell of her life before, during, and after the Holocaust.

I had the privilege of knowing Esther and seeing the work as it appeared on the walls of her daughter's house in Chevy Chase, Maryland, the home of my very dear friend for the last 25 years, Bernice Steinhardt. Most of Esther's works were done in the last 10 years of her life before she passed away at the age of 75 in 2001.

Though Esther intended the art for her family, it was destined to be seen by a wider audience. After Esther's death, her daughters, Bernice Steinhardt and Helene McQuade, created Art and Remembrance, a nonprofit organization dedicated to share this work with the world—through a traveling exhibit, through a book, through a community Web site, through teaching curricula, and through a documentary film.

From the moment that I saw Esther's art, I saw this as a documentary film. Because of its unexpected beauty for a subject of this kind, and its point of view of a teenager as eyewitness, I believed this film could explore the Holocaust, genocide, persecution, anti-Semitism, racism, and even *bullying*, from a fresh perspective in our world *today*. I titled the film *Through the Eye of the Needle* to capture Esther's narrow escape and her method of storytelling.

I knew I wanted to tell Esther's story through her art. But, I wanted to explore not only *Esther's story*, but also *the story of Esther*. What moved her to capture her family's story, down to the most minute detail? How was it possible for her work to hold such beauty and horror at the same time? How did she understand her creative process? Did the many hours and days of stitching and embroidery, alone with her memories, help her come to terms with her enormous loss?

I wanted to understand more about our search for meaning after psychic trauma and the capacity of the human heart to heal.

* * *

Esther was 15 when she kissed her family good-bye and ran away with her 12-year-old sister, Mania. Five of her works deal with this separation: first with the family members standing in front of their farm facing the viewer, all crying (see Plate 16). The next four scenes take a wider and still wider perspective on that day, as Esther came to see this event as happening not only to her family but also to her uncles and aunts and cousins, then the whole town of Rachov, and then her *tour de force*—the picture of the Jews of Europe wending their way through the countryside, to their deaths (see Plates 17–19). Her daughter Bernice told me that Esther found these pieces the most difficult to do. Yet, we can imagine that through the meditative art of stitching, moving and being still at once, in and out, out and in, over many hours and days and months and years that Esther was able to come to grips with her life and her loss. She was able to mend herself and her heart and *externalize* the pain. Esther may not have fully understood the implications of what she was doing, but it provided a way for her to cope with the memories. And by externalizing her trauma, she was no longer the only witness. Through art, now others could also bear witness.

As Elie Wiesel said, "Whoever reads or listens to a witness, becomes a witness."

"Stefan's House" covers a two-day period of dizzying emotions for Esther and Mania (see Plate 20). In this intricately beautiful work, Esther depicts four different memories of place and feeling: momentary *relief* when Stefan takes them in; *worry* for her family as she and Mania dry out in the attic; *fear* for themselves as Stefan turns them out; and unspeakable *terror* in being alone—with no place to go but the forest. But here, as elsewhere in Esther's art, nature—in this case the forest—is seen as a protector, a beautiful protector. By making the most terrifying moment *beautiful*, Esther is able to live with both feelings, that is, to hold both the beauty and the horror in her heart. I think this is key to understanding Esther's art.

During this time in the forest, Esther thinks on her feet—an ability she will demonstrate time and again. She realizes that she and Mania will die if they keep their identities. She says to Mania, "We are no longer Hersh's daughters. We are Catholic Polish farm girls who have lost their family. You are Marisha, I am Juszia." Esther made Mania promise that she would take on this new identity and never speak Yiddish again.

Under the constant threat of exposure and death, the girls kept these disguises for two years. But to do so, they were forced to bury central parts of their identity—as Hersh's daughters and as Jews—and hide them inside. It took its toll, of course. Mania talked in her sleep and cried a lot when she was alone with her sister. Esther told Mania, "We cry inside." Yet Esther also cried. One night, alone, as she worked by moonlight in the garden of an old man whose farm she ran, Esther found herself thinking it was probably around the time of Yom Kippur, and, she recalled the foods her mother used to cook for holidays. She cried for the family she missed and the life that was gone.

It was in dreams that Esther's inner life could speak to her. There, she could become a child again. In one of her works, Esther depicts a dream where her beloved grandfather, who had died some years earlier, appears before her. Although she knew she had to keep her distance from him, she cried, "Oh, Zayde, you are close to God! You have to help me." He said, "Don't worry Esther; you will cross the river, and you will be safe!" Bernice noted that this dream was meaningful to her mother not only because it helped calm her fears but also because it was one of the few times she could allow herself to cry. After hearing this story recently, one psychologist told me that it seemed Esther never lost her sense of *relationship*. She *knew* that her grandfather loved her. And, Bernice added, Esther was always confident in her abilities; she never lost her sense of self.

* * *

A prominent clinical psychologist and personal friend, Dr. Hallie Lovett, who has seen my difficult determination to make this film over several years, recently asked me what accounted for my passion to make this film.

There are two answers to this provocative question.

One, I knew and loved Esther, and I thought a film could bring this tragic and beautiful story to life for a wider public and help heal our world *today*.

The second answer is more personal. The question triggered in me a dawning awareness that *all my life*, I have carried a desire to tell stories from the perspective of those who do not get heard. Exploring this in my own therapy, I realized it began as a little girl, walking alongside my father, who contracted polio as an infant and who walked with a cane and a brace all his life. At a young age, I remember knowing our family was *different*. I saw people point and stare; I wanted to speak—actually to *scream*—on his behalf! I wanted to tell his story; I wanted to tell *my* story—my story as witness.

From that early pain, I have been drawn to tell the stories of those that others dismiss—the *unseen* and *unheard* among us. Thirty years ago, I began my professional work as an anthropologist—conducting fieldwork for my doctoral dissertation. I worked as a solderer in a jewelry factory in Providence, Rhode Island, and documented the stories of low-income women making costume jewelry and their daily struggle for better wages and dignity on the job. For 20 years, I worked as a producer for the Service Employees International Union, making films, *witnessing* janitors, nursing home workers, school bus drivers—across the country—finding their voice and trying to change their lives through their union.

Now, as filmmaker, as witness, again, I tell the story of Esther. Through the transformative power of art, Esther was able to externalize her inner life, transcend her personal tragedy, and bear witness for the world. Through this film, I hope to take Esther's gift further—sharing it with a wider family, for our world, today.

REFERENCE

Clark, M. M. (2002). Oral history: Art and praxis. In D. Adams & A. Goldbard (Eds.), *Community, culture and globalization* (pp. 88–105). New York: Rockefeller Foundation.

Chapter 19

A Photographic Commentary on the Memorial to the Murdered Jews of Europe

Elsa Blum

It is retrospectively impossible to separate my memories of my initial experience of the Holocaust Memorial in Berlin from my later thoughts and feelings about both the memorial itself and the images I had captured. I knew beforehand that it would be important for me to photographically record my experience—to make a memorial of a memorial. I first came upon the memorial during a casual walk, my first day of my first trip to Berlin since its completion. I spotted in Potsdammer Platz the sign ".5 Km—Memorial to the Murdered Jews," written in both German and English, and realized I would have my first view of the memorial. I had planned to visit the memorial, of course, but not at that time. In retrospect, the goal of photographing the memorial was manifold. I wanted to preserve my experiences, express my feelings about them, and share my responses as filtered through my own particular vision.

Thus, my photos are a personal commentary, rather than an attempt to represent exact physical reality. Being behind the lens had an effect on my perceived emotions, both intensifying and diluting my experience. The ultimate goal of my photos is to communicate and perhaps intensify affect, to capture what was for me the essence of the memorial, utilizing formal elements of photography, including composition, shading, and so on. There was perhaps some attenuation of immediate emotional experience. Thoughts about the subject of the memorial itself were deflected at times to issues of light, point of view, depth of focus, and the like, a combination of aesthetic and technical considerations, undoubtedly informed and influenced by unconscious elements. The photographs themselves are my personal commentary, intended to enhance and preserve memory. While my attention was diffused and emotional responses deflected by the act of taking the photographs, later work on the images recalled my experience over and over again.

Any photograph is an abstraction, capturing only part of the surround, compressing three dimensions into two. Converting the colored digital images to black and white was a further abstraction that seemed appropriate for the subject and absolutely necessary to convey what I intended.

My experience of the memorial was markedly colored by the fact that it is in Berlin. I wondered about others' responses: Berliners, other Germans, tourists, Jews, non-Jews. My experience was influenced by these sometimes-distracting thoughts, by my past experience of other Holocaust memorials, personal accounts of Holocaust experience, visits to concentration camps. I was struck by the enormity of the memorial as well as its central location in Berlin. In driving around the city, one would pass by it repeatedly. The integration of the memorial with the city itself, the lack of a surrounding fence or any enclosure, spoke to me as well. This was in contrast to the fencing off and hiding of the concentration camps. One can view the city beyond the boundaries of the memorial, in all directions. In some directions, one sees apartment projects, both completed and under construction. In another direction, rows of stores on the ground floor are evident, eateries, souvenir shops. The message for me was that, despite the past, life goes on and is lived in the present; the surrounding populous is going about ordinary daily actions. My own reaction to this, no matter how long I considered the issue, remained ambivalent. I wondered what people thought as they passed by—did they ignore the memorial, did it become present, but unseen? Does one have to defend against this daily reminder of man's inhumanity to man? These were my thoughts about the memorial—but they were only tangentially related to the subject of the memorial, the Holocaust itself. Were these thoughts about the memorial all a defense against once again experiencing, if only vicariously, the horrors of the Holocaust themselves? Only within the dimly lit underground museum with its more specific printed reminders and photographs did my own sense of horror become more intense. A human face elicited more than the bare coffin-like stones.

The structures, all of which have identical footprints and are regularly spaced, vary in height. Though coffin-like, they are anonymous, reminiscent of the unidentified victims, who in fact had no coffins, and if not incinerated were interred in mass graves. From some perspectives the memorial has a cavernous quality, vertical, almost claustrophobic, deep, yet finite (Figures 19.1 and 19.2).

Rows of higher structures form ominous, prison-like aisles. My reactions were manifold and at times contradictory. As in art, scale is important; "monumental" has of course come to denote huge in scale. The vastness of this Holocaust memorial was daunting. Its variation within the set parameter of the identical footprint afforded multiple views, each with its distinct experience. The image (Figure 19.3) seemed to capture for me the bleak vastness of the site, the repetition of the stark forms.

Naturally, I thought of the millions of victims, the generations of the survivors, the unborn generations of those who had perished. I thought as well of the generations of Germans, the descendants of the perpetrators who had established this memorial. The site and size of the memorial were

Figure 19.1

Figure 19.2

especially telling—during my stay in Berlin, I passed it numerous times, so central is its location. This had great symbolic and emotional meaning for me, as did the extensiveness of the site. The recently constructed buildings that could be seen on the periphery in what had been East Berlin represented new growth from many perspectives. The ongoing life visible from the memorial, including new blocks of apartments, businesses, cars, people, are captured in Figures 19.4 and 19.5.

My second visit took place on a rainy day. I felt gratified to see lines of people from all over the world waiting in the rain for the elevators down to the museum. The museum itself felt sepulchral; dimly lit, inducing an intensely moving experience, as it gave an overview of the Holocaust, but also particularized it with photos and histories of individuals (Figure 19.6).

When I emerged from the museum, the rain had stopped. Water had accumulated on the tops of the stone elements, providing reflections, which became important pictorial elements. The wet stones in a way seemed to create an atmosphere of renewal. Especially poignant was the view of the

Figure 19.3

Figure 19.4

couple seen from behind under an umbrella (Figure 19.7). They are two anonymous enigmatic figures, possible locals going about their daily life, perhaps tourists resting.

Several of my photographs contain reflections, serendipitous, due to the rain. These reflections suggested to me the possible variations even

Figure 19.5

Figure 19.6

in these static concrete blocks as the surface changed with the reflections in the puddles (Figure 19.8).

The hopeful sense that life was continuing in the surrounding eateries, souvenir shops, and residence was mixed with bitterness regarding the lives that had not continued, that had been stifled, smothered, snuffed out.

Figure 19.7

Figure 19.8

Chapter 20

Opening the Mind to Trauma Through Oscillations of Focus

Learning From the Film *Schindler's List*

Nancy R. Goodman

INTRODUCTION

Steven Spielberg's film *Schindler's List* (1993) attracted large audiences around the world in cities made up mostly of people who had never before seen a Holocaust film. Dialogue was opened as newspaper articles appeared and as the film gained popularity and acclaim. In Frankfurt, Germany, where Oskar Schindler had lived for the last 16 years of his life, the film opened on March 3, 1993, with Steven Spielberg in the audience. The *Washington Post* reported this with the statement: "The Holocaust returned to Germany today with the opening of the movie *Schindler's List* and the reopening of a national debate about guilt, courage and the unresolved mysteries of mass murder" (Atkinson, 1993). In the United States, *Schindler's List* won seven academy awards, including Best Director. The degree of attention from the public, media, film critics, and scholars indicates that Spielberg's film invited witnessing in a way that had not occurred previously. Space for an audience was constructed, enabling people to sit in the theater and tolerate the anxiety, fear, anomie, depersonalization, and grief that inevitably accompany acknowledgment of the overwhelming terrible truths of the Holocaust.[1] Through his producing skills, Spielberg was able to bring knowledge of dehumanization and death to cinematic screens without repelling the audience. The way the film was constructed forged a path to realities of the Holocaust, allowing members of the audience to find and keep some movement in their minds. This type of movement is vitalizing and able to create and maintain what I have called "the living surround" (see Chapter 1) that can develop around trauma through witnessing. There was something to try to understand about the way Spielberg

---

[1] Steven Spielberg founded the Shoah Foundation in 1994, collecting video testimony from Holocaust survivors and other witnesses to the Holocaust. It is now housed at the University of Southern California in Los Angeles with nearly 54,000 testimonies in 32 languages and from 56 countries.

made *Schindler's List*. I wanted to find what it was and proceeded to look closely at elements of the film fostering witnessing.

First, there is the personage of Oskar Schindler. He is a rescuer inviting identification from those seated in the audience. He was a businessman who employed Jews in his factories for his own financial benefit and eventually intervened on behalf of his workers to save them from being sent to death camps. Ervin Staub (Chapter 26), who studies bystandership and has developed ways to create active bystanders, considered Schindler, like Wallenberg, to be a "good fanatic":

> The evolution of Oskar Schindler was dramatic. He was a German born in Czechoslovakia who, although not a committed Nazi, became a member of the Nazi Party. An opportunist, he followed the German army into Poland in 1939, took over a confiscated Jewish factory, and proceeded to enrich himself with Jewish slave labor. ... But contrary to others in this position, in many ways he treated Jews who worked for him like human beings. ... To protect his Jewish slave laborers from the dangers of their brutal camp, he created his own camp. He began to endanger his own life in order to help and continued to help even after he was arrested and released. ... Eventually, he sacrificed all his possessions while saving the lives of twelve hundred Jews. (1989, p. 168)

The story of Schindler and the list of Jews he saved from death camps seems to have functioned as a type of mediating transition object for knowing events of atrocity and torment. This provides a transitional location so that the trauma of the scenes on the screen remains a bit at a distance. The viewer can always state: "I am watching a film in a movie theater." An internal narrative develops around both the story and around a relationship with the film, the actors, and the director. Affects are felt and expressed, keeping the ego intact. The viewer is able to speak with reference to self and activity of self with statements such as: "I saw the film," "I admired the film," or "I hated this scene in the film."

Accepting the existence of the film allows a process of symbolizing and a creation of metaphor to take place around the edges of the psychic hole, the 'dead space' (see Chapter 1, p. 5), which exists in the mind of the beholder of truths of the Holocaust. In discussing the set of books *Maus* and *Maus II* by Art Spiegelman (1986, 1991), Laub and Podell (1995) used the idea of mirrors to describe how trauma art helps bring witnessing to the Holocaust. "The book [*Maus*] is like a mirror to memory, which is itself a mirror; and therefore we have an endless series of mirrors facing each other, allowing the reader the freedom to look and imagine as far as he or she chooses" (p. 997). There is the reality, the representation, the perceiving of the representation and dialogue with all levels. The film *Schindler's List* functions similarly to ward off devastating anxiety and allow the mind to turn in different directions, to see different reflections, and to stay alive. The film, like a dream or nightmare, brings about knowing and not knowing of the true anxiety that has threatened and continues to threaten annihilation of psychic functioning itself.

REPRESENTATIONS OF ANNIHILATION

The idea of total annihilation is presented in a speech made by the commandant of the work camp juxtaposed with the scene of the day the Jewish ghetto in Krakow was liquidated (March 13, 1943):

> Today is History. Today will be remembered. Years from now the young will ask with wonder about today. Today is history and you are part of it. Six hundred years ago when elsewhere they were put in the blame for the Black Death, Catherine the Great, so-called, told the Jews they could come to Krakow. They came, they trundled their belongings into the city, they settled, they took hold, they prospered, in business, education, the arts. They came here with nothing—nothing. They flourished. For six centuries, there has been a Jewish Krakow. Think about that. By this evening, those six centuries are a rumor. They never happened.

Listening to this speech and knowing how its aim was almost actualized is absolutely chilling. Psychoanalysts know well that secondary trauma and vicarious trauma (McCann & Pearlman, 1990) can take place, for analysand and analyst, when approaching the places of psychic trauma in patients' and analysts' minds. The idea of an analytic work space is a concept utilized by Viderman (1974) and Poland (1992). Spielberg created something similar concerning the relationship between the audience and the film, a kind of viewing space where the psychic work of receiving and processing the film can occur. To understand how Spielberg did this, I decided to look at the sequencing of the film. I used my recall as a guide. From my theater viewing of the film in 1993, I remembered the red coat. Most of the film is shown in black and white. Yet, of the whole film, I thought of that little girl in the red coat who appears in a sequence of absolute chaos. Every time I thought of this child, I felt a moving emotion of sadness seemingly available because of the sense of aliveness conveyed by the red coat and the innocence of the child wandering alone through the terrified crowd. In a completely devastating scene further in the film, this coat appears again, soiled by dirt, soot, and the limp, dead body of this same little girl. Another point of feeling for me developed around Schindler himself, who always arouses a mix of impressions. Schindler is depicted as a compelling figure, a strange hero, a scoundrel who lusted after wealth and women and at the same time someone who saves lives. His physical presence is large on the screen. The camera often pulls in close so that his facial expressions fill the entire screen. In the chaotic scenes of the roundup of the Jewish population, complete with the SS shooting randomly, dogs barking, children being separated from parents, and blood flowing, the camera turned to focus on the faces of Schindler, who stares, and his girlfriend, who cries. They represent the witnesses who allow registration of the events to take place, which then opens emotional space for the audience to receive the film. In the story itself, Schindler and his Jewish laborers are actual survivors and are not murdered, providing a possible way to enter the story and have some identification with being alive. Survivors and their families appear, in color, in procession at the end of the film. They are tangible, with addresses in New York City, Tel Aviv, Chicago, and Los Angeles. They have histories. Their existence in time with past, present, and future help anchor the scenes of horror, the trains, the terrifying chaos of being wrenched away from family, the ashes, the murdering, the humiliations, the helplessness, and the evil.

Following these preliminary observations, I returned to the film to see how Spielberg moved from events about which one is horrified and numbed to events about which one can experience affect. I found that these types of sequences occurred repeatedly throughout the film, with continuous oscillations between mass, often anomic, brutality to something more human—a closeup of an individual, a gesture, a moment of color, a dramatic use of music. Even the scenes of violent sadistic sexual encounters provide an ability to experience a visceral response and are not totally deadening. Due to the capacity of film, the offering of different types of phenomena does not have to follow in a linear timeline but can occur through the presentation of multiple images, allowing the audience to vary intensity of experience by shifting focus.

To exemplify Spielberg's development of space for viewing and feeling, I define the elements at work in the oscillations taking place in three sequences. By necessity, verbal description collapses in time what was in process on the screen. I attempt in my descriptions to keep the integrity of illustrating the use of variation in focus that Steven Spielberg was able to bring to this film.

The first sequence is from the opening of the film and is in color. A Jewish family is celebrating the Sabbath. They sit around the table while the mother, reciting the prayer, lights the Sabbath candles. The smoke rising from the candles melds into the smoke belching out of a train engine, switching to an achromatic depiction. There is a chilling stereotyped train, anomic crowds of eastern European Jewish families replete with suitcases and terrified faces, typewriters set in front of officious-looking Nazis, who are lining up people to make lists of names. This opening to the efficiency and dehumanization process of the roundup of the Jewish population is followed by the first closeups of Oskar Schindler. He is shown dressing in style for his entrance to the cabaret, where he proceeds to use his personality to bring SS higher-ups to his table, where he wines and dines them and flirts with their women. This scene opens with the maitre d' needing to know his name. After his purposive seduction of their interest, everyone in the restaurant knows his name as if he were their best friend. The charisma of Schindler has been introduced to all, including the audience.

The second and third sequences I studied demonstrate similar camera movement between elements of color and black and white but with greatly increased levels of horror. As the events gain more traumatizing impact, the representation of Schindler gains heroic and even savior-like qualities. In the second film clip, the violence of the liquidation from the Ghetto is presented, including the chaos of breaking into people's homes, tearing family members from each other, lining people up in a vertical line to shoot and murder them all. There are dogs barking, screams from individuals seeing their loved ones killed, orders being shouted, and a procession of people looking terrified as they are herded out of town. All of this happens at once so that the film screen is a scene full of horrors, and the viewer's eyes are drawn from one type of violence to another. This visual melee of terrifying imagery and the cacophonous sound of atrocity are almost impossible to bear. Spielberg provides the audience with two alternating possibilities that allow the movement of the mind not provided within the totality of disaster. We see the girl in the red coat, and we see the facial expressions of Schindler and his lover on horseback high on a hilltop watching and reacting. This establishment of witnesses, who are a bit removed and turn and retreat from the scene, is truly a brilliant move to give relief to the audience.

The third sequence I use to demonstrate Spielberg's technique is the surreal horror involved in the absurd digging up and burning of the dead to annihilate further their existence and their murders. In this scene, we are confronted with a drunken, screaming Nazi, a fiery smoky mound, transportation of bodies on wheelbarrows, a moment of muted color (the little girl in her red coat), and a large closeup of Schindler's facial expression. In the film, the haunting surreal inhumanity of this scene is followed by Schindler wheeling and dealing to buy the workers and take them to Czechoslovakia. Again, stunning devastation and an inability to take in what is being portrayed are followed by the activity of saving lives, which keeps one believing in activity and maintains movement in the mind and opening of space for knowing more.

DISCUSSION OF THE FILM SEQUENCES

In the film, Spielberg filled the blankness of the screen with remarkable artfulness, establishing an environment in which an audience can be formed. The film's capacity to move attention continuously allows the viewer to become a witness to traumatic truths. Unlike a psychoanalyst, who is involved in verbal exchange, a filmmaker tells a story with multiple visual images and sound effects. The holding environment capable of managing trauma has been crafted in the editing room so that the story can be presented without destroying experience of memory and feeling. Without creative use of the film space, there would be nothing to take in and metabolize. There is something to learn from Spielberg's *Schindler's List*, not only about the Holocaust, but also about a process through which the unspoken becomes speakable and traumatic states are ameliorated.

Auerhahn and Laub (1984) put forth the belief that the survivor of trauma, particularly of Holocaust trauma, is able to restore memory function by reconnecting to representations, in memory and affect, of life occurring pre-trauma. They consistently refer to the need for revivification, a reenlivening of what could be called basic properties of ego or of one's selfhood. Through recollections of life before the traumatic events, the person reconnects to an ability to feel variations in affect and a sense of the intactness of one's memory. Elements of the story of Schindler and elements of the film production enable ego functions to remain intact in similar ways to the revivification process. The cinematic techniques of shifting images, of simultaneously presenting multiple images and of mixing sense perceptions (visual and auditory) titrate the overwhelming experience of massive trauma. The ego is not completely overwhelmed but remains able to move between past and present and between blankness and affect.

I learned many lessons from Spielberg's production techniques that I make use of with my patients who are working with deep anxiety and trauma. It is important to know that oscillations are not only possible but also necessary to keep the psyche alive. Often, patients feel guilty that they want to look away from the terribly painful work in the therapy. It is not stopping the work. Looking toward and away often allows the work to take place and to be processed. The psychoanalytic term *working through* generally applies to transformations of the resistances that are operative in bringing about repression and repetition. Concerning trauma, working through applies to a change in the repetition of the "nothing" of being overwhelmed and helpless. Movement of the mind, oscillations like those created by Spielberg, makes for the working through of trauma.

When I present this material to psychoanalytic groups, it invites the opening of a possibility of speaking of the Holocaust and therapeutic work with patients. Therapists feel invited to speak of countertransferences to their patients' traumas. In South Korea in 1998, members of the Korean Psychoanalytic Study Group spoke about the transmission of trauma from brutalities, including rape, during the Japanese occupation and their countertransferences to such traumas as they appear in treatments. I reported in *The American Psychoanalyst* (Goodman, 1999) that "how to acknowledge and work through first denial and then the affects, such as intense shame, related to trauma was the theme that emerged from the presentation" (p. 19). In Peru in 2001, the audience spoke of Jewish people who survived through emigration to Peru and of pain and fear related to the contemporary kidnappings, murders, and terror from the Shining Path.

Movement of the mind, like movement of the camera, creates greater possibility for knowing trauma on the film screen and in psychoanalytic treatments. For many, Spielberg's oscillating movement of the camera in the film *Schindler's List* invites the beginnings of a process for witnessing the Holocaust.

REFERENCES

Atkinson, R. (1993, May 3). Germany views its past through *Schindler's List*. *Washington Post*. Retrieved from http://www.washingtonpost.com

Auerhahn, N., & Laub, D. (1984). Annihilation and restoration: Post-traumatic memory as a pathway and obstacle to recovery. *International Review of Psychoanalysis, 11*, 327–344.

Goodman, N. (1999). A visit with the Korean Analytic Study Group. *American Psychoanalyst, 33*(2), 18.

Laub, D., & Podell, D. (1995). Art and trauma. *International Journal of Psychoanalysis, 76*, 995–1005.

McCann, I. L., & Pearlman, L. A. (1990). Vicarious traumatization: A framework the psychological effects of working with victims. *Journal of Traumatic Stress, 3*(1), 131–149.

Poland, W. (1992). From analytic surface to analytic space. *Journal of the American Psychoanalytic Association, 40*, 381–404.

Spiegelman, A. (1986). *Maus: A survivor's tale: My father bleeds history*. New York: Pantheon Books.

Spiegelman, A. (1991). *Maus II: A survivor's tale: And here my troubles began*. New York: Pantheon Books.

Spielberg, S. (Director). (1993). *Schindler's list* [Motion picture]. United States: Universal Pictures.

Staub, E. (1989). *The roots of evil: The origins of genocide and other group violence*. New York: Cambridge University Press.

Viderman, S. (1974). Interpretation in the analytic space. *International Review of Psychoanalysis, 1*, 467–480.

Chapter 21

Giving Voice to the Silenced Through Theater

Gail Humphries Mardirosian

INTRODUCTION

The artistic life of Terezín has been explored in a project that is titled, "Voices of Terezín," beginning in spring 2009 in Prague and at Terezín and continuing at American University and the University of New Hampshire; it is ongoing. The reflections in this chapter on the theatrical experience at Terezín and the various components of the project emanate from a perspective of theater as a means of seeing and knowing. The theater can provide possibilities connecting to each of us at a level transcending intellectual and emotional paradigms to penetrate into our personal "essence." As a conduit for the voices of others, theater can exert generative power, both for the creators (playwrights, directors, actors, designers) and the audience who shares in the performance. The theater experience engenders a collective occurrence that has the potential to be transformative, to empower, and to function as a catalyst for insight and action. Theater for those in the ghetto of Terezín/Theresienstadt (transit and forced labor camp during the Nazi occupation of Czechoslovakia) appeared to have a deep impact for both the creators and the audience. It is an important reminder on a continuum for us today, as we witness, connect, experience, and hear their voices across time.

While there are many mechanisms for remembering those at Terezín, this project is about the arts as a means of connecting to and telling some of the stories. These stories resonate with messages that are sobering, harsh, and challenging. The realization of the arts provided those who were confined at Terezín with something extraordinary. Perhaps the artistic outlay gave individuals vitality or an affirmation of a sense of identity—art seemed to function as both weapon and feeling agent. Today, the artistic creations from Terezín provide us with a connection that can reverberate in personal and substantive ways.

As an artist, I found the process of approaching theatrical material from Terezín to be daunting. Whether reading the poetry of the children, gazing on their drawings, listening to the music of the composers, or reading the scripts of the dramas and cabarets, I was reminded of the potential for art to sustain, uplift, challenge, provoke thought, and inspire. It is affirming that in the midst of a world of repression, the arts and voices of Terezín resonate with an affirmation of humanity, exceeding the most horrific of circumstances and asserting a spirit of creativity that goes beyond time and space through the integrity of art.

This thought from Vaclav Havel struck me several times throughout the artistic journey: "Art springs from truthful and extreme experience perhaps even more than it does from talent and it has the capacity to be stronger than death" (1995, p. 10).

Many of those who did survive the terror of Terezín soon will pass away. Their stories and others', however, can live on through the telling power of the art that was created there. Theater not only generates fodder for thought and even emotional nourishment for the present but also feeds forward to us. It engages us in the past (creation of script and rehearsal), connects to us in the present (audience and performers are witnessing), and provides a conduit for the future (we ponder, feel, think about the content and can be provoked to further action). Theater in Terezín demonstrates the generative capacity of art, simultaneously providing a striking contrast of the human capacity to destroy, given the very circumstances of the creation. Perhaps this component is what makes the work so challenging for me. Many of the artists never survived to share their work in person, but the vibrancy of their messages continues to resonate today. As a director, I witnessed multiple actors and audience members, both in the United States and in the Czech Republic, as they experienced the unique "in-the-moment" phenomenon of theater and connected to the theatrical content.

Aristotle wrote centuries ago about the "willing suspension of disbelief" and the potential for theater as a catalyst for us to experience something beyond our own personal immediacy. As we engage, we experience the "roles," in essence, the lives of others. As the roles unfold in performance, we invest something from our own emotional lives in a process that is conscious (as performers we decide to act the part or as audience members we decide to attend the theater and "accept" the events on stage), but that takes us to a level that is subliminal and perhaps pervades the unconscious. As a director, I have witnessed that transcendence, time and again, experiencing the power of connection from text to stage to audience, sometimes with a striking impact.

Judy Yordon (2002), in *Roles in Interpretation*, discusses the idea of empathy and sympathy, describing empathy as "the ability to experience vicariously the feelings, thoughts, responses, and attitudes of another individual." She goes on to explore this outlook: "When you sympathize with someone, you understand what the other person is feeling, but you maintain a bit more distance, instead of feeling with someone, you feel for someone" (p. 141). Work on the Terezín project generated many dimensions of empathy and sympathy for me—often intricately intertwined—even as I tried to maintain an objective distancing. As a young director, it made the responsibility of directing rugged because of the type of plays that I was drawn to and my innate sensitivities and sensibilities. Over the years, I have attempted to accept the mantle of responsibility of directing substantive and provocative drama by simply focusing on the creative circumstance, connecting to the role making and role taking for the actors, and consciously encouraging audiences to come to the theater experience to assimilate whatever echoes in a personal, even visceral, manner.

I cannot fully explain what it is that happens during theatrical moments, whether formally or informally, that allows us to surpass who we really are in that given moment and to assume or to accept a theatrical role. Perhaps it is the "you" in the process of theater that is the key: You bring to the theatrical experience your personal repertoire, your history, and your life resonances—whether on the stage or in the audience—and then you become someone else as an actor (either formally or informally) and accept the on-stage role (either informally or formally) as an audience member. To experience and to accept "in role" is fascinating for the actor and the audience. We vicariously enter into worlds that extend beyond our own, and if the moments are effective, we exceed the real present.

Recalling the various talk backs in response to the performances, both in the Czech Republic and in the United States, reminds me of the power of theater to engage us effectively with sensitive and difficult topics. Audience members regularly commented on how the actors gave a face to Terezín for them and how the circumstances of Terezín became palpable to them. Likewise, actors regularly commented on the magnitude of responsibility they felt when approaching their roles and the connections that they experienced as they performed. In talk backs after our productions in the United States, it was clear that our audiences had, at best, limited acquaintance with the arts at Terezín. However, it also was clear that our audiences were exceptionally interested in expanding their knowledge and did so through the artistic encounters.

Finally, my overarching goal in presenting theater and developing the "Voices of Terezín" has not been the generation of empathy for the sake of feeling, but empathy for the sake of understanding, respect, and ultimately action. As such, this goal is implicit in all of my work on the project. I believe in, and have, in nearly 30 years as a theater practitioner, witnessed theater as a provocateur, enlightener, inquisitor, reminder, and catalyst for action in circumstances when social justice and human rights are at stake.

THE ONSET OF THE JOURNEY: ENCOUNTERING
THE STORIES AND THE PLAY *THE SMOKE OF HOME*

The impetus for the "Voices of Terezín" project was the work of Fulbright scholar Lisa Peschel. In the course of her interviews with Terezín survivors and their families, she found that the widow of imprisoned playwright Zdenek Eliáš had preserved a copy of the play *The Smoke of Home* (2006). Scenes from the play were first performed at Divadlo Komedie in Prague in June 2008. I subsequently directed the play in Prague and at Terezín as part of a Fulbright appointment in spring 2009.

The play provides a lens into the challenges, tensions, ruminations, and despair within prison walls during the Thirty Years' War. The text seems to resound to the confines of the ghetto of Terezín, reflecting the oppression of confinement as the characters in the play reminisce and long for home. It begins with the prologue providing the context for the play, set in a prison cell during the Thirty Years' War, describing these prisoners who "were forgotten." Perhaps this prologue captures how the playwrights Zdenek Eliáš and Jiri Stein actually felt at this point in their lives, as young men confined to Terezín, or that they captured in writing what others around them felt at this point—"imprisoned and forgotten."

In the play, the two main characters, Casselius and Christian, reveal diverse perspectives about life and the means of dealing with their circumstances. Christian can be interpreted as a romanticist and idealist as he struggles poetically for meaning and an understanding of his life and his confinement. Casselius, on the other hand, deals with the adverse circumstances rationally and logically. Father Anselm, a priest and the third prisoner, is absorbed in religion and his calling. When a fourth prisoner is added—Waldau, an officer of the army of the emperor's general—there is additional tension, and other outlooks are provided. Waldau and Anselm argue passionately about the practical limitations of the cell and their repression, each with differing paradigms of thinking and beliefs. The only female in the play, Veronika, brings soul and compassion to the harsh situation. When speaking with Christian, she tells us, "I walked from city to city, from camp to camp … always asking about you. … What suffering I've endured through it all!" (p. 15).

What only Casselius knows, and the other characters do not discover until the end of the play, is that the homes they reminisce about and that they long for do not exist—all of the countryside has been destroyed. As the bells of the city ring out a cry of relief, with the people shouting, "It's over, it's over," celebrating the end of the war, the characters exit the prison cell with the knowledge that they will return to a different world, a different life, and a home that is profoundly changed.

In a particularly poignant monologue, Casselius reveals the devastation that has occurred during their confinement:

Casselius: Fools! Get a hold of yourselves! Blind, thoughtless! Fools! (Pauses, then silence.) Should I have told you after all, what that Walloon actually told me? Should I have told you that three weeks ago General Wrangel lost his brother when they were defeated near Dachau, and that in vengeance he tore through Bavaria like death incarnate, sowing all the horrors of war? That he torched a number of your towns and villages? That even the cynical Walloon who marches back and forth in front of our cell still recalls with horror the havoc that was wrought. There are no stones left standing in your Rine—today your church and parsonage, Father Anselm, are shattered ruins. And Waldau? It has long since stopped smoking amidst the trampled and ruined fields! And you, Christian, were you to go from Rine up to Stetten, at the cross-roads by the three firs you would see a thread of smoke from the conflagration where Stetten used to stand! That is your smoke of home today! You want to go home? Fools! The home you left is in the past, irrevocably buried in the abyss of time! There's a different world out there, behind these walls! Do you hear? A different world! There won't be any comfort, leisure, or carousing at Waldau, there won't be time for pious meditation in a quiet corner of your little parsonage garden, Father Anselm! Your romantic idyll will remain unfinished, Christian. There won't be time! Do you hear? There won't be time! (p. 18)

The Smoke of Home went unseen at Terezín and during the lifetime of the playwrights Jiri Stein and Zdenek Eliáš.

Katherine Schmitt Elias (wife of Zdenek) and Dorothy Elias (daughter of Zdenek) readily shared details about the authors of this play.[1] These details informed our work in the process of bringing the play to the stage and to our audiences. They made me all the more cognizant of the burden of accountability I was shouldering in presenting the play. Katherine, or Kate, as I know her, sent photos of both of the men. Their eyes penetrated my being. I recall sighing deeply as I considered the magnitude of the responsibility.

Realistic idealist that he was, Zdenek met a soul mate in the Hannover Barracks (a dormitory for men "fit for work") in Terezín. Jiri Stein, also born in 1920, was a practical-minded engineering student with a poetic heart. Through luck and ingenuity, the two friends were able to build their own tiny room in the barracks, which afforded them a degree of privacy and comfort in which to share wide-ranging ideas and do a little writing, including The Smoke of Home. In May 1944, Zdenek was transported first to Auschwitz-Birkenau and then to the Schwarzheide labor camp in Germany. ... A few months later, it was Jiri's turn. Of the 1,500 people in that transport, only 79 survived; Jiri Stein was not

[1] Taken from the "Voices of Terezín" program notes, American University, March 2010.

among them. He passed the initial selection at Auschwitz, but then was sent in a labor transport to Dachau, where he died December 19, 1944.

At the end of the war, Zdenek was repatriated to Prague, where he recuperated for many months. ... Two years later, the Communists came to power in Czechoslovakia and Zdenek escaped over the mountains back into Germany rather than live under another totalitarian regime. Eventually he arrived in America and became a journalist with Radio Free Europe. ... After a long and peaceful retirement in Seattle, Washington, he died in his easy chair February 2, 2000.

In an interview conducted by American University honors student and religion major Kera Package in April 2010, Katherine Schmitt Elias and Dorothy Elias shared significant thoughts that I continue to ponder as I work on the project.

> Dorothy: Art, especially in the context of Terezín, is not sacred *as art* and certainly can't be separated from resistance or survival. For people who had been stripped of nearly all personal power, who had been deprived of every vestige of their former lives, who had lost everything, having a means to express a sense of self would be enormously empowering.

Dorothy also expounded, and I concur, that through her father's voice, we can "learn to face reality without illusions ... in any conflict, both sides are capable of wrong and, possibly, brutal behavior. Individuals must maintain ethical standards that adhere to human values, and rise above partisan thinking."

Likewise, a viewpoint that Kate Elias expressed captures some of my own thinking as an artist and, perhaps, was even a key factor in my calling to the project: "I think art arises out of personal imperative: artists create first of all because their souls demand it. Then, I think the most logical secondary motivation is psychological, spiritual survival, and this is what I think motivated most of the artistic expression in Terezín."

While the "Voices of Terezín" project centered on *The Smoke of Home*, it became an important catalyst for a multiyear, multidisciplinary exploration of the arts, history, memory, and identity at American University. The project also served as a conduit for difficult dialogue around human rights issues. It expanded to include performances at the University of New Hampshire and will surely continue at other institutions during the upcoming years.

BACKSTORY OF THE "VOICES" PROJECT IN PRAGUE AND TEREZÍN

The impetus for the project, as presented previously, was the play discovered by Fulbright Scholar Lisa Peschel. It was presented by this author at the Divadlo Inspirace in Prague in 2009 through the collaboration of the Academy of Performing Arts, the Spitfire Company, and the Prague Playhouse, with a cast consisting of three Czech actors, one American, and one British actor, all living in Prague at the time. Subsequently, the play was staged on site at Terezín, with the same cast, in the Attic Theatre of the Magdeburg Barracks, as part of the inaugural Raphael Schaechter Institute of Arts and Humanities. It was a haunting and enveloping experience to present the play at Terezín. Everyone involved with the production connected in personal ways.

Nothing had quite prepared me, or I can safely say any of us, for the witnessing that we experienced as we rehearsed and presented the play at Terezín. We each experienced various reverberations throughout the day of rehearsal and performance in the Attic Theatre. After our dress rehearsal and before the performance, I had to just walk the streets of Terezín by myself to gain my composure. I sat on a bench in the town square on a bright sunny day in May. I looked around me and was haunted by the thought of the repression and waste of lives at Terezín. My only comfort was to focus, yet again, on the generative power of theater.

In an e-mail (May 2011), Mirenka Cechova, the professional Czech actress who played Veronika and assistant director for this production, witnessed and described the experience in a profound way:

> For those of us who live in the direct heritage of experiencing the Holocaust, either through close relatives or through the place where we were born, this memory is something that is a part of our collective consciousness and subconscious. There are many things that cannot be pronounced aloud, because we already know them. We have already experienced the pain. This pain returns from the past and is always sensitive and uneasy, but without speaking about the things, without witnessing, there is a danger that they will be forgotten.
>
> This project was incredible for me in many ways, mainly as a trigger for cross cultural dialogue, an aim that was common for all of us—to speak loudly about the past, to share the experience with others, and to give a voice to those who were forced into the silence.

The performance was attended by an eclectic audience, ranging from theatergoers in Prague, including Terezín survivors, to different generations of Czech and American theatergoers, including doctoral students from the United States who were in Prague for a summer semester. It seemed as if each individual witnessed the production in a personal way. Dr. Linda Donahue, head of arts administration and associate chair of the Department of Theatre and Dance, Texas Tech University, attended the production with her students. She had this comment: "We had an extraordinary and once-in-a-lifetime experience at Terezín, viewing *The Smoke of Home*. That is the wonder of theatre—the temporal art event happens once and then it only lives in memory" (personal communication, 2011). Donahue's thinking about the temporal power of theater that continues to live in memory is a key contributing factor in terms of why I embraced this project—to connect contemporary memory to the past through theater.

EXTENSION OF THE JOURNEY

As the project continued to expand, the many components appeared to provide a face for and to personalize the experience for students and faculty at American University and the University of New Hampshire. Students in the honors course at American, who were majors in varied disciplines, including psychology, criminal justice, history, international studies, religion, as well as performing arts, focused on the Holocaust and the wartime experiences of the inmates at Terezín. When responding on an anonymous postcourse survey, students spoke eloquently about the power of the arts, noting that the arts had "enormous power to teach complex content, "to further genuine understanding" and "depth of investigation," providing a "pathway between the message and true personal knowing ... a more lasting and meaningful learning experience." The students consistently spoke about the lessons of responsibility gleaned from their study of the Holocaust through the lens of Terezín. Personal linkages mattered to me, as students assimilated the course material. During one exercise and small-group discussion, I challenged the students to assume some personal responsibility for witnessing. One student, synthesizing her small-group discussion, commented (April 2010):

> What will we do? While we may not leave this semester with the motivation to start a new program or initiative, we will be leaving this class with a sense of responsibility. That responsibility is to apply what we have learned in this course to the rest of our academic careers and beyond. The responsibility is to use our talents, whatever they may be, to share with the world the things we know to be true—whether that be the hope of humanity and self-expression or the pain and hard reality of genocide halfway around the world. The consensus within our group was that we have the responsibility to do our best to use the skills and resources we have to be a voice within our spheres of influence.

In a final response paper (May 2010), another student noted, "In a culture where knowledge comes from data and learning from reason, this is a valuable lesson: It is one thing to know with your mind, another to know with your heart and to act upon that knowledge." Perhaps this is the essence of the potential for a meaningful theatrical experience. It can cue and prompt us with remembrances, generate authentic interaction in the moment, and then afford the possibility of honoring the integrity of the immediacy of the work, even challenging us to hear a call to action for the present and future as we "know with our heart."

When the project was replicated at the University of New Hampshire, similar outlooks emerged. Raina Ames, assistant professor of theater, directed a production of the "Voices of Terezín" and included talk backs that produced dynamic dialogue. Professor Ames spoke of the power of the theatrical experience for her. It was remarkable for me to hear how similarly we both felt:

> Art has the power to transform lives, but in Terezín the arts were a mode of survival. I am truly humbled and inspired by the artists, musicians, actors, and composers who continued to practice their respective arts even in the face of horrendous, unimaginable circumstances. The body can be imprisoned, but the soul can be given wings to fly. Directing "Voices of Terezin" at the University of New Hampshire is just one small way to honor those who upheld their artistic ideals even as they faced hard labor, disease, and deportation to death camps and to testify for those whose voices were silenced.

As the project evolved at American University, I decided to heed the children's voices silenced at Terezín by mounting (in fall 2010) a production of *I Never Saw Another Butterfly*, a musical based on the play by Celeste Raspanti, with book and lyrics by Joseph Robinette and music by E. A. Alexander—all inspired by Hana Volavkova's book (1994). We were able to reach out to children and teachers in the Washington, D.C., metropolitan area to consider the messages, giving voice to the silenced children.

This powerful musical had messages for children and adults *from* children and adults. Based on the stories, drawings, and poetry of the children of Terezín, the title originated from a poem by Pavel Friedman, who was deported to Terezín on April 26, 1942, and then died in Auschwitz on September 29, 1944.

Again, there was a discernible impact from the production, this time not only for the college students and adults who attended the production, but also for elementary and middle school audiences. It seemed to me that the production provided a conduit to and personal connections for these audiences, connections that were provocative, troubling, and haunting.

Both the schoolchildren and the university students appeared touched, surprised, and connected to the content of the workshop exercises and the content of the performance. As one young student noted, "I put myself in the shoes of someone being sent to Terezín, and it was frightening and sad and seemed too real." Another young student noted, "It's like we feel how the people felt leaving their homes. I would have been confused, sad, and very angry." The university student actors also spoke about "having a moral obligation to tell these stories" and "making them immediate through theater." They discussed the difficulty of imagining the creative process unfolding in these ghastly circumstances. One cast member aptly remarked: "It seemed as if their art provided something beyond description while everyone was surrounded by death, illness, malnutrition, and the fear of the transports to the East." Another university student, Jessica Therriault, who attended the production, cogently commented, "This play uses art as a conduit to keep history alive. It physically and emotionally shows humans what happened during this very dark period of time. This art will survive time and remind people of what happened. ... Most importantly, this play reminds people to always search for the truth."

CONCLUSION: THE STORY WILL GO ON

Theater allows us to observe, view, perceive, and behold, to truly witness through another lens, walk in someone else's footpath, breathe through other beings, and transcend the here and now through the here and now. A few years ago, I walked up a hillside in Delphi, Greece, and saw the ancient Greek words for "know thyself" (γνῶθι σαυτόν) still etched in classical Greek in the stone high above me. I have thought about that moment often. What does it really mean to look within and maintain the sphere without? What does it mean to embrace spirituality that transcends rationality? I believe that theater affords us this possibility. My journey with the "Voices of Terezín" constitutes a look within connected to many spheres without, and it continues. The project propels me forward with its own life, and I am continually drawn to it.

In the introduction to the anthology of *I Never Saw Another Butterfly*, in "A Note from the United States Holocaust Museum," there is a significant quotation from Israeli novelist Aharon Appelfeld, himself a child survivor of the Holocaust:

> Art constantly challenges the process by which the individual person is reduced to anonymity. ... Through their artistic expressions, the voices of these children, each one unique and individual, reach us across the abyss of the greatest crime in history, allow us to touch them, and restore our own humanity in doing so. (p. ix)

Perhaps this challenge of reaching into the abyss and exploring the essence of humanity within this horrific circumstance is what has drawn me to this work.

This chapter is dedicated to the memory of those who suffered and those who created at Terezín and to all those individuals who will try to understand and embrace a vision of a better world.

REFERENCES

Eliáš, Z., & Stein, J. (2006). *The smoke of home* (D. Elias, Trans.).

Havel, V. (1995). Foreword. In M. R. Krizkova & P. Wilson (Eds.) and R. E. Novak (Trans.), *We are children just the same: "Vedem," the secret magazine by the boys of Terezín* (pp. ix–xii). Philadelphia: Jewish Publications Society of America.

Volavkova, H. (1994). *I never saw another butterfly*. New York: Schocken.

Yordon, J. E. (2002). *Roles in interpretation*. New York: McGraw-Hill.

Chapter 22

Witnessing the Death of Yiddish Language and Culture
Holes in the Doorposts

Arnold Richards

> This was the end. This was the sum total of hundreds of generations of living and building, of religion, of Torah, of piety, of free thinking, of Zionism, of Bundism, of struggles and battles, of the hopes of an entire people—this, this empty desert.
>
> I looked around me at what had been the Jews of Warsaw. I felt one hope, and I feel it now. May this sea of emptiness bubble and boil, may it cry out eternal condemnation of the murderers and pillagers, may it be forever the shame of the civilized world which saw and heard and chose to remain silent.
>
> Goldstein (2005, p. 248)

To bear witness to the Holocaust is to look both ways. We not only must acknowledge heartbreaking destruction and loss but must celebrate the enduring power of life. Not every individual witness is privy to both perspectives, however. Some witness only destruction; some are themselves destroyed. Some witnesses come so close to destruction that they can endure their experience only by separating as much as possible from what they have seen, keeping it to themselves and passing it on (if at all) as a tale told at a remove. Some manage to continue to grow even with traumatized roots; they put out new shoots and look to the future. Destruction and creation—witnessing includes both. So, when the editors asked me to contribute to this volume a personal view of what the Holocaust meant to Yiddish culture, I found myself contemplating that tension between absence and presence, death and life, destruction and creation. I grew up in a family that did not hide what was happening, which allowed me to be openly interested. At the same time, I saw the intensity of pain the events of the 1930s and 1940s caused in my family and my community, and I learned to appreciate why some people felt the need to separate themselves from it, and why others were disconnected from it by fiat, because their parents could not bear to engage with their experience intimately enough to pass it on.

I think that my choice of profession had a lot to do with my own issues about coming to terms with the past. I am a psychoanalyst, committed to helping people find ways to discover and tolerate their own histories (whatever they may be) so they are free to build their futures. I grew up bilingual in Yiddish and English in Brooklyn, New York, and have been involved since 1978 with YIVO (Yidisher Visnshaftlekler Institut or Yiddish Scientific Institute), an organization dedicated to the preservation of Yiddish language documents and cultural history; I served as chairman of the board of directors between 1987 and 1990. I have gained an expansive, intricate, and very privileged view, not only of the catastrophe of the Holocaust, but also of the extraordinarily creative ways that the Jewish people had found and continue to find to develop.

In this chapter, I act as a witness to honor the history of Yiddish culture and memorialize some the writers and poets who were killed. There is absence where a vast wealth of literature and a tradition formerly flourished.

TRAVELING TO KRAKÓW: HOLES WHERE MEZUZAHS USED TO BE

In the early 1980s, I traveled to Kraków with a YIVO group for a special showing at the Jagiellonian University there. That exhibit gave rise to the collection published as *Image before My Eyes: A Photographic History of Jewish Life in Poland, 1864–1939* (Dobrosczycki & Kirshenblatt-Gimblett, 1987) and to Josh Waletsky's 1981 documentary of the same name. There was an official opening ceremony for our contingent, followed by a tour of the displays documenting Jewish life in the Polish territories before the Holocaust. The Polish visitors to the exhibit, of all ages, responded to the photographs as if they were archeological documents, records of an ancient civilization. They did not seem to feel any close connection between these pictures and their history—in some cases, their lives. But to those of us from YIVO, it was a moving and gripping evocation of the vibrancy of Jewish life in Poland not so very long ago—certainly within our parents' memories and, for many of us, our own.

I thought about this as we drove from Kraków to Warsaw, stopping to visit the formerly Jewish villages—the shtetlach—we passed through along the way. On the doorposts of houses formerly occupied by Jews, there were nail holes you could see and touch, ghosts of mezuzahs that were no longer there.

But, it was not all that long ago that they had been there, and I felt the connection acutely, looking at those photographs in Kraków, and walking through those once-Jewish, now Polish, villages. My mother came from a village like these. She spoke the language that the people who lived here spoke; she read the books that the people who lived here read. I read them, too. We had them at home while I was growing up in Brooklyn. My father's story is different, but that is part of the point of my assignment for this volume, which is to bear witness to the fate of the Yiddish literary culture in eastern Europe from a personal point of view, in the context of my own history.

A BRIEF BIOGRAPHY

I grew up in Brooklyn in the 1930s and 1940s, hearing and reading about the Holocaust in English, Yiddish, and Russian. My parents' marriage was a microcosm of the sociological stew that was eastern European Jewry. They came from towns that are very close together on the map, and their Yiddish was very similar. But, my father spoke Russian, and my mother spoke Polish. My father's family had been more or less integrated with the Russian world for generations—his great-grandfather, who was killed in the Crimean War (1853–1856), was the only Jewish noncommissioned officer in the Russian army, and his grandfather was manager of a Russian estate of an absentee Polish landowner. My father graduated from a gymnasium where he had been excused from religion classes because he was Jewish. My mother came from an Orthodox shtetl family; her family kept kosher, and the schools there were traditional *kheyders* (literally, "room"), the common name for the old-fashioned elementary school for the teaching of Judaism. My mother left Galicia with her family in the 1920s when she was 11 years old. She worked as a milliner and learned English in night school. My father came here by himself in 1924. He was a Bolshevik atheist who joined the Russian revolution and became a librarian in the Red Army. It was the job of the librarian of each unit of Trotsky's army to drive the horse and the cart full of books for the soldiers to read. That was my father's job. Guns were not enough, Trotsky thought. You also had to know Marx.

My earliest lexical memory dates from 1939. I was 5, reading the *Forward* (*Forvets* in Yiddish), a Jewish American newspaper published in New York beginning in 1897, and there was a picture of a bearded man and a caption: "Barimpta yiddisher professor geshtorben": Freud had died.[1] Yiddish culture was an integral part of my growing up, as I know it was not for many Jewish children at the time. But, it was not until I was an adult that I became really aware of the magnitude of what had been lost.

---

[1] Freud died on September 23, 1939, which was a Saturday, and the *Forward* did not publish on Saturday. On Monday, September 25, 1939, on the front page of the *Forward*, was a picture of Freud with the heading "Yiddisher Gelerter Tot," and on page 9 a small article. The following day, September 26, on page 4 without a picture, there was a larger article, "Velt Barimter Zigmund Freud Velecher Iz Yetzt Geshtorben."

YIDDISH: A LOST LANGUAGE

So, let me start with the language in question, Yiddish. The origins of Yiddish are not absolutely clear, but it is thought to have arisen in the 10th or 11th century in the Rhineland, the fruit of generations of migration back and forth between Palestine and Europe after Rome destroyed Judea in the first century AD. It was an inclusive language, open to elements of the various other Jewish linguistic traditions that intersected with it, so it grew in time into a communicative thread that connected many Jews of very different backgrounds.

But its universality—as a language and as the marker of a traditional and separate Jewish culture—was on the wane long before the Holocaust. There were various reasons for this, but they mostly had to do with pressures for assimilation. Convenience was one of these pressures. Yiddish was still the main, and often the only, language of the provincial Jews living in shtetls in the Pale of Settlement (the Pale of Settlement as a legal area of Jewish settlement was abolished with the Russian Revolution in 1917). Many of these people for religious reasons kept themselves apart from the "secular" world and perpetuated their isolation with the traditional religious kheyder education that followed a curriculum centuries old. But, an increasing number of Polish Jews spoke Polish as well; it was a necessary tool for doing business with the Poles. My mother's father by traditional lights was a rather worldly person, and he spoke German as well as Polish and Yiddish.

Some Jews just wanted to feel like part of the world that surrounded them; this was true all over eastern Europe and elsewhere. The great Sholem Aleichem wrote in Yiddish because his audience spoke and understood it, but he wanted his children to be part of Russian civilization and Russian society, and to them he spoke Russian. Fear was another reason for assimilation and the thinning of the population of Yiddish speakers in Eastern Europe, leaving it less concentrated than it had once been. In the wake of the financial crisis that followed the Panic of 1873, pogroms became more frequent within the Pale of Settlement. Times were hard after the booming mid-1800s, and in some quarters the Jews were blamed for it. This was the same period in which the term *anti-Semitism* came to prominence with the publication of a propaganda pamphlet by Wilhelm Marr in 1879, *Der Weg zum Siege des Germanenthums über das Judenthum* (*The Way to Victory of Germanicism over Judaism*). Many Jews felt the need to distance themselves from the distinguishing cultural, religious, and linguistic markers that made Jews so easily recognized—and so easily demonized. Another reason was pride. Yiddish was kept carefully under wraps by many of the Jewish urbanites who settled in Europe's great cities, or who grew up there as the children of immigrants, and wished to assimilate themselves as perfectly as they could to their cosmopolitan surroundings.

Sigmund Freud was an example of this. Like many Austrian Jews, he aspired to membership in what he saw as a great cultural tradition, and certainly this possibility was becoming ever less remote as the Enlightenment progressed. But, every movement that Freud and Jews like him made toward establishment culture meant a movement away from the culture of their parents. They were ashamed of their parents—with their odd dress and odd appearance and odd language—and guilty for being ashamed. I think that Freud's much-vaunted "godlessness" had as much to do with embarrassment as with religion. His wife's grandfather was the chief rabbi in Hamburg, and he did not want his status as an enlightened Jew in sophisticated Viennese society to be undermined by identification with those scruffy and primitive Jews from the shtetl. Following a lecture given by Dr. M. Grinwald in Vienna on "Yochanan" by Zoderman, Freud expressed negative attitudes against religious Jews. According Dr. Grinwald, Freud "preferred the man in the elegant tuxedo to the one dressed like a prophet."[1]

Freud later said that it was anti-Semitism that made him a Jew: "My language is German. My culture, my attainments are German. I considered myself German intellectually, until I noticed the growth of anti-Semitic prejudice in Germany and German Austria. Since that time, I prefer to call myself a Jew" (Gay, 1988, p. 448). But, some prosperous German and Austrian Jews actually came to blame the shtetl Jews for the Holocaust, believing that it was their foreignness that attracted such dangerous attention. I heard this said by German Jews in the United States and by some of the Viennese psychoanalysts who I knew in New York City. They did not recognize this as anti-Semitism themselves, or that the very success that they thought would insulate them had made them envied, and that when hard times returned again in the 1930s envy contributed a great deal to conventional anti-Semitism and support for Hitler's Final Solution.

Sociological factors like these shaped the Yiddish literary and intellectual world, in which the traditional, the assimilationist, the religious, the worldly, the political, the highbrow, the trashy, and the avant-garde were all represented. Assimilationist pressures and temptations being what they were, the halcyon days of the 1930s would likely have been the peak of Yiddish literary culture even if there had never been a Holocaust. But while they lasted, they were glorious. If not for the destruction, this literary tradition would have influenced development of the arts for generations to come.

Eastern Europe before the war was rich with gifted poets, novelists, playwrights, journalists, historians, artists, musicians, and philosophers. In 1931, Poland had the highest percentage of Jews anywhere, more than 3 million of the 17 million Jews worldwide, about 18%. I use Poland here as a focus, partly because it was home to the greatest number of Jews in Europe

---

[1] "I'd rather be the Jew in the tuxedo than the Jew in the caftan."

and partly because its cities were centers of the Yiddish literary life that I discuss. Poland's Yiddish literary culture was the largest and most active in the world; it was the only country in which successful Yiddish authors could support themselves by writing. Isaac Bashevis Singer has talked about the intellectual life of Warsaw, its newspapers, the coffeehouses where patrons could sit and talk about the great Yiddish and Western writers for hours at a time. Many of those great writers died before World War II—the likes of Y. L. Peretz, Sholom Aleichem, and Mendele Mocher Sforim, who has been called the grandfather of Yiddish literature. These men were read everywhere within the Pale of Settlement, and I read their work myself as a child here, in my Yiddish school. At home, we had a bound set of the collected works of Sholom Aleichem and a volume of Peretz as well.

By 1906, there were five Yiddish dailies in Warsaw with a circulation of 100,000 and double that circulation by the end of the decade. They serialized the work of Yiddish writers and published theater reviews and schedules. There were Jewish literary magazines. There was an Association of Jewish Writers and Journalists in Warsaw and a Poets, Essayists, and Novelists (PEN) club in Vilna. So, Yiddish speakers in eastern Europe between the wars had plenty to choose from. Readers could find everything from serious novels to avant-garde poetry to escapist junk. Theater repertoires included not only musical comedies and tearjerkers, but also drama and performances in Yiddish translation of Shakespeare and such modern playwrights as O'Neill and Dreiser. There were Yiddish movies, cabarets, and marionette theaters. A Yiddish version of the Pushkin/Tchaikovsky opera *Eugène Onegin* was produced in Vilna in 1920. Clearly, not all of these offerings were by Yiddish authors or composers, but a vast number of them were, and the fact of the others attests to the appetite and the cosmopolitan temperament of Polish urban Jewry.

DESTRUCTION

But, by the middle of the 1940s, the Yiddish culture in eastern Europe was almost completely destroyed by the Germans with the collaboration of Ukrainians and Poles. And the question to which I address the rest of this chapter is: What happened to the Yiddish writers? We can divide the Yiddish literati into groups according to the date of their deaths. The first group includes the early greats, who were dead by the time the war began. A second group survived the Holocaust and developed a Yiddish readership (significant, if dwindling) in the United States and Israel. Among these were the likes of Itzik Manger (Itsik, according to the *YIVO Encyclopedia*; Hundert, 2008), Chaim Grade, and Abraham Sutzkever. There also had been a very creative and vibrant group of Yiddish poets called the Yunga, the young ones, who were developing an avant-garde Yiddish poetic sensibility.

Some of them survived the war in the Soviet Union but were subsequently killed by Stalin. In Joseph Leftwich's anthology *Great Yiddish Writers of the Twentieth Century* (1969), both of these groups are generously represented. Leftwich included many of the early giants who died before 1940, including Y. L. Peretz (Leftwich used I. L. Peretz), Sholom Aleichem, and Isidor (Yisroel) Eliashev (Leftwich used the pen name Baal Machshoves). Among the postwar greats who survived the Holocaust, Leftwich included, for example, Grade, Sutzkever, and Sholem Asch.

The group I want to speak of and memorialize here is barely represented among Leftwich's 81 authors or in any other anthology or classification that I know. These are the Yiddish writers who were murdered in eastern Europe between 1940 and 1945, particularly those who were not granted the time to develop their craft fully or to establish enduring reputations. They were acclaimed and reckoned significant among the Jewish eastern European literati of their time. But, their work had not yet been disseminated widely, and it was lost, for the most part, when the audience of readers and theatergoers who knew it best disappeared. It is these writers who call up so poignantly the bittersweet awareness of what might have been.

Of the group who were murdered during the war years, Leftwich included two, one of whom was an old man who had fully developed his skill and renown. Hillel Zeitlin, the scholar, writer, and journalist, died in 1942 in the Warsaw Ghetto at the age of 72. Leftwich's second choice was the poet and critic Yisroel Shtern, who perished in Treblinka in 1942 at the age of 46.

These three, however, are only a few of the dozens, perhaps hundreds, of Yiddish poets, novelists, playwrights, historians, philosophers, and journalists who were lost between 1940 and 1945, dying of starvation in the ghettos of Poland and the Pale, shot in the fields and forests of Russia and Lithuania, or otherwise murdered in concentration camps. They are only a few of the people whose names we do not recognize, whose productions we have never heard of, whose books are not fondly remembered by our parents. They had not written enough, or written long enough, before the war to be known outside their immediate community, and they did not survive the war to promote their work afterward to the world's tragically destroyed audience of Yiddish speakers, readers, and theatergoers.

Leftwich's list is sobering, and it is very hard to add to it. I hope I have made clear that this is not because there was not much going on in the arts in Yiddish-speaking Europe. It is because the documentation of the period was decimated along with the people themselves. What little we know comes from material saved from the conquering Nazi armies by courage, guile, and luck and then in some cases saved again from the tightening grip of Stalin. These efforts at preservation are yet another aspect of witness, and I mention two of them here: YIVO and Ringelblum.

YIVO was founded in Vilna in 1925 by Max Weinreich and other European Jewish intellectuals (Edward Sapir, Albert Einstein, and Sigmund Freud among the trustees), who wanted to make available for study the history, language, and culture of the Jews of eastern Europe before they were swamped by change and assimilation. YIVO sent emissaries throughout the Pale of Settlement to collect the stuff of the culture. Its initial mission was collection and scholarship, not preservation. But, given what happened so soon afterward, their foresight turned out to be a great blessing. When the German army took Vilna in March 1942, the Einsatzstab Rosenberg task force, started by Nazi ideologue Alfred Rosenberg for looting the Jewish world of its cultural treasures, established a sorting center in the YIVO building. It was supposed to identify the most valuable materials there and ship the plunder to Rosenberg's Institute for the Study of the Jewish Question in Frankfurt. Rosenberg's functionaries could not distinguish between the gold and the dross, however. They impressed Jews who knew the material into this bitter task, but their unwilling accessories soon set their minds to saving YIVO's most valuable holdings. Dubbed the Paper Brigade, they disguised, removed, and hid as many important documents as they could. They were led by the poet Abraham Sutzkever and the writer and cultural historian Shmerke Kaczerginski, and they risked their lives to cache materials in the ghetto, in YIVO's attics, and with non-Jewish contacts for safekeeping.

In 1987, despite the ravages of war and Communism, a huge collection of YIVO materials that had been spirited into the hands of gentiles were discovered in a book depository, the Lithuanian National Book Center. This accounts for a significant percentage of YIVO's archive today. David E. Fishman has told this story in his book *Embers Plucked from the Fire: The Rescue of Jewish Cultural Treasures in Vilna* (Fishman, 2009). Perhaps most miraculously, or at least most ironically, the materials dispatched from YIVO to the Nazis in Frankfort were discovered in 1946 by a U.S. Army officer in a freight car at a railway siding outside Frankfort. These were sent to New York and reconstituted as the American YIVO collection.

Emanuel Ringelblum, the organizer of relief in the Warsaw Ghetto and of Oneg Shabes, the Warsaw Ghetto archive, tried to accumulate materials that would portray all facets of Jewish life from many different perspectives. He also wanted to document the destruction of Polish Jewry, to which he was an eyewitness. He and his colleagues collected questionnaires, memoirs, and interviews administered by amateur field-workers, as well as input from professional historians and sociologists. David Roskies, author of *The Jewish Search for a Usable Past* (1999), includes him among the eyewitness chroniclers of modern Jewish catastrophe. His work is an example of what Roskies called "the Literature of Destruction," another name for the tradition of witnessing that is the subject of this volume.

By some estimates, about half of what was written by Jews during this time was saved through the efforts of committed individuals like Ringelblum, who had opportunities to escape but who chose to remain in the Warsaw Ghetto to continue his work (see Kassow, 2007). Ringelblum finally left the ghetto on the eve of the uprising, but he was discovered by the Gestapo and killed, along with his family and the gentiles who had hidden them. The archive was maintained until February 1943. Two of the three Oneg Shabes caches were found after the war; the last is still missing. My mother was still alive at the time of the discovery of our YIVO materials in Vilna; when I told her about this discovery and the amazing accomplishments of the Paper Brigade, she said in Yiddish, "Better they had saved fewer papers and more people." That was not within their power. But mindful of my mother's comment, my intent in the rest of this chapter is to speak of the Yiddish poets, playwrights, and novelists of Poland who were murdered between 1941 and 1945. In some cases at least, thanks to those who documented their lives and to those who courageously managed to preserve the documents, their names will live on.

Yet, there are others whose names do not live on—whose names, even, have been lost, along with their lives and their work. Witnessing works both ways—we witness what is present, "before our eyes," as the Kraków exhibition had it, and we witness also the fact of absence and the fact of the loss of the future. Some of these names are lost to us because it was not only the people who vanished but also those who knew them. They also might have grown into greatness had their world not been destroyed. But, like the mezuzahs that once graced the doorposts of village homes, they are gone; we can know that they were there only by the holes they left behind.

A COMMUNITY ERADICATED: CREATIVE VOICES LOST

Some of the holes in the doorposts are large and deep; some are small and barely discernible. But, they all attest to a community destroyed, to an irreversible loss of life and of creative force. What follows here are two lists. The first is a list of Yiddish writers murdered between 1940 and 1945 about whom a significant amount is known. I offer it to establish a more detailed picture of these people and the lost riches that can never be recovered. I then follow with a Yizkor list, a list of remembrance, of those whose names we know but whose work we do not. All this material is excerpted from the wonderful *YIVO Encyclopedia of Jews* in Eastern Europe Web site (http://www.yivoencyclopedia.org). Anyone interested in this vanished world will find a visit there very rewarding. Yet, the list still is not complete, and it never will be. Part of the tragedy we are witnessing here is the fact

that we do not even have names for so many of these people, and yet surely
many of them contributed in measure as full as those who are remembered.
The names we do have, the ones I memorialize here, are listed with the little
information available about them on the YIVO Web site. My hope is that
anyone with historical connections to this vanished civilization will look
at that list and offer to YIVO any further information they may possess,
either of names that should be added or of knowledge about the people who
are already included there.

Mordkhe Gebirtig, poet and songwriter: born 1877, Kraków; died
1942, by random German fire while being marched to the Kraków
train station for transportation to the Belzec death camp. Gebirtig
is best known for his song "S'brent" ("It Is Burning"), which was
written in 1938 in response to a pogrom, and became a favorite of
the Jewish Resistance movement. The first collection of Gebertig's
songs, *Folkshtimlekh* (*In the Folk Style*), was published in 1920 and a
second, *Mayne Lider* (*My Songs*), in 1936. In 1940 or 1941, he wrote
"A Tog fun Nekome" ("A Day for Revenge"), a song about hope for
the downfall of the perpetrators of the Holocaust.

Shimen Horontshik, novelist: born 1889, Wieluń; died 1939, Kałuszyn,
a suicide, to forestall being murdered by German troops engaged in a
pogrom. Horontshik lived in Łódź during World War I and in France
and Belgium during the early 1930s. He wrote 11 novels, 5 of which
were primarily autobiographical. Two—*In Geroysh fun Mashinen*
(*Amid the Noise of the Machines*, 1928) and *1905* (1929)—are set in
the lace-making district of Kalisz, where industrialism and capitalism
were making inroads on shtetl life. *Baym Shvel* (*At the Threshold*,
1935/1936) looks at the conflicts between Jews and Poles and among
Jews themselves, as seen through his young eyes. In other novels, he
considered the damage to the Jewish way of life wrought by greed and
the loss of moral structure.

Alter-Sholem Kacyzne, novelist, playwright, and photographer: born
1855, Vilna; died 1941, Tarnopol, killed with thousands of other Jews
who were fleeing the German advance. Kacyzne's great two-volume
novel, *Shtarke un Shvakhe* (*The Strong and the Weak*, 1929/1930),
dealt with the 1905 Polish uprising and the conflict between Bohemian
Jews and the rising generation of Poles. He also wrote three plays,
Dem Yidns Opere (*The Jew's Opera*), *Ester* (*Esther*), and *Shvartsbard*
(about Sholem Schwartzbard, who assassinated the Ukrainian nation-
alist Symon Petliura in 1926). Kacyzne was probably one of the most
prolific of the prewar Yiddish writers in Poland and was considered
by many the literary heir to Y. L. Peretz. Despite these accomplishments, he is better remembered as a photographer than as either novelist or playwright. In 1921, he was commissioned by the Hebrew

Immigrant Aid Society to photograph Jewish life in Poland, and his work was published regularly in the New York *Forward*. Kacyzne's photographic archive in Warsaw was destroyed in the Holocaust, but the 700 photographs he had sent to New York are at YIVO.

Yitshak Katzenelson, poet, educator, writer: born 1885, near Minsk; died 1944, Auschwitz. Katzenelson was a major Hebrew and Yiddish poet (called by some the Poet of Destruction). His first anthology of Yiddish poetry, *Die Zun Fargeyt in Flamen* (*The Sun Sets in Flames*) was published in 1909. He was a man of many accomplishments. He established a network of private Hebrew schools that continued until 1939 and for it wrote children's literature and Hebrew textbooks. He started a Hebrew theater company and wrote plays on contemporary and biblical themes. He translated the poetry of Heinrich Heine into Hebrew and published his collected Hebrew poems in three volumes in 1938. These were much darker in tone than his early work. But at the time of publication, the political situation made for poor distribution, and few copies survived the war. Later, however, they revealed Katzenelson to be what the *YIVO Encyclopedia* calls "the great eulogist in verse of the murdered Jewish people." In December 1939, Katzenelson escaped from Łódź and became a central figure in the pedagogic and cultural life of the Warsaw Ghetto. He continued to teach, direct plays, and write, and he contributed to the underground press. Forty of his own works were composed in the ghetto, including two long poems, "Dos Lid vegn Shloyme Zhelikhovsky" ("The Poem About Solomon Zelikhovsky") and "Dos Lid vegn Radziner" ("The Poem About the Radzhin Rebbe"). Both of these were about spiritual heroism in the face of death. He was now writing in Yiddish, seeking to reach the largest audience he could in his current circumstances. But in August 1942, his wife (Hanna) and two younger sons (Ben-Tsiyon and Binyamin) were deported to Treblinka, and his poetry turned very dark again. He took part in the first Warsaw Ghetto uprising in January 1943 and escaped briefly. Katzenelson obtained Honduran documents and was sent to a German camp for Jews with foreign passports in Vittel, France, but was caught and sent to a German detention camp and then to Auschwitz, where he and his oldest son, Tsevi, were murdered. In Vittel, Katzenelson wrote two of the Holocaust's most important works: *Pinkas Vitel* (*The Vittel Diary*) in Hebrew and "Dos Lid fun Oysgehargetn Yidishn Folk" ("The Poem About the Murdered Jewish People"). These capture the terror, pathos, and rage of his people and lament his own impending death.

Miryem Ulinover (née Manya Hirshbeyn), poet and journalist: born 1890, Łódź; died 1944, Auschwitz. Ulinover was a prolific poet and active in Yiddish literary circles during the 1920s. Her first poems were published in Polish when she was 15. She also wrote in Russian and

German. Her Yiddish work began to appear 10 years later. Her best-known collection of poems is *Der Bobes Oytser* (*My Grandmother's Treasure*, 1922). There is disagreement among literary critics about whether Ulinover was a modernist or a naïve folk poet and about whether her poetry is secular or religious (an article in the *YIVO Encyclopedia* states that unlike modern Yiddish poets, she was "so sensitive and so Jewish"). Kathryn Hellerstein wrote in the *YIVO Encyclopedia* that "Miryem Ulinover wrote poems designed by a modern sensibility that sought to preserve the folk diction, sayings, and customs of pre-modern Jewish life in Poland."

Oyzer Varshavski, novelist: born 1898, Sochazcew; died 1944, Auschwitz. Varshavski's first novel, *Shmuglars* (*Smugglers*), published in 1920, is considered the finest example of Yiddish naturalism. It is a raw tale of Jews in a Polish town trying to make a living during World War I by distilling illegal whiskey and smuggling it into German-held Warsaw. Varshavski portrayed the implosion of shtetl life as it came into increasing contact with the outside world. In his *Study in the Mirror of Literature: The Economic Life of the Jews in Poland as Reflected in Yiddish Literature (1914–1939)*, William Glicksman (1966) described Varshavski's vision as the vortex of a world at the brink: "Warshavsky showed the *shtetl* at the brink of the abyss" (p. 73), spelling his name with a W. His second novel, *Shnit-Tsayt* (*Harvest Time*, 1926), was about shtetl life in the years between the outbreak of World War I and the beginning of the German occupation. There is a tragic irony to Varshavski's last book, *Rezidentsn* (*Residences*), which described the efforts of various Jewish characters to escape the Nazis in occupied France. Varshavski settled in Paris in 1924, but after the occupation fled first to Vichy France and then to Italy, where he and his wife were seized and sent to Auschwitz.

Dvora Vogel, philosopher and art critic: born 1900, Burshtyn, Galicia; died 1942, together with her husband, mother, and small son, in the Lwów Ghetto during the Great Action of 1942. Vogel was educated in Vienna, in Lwów, and then at Jagiellonia University in Kraków, where she completed a dissertation on Hegel's aesthetics. She was an accomplished academic as well as a writer; she taught psychology at Hebrew Teachers' Seminary in Lwów and was a central figure in the Polish literary and artistic avant-garde. She corresponded widely with other writers in a circle of mutual influence. Her first volume of poems, *Tog-Figurn: Lider* (*Figures of the Day: Poems*, 1930), is free verse poems on concrete and abstract themes. *Manekinen: Lider* (*Mannequins: Poems*, 1934) was openly constructivist in principle. Her work was little regarded in her time; if she and her audience had lived long enough to become familiar with the new literary forms, her literary fate would likely have been very different.

GRIEVING THE DEATH OF WRITERS LOST

Finding this list has changed what was intellectual insight to a profoundly emotional feeling. The sadness and sense of loss to all of us must be overwhelming to me. The number and the details of who they were and what they had written follow, taken from the *YIVO Encyclopedia* on its Web site.

Apshan, Hertsl (1886–1944), prose writer and journalist. Apshan was born near Sighet, Hungary; as an adult he was a businessman and insurance agent in that city. After 1918, he lived in Romania. Apshan's depictions of Hasidic life in Transylvania were praised for their artist observations and soft irony. He was murdered in Auschwitz.

Aronski (Zak), Moyshe (1898–1944), prose writer and educator. Born in Ovruch, Ukraine, Aronski (originally Zak) graduated from Kiev University in 1930 and subsequently taught literature and history in Yiddish schools in Ukraine. From 1926, his prose appeared in periodicals in Kharkov, Kiev, and Moscow. Aronski enlisted in the Soviet Army and was killed in action. He published more than 15 novels and collections of stories about Jewish life in the Soviet Union.

Beylin, Moyshe-Zisl (1857–1942), scholar and folklorist. Born in Novogrodek, Belorussia, Beylin served as a crown rabbi in Rogachev (Belorussia) and Irkutsk (Siberia) and from 1920 lived in Moscow. Throughout his life, he collected and studied Yiddish proverbs, songs, and children's rhymes and riddles; his studies appeared in Russian, German, and Yiddish scholarly and literary periodicals. Beylin's last collection of Yiddish folk jokes and anecdotes was ready to be published in 1941 but was not released because of the war. Some of his unpublished materials are preserved in the YIVO archives. He died in Siberia.

Dreykurs, Leybush (Leon; 1894–1941), prose writer, journalist, and actor. Born in Lwów, Dreykurs began to publish poetry in the *Po'ale Tsiyon* press in 1911. After World War I, he went to Czechoslovakia, where he founded a traveling Yiddish theater company. He returned to Lwów and contributed short stories, essays, and poems to the Yiddish press under various pseudonyms. Living in Riga and Warsaw, Dreykurs edited Yiddish and Polish periodicals; published a novel about actors, *Kulisn (Behind the Stage,* 1927); worked in theater and on the radio; and in 1939 returned to Lwów. He died in the Janów concentration camp.

Dua, Yankev-Kopl (1898–1942), writer and journalist. Dua was born in Warsaw and attended a Russian school. He became involved in socialist politics and contributed numerous articles on art, theater, literature, and music to the left-wing Yiddish press. His novels about Polish Jewish history were reprinted in installments by Yiddish newspapers in the United States, Argentina, and South Africa. He was the main editor and author of *Groshn-Bibliotek* (*Penny Library*), which published popular brochures and produced numerous translations from world literature. Dua continued his literary work in the Warsaw Ghetto; a German officer shot him on the street.

Dubilet, Moyshe (1897–1941), literary critic and educator. Born in Ekaterinoslav province, Ukraine, Dubilet served in the Red Army during the Russian Civil War and later graduated from the Yiddish department of the Odessa Pedagogical Institute. He taught Yiddish language and literature in Yiddish schools and in 1933 began graduate studies at the Kiev Institute of Jewish Proletarian Culture, researching 19th-century Yiddish literature (Yisroel Aksenfeld, Shloyme Ettinger, Sholem Yankev Abramovitsh, Sholem Aleichem). Dubilet's collection *Kritishe Artiklen* (*Critical Essays*) was published in 1939; in 1941, he enlisted in the Soviet Army and was killed in action.

Eliashev, Ester (1878–1941), literary critic, journalist, and teacher. Eliashev was born in Kaunas and studied philosophy at the universities of Leipzig, Heidelberg, and Bern (receiving a doctorate in 1906) and taught at the Higher Women's Courses in Saint Petersburg. She returned to Kaunas in 1921, where she worked as a teacher and was a prolific literary critic and journalist. Eliashev died on the eve of the German invasion. She was the sister of Isidor Eliashev (Bal-Makhshoves).

Gilbert, Shloyme (1885–1942), prose writer and poet. Born in Radzymin, near Warsaw, Gilbert began to publish neo-romantic poetry and novellas in 1907. His first collection of stories appeared in Warsaw in 1922, followed by two additional books of poetry and drama inspired by religious and mystical motifs. He was deported from the Warsaw ghetto to Treblinka.

Glik, Hirsh (1922–1944), poet. Born in Vilna, Glik began to write under the influence of his older friends from Yung-Vilne; he issued his first publications in 1940. Glik is famous for his ghetto poetry, especially the "Partisaner Lid" ("The Partisan Hymn," 1943), which became a symbol of Jewish resistance.

Goldshteyn, Moyshe (1900–1943), prose writer. Goldshteyn was born near Siedlec, Poland, and lived in Warsaw. In 1923, he immigrated to Argentina and published short stories in the Yiddish press. In 1932, he arrived in Birobidzhan, worked in an agricultural colony, and published reports about Birobidzhan and Argentina in the Yiddish press. Two collections of his short prose works were published in Moscow. He served as an officer in the Soviet Army and was killed during World War II. A number of his war stories were published posthumously.

Gotlib, Yankev (1911–1945), poet. Gotlib was born in Kaunas and received a traditional education. His first poem was published in 1925; subsequently, he published four collections of poetry and a book about H. Leyvik; he also edited literary publications in Kaunas. He died under evacuation in Central Asia.

Grin, Yerakhmiel (1910–1944), prose writer. Grin was born in a village near Kolomyya, Ukraine; he lived in Warsaw. He wrote stories and novels about Jewish life in the Carpathian Mountains and died in the Janów concentration camp together with his wife, Hinde Naiman-Grin (1916–1944), a Polish and Yiddish writer and journalist.

Grodzenski, Arn-Yitskhok (1891–1941), poet and journalist. Grodzenski grew up in Vilna and published his first poem in 1906. From 1910 to 1913, he lived in Antwerp and then returned to Vilna, publishing his first collection of poetry in 1914. In 1916, Grodzenski fled to Ekaterinoslav, where he lost his legs in an accident. He contributed to various Yiddish publications in Ukraine as well as translated Russian and German poetry. In 1921, he again settled in Vilna, where he worked as an editor and translator. His most popular work was the novel *Lebn* (*Life*, 1923). Tchaikovsky's opera *Eugène Onegin* was performed in his Yiddish translation in Vilna in 1923. Grodzenski was murdered in Ponar.

Hartsman, Motl (1908–1943), poet. Born in Berdichev, Hartsman attended the Yiddish school headed by Nina Brodovskaya, who encouraged his first literary and theatrical attempts; he received his higher education in Odessa and Moscow and completed graduate study in Kiev with Maks Erik. Hartsman's first poems were printed in Berdichev's Yiddish newspapers and quickly became popular; a few collections of his poems were published in the 1930s. His last long poem, "Der Toyt-Urteyl" ("The Death Sentence"), was written during the war while he served in the Red Army. He was killed in action.

Hershele (1882–1941), poet, prose writer, and journalist. Hershele (pseudonym of Hersh Danilevich) was born in Lipno, Poland. As a textile worker in Warsaw, he joined the socialist Zionist movement, was arrested, moved to Switzerland, and then came back to Poland, where he eventually settled in a town near Warsaw. His first publications, in 1904, were greeted warmly by Y. L. Peretz. Beginning in 1910, Hershele contributed poetry, short stories, children's literature, and translations to various Yiddish periodicals; he collected and published Yiddish folklore, and some of his poems became folk songs. His earliest book of poetry came out in 1907; he also published and edited several other collections. His poetry from the Warsaw ghetto appeared in illegal publications.

Heysherik, Kalmen-Khayim (1900–1941), prose writer. Heysherik was born near Łódź, Poland. As a prisoner of war in Germany during World War I, he kept a diary that later served as the basis of his memoirs and fiction, which became popular during the 1920s. He published stories and essays in major Polish Yiddish newspapers. After the occupation of Warsaw in 1939, he fled to Vilna. He was murdered in Ponar.

Kava, Shloyme-Leyb (1889-?), critic and journalist. Born in Warsaw, Kava (main pseudonym of Moyshe-Yosef Dikshteyn) served as Y. L. Peretz's secretary and later became vice president of the Association of Jewish Writers and Journalists in Warsaw. From 1905, he published numerous articles and essays in the Yiddish press, some of them sharply satirical and critical. In 1923, he published a collection of Yiddish folklore and was involved with various Yiddish publications in Poland. He died in the Warsaw ghetto.

Kirman, Yosef (1896–1943), poet. Kirman grew up in Warsaw in a poor family and was a worker; his first poetic publication appeared in the collection *Ringen* (*Rings*, 1919); he later contributed to various periodicals and published one collection of poems. He was arrested for his political activity by the Polish police. In the Warsaw Ghetto, he continued to write poetry and prose, which was partly preserved in the Ringelblum Archive. He was murdered in the Poniatów concentration camp.

Kreppel, Yoyne (Jonas) (1874–1939), journalist and writer. Born in Drohobycz, Galicia, Kreppel was active in the Zionist movement and later became a leader of Agudas Yisroel. He also participated in the Czernowitz Conference. Beginning in 1914 in Vienna, he served for many years as an adviser for the Austrian Foreign Ministry. He contributed to *Der Yud* and other Yiddish publications in Galicia and from 1919 was a Vienna correspondent for New York's *Yidishes Togblat*. A prolific Yiddish language author of crime and historical fiction in Poland and America, he published more than 100 small books of stories and novels that were popular among a mass readership. He composed a comprehensive overview of contemporary Jewish life in German with *Juden und Judentum von Heute* (*Jews and Judaism Today*, 1925). Kreppel died in the concentration camp at Mauthausen.

Olevski, Buzi (1908–1941), poet and prose writer. Born in Chernigov, Ukraine, Olevski's primary focus was on the economic and social transformation of shtetl youth; he also wrote for children. He wrote his dissertation on the poetry of Dovid Hofshteyn in Kiev and later lived in Moscow and Birobidzhan. As an officer in the Soviet Army, Olevski fought in World War II and was killed in action. His autobiographical novel *Osherl un Zayne Fraynd* (*Osherl and His Friends*) was published posthumously in 1947.

Pitshenik, Moyshe-Leyb (1895–1941), writer and journalist. Pitshenik was born in Złoczew, Galicia; spent 1920–1922 in Katowice; and was the director of the Jewish school in Łowicz from 1923. He published poetry, stories, and articles in the Polish Yiddish press as well as historical novels about the Haskalah and Hasidism. He was murdered by the Nazis near Chełmno.

Rashkin, Leyb (1903?–1939), prose writer. Born in Kazimierz (Kuzmir), Poland, Rashkin (Shaul Fridman) began writing stories in the 1930s. His major work, *Di Mentshn fun Godl-Bozhits* (*The People of Godl-Bozhits*, 1936), a realistic panoramic portrait of the Polish shtetl, was one of the most important Polish Yiddish debut novels in the 1930s and was awarded a literary prize. Rashkin was murdered while attempting to escape from German occupation to the Soviet Union.

Shaevich, Simkhe-Bunem (1907–1944), poet and writer. Born in Tęczyce, Poland, Shaevich grew up in Łódź. From 1933, he published poetry and short stories, mostly in left-wing papers in Łódź and Warsaw; his first collection of stories was ready for publication in 1939 but was not issued due to the start of the war. In the Łódź Ghetto, Shaevich composed profound Holocaust poems that explored traditional concepts such as exile and martyrdom. These works were preserved by survivors and published, posthumously, in 1946.

Shalit, Moyshe (1885–1941), journalist and communal activist. Born in Vilna to a well-off family, Shalit was actively engaged in a wide range of public and philanthropic activities in Russia, Poland, and abroad, among them the PEN club and the Association of Jewish Writers and Journalists. In 1906, he published a historical study of the BILU movement in Russian (translated into Yiddish in 1917) as well as articles and reviews in the Yiddish and Russian press, and he edited a number of books and periodicals on politics, culture, and education. He was arrested and murdered immediately after the German occupation of Vilna in July 1941.

Sito, Fayvl (1909–1945), prose writer. Sito was born Rovno, Volhynia; lost his family during the civil war; and grew up in an orphanage. He studied in Odessa and at the Kharkov Conservatory. His stories about the lives of Jewish orphans in postrevolutionary Russia were based on personal experience, written with warmth and humor, and made him popular with a Yiddish readership. Also popular were his parodies of various Soviet Yiddish writers, which were collected in two books (1934, 1938); he also wrote plays and translated from Russian and Ukrainian into Yiddish. In 1939–1941, Sito edited a Yiddish magazine for teenagers in Kiev. During the war, he edited an army newspaper and worked for the Moscow Yiddish newspaper *Eynikayt*.

Umru, Dovid (1910–1941), prose writer. Born in Alitus, Lithuania, Umru lived in Kaunas. He began to publish short stories in the Yiddish press in the 1930s; two collections of his short stories appeared in Kaunas in 1937 and 1938. In 1940–1941, he edited the newspaper *Vilner Emes* and served as the director of the Vilna State Yiddish Theater. He was murdered by the Gestapo in July 1941.

Varshavski, Yakir (1885–1942), writer and journalist. Born in Mława, Poland, Varshavski contributed to the Hebrew press (from 1908) and to Yiddish periodicals (from 1909); he also taught Hebrew in Warsaw's schools. Varshavski published his travelogue to Palestine and Egypt in 1919, as well as a number of other books in Hebrew in Poland, including short stories for children. His two Yiddish collections were ready for publication in 1939 but did not appear due to the outbreak of World War II. He continued writing in the Warsaw ghetto until the Nazis murdered him in the summer of 1942.

Vaynig, Naftole (1897–1943), literary critic and folklorist. Born in Tarnów, western Galicia, Vaynig studied philology at Kraków University and art in Vienna. He also taught in Polish and Jewish schools. From 1917, his critical essays appeared in the press of Vienna and Warsaw, and he contributed studies of Jewish folklore to academic Yiddish publications in Poland. From 1941, he was in the Vilna Ghetto, where he continued to teach, write, and collect folklore. His study of Leyb Naydus's poetry won a literary prize of the Judenrat.

Vulman, Shmuel (1896–1941), prose writer. Vulman was born in Kaluszin, Poland. From 1917, he lived in Warsaw and contributed poetry, articles, reviews, and translations to numerous Yiddish periodicals in Warsaw, Lwów, and Czernowitz. He published collections of poetry, memoirs of the German occupation during World War I, an autobiographical novel, and a number of popular books on history, literature, geography, and other subjects. He was murdered by the Nazis in Kremeniec, Volhynia, where he had fled from Warsaw.

Zhitnitski, Hersh-Leyb (1891–1942), writer and journalist. Zhitnitski was born in Szeradz, Poland, and lived in Łódź. From 1920, he lived in Warsaw and fled to Lwów in 1939. He fell into the hands of the Nazis in 1941 and was deported to a death camp a year later. His first short story appeared in 1913 in *Łódźer Morgnblat*. Zhitnitski worked as an editor of the *Warsaw Haynt*; contributed to the Yiddish press of Poland, the United States, Argentina, and Palestine; and published two collections of novellas and a novel about World War I in installments. His last book was ready for publication in 1939 but was never published due to the outbreak of the war.

Zilburg, Moyshe (1884–1941?), literary critic and translator. Born in Molodechno, Belorussia, Zilburg took part in revolutionary activity, was arrested, left Russia, and moved to Galicia. He lived in Kraków, Lwów, and Vienna, where he edited the Yiddish literary magazine *Kritik* (1920–1921). In 1923, he returned to Vilna and worked on various Yiddish literary publications. He began to publish literary criticism around 1908 and later produced several translations from Hebrew, German, and Russian. After the German occupation of Vilna, he was killed in Ponar.

The contribution of this chapter is to bring to our awareness the Yiddish writers listed in an encyclopedia but otherwise not widely recognized and their loss not mourned. This is my Kaddish for them.

REFERENCES

Dobrosczycki, L., & Kirshenblatt-Gimblett, B. (1987). *Image before my eyes: A photographic history of Jewish life in Poland (1864–1939).* New York: Schocken Press.

Fishman, D. E. (2009). *Embers plucked from the fire: The rescue of Jewish cultural treasures in Vilna.* New York: YIVO.

Gay, P. (1988). *Freud: A life for our time.* New York: Norton.

Glicksman, W. (1966) *In the mirror of literature: The economic life of the Jews in Poland as reflected in Yiddish literature* (1914–1939) New York: Living Books.

Goldstein, B. (2005). *Five years in the Warsaw ghetto: The stars bear witness.* Oakland, CA: AK Press.

Grinwald, M. (1941). *Ha'aretz.* September 21st, 1941.

Hellerstein, K. (2010). Miryem Ulinover. In *YIVO Encyclopedia of Jews in eastern Europe.* http://www.yivoencyclopedia.org/article.aspx/Ulinover_Miryem

Hundert, G. D. (Ed.). (2008). *The YIVO Encyclopedia of Jews in eastern Europe.* New Haven: Yale University Press.

Kassow, S. D. (2007). *Who will write our history? Rediscovering a hidden archive from the Warsaw Ghetto.* Bloomington: Indiana University Press.

Leftwich, J. (Ed.) (1969). *Great Yiddish writers of the twentieth century.* New York: Aronson.

Marr, W. (1879). *Der Weg zum Siege des Germanenthums über das Judenthum (The way to victory of Germanicism over Judaism).* Berlin: Otto Verlag.

Roskies, D. (1999). *The Jewish search for a usable past.* Bloomington: Indiana University Press.

Waletzky, J. Director (1981). *Image Before My Eyes,* documentary film. Written by J. Badanes, L. Dobroszycki (book) and B. Kirshenblatt-Gimblett (book). Produced by S. Lazarus and the YIVO Institute for Jewish Research. 88 minutes, USA.

Part 5

Links

Chapter 23

Trauma, Therapy, and Witnessing

Marilyn B. Meyers

INTRODUCTION

In this chapter, I link our conceptualization of the power of witnessing to the therapeutic encounter. I emphasize the creation of an atmosphere in which the therapist is a willing witness to moments of trauma. When speaking of trauma, we are faced with specifying an adequate and specific means of defining what we mean. The dictionary definition of psychic trauma is "a disordered psychological or behavioral state resulting from mental or emotional stress or physical injury." In light of the increasingly broad use of trauma as applied to virtually every aspect of life, I intend to restrict the definition to the feelings of utter helplessness, annihilation terror, despair, and failure to be seen as a worthwhile human being as represented by the Holocaust. That is not to suggest that the Holocaust alone "qualifies" for this definition, but rather that it represents the extreme psychological aftermath of unspeakable atrocities.

In working with severe trauma, the therapist must be open to the potential of accompanying the traumatized individual to the darkest and most terrifying places in the psyche. The therapist, while willing to travel this road, will also be in a regressed and frightening state of mind. Shabad (2001) stated that the "credibility of the therapist as witness is something that cannot be conveyed by words alone. For the patient who has huddled in self-enclosed isolation, waiting for someone to retrieve him, words are insufficient" (p. 154). I posit that the person who has been exposed to terror and annihilation anxiety can face that exposure through the empathic listening that a therapist provides.

Russell (1993) employed the metaphor of the camera, stating:

> The photographic perceiving and recording apparatus itself is damaged while it is being built. The camera cannot photograph its own injury; it needs to be fully developed, operational, and somehow separate from itself in order to do so. It needs, in short, to be what it would become had it not been damaged. (p. 515)

The metaphor of the camera suits my concept of the witness for mass trauma. I am emphasizing the psychoanalytic concepts of holding, containment, and intersubjectivity as a means to that end. The concept of "holding" and the "container and the contained" was presented by Bion (1962) as a function of both the intrapsychic and intersubjective. Bion (1984) also spoke of the "feeling that there was someone to go to" (p. 5). The role of the mother with her baby as a container for intense affect was emphasized by Winnicott (1945). He saw the work of the analytic process in terms of a reawakening of frozen parts of the self. The holding function of an empathic "other" provides an opportunity for the "true self" to emerge from hiding. The sequestered "true self" went into hiding to protect it from emotional neglect or abuse of the parents.

More recently, the notion of the "analytic third" has entered our clinical ideas of the space "between" in the psychotherapeutic relationship. Thomas Ogden (1999) defined the analytic third as the experience of being simultaneously within and outside the intersubjectivity and the notion of the "surrender to inevitable danger" (p. 463). Jessica Benjamin (1995) emphasized the importance of recognition of the "other" as "another subject in order for the self to fully experience his or her subjectivity in the other's presence" (p. 30).

Other authors have written about the difficulties with affect regulation as sequelae to trauma. In the section of his article "Surrender, Psychogenic Death, and Trauma," Krystal (1978) wrote that in the face of massive trauma there is "a disturbance of affectivity consisting of a vagueness and loss of specificity of emotional responses, so that the patient cannot tell what feeling they are experiencing" (p. 87). It is often the therapeutic task to help patients who have suffered severe acute or chronic trauma find a way to put their unformulated affective states into words. This, of course, resides to a great extent in the transference/countertransference matrix. The therapist's capacity to contain, experience terrifying states, and metabolize those states is often a great challenge; however, this is a crucial task in assisting the patient to enhance his/her own capacity to confront and contain traumatic states.

In an early phase of treatment, Wendy, a child of Holocaust survivors—both of whom lost virtually their entire families—reported a dream that had transference/countertransference implications. This dream followed a session in which she had begun to talk of the impact of her parents' Holocaust trauma on her life. In the dream, she is coming to a session with me. I am in the office. I am small, cute, and radiant—wearing a shawl. In the dream, I tell her that I will no longer be working. She does not actually hear me saying that—then she leaves and comes back. I am "burned out." I offer her two books that I take from a drawer. She thinks I am giving her both books, but in fact she must choose one. She chooses the smaller of the two books so as not to appear greedy, and then she leaves. She associates to her fear that she will "burn me out." She has further associations to the dream. I hear it as containing both the fear and the wish to be witnessed. Is she afraid that her trauma will destroy me and thus I will abandon her in the face of her trauma? Will she have to choose between knowing and not knowing (the two books)? Of course, there are many other associations to the dream for both of us (and as I write this); however, I present this dream as an illustration of the powerful transference/countertransference matrix that can emerge from the outset in clinical work with the history of massive trauma.

The work of Beebe (1986) and others has shed light on the centrality of the mother–infant dyad in the regulation of affect and its subsequent effects on self-organization and mutual regulation. This work is linked to the study of attachment styles and patterns. In her studies of the "strange situation," Mary Ainsworth (Ainsworth, Blehar, Waters, & Wall, 1978) developed a model for understanding patterns of attachment between young children and their mothers. This work has proven to be central in our current understanding of psychological development, although it has yet to be widely applied to our comprehension of the effects of severe trauma. It is likely that a person who has had secure and safe experiences as a child is more capable of drawing on inner psychological resources to allow for coping with posttrauma life relatively well. This can be thought of as resilience, but I think that the process is very complex. However, the attachment system is unavoidably disrupted by such massive trauma as the Holocaust. (Of course, this would apply to other traumas as well, such as torture, rape, being held hostage, battlefield exposure, acute and chronic childhood neglect and abuse, etc.) Specifically, survivors of the nightmare of the Holocaust, who may have had a secure attachment system in place, are nonetheless unavoidably affected in their attachment system.

The poignant description by Elie Wiesel (2006) of his father's death in Buchenwald describes a wrenching disruption in his attachment to his father:

> "Eliezer, my son, come here ... don't leave me alone. ..."
> I heard his voice ... yet I did not move. It had been his last wish to have me next to him in his agony ... yet I did not let him have his wish. ... I was afraid. Afraid of the blows. That was why I remained deaf to his cries. ... I remained flat on my back, asking God to make my father stop calling my name. ... In fact, my father was no longer conscious. ... I shall never forgive myself. ... Nor shall I ever forgive the world for having me pushed me against the wall, for having turned me into a stranger, for having awakened in me the basest, most primitive instincts. (p. xii)

As a consequence of severe trauma, early capacities for self-regulation are likely to be disrupted, thus also disrupting relational capabilities: "The breakdown of the empathic process leaves many survivors with a sentenced to death feeling..." (Auerhahn, Laub, & Peskin, 1993, p. 434). This "sentenced to death feeling" can be somewhat countered via the empathic willingness to witness. While a full return to pretrauma self-organization and relational capacities is most probably not achievable, the individual can recover or rediscover vital parts of the self. A child of survivors stated early in the treatment, "I feel that the experiences that they had are inside of me, as if I lived them." This man wished that his parents would give oral testimony to the Yale Video Archives or the Holocaust Museum. He felt that this would free him from the psychological burden he carried. They, however, refused to participate. His relationship with me felt distant, dead, and robotic. He faced the seemingly insurmountable dilemma of wanting to feel alive and feeling guilty about this wish, as if to enliven himself would betray his parents' trauma. Telling his own story to me was experienced by him as a betrayal of his relationship with his traumatized parents. He was caught in the midst of divided loyalties. His early departure from therapy signified and enacted this dilemma.

Thus, the willingness of the therapist to engage, listen, and be alive to the story is only one side of the equation. There must be at least an adequate measure of a drive to "know" on the part of the person seeking help. The fact that he or she comes to a therapist demonstrates a willingness; however, my experience is that there is conscious or unconscious ambivalence in this process. The therapist must be able to endure the wall that surrounds the trauma and gently but persistently pursue. Conversely, the therapist's interest can be experienced as voyeuristic and exploitive. Of course, any therapy has, as its first step, the establishment of a therapeutic alliance. The provision of a safe place (a secure base) allows both to face the trauma. The therapist can also help to modulate the moving close and finding safe distance from the psychic trauma.

The therapeutic work can be compromised by the unconscious feeling that to be fully engaged with the therapist is to betray the bond to the traumatized parents or lost others. All too often there can be an unspoken collusion to avoid the flame of trauma—to not know. Some of the possible countertransference responses in work with survivors include "anger at the victim, withdrawal and numbness, awe and fear ... hyperemotionality, philanthropy (positioning oneself in a giving, healing way), foreclosure through facts, and foreclosure through already knowing" (Auerhahn et al., 1993, p. 438). It is unavoidable that some of these countertransference responses will emerge. It is the therapist's responsibility to have an awareness and capacity for reflection to know when the countertransference resistance interferes with the therapy. The patient both seeks a "new," empathic presence and defensively retreats from this new relationship. The transference is certain to be rife with projections and counterprojections. The patient can experience the therapist as untrustworthy and dangerous—possibly as a defense against the terror of intimacy, although safety is always a paramount concern for the massively traumatized patient. The triangle of roles—rescuer, abuser, and passive bystander—are all bound to be evident in this complex work. Thus, in the transference the patient consciously desires a fully present "other" who will listen and help actively in constructing a narrative in which there were only fragments; this conscious desire is countered by the unconscious loyalty to the traumatic past. The establishment of such a collaborative and trusting dyad must evolve over time.

Donnel Stern (2009) posits that both developmentally and in trauma there exists what he calls "partners in thought." He states that:

> The witness is one imagined, consciously or *sub rosa*, to be listening. … To know what our experience is, to think and feel, we need to tell our stories of our lives, and we need to tell them to someone to whom they matter, listening to ourselves as we do the telling. If we have to make up our audience, so be it. Our need for a witness goes so deep that imaginary witnesses must sometimes suffice. (p. 723)

Illustrations of this phenomenon are captured in the chapter by Sophia Richman in this book. In Chapter 7, she writes about her invention of her imaginary friend, Françoise, to help her through her loneliness and trauma. Anne Frank also created an imaginary witness named Kitty in her diary.

Sam Gerson (2009) focused on the presence of an absence in the mind of the survivor of mass psychic trauma. He referred to this phenomenon as a "dead third." While I am not denying or minimizing the effects of such devastating experiences as the trauma of the Holocaust, I believe that there can be, and usually is, the presence of a life force, a drive to know in order to fend off the deadness and provide a degree of balance. Nancy Goodman (Chapter 1) speaks of the "living surround." The various forms that this balance takes are multidetermined by such factors as pretrauma life experiences, preexisting ego strength, and posttrauma help. I see this not as a dichotomy between life and death forces but as a "both/and" phenomenon. I do not ascribe to the notion of healing as an end point; however, I do believe that a drive toward revivification (Auerhahn & Laub, 1984) is often present. This is not "getting over" the trauma or even "working through" in the traditional sense, but rather an attempt to integrate both the deadness and aliveness in the wake of the trauma. The language for this process is problematic; the often-used language of "healing" falls short of capturing a complex process. If we draw a comparison to a physical wound, for example, a broken bone, we can say that there will always be a remnant and reminder of that wound. Given good treatment, the wound will heal well. In the absence of proper treatment, there may be a crippling effect. The "damaged" part also serves as a reminder and link to one's life and past. Perhaps the best word for this process is that the survivor "prevails."

A potent model for the capacity to know massive psychic trauma has been put forth by Laub and Auerhahn (1993). They proposed a continuum of eight forms of knowing. The first form is designated as "not knowing." It is characterized by varying degrees of splitting of reality. Depersonalizing and derealizing defenses are employed to cope with unbearable reality. An extreme example of this phenomenon was described by Laub (2005), who worked with psychotic patients in an Israeli mental hospital. These patients were Holocaust survivors who had been essentially "dumped" in a hospital. Many of them had been mute for years; the traumatic experiences were represented as an absence and withdrawal to psychosis. Laub pursued engaging these patients and for the first time asked them what had happened to them in the war. Several of them responded by telling some of their story. Laub stated that these people who had been diagnosed as schizophrenic were actually suffering from what he called extreme cases of speechlessness of trauma.

The next form of knowing is "fugue states." This is characterized by a lack of "content or of a connection to an experiencing 'I'" (p. 293). The traumatic memory is not integrated, and the person is essentially without access to their own experience. Next is "fragments," which involves the "retention of parts of a lived experience in such a way that they are decontextualized and no longer meaningful" (p. 293). When Francesca Bion, wife of Wilfred Bion, edited her husband's account of his traumatic war experience, she titled it "Fugue." She indicated that this meant the "loss of one's identity" and understood it to be an account of psychic flight and catastrophe (Souter, 2009). The next point on the continuum is "transference phenomena," in which "unintegrated fragments from the past are enacted on the level of object relations, the survivors' knowledge is in the form of transference experiences" (p. 293). The fifth form is "overpowering narratives," in which there is "memory that can be described and the event narrated. ... There is an 'I' present" (p. 293). These are conscious memories, but they tend to be unintegrated. The sixth form of knowing in this schema is "life themes," a "more complex degree of personality organization and sublimatory processes form a nucleus for one's identity" (p. 293). The seventh form is "witnessed narratives." This form involves witnessing, "in which the observing ego remains present as a witness ... knowing takes on the form of true memory" (p. 293). At the highest level of knowing is "trauma as metaphor and more" in which the "there is the use of imagery and language." There is a richness of expression at the level of the symbolic. This level is represented by visual arts, poetry, and other creative expressions. Laub and Auerhahn (1993) concluded by stating that "therapy with those impacted by trauma involves, in part, the reinstatement of the relationship between event, memory and personality" (p. 293). Their model captures some of the complexity of the capacity to know but at its core emphasizes the need for a witness, specifically as therapist.

CLINICAL VIGNETTES

The following clinical vignettes illustrate various points along the continuum of "knowing and not-knowing" depicted by Auerhahn and Laub (1993). Each of these cases touches on the complexity of the desire to know and the levels at which knowing is possible. It is evident that the continuum of levels of knowing overlap each other and can ebb and flow within the context of having a witness and hearing oneself speak.

Fragments

Michael described the scene at his family dinner table. No one talks or connects in any meaningful way. People have anxious looks on their faces. The tension of the meal is painful. "I can't breathe, I feel suffocated. My hands are hot, my stomach feels weird. Nothing makes sense." He turned to me and asked, "What do you do when something makes no sense?" He has embodied sensations, but in the face of the "nonsensible" experiences at the dinner table—over and over again—he numbs out into a dissociated state. This defensive maneuver/strategy allowed him to tolerate the discomfort that he experienced but did not provide him with any way to make sense of his experience. No one was there to help him. In his adult life, he often felt psychically under attack, suffered confusion between his own self-states and those of others. He had both trouble tolerating being alone and enormous difficulties in his relations with others. These problems manifested themselves with me. Any interaction with me—so much as saying "Can you go on?"—was experienced as an invasion of his mind. For a long time, my presence as representing another mind was unbearable to him, while paradoxically he desperately sought and wanted my help. I had to tolerate a kind of self-annihilation for long stretches of time. I came to understand this as a re-creation and unconscious communication of his experience in his family. He turned to me with a question: "Can you explain to me what was going on?" I reply, "There are some things that make no sense, and you are left with that knowledge. As a child, though, you can't find ways to make sense of something that makes no sense."

He then associates to a parable about a man with an ax. The man has an ax that he wants to make shiny. It is dull but for the edge. The blacksmith who is supposed to repair the ax says that he cannot achieve what he wants. The part that cuts is shiny, but the rest is rough. The man wants the ax made shiny and smooth all over. The blacksmith tries very hard and manages to make a small part of the ax shiny. He, however, realizes that the task is not possible. Michael associates to his dream: He will never be able to make complete sense of his experience. In my mind,

I think of the transference, in which he wishes that I could make it "all shiny and new," but we both know that I cannot.

Life Theme

Susan survived during the Nazi reign of terror by hiding in the attic of a barn with her parents and other family members. She was between the ages of 5 and 7 at that time. Childhood play was out of the question for her. The usual childhood noises—laughter, giggling, shouting—were, by necessity, silenced. Her extremely anxious parents responded to childlike enthusiasm with frightened and frightening responses. In a session, Susan stated, "I never live in the future. I can't picture a future. I am always looking back. What have I done wrong? What else could I have done?" I respond: "I have an image in my mind—it's a body feeling, when you have the taste of vomit in your throat—it's not quite throwing up, but you taste and feel the vomit." (This was the embodied image that came to mind for me, and I chose to share it with her even though it felt to me pretty out in "left field.") Susan responded: "That's exactly right. I never get rid of the bad stuff."

Susan's "life theme" is not to allow for pleasure and not be able to visualize a future. This, of course, entered the therapy in the form of defensively undoing the good experiences with me. For example, she reported a success at work—she moved and spoke in a lively, expansive manner. I felt good with her, joining her in the pleasure. Suddenly, she slumped over, curled up, and went to worry and anxiety. Something is certain to go wrong. I notice the shift and comment on it. Susan associates to her mother's warnings of danger whenever she ventured out. Life is dangerous; the outside world is full of danger and carries the threat of annihilation.

Transference Phenomena

Adam entered treatment for feelings of emptiness and futility. He introduced himself by telling me literally countless losses suffered by his parents during the Nazi regime. In our first session, I dutifully recorded his "list" of losses. I lost track and went numb during this. He delivered these facts totally without affect—one horrific loss followed another. They were a series of sound bites without context or feeling—the words without the music. He is an appealing young man, successful in his profession, but with a life without close relationships. This was evident in the transference/countertransference matrix from the outset. I found myself wanting to breathe life into him by getting more active in the sessions. One of his stated problems was a seeming inability to allow himself pleasure. He wanted a new "cool" car but kept himself in a perpetual state of longing. He was worried about his parents' reaction if he were to show up with this car. He expected them to be critical.

They were stuck in a life of self-deprivation. I heard these conflicts as transference themes from the start. Could he allow something new with me? Could he allow himself the pleasure of receiving something markedly different from his parents? In a concrete sense, he described his parents as never getting anything new and holding on desperately to what they had lost. They held on to the fantasy of recovering the home and possessions that were taken as the reign of terror took over their lives. It was as if time stood still. My struggle in this therapy was to make authentic contact with him. I did not succeed in this effort, and the treatment ended without much progress. I was unable to "hold" him, and he was terrified of living his own life in the present and imagining a future.

Metaphor

This level of knowing is represented by poetry, artwork, literature, memoir, memorials, and the like. It has been my experience that the therapy can lead to metaphoric symbolizations of trauma. Patients start to create artwork, write poetry, paint, and write. I discuss this phenomenon in the section on the psychic timeline in Chapter 2, with an emphasis on sociocultural context that allows for this level of knowing. This book is comprised primarily of metaphoric ways of knowing. Each of the contributors had the capacity and willingness to know at this level. We hope that in this way of knowing we honor the legacies of the lives lost and those who survived are to bear witness.

INTERGENERATIONAL TRANSMISSION OF TRAUMA

One area of particular interest to clinicians has been the intergenerational transmission of trauma. Specifically, children of Holocaust survivors are seen to either consciously or unconsciously carry the unformulated and unmourned losses and trauma of their parents' experiences of massive trauma. Eva Hoffman (2004) wrote:

> The Holocaust, in my first childish reception, was a deeply internalized but strongly unknown past. … We who came after do not have memories. … I took in that first information as a sort of fairy tale deriving not so much from another world as from the center of the cosmos: an enigmatic but real fable … something closer to enactments of experience or sometimes embodiments of psychic matter. (p. 6)

Others speak of the multiple ways in which the horror and survival are passed on to the next generation. It is important to recognize that not only the trauma but also the survival and hope are capable of transmission.

The concept of the memorial candle child who grows up feeling "responsible for continuity between generations" is widely thought of as useful and strikes a chord with patients in this work (Wardi, 1992). Mindy Wiesel (2000) wrote: "Only in my studio, while painting, was my authentic voice disclosed to me. ... Painting became a form of prayer, a form of dance, of song, a life itself" (p. xix).

David, the only child of Holocaust survivors, stated in an early session, "I am the translator, between mother and father, past and present, between the living and the dead, between generations." He described his father as stuck in the losses of the past, certain that the Germans will return what they took and that life will return to as it had been. He cannot live his own life in the present or imagine a real future. In this case, as a child of survivors, this man was acutely aware of the damaging effects of his parents' trauma on his psyche and consequently on his life. He literally kept his bags packed, ready to leave home, work, or relationships at a moment's notice, thus, actually living out his parents' trauma. My early interpretation of this potentiality seemingly helped him to recognize this and remain in the therapy. It was an ever-present threat to the continuity of the work; however, it was important for him to know that he could leave—that he could take action and not feel trapped.

NEUROSCIENCE: CONTRIBUTIONS TO UNDERSTANDING THE NEUROSCIENCE OF EMPATHY AND TRAUMA

Advances in neuroscience have contributed greatly to our understanding of the neurological underpinnings of empathy and trauma and some postulates regarding the contributions of that knowledge to psychotherapy. For example, the role of mirror neurons, discovered by Rizzolatti and others (Rizzolatti & Craighero, 2004; see also Gallese, 2001), has influenced our thinking about empathy, trauma, and treatment. The accidental discovery of mirror neurons is interesting: While Rizzolatti was studying the premotor cortex in monkeys, he happened to eat an ice cream cone in the midst of his experiment. As he was licking the cone, Rizzolatti observed that the electrodes implanted in the monkeys' brains were activated. Rather than ignore this phenomenon, he studied it further. He came to the conclusion, after extensive study, that certain neurons in the visual motor cortex that are activated when a monkey performs a "goal-directed" action are also activated when another monkey observes the same action. Numerous investigators have extrapolated from these studies to conceptualize empathy as a function of the mirror neuron system. This knowledge of the neurobiology contributes to notions of the act of witnessing—how the witness can engage with the traumatized person. While caution should be exercised in drawing conclusions from studies performed on the brains of monkeys, it is tempting to do so. It has been postulated that "the shared neural activation pattern and the accompanying embodied simulation constitute a fundamental basis for understanding another's mind" (Gallese, Eagle, & Migone, 2007, p. 131). Other studies of the neuroscience of trauma have demonstrated that when trauma is extremely severe, damage to the hippocampus (the memory center of the brain) may occur—resulting in an absence of memory formation such that memories of the trauma are not consciously available. The processing systems in the brain are the amygdala and the hippocampus. The amygdala controls the somatic reactions to fear, and the hippocampus is responsible for memory formation and recovery. It has also been found that in trauma there is a decrease in activation of the center of the brain involved in speech, Broca's area (Parens, Blum, & Akhtar, 2008). Allan Schore (1997) has emphasized the unconscious connection of right brain to right brain in the therapeutic relationship. It is well beyond the scope of this book to provide a review that would do justice to this emerging and important field of study. Positron emission tomographic (PET) scans and functional magnetic resonance imaging (fMRI) and other technologies applied to study of the brain have contributed to our knowledge of brain structure and function. Much remains to be studied. The new field of translational neuroscience is in its infancy (Baughman, Farkas, & Guzman, 2006). Among the many goals of this area of research is to bridge the gap between basic research in the field of neuroscience and clinical applications of this research. We can assume that this work may help in understanding the complexities of the neuroscience of trauma and the clinical applications of this knowledge.

RELATIONSHIP BETWEEN TRAUMA THEORY, CLINICAL PRACTICE, AND WITNESSING: WAR TRAUMA

As the evolution of witnessing has occurred, the notions about trauma and its treatment have changed over the past 100 years. Judith Herman (1997) has provided an historical perspective on trauma. In her chapter, "Remembrance and Mourning," she quotes Freud as stating, "[The patient] must find the courage to direct his attention to the phenomena of his illness" (p. 175). I conceive of two parallel lines—the importance and centrality of witnessing as process and how the conceptualization of trauma has evolved. These two have intersected and influenced one another even as they appear to be separate. One notable example of the relationship between witnessing and trauma theory is related to war trauma.

I trace those developments as a way to focus our attention on the history of trauma. It is important to recognize that wars, particularly the modern world wars, were characterized by fighting between known enemies, with certain "rules of war." This differs dramatically from the purposeful genocide carried out by the Nazis, with the explicit intent to round up and murder millions of men, women, and children based on nothing other than their Jewishness, their ethnicity, political affiliation, sexual orientation, or so-called defects (mental or physical). This distinguishes Holocaust trauma from war trauma; however, I think that the study of war trauma concepts can be useful in tracing the history of trauma and its treatment.

In World War I, soldiers suffering what was then known as "shell shock" or "combat neurosis" were rapidly sent back to the battlefield. The idea that they needed help with their traumatic experiences was systematically dismissed. In fact, they were often thought of as malingering or as merely suffering physical injuries. The soldiers were sometimes characterized as "moral invalids" (Herman, 1997, p. 21). There were, however, some progressive thinkers who recognized the reality of war trauma from the war combat experience. A prescient thinker (Rivers, 1918) wrote that the avoidance of remembering traumatic combat experiences was not helpful to soldiers and, in fact, was harmful to their psychological well-being. The concern with and interest in psychological trauma receded, however, after the end of World War I, and many of the men who suffered were essentially hidden in back wards of veteran's hospitals (Herman, 1997, p. 23).

Following World War I, an American psychiatrist, Abram Kardiner, returned from Vienna, where he had been in analysis with Freud. His important contribution to the study of war trauma has not been widely recognized. He worked with men with combat neurosis and was troubled by the lack of help for them. In 1941, he wrote a book, *The Traumatic Neurosis of War*, in which he developed his ideas about war trauma and its treatment. In a later edition of this book (coauthored with Herbert Spiegel), Kardiner emphasized the central role of relationships with comrades in recovery from the effects on war trauma. Thus, he was aware of the importance of witnessing in the wake of trauma (Herman, 1997, p. 27).

Attitudes about war trauma changed somewhat during and following World War II. Nonetheless, many soldiers who were traumatized by their combat exposure went unrecognized and therefore untreated. Furthermore, many of the troops who liberated the concentration camps were profoundly impacted, with little or no attention paid to the effects of that exposure. Young men witnessed the horrors of Buchenwald and Auschwitz and other concentration camps with virtually no acknowledgment of the trauma of witnessing these atrocities (see historic and psychic timelines, Chapter 2). The unspeakable went unspoken. The idealization that surrounded World War II contributed to the denial of trauma. In fact, it is my clinical experience that many patients had fathers or grandfathers who suffered unacknowledged combat trauma that had severe deleterious effects on their families. The soldiers of that war were clearly delineated as heroes, often without recognition of the complexities of that distinction. Only the most severe cases were of note, with the possibility of treatment, while many soldiers were too ashamed to speak.

Kay Souter (2009) cited Bion's traumatic war experience as influential in his thinking, specifically his "shattering insight into the extent to which mind is inter-mind, self is inter-self" (p. 795). Drawing on his wartime experience, Bion (1984) described how a mother must be able to withstand the onslaught of the baby's terror and return it to him detoxified. In the absence of this capacity, the baby "reintrojects ... a nameless dread" (p. 116). Thus, for Bion "minds, especially minds under stress, need other minds" (Souter, 2009, p. 805).

The Vietnam War was in sharp contrast to World War I and World War II. In fact, it could be thought of as the polar opposite of the attitudes toward the veterans of those wars. The atmosphere in the United States was very divisive during that time. Families were alienated from each other, and the country was in turmoil. The war itself was fought under very different conditions from either of the two European wars. The culture of Vietnam was vastly different from that of the United States, and the reality of guerilla warfare was unlike anything seen before. Brutal, terrifying, and unpredictable conditions were faced by the troops. Young men killed innocent women and children under dire conditions, and many felt extremely guilty about their role in the war. There was controversy whether one could be opposed to the war but still support the returning troops. There was a split in which it was viewed as not supporting the troops if one were opposed to the war. "Love it or leave" was the predominant sentiment.

Returning soldiers were often seen as tainted and were isolated and shunned on their return. One returning veteran said that he preferred to say that he had been in prison rather than to acknowledge and share his war experience. Women recoiled at his Vietnam War experience, thus confirming his feelings of shame. The diagnosis of posttraumatic stress disorder developed in the wake of the post-Vietnam era. Much of the impetus for that recognition came from the soldiers themselves, who did not trust the "system" of the Veteran's Administration to meet their needs. A network of storefront centers and informal rap groups developed as a grassroots movement often in defiance of the Veteran's Administration policies (Arthur Blank, personal communication, 2011). Ironically, this led to recognition by the Veterans' Administration of the psychological needs of the veterans. In 1980, posttraumatic stress disorder was first included as a syndrome and diagnostic category. Subsequently, the entity of posttraumatic stress disorder and the clinical and social implications of this recognition have been wide ranging. In the current milieu, war trauma remains largely untreated but more readily recognized. The wars in Iraq and Afghanistan have received attention for the effects on our soldiers, and yet the psychological needs of these men and women remain frequently unmet or unrecognized.

Ironically, it could be said that the more we recognize the trauma, the fewer resources there are available to meet the needs. This sometimes, within the military system, serves as a disincentive for recognition of war trauma. In addition, there is still shame and stigma surrounding this—sometimes reflected in negative reports on service people who demonstrate psychological stress.

In this brief review of the changing attitudes toward war trauma, one of the features that stands out is the increased recognition of the central role of witnessing. As with the Holocaust, I want to highlight the notion that one needs a willing witness, whether an individual or society at large, to honor the trauma or, at the very least, to "know" it. The absence of recognition serves as a double trauma that is exemplified by the following statement: "The failure of empathy not only destroys hope of communication with others in the external world and expectation of resonance with the internal other, it also diminishes the victim's ability to be in tune with themselves, to feel that they have a self" (Laub & Auerhahn, 1989, p. 378).

REFERENCES

Ainsworth, M. D. S., Blehar, M. C., Waters, E., & Wall, S. (1978). *Patterns of attachment: A psychological study of the strange situation*. Hillsdale, NJ: Erlbaum.

Auerhahn, N. C., & Laub, D. (1984). Annihilation and restoration: Post-traumatic memory as pathway and obstacle to recovery. *International Review of Psychoanalysis, 11*, 327–344.

Auerhahn, N. C., Laub, D., & Peskin, H. (1993). Psychotherapy with holocaust survivors. *Psychotherapy, 30*(3), 434–442.

Baughman, R. W., Farkas, R., Guzman, M., & Huerta, M. F. (2006). The National Institutes of Health Blueprint for Neuroscience Research. *Journal of Neuroscience, 26*, 10329–10331.

Beebe, B. (1986). Mother-infant mutual influences and pre-cursors of self-object representations. In J. Masling (Ed.), *Empirical studies of psychoanalytic theories* (Vol. 2, pp. 27–48). Hillsdale, NJ: Analytic Press.

Benjamin, J. (1995). *Like subjects, love objects: Essays on recognition and sexual difference*. New Haven, CT: Yale University Press.

Bion, W. R. (1962). *Learning from experience*. New York: Basic Books.

Bion, W. R. (1984). *Second thoughts*. New York: Aronson.

Gallese, V. (2001). The "shared manifold" hypothesis: From mirror neurons to empathy. *Journal of Consciousness Studies, 8*, 33–50.

Gallese, V., Eagle, M., & Migone, P. (2007). Intentional attunement: Mirror neurons and the neural underpinnings of interpersonal relations. *Journal of the American Psychoanalytic Association, 55*, 131–176.

Gerson, S. (2009). When the third is dead: Mourning, memory, and witnessing in the aftermath of the Holocaust. *International Journal of Psychoanalysis, 90*, 1341–1357.

Herman, J. (1997). *Trauma and recovery*. New York: Basic Books.

Hoffman, E. (2004). *After such knowledge: Where memories of the Holocaust ends and history begins*. New York: Public Affairs.

Krystal, H. (1978). Trauma and affects. *Psychoanalytic Study of the Child, 33,* 81–116.

Laub, D., & Auerhahn, N. (1993). Knowing and not known massive psychic trauma: Forms of traumatic memory. *International Journal of Psychoanalysis, 74,* 287–302.

Laub, D. (2005) From speechlessness to narrative: The cases of Holocaust historians and of psychiatrically hospitalized survivors. *Literature and Medicine, 24,* 253–265.

Laub, D., & Auerhahn, N. C. (1989). Failed empathy: A central theme in the survivors' Holocaust experience. *Psychoanalytic Psychology, 6,* 377–400.

Ogden, T. (1999). The analytic third: Working with intersubjective clinical facts. In S. Mitchell & L. Aron (Eds.), *Relational psychoanalysis: The emergence of a tradition* (pp. 459–492). Hillsdale, NJ: Analytic Press.

Parens, H., Blum, H., & Akhtar, S. (2008). *The unbroken soul*. New York: Aronson.

Rivers, W. H. R. (1918). An address on the repression of war experience. *Lancet, 171,* 173–177.

Rizzolatti, G., & Craighero, L. (2004). The mirror-neuron system. *Annual Review of Neuroscience, 27,* 169–192.

Russell, P. L. (1993). The essential invisibility of trauma and the need for repetition: Commentary on Shabad's "Resentment, indignation and entitlement." *Psychoanalytic Dialogues, 3,* 515–522.

Schore, A. N. (1997). A century after Freud's *Project*: Is a rapprochement between psychoanalysis and neurobiology at hand? *Journal of the American Psychoanalytic Association, 45,* 807–840.

Shabad, P. (2001). *Despair and the return of hope: Echoes of mourning in psychotherapy*. New York: Aronson.

Souter, K. M. (2009). The war memoirs: Some origins of the thought of Bion. *International Journal of Psychoanalysis, 90,* 795–808.

Stern, D. B. (2009). Partners in thought: A clinical process theory of narrative. *Psychoanalytic Quarterly, 28*(3), 701–731.

Wardi, D. (1992). *Memorial candles: Children of the holocaust*. New York: Routledge.

Wiesel, M (2000). *Daughters of absence: Transforming a legacy of loss*. Herndon, VA: Capitol Books.

Wiesel, E. (2006). *Night*. New York: Hill & Wang.

Winnicott, D. W. (1945). Primitive emotional development. In *Through paedeatrics to psychoanalysis* (pp. 145–156). London: Hogarth Press, 1958.

Chapter 24

"We're in This Too"

The Effects of 9/11 on Transference, Countertransference, and Technique

Nancy R. Goodman, Harriet I. Basseches,
Paula L. Ellman, and Susan S. Elmendorf

INTRODUCTION

A few days after the terrorist attacks of 9/11, we decided to begin a study of our reactions, our patients' reactions, and the way we worked therapeutically at this time of terror. We were at a meeting together looking out a window over the city of Washington, D.C., remarking at the beauty of the monuments and the horror of the destruction and deaths at the Pentagon. We spoke about fears of what else could happen here in the Capital. We had a personal need to believe there was a place to think and feel and discover and set out to do so. Our own psyches were steadied at knowing we could reflect on our psychoanalytic work at this time and planned to meet regularly. We had previously collaborated in study group explorations of psychoanalytic listening (Goodman et al., 1993) and female development (Basseches et al., 1996; Fritsch et al., 2001). We now see our activity as the creation of a witnessing group. We formed a type of Anti-Train (Chapter 3), a place of Anti-Trauma to help live with the terror outside and inside each of us and our patients. Most of all, we knew we could be better therapists when our fears were being held and contained through the group endeavor.

* * *

When the planes struck the Twin Towers, the explosion shattered our view of the world. Day and night, sirens blared and military jets flew overhead, signals of protection but also reminders of danger. During the weeks and months that followed the attacks, we and our patients were subject to news of the anthrax scares, of suicide bombings, news from New York at Ground Zero, and later, about sniper attacks fueling speculations about further harm. We noticed our patients were responding to the events, from the first day of shock and many cancellations, to the ensuing responses that ran the gamut from terror to numbness to denial. We oscillated between acknowledging our patients' terror and making interventions to distance them and us from the horror. We became increasingly aware of the unique impact of these events on our work, in that both we and our patients were experiencing the same traumatic reality situation together.

We offer case vignettes from psychoanalyses and psychoanalytically oriented therapies to illustrate our evolving understanding of the effects of the terrorist attacks on our analytic work. We begin with snapshots of what took place in our four analytic offices and in our study group as we and our patients responded to the events of September 11. Then, we describe ways that the traumatic affects opened avenues for exploration and growth and illustrate ways that 9/11 imagery entered the world of metaphor for patient and therapist. Only recently were we able to conceptualize a difficulty that had been plaguing our group—a form of survivor guilt. Although we were at the symbolic hub of the U.S. government, we were not in New York. Since we had not suffered as much harm, were we entitled to claim this trauma as our own and to study and write about it? With some relief, we have worked with this inhibition to our creative process and share with you the result.

PART I: A VIEW OF 9/11 FROM FOUR ANALYTIC OFFICES

Analyst I

9:30 a.m., Tuesday 9/11. My patient walked in and sat down and said he had heard something unbelievable on the radio on his way to his hour—that two airplanes, one after the other, had just hit into the Twin Towers in New York, and he does not understand why. I could not understand, thought he had made a mistake, or that it was some accident. We proceeded with the hour as if nothing had happened. That which is outside our usual experience remains unabsorbed, unintegrated, rejected, split off from our present moment's consciousness. Patient and analyst were in the trauma together: rejecting the foreign, the unexplained, denying what is too horrific even to be able to imagine.

The next patient, at 10:20, who never misses an hour, entered, lay down, and said he just heard that the Pentagon was hit, and "They think it is terrorism." He wanted to stay and talk, but also wanted to go home and be close to his family "since we do not know what is happening and we may be under attack." Unusual for me, I said I understood (eager to get access to my own television)—allowing, even encouraging action, rather than asking him to speak and reflect further about his wish to leave the hour.

This was the start of my noticing how differently I was responding—my readiness to act and gratify, rather than preserve my "analyzing function" with my patients. I had been ready to respond in reality, rather than in the "as if" relationship. Was my readiness to appreciate the realities an abandonment of my analytic stance, or was this "analytic" in a time of terror?

I was ready to appreciate the realities—the shared concern with the sounds of fighter jets outside my window overhead, the frequent acknowledgments of the "we" and the "us," rather than the "you" and the "I." Even more of a challenge to my analytic position were questions about my own view of reality that my patient's associations called into question. My patient described his family's preparation for an emergency departure from his home; he loaded the trunk of his car with a suit-case of clothes, water, flashlights, extra batteries (the emergency "kit" that the gov-ernment recommended to have on hand), and kept it there should the necessity for a rapid departure from the Washington area arise. On hearing about his prepara-tions, I began to question my not wanting to prepare my family for an urgent flight. For the moment, I was lost in my own personal questioning. I had then to grapple with my guilt for losing track of my patient's associations as my thoughts moved between his words and affects and my own. Was I like the many upper middle class European Jews who stood by in disbelief as Nazi Germany conducted the Final Solution, while a few others responded by leaving their comfortable professional lives and saving themselves from death? This was a trauma for me and my patient and infringed on the usual analytic process.

Analyst 2

At 10:30 a.m., I drove to my office under the bluest sky I had ever seen. Everything I looked at had a visual clarity at odds with the wordless uncertainty I was feeling since watching the televised images of destruction from the terrorist attacks. My first patient wondered when to pick up her children from school and then immedi-ately spoke of the Holocaust: "How did people know when to leave?" Her mother was a child survivor who had been sent from country to country and almost died. My patient had never imagined being in this situation in the United States. I began wondering if I would ever be telling patients I was leaving Washington or telling them they should. (Do psychoanalysts say such things?) This was a new terror, and I felt at sea on a boat with an uncertain destination. My patient's wonderful capacity to take charge when chaos prevailed served both of us as she found a way to rec-ognize the immediacy of our new reality. She looked at me at the end of the session and said in a lilting voice: "I hope we will be meeting at our next session."

Later in the day, I pointed out to a patient that she was speaking about everything but the terrorist attacks. She told me that she was concerned that I must have been listening to everyone else's fears and would welcome a rest. She said this in an empathic, caring way that moved me, and I also recognized her statement as an exquisitely beautiful example of the special bond she had formed with her mother in just this way as she subdued her own needs to take care of her. I gave her this interpretation of the repetition with me on this day, and we were able to think about it. Her actual gift to me that day was not silence on 9/11 but the chance to work in the midst of it. Only 7 hours after the collapse of the World Trade Towers, this analytic patient and I were attending to how the present contains aspects of the past especially in the affects, wishes, and fears appearing in the transference in the here and now of 9/11.

Mr. W arrived for his first meeting after the attacks on Wednesday, 9/12. Having grown up in a country where threats of revolution and upheaval were constant, he said, "This is nothing unusual; it's just naïve Americans who feel so surprised." He went on to admit, however, that when he had arrived home the previous night, he had experienced what he called the ridiculous fear of not knowing if he should open the window or keep it closed—how was one to know where the dangers would come from, the ventilation system in the building or something put in the air outside? He said this in an exaggerated way, worthy of Woody Allen, even gesturing with a well-timed shrug of the shoulders and hands put in the air. He laughed slightly, and I laughed slightly with him, commenting on his ability to engage me in this humor as we talked about such awful possibilities. I thought his confusion of whether dangers were outside or inside spoke to the experience of how psychic reality was taking place moment by moment within the shock waves reverberating around us.

Analyst 3

My first two patients' hours preceded my learning of the shocking events of 9/11. Immediately after these sessions, I received a disturbing call from my husband telling me that an airplane had crashed into one of the New York Twin Tower buildings. Only two of my remaining nine patients of the day showed up for their hours. I felt isolated and unable to concentrate on anything. I got out an old rickety radio that had formerly functioned as a white noise barrier. I remained glued to the radio reports much of the day, as I heard about the second tower, then the Pentagon, then the horrifying collapse of the towers.

One of the absent patients, who had never "no showed" before in the many years we had worked together, did so on this day. "What is happening?" I worried. That patient, in her next day's hour, explained that, coincident with the terrible news, her phone had been out of order. She had been too frightened to leave her apartment to come to her appointment or even to go out to make a call. In the days that followed, she was agitated in each hour, describing frightening nightmares and feeling terrified. "At any moment we are all going to die!" she repeated in various forms. Retrospectively, I reflected on my reactions, and they seemed odd to me. I became very clinical, perhaps denying my own fear, which was contagiously building in me. I listened with emotional distance, as if to reassure myself that this was her problem and not mine. I was quick to think in terms of her history, and ironically her prehistory, perhaps in an attempt to move far away from current events of history. She was the child of a European mother, whose father may have been a Nazi, and a South American father, whose forbears were slave holders. She was an only child of privilege, neglect, and loss. I listened, explored genetic roots; I listened, while we heard the sirens blaring and planes constantly flying overhead. Her distress escalated; she became more agitated with each hour and complained of not sleeping. With a sense of helplessness because nothing that usually "worked" in our interaction seemed to be working, I suggested a medication consultation to ease her anxiety during this crisis. In making this recommendation, I thought I might be doing something "destructive" to the analytic process, and yet I could not seem to ride out living with her pain and terror without taking action. She readily agreed to my recommendation and went the following day to the psychiatric consultation. The next day, she was calmer and barely spoke of her meeting with the psychiatrist. Dismissive of him, she said she had not taken the medication, and that was the end of that. It was as if what she needed was for me to take her seriously, and then she could be calmed enough to settle back into the analytic mode. My thoughts about this one patient epitomized my state of mind. I came to realize that my readiness to suggest outside "help" (i.e., the consultation) reflected how terrified I myself felt but was not acknowledging.

Analyst 4

I met with two patients early in the morning of September 11 prior to the terrorist attacks. In a break between appointments, I found myself riveted to the TV, while I tried to contact members of my family, none of whom were in D.C. Remaining patients scheduled for that day phoned to cancel their appointments; they said that they did not know what was going to happen next. Sharing my patients' anxiety, I did not question their decisions or subsequently charge for these initial cancellations. It seemed important to acknowledge the "reality" of what was happening. Yet, I experienced an eerie sense of "unreality" during that day and that week. Time seemed suspended as I struggled to take in the horror of what had just occurred and the prospect of future attacks.

When Mrs. T arrived for her appointment on September 12, she freely talked about her terror—her sense of helplessness, rage, and lack of protection from future attacks. Characteristically, she was conflicted about revealing her upset, for she did not want to appear like a helpless little girl. While her colleagues had gone home immediately after the attacks, Mrs. T said she had been determined to stay at work and stick to her routine. In hindsight, I was surprised not to have questioned this decision. Perhaps, I identified with Mrs. T's resolve, for I, too, had been determined to continue my regular work routine in a D.C. office. Moreover, in response to Mrs. T's outbursts of helplessness and rage at the terrorists, I quickly invited genetic associations. And when she remarked I seemed upset, I did not encourage elaboration of this observation. Clearly, my responses reflected my own attempts to defend against terror. Only at the end of the hour did I regain some analytic balance when I addressed the transference ignited by the terrorist attacks. Mrs. T declared: "Zealots have just begun. There may be a lot more people affected. There's no stopping them!" I replied, "You felt your mother wasn't able to stop your brother and provide the protection you needed. Now I'm not able to stop what might happen, not able to protect you from future terrorist attacks." "That's right!" she exclaimed.

Later that day, several other patients tried to distance themselves from the trauma. When I noted that Mrs. C had not mentioned the terrorist attack, she declared that it was just a "riveting story," which had no personal impact on her. Mr. D mentioned the attacks, but he defended against his vulnerability by being contemptuously scornful of other people's hysteria. Both of these patients were dismissive of my observations of their wish to shield themselves from the trauma.

Commentary

These snapshots are as varied and diverse as we and our patients are. In an effort to grasp and cope with the trauma and its immediate aftermath, affects and defenses appeared, ranging from shock, disbelief, fear, terror, anger, denial, humor, and intellectualization. Some patients readily spilled out their reactions, flooding the hour with anger and helplessness. Other patients held the trauma at a distance. At times, we found ourselves joining with our patients' emotions, as well as with their defenses, especially intellectualization and humor. We felt a pressure to communicate that we were in this together and acted, often without reflection, to alter our customary frame by not charging for canceled hours, offering telephone sessions, or making medication referrals. We were confronting a new reality—that in a climate of terror, analysis could not provide the illusion of safety or the promise of a hopeful future. Yet, at the same time, we and our patients experienced the routine of appointments and the analytic space as a refuge from the noise and chaos filling the air and airwaves outside our offices and in our minds.

In spite of the many pressures to merge in sharing our patients' experiences, we were surprised to discover that even in the early days following the 9/11 attacks, there were moments we set ourselves apart through our capacity to analyze. We questioned what was occurring between us and our patients. We intervened to contain patients' flooded affects or to point out their defenses against terror. Analyzing, being curious, being reflective, and creating interpretations also seemed to serve as a personal defense for, at these times, we often experienced a sense of relief.

PART 2: THE STUDY GROUP

Shaken by the attacks and ongoing threats, we launched our study group 3 weeks after 9/11 to provide a structure, a safe place, to view the traumatic sequelae taking place in our lives and in our work with patients. From the first meetings, we spoke of concern for our patients and concern for ourselves and our families. We asked each other: Were we focusing too much on patients' affects, encouraging flooding? Were we too quickly diverting patients from their terror and our own? Was our thinking too paranoid, too extreme, too filled with denial? We asked ourselves: What is analytic in a time of terror? We experienced an ongoing tension between feeling relieved that our own experiences of terror were so similar, "We're in this together," and wanting to assert differences, "Well, I'm not like you." We were witnessing horror, fear, death, and experiencing retraumatization after meetings, including nightmares and difficulty sleeping. Humor helped ease the tension.

Some months after the attacks, we began to find it difficult to schedule group meetings. September 11 was floating out of sight, like a storm that had blown over. As we continued to discuss clinical material, we realized that many of our patients seemed to share this avoidance. Rarely were our patients referring to the recent trauma, and we were not interpreting or linking their emotions to it. We questioned whether our own avoidance sprang from a fear of retraumatizing our patients or ourselves.

We turned to history. What did analysts do in Vienna and Berlin under the threat of Hitler and the SS? What did analysts do in London when the bombs were falling and in Buenos Aires, Santiago, Bogotá, and Lima in times of terror? We turned to Freud. Under the press of colleagues leaving for the United States, Israel, and England and anticipating catastrophe, Freud kept working on *Moses and Monotheism* (1939) even though this work could place him in further danger. While our group meetings continued to heighten our anxiety, they also helped us to reestablish our footing, to engage our observing egos. We had a compelling view of the unique ways each patient was transforming a "real trauma" into psychic reality. Like the blue lights marking the empty New York skyline, the mind was finding ways to represent and rework what was traumatic—through dreams, fantasies, and the creation of metaphor.

PART 3: FURTHER REVERBERATIONS

We now present vignettes illustrating some of the ways representations of the September 11 trauma and subsequent terrorist threats entered the psychic reality of our patients and ourselves and affected our analytic dialogue.

Case 1

In a session 10 months after the September 11 attacks, and shortly after I had informed Mrs. Q about an unexpected absence, she displayed a greater freedom to express her anger toward me, including a wish to attack me. Then, Mrs. Q went on to describe raw feelings: "I feel like those people who were caught on the floor just above where the planes hit the tower—the whole building is going to collapse in just another minute." I replied, "What a horrible idea. I'm wondering whether you are recalling this image right now might have to do with the anxiety you feel when you get in touch with your anger, your wish to lash out at me, wish to attack me?" Mrs. Q replied, "Well, I'm angry about your absence. This is a terrible time for you to be away!"

In this vignette, Mrs. Q conjured up a terrifying image of being caught in one of the Twin Towers just before the building's collapse. This image represented a masochistic retreat from her destructive wishes toward me as well as her acute sense of vulnerability in response to my unexpected absence. Typically, this patient retreated from her aggression by recalling a salient childhood humiliation. Because the 9/11 imagery was affect laden for both of us, it served as a particularly vivid communication of her narcissistic vulnerability.

Case 2

During a session the week after the September 11 attacks, Mrs. G began with a long silence. She quickly dismissed several of my attempts to understand what was going on. I observed that Mrs. G looked sad and upset and commented that I seemed unable to provide any relief. In the following extended silence, I became aware of images of the planes tearing into the Twin Towers and the huge, fiery explosion that followed. I realized that I was experiencing the patient as a terrorist who, through her silence, appeared to be spoiling, damaging the analytic process. I thought that Mrs. G must be taking satisfaction in shooting me down again and again. Only later did I consider that Mrs. G might have perceived me as a terrorist who was attempting to break through her protective, silent cocoon. Near the end of this mostly silent hour, Mrs. G finally remarked, "I don't feel sad and upset—just diluted anger." Connecting the fiery explosions and the patient's rage, I said, "You say 'diluted' anger. Perhaps you wish to dilute your anger because you fear its full force." Mrs. G tensely replied, "I'm not afraid of my anger." In this hour, the vividness of my associations to 9/11 imagery gave me access to the rage of this patient, who rarely acknowledged any emotional response toward me.

Case 3

On Thursday, September 13, Ms. S came to her session having canceled the meeting on September 11. She wept the entire session and spoke of frightening possibilities of what could happen to her children and her husband, who worked in downtown D.C. She was afraid to sleep and kept imagining herself falling through the World Trade Towers. Like painters mastering a vision of horror, we used words to depict the events of 2 days before. I was aware of feeling pain in my back and shoulders and wondered if I would scream at her to stop because I had a daughter in New York City and a husband who would soon be traveling to Latin America. I was so close to her fears—these were our fears—and yet I was the therapist.

Three weeks post-9/11, this patient stated, "I need you to help me; I cannot stand feeling this way anymore." I also felt the need for a "break" from the continuous, vivid images of destruction. I told her of something I had learned about trauma from a study of the film *Schindler's List*—the necessity of allowing the mind to shift focus from that which is overwhelming to other events. I had found a way to tell her to stop. I was also reinstating my position as an active therapist who could help my patient. In the next session, Ms. S sobbed and told me her terrible dream of the night before in which she could not find her children after an atomic bomb warning. Working with these internal images of trauma put me on more familiar ground. As we worked with the dream, I asked if she had ever felt similarly at other times. She went on to tell me of a tragic event of her adolescence when a favorite aunt died, and she felt she could not speak about the depth of her grief because it hurt her parents and grandparents so much. She now told me how she had felt then. Analysis of the shattering impact of 9/11—as symbolized in the dream—led to the recovery and working through of deeply buried psychic pain. Sharing the trauma of 9/11 together greatly facilitated this process and brought to the transference her deep doubt that anyone, and now her therapist, would want to know her pain and could tolerate her pain.

Case 4

With Mr. W, an intense transference/countertransference configuration appeared around the anthrax scares. Mr. W tracks potential bioterrorist attacks for his agency. He started or ended sessions with comments such as, "Don't sniff your letters," or "No one with Ebola virus has shown up on airplanes," or "Have you gotten your antibiotics?" I was already finding myself terribly troubled about potential bioterrorism and reading information that was far too scary on the Johns Hopkins bioterrorism site. This patient's demeanor was unusually calm, seeing himself as someone who could organize and disseminate information. He was placing all of the panic in me, and I was receiving it. We began to understand that he was attempting to frighten me and treat me as he felt he had been treated as a child when he was alone and quite helpless. This was a profound insight for him.

During the height of the scare, he missed many appointments and left me messages like, "Two new cases today, unlikely to be positive," "Nose swabs taking place, nothing much to report today," or "A bunch of false alarms today." I found myself waiting intently for every bit of information. I was developing a "savior" fantasy about this patient, whom I imagined had access to medical interventions such as smallpox inoculations. When I wondered with him about what effects his reports could have on me, we began to uncover core fantasies of destruction and salvation. There was a heightened here-and-now significance to quick-moving wishes and fears about who would save and who would be abandoned and destroyed because we were living together in a time of terror.

PART 4: THE FIRST ANNIVERSARY

The first anniversary of September 11 brought a return of some of the emotional intensity of the early weeks following the attacks. Yet, even though the press, TV, and a series of sniper attacks in the Washington area also heightened our fears, we felt less emotionally labile and less defensive than we had 1 year previously. Our observing egos seemed more resilient. We had a keen curiosity about how this anniversary would affect our listening and interventions with our patients. And, of course, this study kept us focused.

Case 5

A couple, married for many years, called for a consultation on 9/11. The husband had discovered his wife had been having an affair with a colleague. She insisted that she was not involved sexually with this man. Even after the husband threatened to leave her, the wife continued her extramarital involvement. To begin to heal and to regain his trust, the husband said that he needed to hear what was on his wife's mind. The wife expressed her grave reluctance to having her private thoughts intruded on, stating she never took the involvement seriously or questioned her love and commitment to her husband. She wondered why he needed to hear from her in this way since, in all their years of marriage, he had never done so before. The husband expressed that their world had changed, that the landscape was completely different and the old rules no longer applied.

I could not help but think that the husband's descriptions of his new surroundings were spoken in terms of a 9/11 metaphor: The terrorist attacks had eliminated the trust and security previously built into our country's foundation, as the wife's betrayal seemed to have destroyed the foundation of their marriage. Old rules no longer applied since our landscape, our world, was forever changed. Here, the use of metaphor enhanced my empathic position with the husband. Perhaps I, in the countertransference, identified too easily with the husband's difficulties grappling with the aftermath of the shock of his wife's attack on what had seemed a secure and trusting foundation, further setting me apart from an empathic position with the wife.

The following case illustrates an uncanny psychoanalytic moment when, on the first anniversary of 9/11, analyst and patient were joined together, experiencing life's fragility.

Case 6

I began my morning hours preoccupied. My 10-year-old daughter had gone to feed her beloved pet rabbit (her baby) before school and was distressed that the rabbit was lying down, with a peculiar odor, not eating or startling. Both she, and secretly I, believed the rabbit was dying. Concerned about my daughter's possible loss, I urgently arranged a veterinary appointment during my morning break.

Ms. R began her hour, "I was scared last night, didn't think I would be alive today. It was so silent. The past few nights, there have been a lot of military planes but not last night. I listened to the list of names of the dead. I was certain I must know someone. I read about a man who worked at the Pentagon and didn't want to go back to the building last year. I felt ashamed for what I had thought. 'You're one of our Marines, and you can't go back to the building.'" I commented, "If he didn't go back, you would not be protected." Ms. R went on, "I had some anxiety about sending my child to school. I am so angry that they haven't caught Bin Laden nor solved the anthrax problem. The leaders are not taking care of me. There's an orange alert, we are definitely a target. I didn't clean my child's rabbit's cage yesterday. When my daughter takes it out to play, it's jumpy and startles easily. Today, something was wrong; the rabbit was too still. It was not eating much, not active as usual. I think it's dying."

Having no memory of hearing before about Ms. R's daughter's pet rabbit, I felt this uncanny sense of too close a coincidence. On this anniversary day, "we were both in this, too," feeling overwhelmed with worries about life and death. Ms. R spoke of feeling victim to the night noises, to waiting for the protection of the "leaders" and marines, and to waiting for her daughter's rabbit to die. My patient's feelings of helplessness and yearning for protection mirrored the way I had felt on this day and 1 year earlier. Now I, in a more activated state, wanted to do anything I could possibly do to protect life.

Case 7

A couple who lost their only daughter in the 9/11 tragedy—a daughter who began working at the Pentagon just 2 weeks before the attacks—entered therapy because they could not seem to get past this traumatic loss. Obsessed with thoughts of "if only" and "what if," they were wracked with guilt and self-torturing aggression. They reported that, on the first anniversary, they had gone out to the country to avoid radio, TV, newspapers, public places, and other people. "Going off by themselves achieved what purpose?" I wondered aloud. "Because," they said, "we can't stand it—the constant public outpourings, ceremonies, headlines, radio encomiums to the heroes of that day. They won't let us forget!" Rather than feeling recognized and supported in their grief, they felt that the publicness was an unrelenting intrusion on their ability to metabolize the trauma and to mourn their daughter in peace. It was as if the repeated emphases, by many voices, on many losses minimized their own personal loss. Moreover, they seemed to need to find some wrong to rail against as a road back from their grief and rage. Their idea of mourning required space to forget as well as to remember.

Case 8

Mr. B, a patient who suffers from strong feelings of vulnerability, described his activity on the night of the 9/11 first anniversary. He and a girl were walking near Dupont Circle when they came upon a street band. They saw that a crowd had gathered to hear the band, so they sat down on the curb to watch and listen. More people began to congregate. People began to dance on the broad sidewalk and even in the street. They danced in couples and in threes and fours. Others began to sing. This, he thought, had not happened at other times when he had heard the band playing. It felt to my patient as if these strangers had joined together to remember those lost on 9/11. But more, he felt that the group was saying: "We can dance, sing, play music; we can remember, but we also can go forward."

Listening to him, I felt both uplifted and almost moved to tears, so touched by a feeling of hopefulness and maybe resiliency, not only for this patient, who often feels so damaged, but for us all. I was surprised by the intensity of my emotional response, as if my own anniversary reaction was evoked, complete with my own longings to mitigate the feelings of loss with thoughts of hope.

Commentary

Throughout the year after 9/11, we watched the symbolic use of the attacks take on evocative significance in the psychic realities of our patients. Patients' overwhelming affects once split off from traumatic events and fantasies were reconnected as 9/11 responses led the way back. Core fantasies such as fantasies of destruction and salvation were played out on the 9/11 stage. Patients depicted old compromise formations with the vivid imagery of the terrorist attacks, thereby facilitating further work on these conflicts. Analysts' experiences of their own terror, just following 9/11 and at the 1-year anniversary, brought an emotional immediacy to the work as "we were in it, too." At moments, this shared trauma offered analysts access to the patient's emotional state and often led to powerful identifications with the patient.

DISCUSSION

This chapter has explored the effects of the 9/11 attacks and their aftermath on the work of four psychoanalysts. The question, "What is psychoanalytic in a time of terror?" continually surfaced as we processed our collected snapshots of responses to trauma in our patients and in ourselves. What is analytic is the capacity to witness and acknowledge the shared trauma, "We're in this, too," as well as to explore its unique impact on the psychic reality of each patient to help develop more adaptive, creative responses. Immediately following 9/11, we experienced a greater tendency to merge with our patients' fright and terror as well as to share similar defenses. At times, in our own states of shock, there was a struggle to maintain free-floating capacity to oscillate between empathic identifications and analyzing. Yet, even during the first days and weeks, the ability to acknowledge the images and affects of sessions and to reflect on their multiple meanings was available as we used our observing egos. We were surprised and comforted by the resilience of the analytic work in the midst of these days of terror.

Over time, we watched with excitement how our patients made symbolic use of the trauma to express and rework previous traumatic events and core conflicts. The way trauma appeared gathered intense affect and fantasy around it and was felt deeply. We could observe firsthand, with immediacy, what was taking place for our patients, ourselves, and between us in our offices. Retraumatization for patients and ourselves was a recurring aspect of the work, particularly with the occurrence of the new threats of anthrax and sniper attacks in the Washington, D.C., area. Retraumatization was also an unexpected and constant presence in our group meetings as we examined our analytic hours and discussed their content and our own affective responses.

Countertransference reactions ran the gamut from joining patients in fear to distancing ourselves. We recognized that when we focused only on analyzing patients' responses and failed to acknowledge the actual horror, we were defending against the intensity of our own fear with intellectualization and compartmentalization. Both with patients and in the group discussion, there was continual tension between when "we were in this together" and when we individuated from patients and each other, "my response is different from yours." Working analytically in a time of terror heightened the emotional intensity of our work and presented us with a unique view of the way the psyche, our patients' and our own, responded to traumatic events. Ultimately, the answer to the question, "What is analytic in a time of terror?" was found to be the ways we assisted our patients on the journey of creating meaning after 9/11. We are grateful to psychoanalysis for giving us the tools to think about these complex issues, for providing us the framework for work with patients, and for offering us a forum to discuss our ideas with each other when facing terror.

REFERENCES

Basseches, H., Ellman, P., Elmendorf, S., Fritsch, E., Goodman, N., Helm, F., & Rockwell, S. (1996). Hearing what cannot be seen: A psychoanalytic research group's inquiry into female sexuality. *Journal of the American Psychoanalytic Association*, 44(Suppl.), 511–528.

Fritsch, E., Ellman, P., Basseches, H., Elmendorf, S., Goodman, N., Helm, F., & Rockwell, S. (2001). The riddle of femininity: The interplay of primary femininity and the castration complex in analytic listening. *International Journal of Psychoanalysis*, 82, 1171–1183.

Freud, S. (1939). *Moses and monotheism*. In J. Strachey (Ed. & Trans.), *The standard edition of the complete psychological works of Sigmund Freud* (Vol. 23, pp. 1–140). London: Hogarth Press.

Goodman, N., Basseches, H., Ellman, P., Elmendorf, S., Fritsch, E., Helm, F., & Rockwell, S. (1993). *In the mind of the psychoanalyst: Capturing the moment before speaking*. Paper presented at the International Psychoanalytic Association, 38th Congress, Amsterdam.

Chapter 25

What Do You Want? On Witnessing Genocide Today

Bridget Conley-Zilkic[1]

INTRODUCTION

The U.S. Holocaust Memorial Museum's permanent exhibition, "The Holocaust," begins with an ascending elevator and a voice stating these things "just don't happen." It ends with voices of individuals describing the sometimes-painful, sometimes-beautiful realization that they had survived. In between is a relentless and overwhelming presentation of the history of the Holocaust. "This happened," the exhibition intones with the searing injustice of millions of shattered voices. Those who enter this space are asked to become witnesses, not merely exhibition visitors.

The hushed crowds exit the exhibition and face an austere memorial hall, where an eternal flame and candles flicker in honor of those who suffered and died. Then, visitors face a long hallway that is connected by an intimidating, steep, and dramatic black stone stairway to the main atrium, the Hall of Witness. It is generally noisier there, groups are getting ready to enter or are re-forming on leaving; it is a space that transitions the visitors back to their everyday lives.

* * *

In April 2009, I led an effort[2] to alter this pathway by inviting the Museum's annual 1.7 million visitors to stay longer to learn about contemporary genocide and their potential role in changing response to threats of genocide. The first sign of this change appears with the words "From Memory

---

[1] The views expressed in this chapter do not necessarily reflect those of the U.S. Holocaust Memorial Museum or its council.

[2] I was privileged to work with amazing colleagues from the museum, among the core team were Belinda Blomberg, Nancy Gillette, Traci Sym, Timothy Kaiser, Jamie Bresner, and Ariana Berengaut. We also had the honor of sharing this project with outside designers and developers. Those who played central roles in the conceptual development were David Small and Justin Manor from Small Design Firm; Philip Tiongson from Potion, Inc.; and Jonathon Alger from C&G Partners.

to Action" painted in a simple and bold statement at the end of that final hallway, over the entryway to a new space that is encountered if, instead of going down the stairs, one simply kept walking straight ahead.

The Museum's reputation is founded on relentless pursuit of history with the foremost goal to create a deeply impactful encounter with layer on layer of narrative, photography, video, artifacts, and testimony bearing witness to the history of the Holocaust. The exhibitions do not make the history a palatable morality tale but assert again and again the finality of this terrible past. With harsh angles crafted from granite, industrial brick, and metal, even every detail of the architecture feels as if it will never change.

This new space had to convey a story that was not yet completed—responding to the challenge of genocide in our lifetimes. *Genocide* is a legal term meaning, essentially, the intent to destroy in whole or in part an ethnic, national, racial, or religious group, as such. The legal or conceptual story of genocide is important, but it is not the whole story. Genocide never occurs; it manifests only through the actual assaults in specific places and times, against specific groups of people. There are inherent tensions in the task of exhibiting genocide with a goal of moving visitors to consider their own place in unfolding history. These tensions exist between telling a story of genocide and telling the stories of what happens in places. They are present in the differences between any single case of genocide and the unique experiences the individuals who suffered in it. Finally, such tensions are also present in the distance between the reality of extreme violence and the attempt to inspire response to it from afar.

The strategy we chose was to present these tensions without resolving them. The room is a deconstruction of what it means to exhibit genocide. It offers three modes of organizing content, each intended to challenge the other. Along three walls of the room as top-level headlines is a story of genocide. It can be read as a series of statements regarding the phenomenon: "When genocide occurs, there are always warning signs, groups are destroyed person by person, there is more than one way to respond, societies struggle with the consequences, and the future can be different." Running on three bands under these headlines are major cases of genocide: green for Rwanda, blue for Srebrenica in Bosnia-Herzegovina, and brown for the Darfur region of Sudan. Suspended from the ceiling in the center of the room, like a beating heart, 15 video screens cycle through 25 videos of eyewitnesses to these genocides. The personal stories both reinforce and complicate the conceptual and historical narratives told through the headlines and on the bands. Spanning the fourth wall is a "pledging area," where visitors are asked to write themselves into the problem by responding to the question: "What will you do to help meet the challenge of genocide today?" The wall also introduces today's ongoing threats of genocide: headlines, alerts, as well as model pledges about taking action.

Conveying knowledge, however, would not be the crucial ingredient. We did not have enough time with the visitor or enough space ever to convey all the knowledge that could be gained about any of these cases—it could not be achieved over three floors about the Holocaust, certainly it could not be done in one room about three other cases. Could we invite serious reflection on the complexity of the problem and still shift the visitor to thinking about personal actions? In short, could we bring this problem of genocide closer to our visitors?

* * *

Proximity, in truth, is the real dilemma. The challenge is to understand where one is in relation to a threat of genocide. It is here with us now, but of course, we are not at risk, our authority to have an impact on events is limited, and our knowledge is always incomplete. Is it possible to introduce the reality of genocide in our time while asking visitors or the general public (let alone the policy "experts") to recognize as well their distance from it? Can urgency and ethical imperative coexist with intelligent policy analysis? Does understanding the risk of genocide convey understanding of what might be done to prevent, halt, or mitigate its effects? The challenge of responding to threats of genocide today is not mere amplification of ethical stakes, but the work of translating ethics into informed political action. Could the exhibit provide a first step in conveying this message?

In my experience, the stories that haunt and compel a search for better responses are not the ones that make genocide easy for a distant audience to understand; they are always the ones that make it painfully difficult. No story of genocide can be accurately told by reducing it to some service it does to the concept of genocide or to the actions that those who are far away might have, could have, or wish they had taken. Not Rwanda, Bosnia, Sudan, or any emerging threat can be subsumed into a morality play or mirror for self-righteousness today without doing additional violence. This, however, is not to say that our distance can serve as an alibi for decisions that enable genocide. Balancing the call to action with respect for the alterity of such violence is the struggle of proximity.

* * *

How do we measure the space between (a) the story that ultimately cannot be told (it is impossible to imagine the end of a social world; it destroys the terms for discussion) and the burden that nonetheless all witnesses have to tell it; and (b) the events themselves and any actions that might be undertaken—particularly from afar—to change the story?

It is of course possible to get lost inside the labyrinthine task of measuring such distances. But, there are limits to our proximity to genocide, and it would be a display of dishonorable hubris to forget this. Such forgetting is always a risk, just as getting lost is a risk.

* * *

In April 2004, I boarded a small plane from Nairobi, Kenya, to Kigali, Rwanda. Seated next to me was Linda Melvern, an investigative journalist whose writing on the 1994 Rwandan genocide was among the early examinations of the violence. Her work, astonishingly angry and focused, detailed the failures of the outside world to help when the extremists took over the state and systematically murdered at least 500,000 of the country's Tutsi minority in 100 days. We chatted a little; she turned silent as we approached the Kigali airport and started softly crying. She quietly explained, "I cannot help it; I always cry when I arrive in Rwanda."

Years later, I met Jean-Philippe Ceppi, a journalist who was there in 1994. He was among the few who made his own way into Kigali in the early days of the violence, intrepidly finding a taxi driver willing to drive him from Burundi across the border and then somehow making his way into the epicenter of genocide. He cried as he spoke about an incident that was not at all violent—approaching a hotel in the middle of the night in southern Rwanda, a place where there was no killing, yet. He would later see horrible things, but it was his attempts to describe two teenage girls he had awakened to check into the hotel that triggered his emotional response. He explained to me: "You don't know why I am crying now—there will be worse things in my story, don't worry. But while it was quiet that first night when I came to the hotel, I know what happens to them later, those beautiful, young, innocent girls. I remember them so sleepy ... but I also know how they died later" (U.S. Holocaust Memorial Museum, 2009b).

And a few scattered words: *so much blood, rape ...*

It was enough to tell me that there was an enormous abyss between what he saw and what I could understand—an abyss dwarfed by the chasm that separated what the girls experienced from any of us.

Ceppi was the first person to describe Rwanda as genocide in a published article. He used the word on April 11—just days after the violence had begun, while those who could have helped tried their hardest, as Melvern wrote, to avoid grappling with the enormity of the atrocities against civilians in Rwanda. Ceppi never wrote about his personal experiences, despite covering the story for news outlets as it continued for years; from Rwanda, it bled into Zaire, which became the Democratic Republic of the Congo, but retained the crisis along its wound of an eastern border. He told me he just never felt it was his story; he did not have an angle on it, could not capture it as his own. He had a chance, but turned it down, to cover the 10th anniversary ceremonies in Kigali. The anniversary covered him, though—his own stories were played back on a radio program in Switzerland, where he was in 2004. As he listened in his car, the memories rushed back.

* * *

Rwanda's capital city, Kigali, is (or at least was when I visited) relatively clean, calm, and contained. I stayed at a hotel, Chez Lando, owned by the family of a friend of mine in Washington, D.C., Louise Mushikiwabo.[1] Her brother, Lando, was the original owner. Lando had political ambitions as well, and when, in response to outside pressure in the early 1990s, Rwanda's one-party system opened to allow opposition, Lando became active in the Liberal Party.

He was on the lists of those to be killed immediately in April 1994. His Canadian wife, Hélène, daughter, and son were also killed. My friend's family was ravaged by the genocide in other ways as well. I knew her story from over the years she had told it publicly and in private to me. When she published a family history, *Rwanda Means the Universe: A Native's Memoir of Blood and Bloodlines* (Mushikiwabo & Kramer, 2006), Louise had her publisher send a copy directly to me in the mail. I opened it right away, flipping through the pages to the photo inserts in the middle.

There, I found Louise's family smiling out of old photos. The captions gave each one's name and noted which ones had been murdered in 1994. Beautiful nieces, nephews, her beloved brother, sister-in-law. Family. And so many of them violently struck down. They were not my family, and the violence had ended before I "met" them, but understanding them as my friend's family changed how and what I could see. It is one thing to hear the stories of violence, another to know someone caught in them, searching for familiar faces among the photographs of crowds in desperation.

* * *

At a program held at the Museum in March 2005, Brian Steidle, an American who was a member of the African Union monitoring team in Darfur, testified about what he had witnessed. He showed photographs of bodies and of explicit Sudanese government complicity in the looting and destruction of villages. After the presentation, an interesting comment came from the audience. A man stood up and said: "I haven't seen any pictures showing genocide. I don't trust you one hundred percent. I don't believe your pictures."[2]

Believe is an interesting choice of words in this case, and it is precisely the right choice. There are, of course, no pictures that show genocide. Even

---

[1] Mushikiwabo would eventually return to Rwanda and join the government. At the time of this writing, she had risen to the position of foreign minister. I do not know the story of her transition from unofficial advocate in Washington, D.C., to a place of power in Kigali. I have followed it from afar, ever more distant.

[2] Author's notes from the program. A video based on the program, "Eyewitness Testimony: Brian Seidel" (U.S. Holocaust Memorial Museum, 2009a) is publicly available at the museum's Web site.

324 The Power of Witnessing

images of piles of dead bodies can confuse: After the Rwandan genocide, millions fled the country, among them the perpetrators. In the refugee camps, a cholera epidemic killed an estimated 12,000. The piles of bodies from this catastrophe were not from the genocide, although when one searches for images under "Rwanda, 1994" these photos invariably appear.

The crime of genocide cannot be clearly presented in a single frame, or even really in multiple frames, regardless of how illustrative the evidence might be because of the demands of demonstrating the perpetrator's "intent to destroy" a group, not on any number of particular acts (although cumulatively they bolster a case for genocide).[1] Because of this inherent lack of objectivity at the heart of the term, *genocide* as a name given to events calls on a community of believers—those who share the idea that a group of perpetrators are intentionally committing acts that cumulatively pose an existential threat to a group. In addition, and this is the part that gets difficult, these believers share the idea that the violence deserves exceptional attention and response. The name not only names events, but its usage calls into existence a community whose activism too often claims an ethical position beyond politics.

The term operates as shorthand for all the knowledge and debate that would usually accompany discussions of appropriate foreign policy responses and recommendations for use of the military. Genocide's promise of an ethical community created in solidarity with threatened people is worth imagining. However, if this "shorthand" is to avoid being shorthand for uniformed escalation of rhetoric, facts, and action, then its demands must be reconsidered.

* * *

I did not follow the war in Bosnia-Herzegovina (1992–1995) very closely while it was happening, although I do remember seeing *Schindler's List* in the movie theater and wanting to stand up afterward and yell at the crowd to dry their eyes and take a stand against atrocities in Bosnia today. I remember that clearly, but I have no recollection what I thought I knew about Bosnia or why I had such a reaction. My real exposure came in graduate school through journalists' books, translated writings from Bosnia, and scholarly texts. Photographs are the images of the war that I recognize; perhaps the most compelling are those of photojournalist Ron Haviv.

Haviv began covering the wars of the former Yugoslavia in Slovenia (1991), a conflict that lasted barely more than a week. From there, war, with journalists like Haviv following, moved to Croatia (1991), Bosnia (1992–1995), and finally Kosovo (1999).

---

[1] This core difficulty has led many professionals in this field to shift terms, using the legal framework for "crimes against humanity," or the crimes outlined in the *Responsibility to Protect* document, or other less legally specific terminology, like "atrocity crimes."

Some of the most shocking of Haviv's images are from Bijeljina, a small town in eastern Bosnia near the border with Serbia, early in the conflict, April 1992. He gained access to Bosnia by going in with a group of Serbian paramilitaries, the "Tigers," led by Zeljko Raznatovic, known as "Arkan." The Tigers would soon become notorious for the brutality of their assaults, innovators of ethnic cleansing. A local dispute had split the town, and the atmosphere was tense. Then, Arkan's men showed up claiming they were there to liberate the town from Muslim extremists.

The Tigers went house by house, pulled out a few men and women and killed them while Haviv watched. He described the scene as taut: hyper, violent, and dangerous. The soldiers yelled at the civilians to follow orders and at Haviv not to take photographs. He separated himself from the soldiers and, partially hidden, documented the unfolding violence.

Haviv had once before been a witness to an atrocity that he could not document. In Croatia after the fall of Vukovar, he witnessed several executions. When he tried to take photos, each time a gun was placed to his head, and he was stopped. He vowed if ever in that situation again that "if I can't at least help the person to survive it, I have to walk out with a document to hold those accountable."

Among the images he took that day are a series along a street. In the first, a woman is tending to the fallen body of a man. Blurry lines in the foreground bear testimony to Haviv's attempts to hide while taking the photo. In the second, a soldier's foot is raised, on the way to kicking his victims' bodies on the ground—it appears to be the bodies of the first man, with the woman now collapsed beside him and another man's body next to her. The third displays the same three bodies on the sidewalk, a soldier behind them holding a gun examines something outside the frame through a wide door opening into a brick wall.

Perhaps the most terrifying image from Bijeljina is one that depicts a man on his knees, hands raised in surrender, looking directly at Haviv's camera. Behind the man, a gun is held at the ready, and further back is another soldier, patrolling the street. The caption tersely states: "A Muslim in Bijeljina begs for his life after capture by Arkan's Tigers. Spring 1992." In an interview (U.S. Holocaust Memorial Museum, 2009c), Haviv described the photo:

> The Serb soldier had thrown him down and he put his arms up and basically looked at me as if I was the only person that could save him, which probably in his mind I was, but unfortunately there wasn't really anything I could do. They brought him to the headquarters and at that point I was waiting for permission to be able to leave from Arkan himself and as I was standing there, I heard a great crash and I looked up and out of a second floor window this man came flying out and landed at my feet. And amazingly he survived the fall and they came

over, doused him with some water and said something like, "this is to purify Muslim extremists," as they doused him with the water and they started kicking him and debasing him and then dragged him back into the house.

* * *

Once while searching the Associated Press photo database for images from Bosnia for potential use in a new exhibition I was working on, I was shocked to find among the hundreds of photos this same Muslim man pictured in a black-and-white image I had never seen before. Scrolling through frame after frame of photos, I recognized him. In this photo, he was being doused with water (or some clear fluid) from plastic bottles. I was not sure at first if it was the same man; the look of terror on his face from Haviv's portrait had altered his features. In the AP image, he was more dazed, a little further gone. The clothing matched, as did the scene.

I did not save the image, though, and have never been able to find it again. I have searched under all the terms I thought I had previously searched, added more specific ones, and spoke with a representative from the database—all to no avail. Now, I am not sure if I saw the image or imagined it from hearing Haviv's story.

I also tried to find out more about the man's backstory. Bijeljina is not that big. Surely among the survivors someone would recognize him. I found several people from Bijeljina willing to look at Haviv's image, but none could help me discover his name. This "Muslim man begging for his life" had a name, a unique history that should not end as the emblem of a nation's pain, much as his story is caught in that narrative.

* * *

Haviv's images of the soldier kicking a dead body and of the man begging for his life—images of people dead and dying, and for which he risked his life—appeared around the world in major publications. The effect, as Haviv stated, "was no reaction. The war started and four years later several hundred thousand people were killed, millions became refugees." He continued:

> The work that I showed of this brutality is something that holds people accountable; but not only the perpetrators—the western politicians that talked about peace and didn't really put any action into plan and then also hold everybody responsible. Those of us who come from the countries that democratically elect our leaders; we are also responsible for that. We put these people in power and they acted in our name and they did nothing.

* * *

Haviv's images are shocking. There are some, like *New York Times* columnist Nicholas Kristof, who argue that shock is necessary to spur a blasé audience into engagement: "If I can make people spill their coffee in the morning and help put those issues on the agenda, then that's the first step toward getting them resolved" (Conley-Zilkic, 2010). Referencing the literature of social psychology, Kristof posits that to get an American audience to care about terrible situations around the world, the first connection needs to be an emotional one. The next step will be to seek rational modes of engagement.

This is an argument political theorist Judith Butler (2009) has made regarding the potential of searing images to reveal the innate humanity of their subjects. Writing in the context of the Iraq War and deeply critical of the policy of embedding journalists within military units, Butler argues that the inherent power of the image is tied to how it frames reality: to what it both pictures and censors. But, she posits a political kernel buried in the possibility of "alternative frames" that "would perhaps communicate a suffering that might lead to an alteration of our political assessment of the current wars. For photographs to communicate in this way, they must have a transitive function, making us susceptible to ethical responsiveness" (p. 77). For Butler, the image can reveal human vulnerability and spark political response.

Butler wrote in conversation with Susan Sontag's *Regarding the Pain of Others* (2003) work on the photograph, which is more skeptical of the image: "Harrowing photographs do not inevitably lose their power to shock. But they are not much help if the task at hand is to understand" (p. 89). Sontag, unlike Butler, had many contexts in mind, including the war in Bosnia, where the ethical demand issued by images of humanity at risk produced action designed to banish that suffering—humanitarian aid—rather than action designed to engage with the more difficult political issues at hand.

For me, it is unclear if the reaction sparked by shock, be it captured in an image or told in a story, is emotional and is then followed—for those who make the transition—by an engagement to placate emotions. This may not be the best way to think structurally or logically about action, but rather produces consumerist activism—action designed to respond to one's emotions: "Click here to end suffering in Africa"; "Dial 1-800-save-the-world to support armed intervention in X-place;" and so forth.

Ethical exposure is crucial; there can be no denying that. However, Sontag's argument that it is insufficient for informed decisions is compelling. It is time to move beyond thinking that political action can be limited to reimagining the space of the political or to discourse on ethical exposure, safe havens for the cynical who fear compromising policy stands. It is time to translate that initial impulse into a more serious grappling with the limitations and possibilities of response to particular situations. This will, inevitably, mean that one will be wrong from time to time. It is not a task for those who would want to rest comfortably in ideological frameworks or are caught in the undertow of shock and pity. It implies an engagement born of critical insight, realizing its own limitations and how these limits are constructed less by distance than by our own relations to power, and nonetheless takes a stand.

* * *

I will never forget the eyes of a group of Rwandan women survivors who I met with in 2004; their worlds were gone, many had witnessed their husbands and children murdered, and yet they survived to linger in loneliness, poverty, illness, and fathomless sorrow. I cannot imagine the strength it takes to live as a survivor or the injustice to demand that survivors forgive, reconcile, and move on because the attention of the outside has moved on.

The outside world seems to be adept only at disjointed attention—always the wrong place when the violence strikes. Spring 2004 was marked by increasingly disturbing and vivid news of destruction in the Darfur region of Sudan. Villages were being systematically burned to the ground, civilian populations assaulted and displaced into conditions that caused the deaths of hundreds of thousands. It was pretty clear that the targeting was on an ethnic basis. I remember talking in Kigali with some representatives of international organizations and various governments on the 10th anniversary of the Rwandan genocide about the need to respond more emphatically to the violence in Darfur. It was absurd to attend the Rwandan memorial ceremonies, filled with regrets of a world that had failed to engage seriously with the genocide, while Sudan was burning. Patience, I kept being told, we are trying.

My Rwandan friends were all saying, come back sometime when it is not April. Everyone is different in April, a little crazy. Everything is too close in April.

* * *

"Get out of my frame." That is what the photographer said to Emir Suljagic, a survivor from Srebrenica, as he stood by his father's grave. Emir's father, like thousands before him, was being buried at the memorial site for Srebrenica, Potocari, the former headquarters of the U.N. forces who were sent to establish the town as a "safe haven" and who handed over civilians to their would-be murderers. Emir apparently was in the way of the international image producer capturing the moment when survivors would grieve and bury their dead.

When Emir told me this story, I wondered how much international attention to memorialization occurs in spite of, rather than because of, the survivors. Perhaps that is too cynical, but the production of a "survivor" identity at times conflicts with the continued living of people who happened to have survived.

* * *

Although visiting the Avega offices was high on my personal list of priorities for my time in Rwanda, it was only late in the week when I found time to walk down a mud alley to the organization's back gate. Avega-Agahozo is an organization created by women widowed by the genocide to support the survivor community of widows, orphans, the elderly, those who lost their children, children heads of household, and the handicapped. They provide trauma counseling, income-generating projects, health clinics, and more. In my free time, I was working with friends in Washington, D.C., to try to organize a benefit program for them.

I made my inquiry at the front desk: Could I speak with someone about their work and how we might best focus our efforts in D.C. to support them? I was led to the office of a young man, himself a survivor. He was visibly tired, and I started in my rusty French to explain myself. He looked up, with bloodshot eyes, and as if something inside had suddenly broken and there was no more pretending, angrily questioned: "What do you want from us? You people have been coming here all week asking for our stories, and what do we get? What do you want from us?"

I was stunned and stammered through an explanation, again, of what I was trying to do.

He recovered his demeanor, professional and competent—but now all at once exhausted as if he had been running for a hundred days. He apologized and said he had been speaking with journalists and other visitors all week and was just too tired, too tired.

So, what did I want?

* * *

In a very straightforward way, the story of genocide is usually told first by journalists, human rights defenders, and sometimes aid workers. While this last category of responders has as its primary goal the delivery of aid, which can sometimes come in direct contradiction with the need to speak out about abuses, individuals and organizations in this field do often bear witness. In Rwanda, the International Committee of the Red Cross (ICRC), the elder statesman of aid organizations, showed that organizations can learn from history when it made a conscious decision to empower its man on the ground, Philippe Gaillard, to help the press gain access to atrocity sites and information from their network. This move contrasts sharply with their failure during the Holocaust to speak out about the fate of Jews under Nazi occupation for fear it would jeopardize their cross-border programs.

After the crisis brokers, come the first round of books. Often by journalists, these help establish the narrative arc of the day-to-day events they covered. In Rwanda, and in a few other places, the tools of international humanitarian law have also asserted authority over the storytelling mechanisms. Tribunals produce a record of the eyewitnesses, experts, and researchers. In Rwanda, survivor testimonies have come later. This is not always the case; in Bosnia, for instance, there were books published during the conflict by people trapped inside it. But, the war in Bosnia continued for years; Rwanda was a hundred days. Regardless of the duration, once violence ends, survivors face other challenges of surviving. It is no longer the time to think, at least often not for years. And then, the state gets involved, sending out the tendrils of control to coax or coerce the story of violence to match its self-explanatory narrative. Meanwhile, the academicians take their turn, at times digging deeper, other times skimming the surface on the way to a larger theory. And in Rwanda, another phase began of devotees to memory: documentaries, feature films, oral history projects, photojournalists, and so on.

Survivors, meanwhile, struggle. Does the story belong to them? Are they the keepers of honesty for the others? Do we return to them as the closest point of proximity to the truth? Do we want their story to fit into a narrative of "the 1994 Rwandan genocide"? Of genocide as a conceptual term? As a way of illustrating why something else is important, like preventing the next case, creating legal tribunals, funding projects?

* * *

What did I want? Could I have told this man, who lived in the shadow of violent loss, that I could in some small way contribute to the world's understanding of what had happened in Rwanda, and that this would either be of value in and of itself or would help improve the lives of survivors in some material way? Of the former results, I could be confident; of the latter, I had no idea. Would he want to know that Rwanda is being taught to audiences with the goal of improving U.S. or international policy the next time genocide might occur? Would the statement ring with hope or only delusions of a world whose record of failure in Rwanda is as unbearably painful as is the overall record of pursuing policies that are foremost concerned with the rights and safety of any civilians anywhere?

What if I were to say that I and I alone, without any promises for anything else, cannot bear his story and having heard it must tell it. Is my inability to live with the small burden of learning about this history any more honest a reason to ask him to tell the story again, and again, so that I could burn it into my memory and tell others? Is my wanting to tell the story really an expression of wanting relief from its burden? Is this proximity?

* * *

In the work educating about genocide, there are some images that are difficult to use. A catalogue of the human body as nothing other than the object for displays of raw power: a burnt body arched in pain, entrails exposed, from a village in Darfur; a spreadsheet of nightmares from Rwanda; e-mailed images from someone in Congo of his sister's body, found raped and drowned; video of Serbian irregular soldiers forcing Bosnian men to drag the bodies of their murdered neighbors deeper into the woods before befalling the same fate; the long shot through the trees in Rwanda of a murder at a roadblock; the battered body of a colleague's friend beaten to death while in the custody of Sudanese security forces—and others.

On the day that the last image described was e-mailed to me by a colleague, I also attended a meeting at which testimony from a Holocaust-era perpetrator was discussed. The perpetrator, after describing his role on an execution team killing Jewish families, questioned where God was at the time—as if God had abandoned perpetrator and victim alike and taken leave of humanity.

It is wrong, though, to blame God at that moment. The perpetrator and the victim remain only human. The executioner can kill but cannot change the humanity of the victim. At this moment, as Maurice Blanchot (1993) has argued, man can be destroyed but also remains indestructible. There is no inhuman. The implications of this are enormous: "We no longer have the least chance of seeing ourselves relieved of ourselves or our responsibility" (p. 130).

The role of those of us who educate about genocide is not to preach platitudes beyond critical inquiry; we should not ask that audiences "believe" but help them better understand, with great humility before our task and our limitations, the world and their place in it, humanity, and history. Genocide is in many ways a profoundly weak concept; under its heading, enormously complex and compelling human and historical events are tethered together with the binding force of frayed and unraveling rope. As a concept, word, and law, genocide promises so much more than it can fulfill. The ethical imperative issued by exposure to the humanity of those at risk finds no match in the quality and clarity of the political actions that might follow. Our tools for response are always compromised and inadequate. One cannot produce proximity to genocide—neither to its reality nor to adequate response.

There is no alibi in this insight. Rather, it strengthens the call to struggle against genocide regardless of—or perhaps because of—our inability to do justice to the demands of its violence.

Eugenie Kayierere, a Rwandan survivor, was recorded by Jean Hatzfeld (2009) as saying: "We were pursued, we ran all day, we waited through sleepless nights, and we had soldiered on for years since then, yes. But our ordeal stops at the gates of death. What is behind those gates belongs to the dead" (p. 111). And according to another survivor, Ignace Rukiramacumu: "The truth of the genocide is in the mouths of both the killers, who manipulate and conceal it, and the dead, who have carried it away with them" (p. 112).

The rest of us work at the borders of an ever-retreating proximity to the truth of genocide.

REFERENCES

Blanchot, M. (1993). *The infinite conversation*. Minneapolis: University of Minnesota Press.

Butler, J. (2009). *Frames of war: When is life grievable?* London and New York: Verso.

Conley-Zilkic, B. (Interviewer), & Kristof, N. (Interviewee). (2010). *Shining the spotlight*. Retrieved from http://blogs.ushmm.org/COC2/728/

Hatzfeld, J. (2009). *The antelope's strategy: Living in Rwanda after the genocide.* New York: Farrar, Straus, and Giroux.

Melvern, L. (2000). *A people betrayed: The role of the West in Rwanda's genocide.* London: Zed Books.

Mushikiwabo, L., & Kramer, J. (2006). *Rwanda means the universe: A native's memoir of blood and bloodlines.* New York: St. Martin's Press.

Sontag, S. (2003). *Regarding the pain of others.* New York: Farrar, Straus, and Giroux.

U.S. Holocaust Memorial Museum (Producer). (2009a). Eyewitness testimony: Brian Steidle. Retrieved from http://www.ushmm.org/genocide/take_action/gallery/portrait/steidle

U.S. Holocaust Memorial Museum. (2009b). Bridget Conley-Zilkic interview with Jean-Philippe Ceppi.

U.S. Holocaust Memorial Museum. (2009c). Bridget Conley-Zilkic interview with Ron Haviv.

Chapter 26

Bystandership—One Can Make a Difference

Interview With Ervin Staub

Nancy R. Goodman and Marilyn B. Meyers

I rail against the notion of incomprehensible evil.

Ervin Staub (interview, 2011)

Ervin Staub is an exemplary witness of the Holocaust, mass killing, atrocity, and individual acts of dehumanizing behavior. He is not only willing to face all of these terrible events but also fully brings his mind to them. In his scholarly work, he brilliantly creates concepts depicting what factors lead to the horrors of genocide and what can be learned to prevent genocide. Ervin was a hidden child of the Holocaust who was protected by active bystanders who risked their own lives to save him and his family. Ever since, he has been motivated to bring active witnessing and intervention to others. The titles of his recent books speak directly to the aims of his extensive research and direct work on interventions: *The Roots of Evil: The Origins of Genocide and Other Group Violence* (1989); *The Psychology of Good and Evil: Why Children, Adults and Groups Help and Harm Others* (2003); *Overcoming Evil: Genocide, Violent Conflict, and Terrorism* (2011); and *The Roots of Goodness: Inclusive Caring, Moral Courage, Altruism Born of Suffering, and Active Bystandership* (2012). We were determined to end this book by demonstrating the importance of bringing the power of witnessing to all inhumanities and traumas. As we read the work of Ervin Staub, we knew we needed him. We are so grateful to him for helping make his ideas available to the readers of this volume.

On May 28, 2011, we flew to Bradley International Airport (Windsor Locks, CT) and, with Ervin's directions, found our way to him. His home offered a warm space for settling down to conversation at the dining room table. From the window open to the backyard gardens, we could see a beautiful copper beech tree spreading its branches high and wide, creating shade underneath as the leaves shone in the light of the sun. It seemed to us that this magnificent tree symbolized the largeness of Ervin's witnessing and scholarship to understand and prevent genocide and evil.

Ervin is a leading scholar in understanding the bystander phenomenon. As evidenced in the interview, his personal experience as a child in Hungary under the Nazi threat affected him deeply and influenced his life's work. His family was provided "protective passes" and presumed safe housing by the Swedish humanitarian Raoul Wallenberg. Wallenberg was a hero who saved many lives. But, it was his beloved housekeeper, Macs, who was the active bystander who influenced Ervin most. She took Ervin and his younger sister into hiding and then repeatedly endangered her life to feed Ervin and his family and other people in their "protected house." In the interview, he also told us about other breathtaking situations when a family member was able to do something to ensure, for that moment and that day, that they would remain alive. He told us that he understands how fortunate he is. There were so many Jewish people who had received no active interventions from anyone around them and had no chance to take effective action on their own behalf.

The situations of active bystandership in Ervin's life left their imprint in enduring ways that he brings continuously to his worldwide efforts to change what happens for individuals and societies when faced with individual and mass cruelty. His long-standing and consistent dedication to the exploration of the motivation for active bystandership brings him not only to genocide and mass murder but also to bullying and other misuses of authority and power and aggression. He has made 17 trips to Rwanda, working to prevent reoccurrence of mass murder through reconciliation. His determination to intervene led to work with the Los Angeles Police Department after the Rodney King incident and with the city of New Orleans after Hurricane Katrina. He also goes into classrooms to raise awareness in children about treating others kindly and to work with teachers to create caring classrooms that help develop positive behavior by children.

In the interview excerpted here, Ervin emphasizes the interconnectedness of genocide, atrocity, altruism, passive and active bystandership, and perpetration. Throughout, he generously lets us be his witnesses as he interweaves and reflects on stories of his personal and professional life. This interview took place between Ervin Staub (ES), Nancy Goodman (NG), and Marilyn Meyers (MM). We chose segments of the interview that highlight Ervin's work and his personal history as a child of the Holocaust. In the interview, we move between past, present, and future. We return often to felt memories of his childhood witnessing and to his development of ideas defining the evolution of genocide and the evolution of caring, active bystandership and prevention. A better future becomes possible by following how Ervin has brought the power of witnessing to his work and has used it to think fully about atrocity and to prevent further atrocities and genocide.

EVIL IS IMPORTANT

ES: Evil is important to think about, important to comprehend, and important to penetrate. It's not like you are trying to find some mysterious alien substance. It is that you are trying to understand all the layers that are involved. By layers I mean societal conditions, characteristics of the culture, and the psychological impact of the combination of social conditions and culture. I mean the social processes that evolve out of this mix, and then to understand the evolution of hostility and violence and the transformations of individuals, groups, and society. We can transform so that we become better, but unfortunately transformation can take place for evil, and that's what happens to perpetrators. There was this medical thinking among the Nazis, that the Jews were bacilli, the Jews were a virus. What has been written about the Wannsee Conference indicates the consequences of this. Those people, high-level Nazis at the Wannsee Conference, sit around and talk about how to do this, how to exterminate the Jews, and they are not doing it to human beings. They are not thinking about that person as a human being any more. You are now thinking of how to deal with a problem that must be dealt with, and so this is the tragedy of perpetration, that the experience of the other as a human being with feelings and thoughts and needs is lost and gone and negated. To be able to do great violence to people, you have to devalue them greatly, and this happens in every genocide.

"I SAW ALL OF THIS": BECOMING AN ACTIVE BYSTANDER

Ervin talked about what he experienced as a child in having Macs standing by his family and the witnessing and many actions by family members that gave them a chance to hide and survive.

ES: I attribute my interest in the active bystander to a number of things. I was recently thinking about this because, as I mentioned, I wrote a little piece to honor Macs, this woman who was our maid in Hungary. In Hungary, middle-class families had maids, and she helped us as best as she could. She lived with us from the time before I was born. I escaped from Hungary when I was 18. She continued to live with my family, and she was the last survivor of that generation. I think that her actions, her taking action on our behalf, her endangering herself by going out and baking bread and bringing it back to the protected house that we were in at that point, and doing other things to help us, and her loving presence, had a large role in inspiring my work on helping behavior, and altruism, and questions about what leads people to help others, and why people remain passive in the face of other people's need, and how we can create more caring—and what I like to think of as inclusive caring. It is perfectly possible for children to be raised in a way that they care about people connected to them, people in their family and people in their group. But then they can draw a line between their group and the rest of the world, and especially draw a line between their group and some devalued group. They can then not care about the welfare of the people in that devalued group. So that has been for a long time my intense concern.

I think there is also another source of what I do, and I am just realizing some of these things now. It's interesting that I'm thinking about this now, it's a nice coming together. In the huge majority of cases, Jews had very little potential to affect their fate. But, my experience was that my family did all kinds of things that affected our fate for the better. We were lucky to be in such a context. What do I mean by that?

My aunt and my mother went to stand in front of this crowd in front of the Swedish embassy in Budapest, and everybody was trying to get in because that seemed to be the one means of survival, and they somehow managed to get in. Now, in truth, I must say that later on I felt guilty about this, that they got in but other people didn't get in. The tragedy of the Holocaust was that in the limited instances when people had an opportunity to do certain things, often there was competition for survival, and people under those circumstances even if they are really good people, what do you do when there is that kind of competition for survival. The point is that they took action. They got these letters of protection. Macs, this woman, took action and took me and my sister into hiding and then brought us back when we were to move to this protected house. She went out to get bread for us and continued to do that.

Macs took a copy of the letter of protection to my father who was in a forced labor camp. She asked somebody to ask my father to come to the fence and gave my father a copy of this letter of protection. That piece of paper was totally useless to him. Actually in the protected house where we stayed there were constant raids on the house, so it wasn't like we were there and we were safe. In ongoing raids on the house people were taken away, and people were taken away because they were not the right age or they were not something. So while this was of no use to him in a practical sense, my mother and I later believed, we talked about this, strangely, only after he died many years later, that this was probably what gave him the courage to escape. And when his group from his labor camp was being taken to Germany, they had a stopover in Budapest, and during that stopover he escaped.

He came to the protected house where we were, and the superintendent allowed him in. He knew where we were because Macs also told him. So he came there and he was in hiding in the building, and once I saw a group of black-uniformed men marching down the street, and I called out, "They are coming!" I don't know whether my mother had this in mind before or just came up with this plan, but she had my father sit down in the corner of the room, pushed an armchair over him, and threw a blanket over the armchair. And these men came into the house, and they looked at everything, pulled out every drawer, and they didn't find him. The point that I'm making is that her actions saved my father. I saw all of this.

ONE CAN MAKE A DIFFERENCE AND ONE CAN CHANGE THE WORLD

ES: I must have had the feeling at some level that one can take action, one can make a difference, and one can change the world and people can be protected, and violence can be stopped. And all of these experiences probably contributed to my orientation to do work about prevention and active bystandership. From the very beginning, I was doing work to see how things can be changed. As I started to work at Harvard University, for the first few years I was doing—surprise—research on fear and how people can deal with fear and anxiety and how opportunity for control, for exercising control over events, and information about events and so on can diminish fear. So from the very beginning, and all along, I was interested in change processes.

MM: At what point was there for you a conscious connection between your experience as a child in Hungary and the work that you've been doing?

ES: At the very beginning I was working on disconnecting myself actually, disconnecting the work that I was doing from my experience in the Holocaust. I was trained at Stanford, in graduate school, to be a serious experimental researcher. So I saw myself as studying valuable, serious problems, and separating them from my experience. Then some years after I had been doing research on helping behavior, I was reading a book by Leon Uris, maybe it was *Exodus*, maybe it was something else, and I remember feeling teary and I'm thinking I want to do in my work whatever I can so that these things don't happen ever again, and the world will be a different kind of place. And then, as time went on it became very clear that everything that I do has to do with my earlier experience, that all my work and everything grew out of that.

FROM PASSIVITY AND AVOIDANCE TO ACTION
AND RESPONSIBILITY

NG: When did studying bystander phenomena occur to you?

ES: It's so integral now to the way I think, that I'm not sure when it started. I began to think about doing research on helping when I talked at Stanford to Perry London, who was a visiting professor there, and became my friend. He was the first person to do research on rescuers. So when I got to Harvard, early on I began to do some research on prosocial behavior. I was then influenced by the work by Latane and Darley on emergency helping. Before I was doing work on the Holocaust and genocide, as I was doing this research on helping behavior, it was very clear that sometimes people take action and sometimes they remain passive. In the course of that work I began to see the importance of the passive bystander in encouraging harm-doers. When I started to read about the Holocaust I thought I understood on the basis of my earlier work that somebody who is a witness and remains passive can distance themselves from that situation, even avoid taking in information. When I was at Harvard I had these young Harvard students collapse on the street in Cambridge in one of my studies, as passersby were approaching. An incidental observation was to me the most powerful information from that study. Some people walking on the other side of the street after a single look immediately rushed over. But some others turned their head away and never looked back, and sometimes at the next corner, rather than continue down the street, turned away. I interpreted this as meaning that they didn't want to be anywhere near, that they wanted to avoid taking in information so that they have no responsibility.

Such avoidance of responsibility and distancing from events I thought early on was probably an important contributor to the Holocaust and to other genocides. And that seems to be the case. Almost always hostility and violence evolve gradually. Perpetrators change as a result of their own action—but so do bystanders. In the course of the evolution of violence there is often general passivity. That is, witnesses become passive bystanders, they don't take action, they change bit by bit—and only when the genocide actually begins.

MM: Right.

ES: So you are the witness and you can look at it and say, oh well, it's just a small change, and you already distance yourself a little bit from it, from the people who are harmed, and you already begin to justify, because otherwise how do you just stand by? So then, it moves a little further, and having not acted before, you know, when do you decide to act? Then another small thing happens. So it's only when the killing really begins that some people, as we know an extremely small percentage of the population, cannot accept it and they cannot just look on any more.

MM: Yes.

ES: And they take action and become rescuers.

NG: There is action in being a passive bystander.

ES: Internal action, yes. Yes, that's a good point.

NG: And it has implications that are defining of what can happen to people. I mean you could think that you're being passive, but you are doing something.

MM: Making a choice by inaction.

UNDERSTANDING THAT EVIL AND GOODNESS EVOLVE

Ervin told us about his insights about how evil evolves and what the defining features of this evolution are. He developed these ideas through witnessing of atrocity throughout the world. For example, in his book, *The Roots of Evil: The Origins of Genocide and Other Group Violence* (1989), he presented case examples of the Holocaust, the Armenian genocide, Cambodia's autogenocide, and Argentina's mass killings and torture. He also brought his understanding to how rescue behavior comes about. His next inspiration was that since evil human behavior evolves, goodness also evolves, and there are ways to help it evolve, and these ways can be identified and put into action.

ES: Now, as I was doing this work, I came to profoundly believe that at the core to understanding was that evil and goodness evolve. I mean psychological evolution and social evolution. When people begin to do things without constraining forces, they are going to move further in that direction because they learn by doing. They do bad things, then they justify those actions. They also develop communities around those actions that support them in those actions, so they are likely to move in that direction. And the same thing tends to be true of people doing good things.

If you do worthwhile things and if there are no constraining sources, and especially if there are supportive sources, then you are going to move in that direction. Often the rescuers were in connection to other rescuers. I mean at the beginning they might have started off on their own, agreeing to hide somebody for a period of time, sometimes as a result of a request by an intermediary, and often continued to hide them for much longer times. Some of those who then managed to move the people they hid to safe places, and then decided to continue, connected up with others and did it in connection and support. So this relates to what you talk about in terms of witnessing, in terms of whether there is a receptive other and so on. I think that is important. There are single, heroic actors, and many rescuers were such actors. But difficult, challenging things become more possible and are often done in connection and through the support of the shared vision of people.

ALTRUISM BORN OF SUFFERING

MM: I was wondering how you saw Macs's psychology—how you saw her then and how you understand her motivation to be active on your behalf?

ES: In trying to understand Macs's motivation, I do not think it was an intellectual thing. I don't think it was a moral thing to work out, the moral principle in her head and to say, you know, this is what I must do. It was an emotional thing. It was just at the core level, this was the right thing for her to do. I don't think it ever came up in her mind to abandon us. I think we were her family.

One of the things in recent years that I have started to think about and write about is what I call altruism born of suffering. As we know from research, people who are victimized often become aggressive or they become dysfunctional in some ways or they remove themselves from other people, but for some people, when they have certain mitigating experiences, their own suffering becomes a source of caring and altruism. So for Macs, in addition to caring about us, the other thing was, I think, the lesson she took from her own suffering. When her mother died, she had a stepmother who was very cruel to her. She would do some little thing, she was a child, and her stepmother would make her kneel for hours on dried corn, which was very painful, and then from an early age on she was sent out to work as a maid. Fortunately for her, perhaps, part of it was taking care of children whom she loved, and then she came to work for my family and lived with us, starting 5 years before I was born. So by the time I was 6, when these really terrible things were happening, she lived with us for 11 years. So, you know, we were her family, I think she herself suffered, she knew what suffering was like, both of those things were likely to contribute. And basically, also, she was a good person. Not a good person who was holding intellectual values that she was going to live by, but in a very basic and core sense a good, empathic, loving person.

When we are caring, helpful bystanders, apart from helping someone who is harmed, who is suffering, I believe we make another contribution. Being helped at the time of one's suffering is, I think, one of those mitigating experiences that transforms victimization into altruism born of suffering.

REMEMBERING FEAR

ES: My first very clearly held memory is waking up very early in the morning and hearing sounds from the adjoining room and going into the adjoining room and people were sobbing and my uncle had this pink sheet of paper and he had to go and report at the forced labor camp. And so there was this air of anxiety surrounding us. Anxiety suffused our existence. In the summer of 1944 all Jews from the countryside were taken to Auschwitz. We knew about this; we had relatives in the countryside. My father's sister and her family lived there, and they were taken to Auschwitz. So when we saw those German troops, I knew, even though I was not yet quite 6 years old, that something very bad was happening. And we knew about the deportation of the Jews, and so, as I am saying, our life was suffused with anxiety. One story I remember was when we were still in our old apartment, all young men living in the house, boys, teenagers, were supposed to go into the courtyard and line up, and I think we were told that they were going to be taken to do some work somewhere. But, my aunt, not trusting this, told my cousin who was 9 years older than I was, so he was 15 at the time, not to go, and he thought that he should go because he was told to go and the best thing was to go, and my aunt, who never did this, slapped him and said you are not going, and so he didn't go. I don't know for sure what happened, but I think those kids didn't come back.

NG: People did things. They interrupted the March to Death, which is what you keep focusing on.

ES: Yes, that's right. Now this is an interruption under extreme and tragic circumstances, and the point is, my focus is really to interrupt it early, because we can point to the signs that indicate that some form of violence is likely.

INTERRUPTING VIOLENCE AND THE EXAMPLE OF WORKING IN RWANDA

ES: Given that violence evolves, once it begins, we don't know where it will end, and the later you go, the more difficult it is to interrupt it because commitment develops. Ideologies, ways of thinking that support the violence against a group, become more and more influential. Those who are victimized are devalued more and more along the way. Systems are created that maintain and increase harm-doing, so it is extremely important to do these things early to increase the chances that one can actually interrupt. And if you interrupt effectively, that also means that you are transforming circumstances in such a way that the society improves. People sometimes say, well you don't know if actually extreme violence is going to evolve; yes, there may be the likelihood because there are these indicators, but they are not certain so they don't take any action. They don't bother at all. But the thing is that even if it turned out that there would not be serious violence, the kind of actions that we need to take and could take would improve society and the lives of people a great deal. So nothing is lost and everything would be to gain.

NG:　Everything is gained. Have you been able to do this? You and your team of people? Have you convinced a government to take steps?

ES:　Well, you know, it's complicated. We have been working in Rwanda, and we started out doing workshops and trainings for all kinds of groups. We started first working with people who worked with local community groups that worked with groups in the community. And we trained these people and helped them to interweave their traditional approach with our approach. Then we actually did a very elaborate study to evaluate the effects of this training, not on the trainers, on the people we trained, but on the people *they* trained in turn, to see if our training translates into a larger effect when they work with groups. And we found all kinds of positive effects. The attitudes of Tutsis and Hutus in those groups toward each other improved. People showed a more complex understanding of the roots of violence. Their trauma symptoms lessened. Then we did these trainings with media; we did these trainings with high-level national leaders. We talked about the roots of or influences leading to violence; we engaged them in talking about how you prevent violence; we talked about the impact of violence on people, the traumatic impact. You know, my wife and my partner in this work is Laurie Anne Pearlman. She's a clinical psychologist and specialist on trauma. The term *vicarious trauma* was originated with her and one of her co-authors. She is the prime expert on vicarious trauma. So anyway, we did this and we had these leaders work in small groups.

So we did short lectures and then we engaged people in extensive discussion. When I talk in Rwanda about the influences leading to genocide, I never tell the Rwandese this is how it happened here, what happened to you. I tell them in general how these things come about; I give them examples from other places, which in itself is very important to them because it makes them feel that they are not alone, it has happened in other places also. But then they apply it to their own experience. I think the result is experiential understanding, when people take information and knowledge and apply it to their own experience, and then I think that has a different kind of power than just information.

NG:　And, people who have been so traumatized.

ES:　You begin to ask: How can genocide happen when there is this influence and that influence, how did it happen here, to us? And then you look at the whole society and what happened there, and you see that that element was present, and somehow I think it becomes more part of you, that knowledge. So, one of the things that we did with leaders was to have them work in small groups, to look at policies that they have been introducing and to consider whether these policies are likely to make violence more likely or make it less likely.

Then we did something that it seems was a good thing. Everybody wanted us to expand the range of our work so that it could reach more people. Leaders also wanted us to do this; so we decided to go to educational media, and we got somebody involved, George Weiss, a producer who lives in the Netherlands, who not long before got in touch with me. He had this vision of creating 10 TV programs, *Hate in Ten Lessons*. He was interested in the roots of hate and the prevention of hate, very much along the lines of what I had been doing In fact, he got the inspiration from reading *The Roots of Evil*. So we invited him, and instead of doing that television series he came to work with us in Rwanda and we set up educational radio programs. Our radio drama immediately became very popular. It is called "*Musekeweya*," "New Dawn." Just about everybody in the country, well, about 90% of the people listen to. It has been going on since May 2004 continuously. It is the story of two villages in conflict, with hostility, violence, active bystanders, slowly over the years moving on to reconciliation and all kinds of positive processes. There is evidence, again from a careful evaluation study, that it had a variety of positive effects even at the end of the first year, from increasing empathy to leading people to speak their minds, to be more independent of authority, since overly strong respect for an obedience to authority contributes to group violence. And the whole community is very involved with it. Children talk to their parents about it.

In addition to the radio drama, we also have straightforward educational programs. Since 2006, we have been doing all these things in Burundi and the Congo as well. All these programs are ongoing.

"FACING HISTORY": TEACHING CHILDREN ABOUT THE HOLOCAUST AND OTHER INHUMANITIES

We talked with Ervin about the specific ways in which he has reached out to children to teach them about bystandership and how to be caring people. He told us about Facing History, an organization that he has worked with at times, and how it engages children about lessons in the prevention of cruelty.

ES: Facing History is a very wonderful organization that was started many years ago by Margot Strom, a woman who at that time was a teacher in a school in Brookline, Massachusetts, to teach about the Holocaust. It evolved into a very substantial organization that develops materials, trains teachers to teach courses all around the country and also some internationally on the Holocaust. It also evolved from a focus on the Holocaust to using the Holocaust as an avenue to have students understand the role of the individual in the face of these events and concern with human cruelty and violence in general. So they are concerned with other kinds of genocides; they are concerned with racism and so on. It's the individual facing historical events, and the issue for them, like for me, is not to be passive bystanders. By helping students understand what happened in the Holocaust and how this evolved, it is more likely they hope and believe that a person will relate to events in a different way.

NG: How do you engage children and teach them to be active bystanders?

ES: Well, one thing that you can do is, you can talk very directly about "us" and "them." That we create divisions between "us" and "them," and we tend to look at some others in a negative light, whether we have a reason to or whether it is because other people tell us things. They recognize that this happens. I give many talks about these things. Sometimes also in the area where I live as a kind of volunteer activity. Just a few days ago I gave a talk to people in Greenfield, about harassment, intimidation, and bullying.

I actually developed a training program with some people here, an organization in the area. They read *The Psychology of Good and Evil* where I have written about bullying, harassment and intimidation, and raising caring children. So they approached me to work with them to develop a training program to train active bystanders, kids as active bystanders. So, one of the things that you can point out to kids, because they don't really think about this, is how when you do certain things it affects and harms others. What's the impact of this on other people? What happens? As part of this training program, we trained kids to be trainers of others. So one of the trainers said afterwards, "I used to do these things. I never thought about the effect of it, of what I am doing."

MM: Right, exactly.

ES: So, you know.

MM: To plant the seed to think about it.

ES: To have them understand how devastating it is. Actually, one of the important contributions to raising caring children is to point out the consequences of their behavior on other people. Not to tell them to be good, but to tell them when you do things, what is the effect on another person; also, to engage children in a conversation about these things. Does it ever happen that something is going on or something is happening to you and nobody is doing anything to help you? And so then they are right there.

MM: They get it.

ES: They understand these things, because it's happening to them—when they need help and somebody else doesn't do anything. Then as they think about it, this can contribute to changing their orientation to such situations.

As part of our training active bystanders we also help young people understand what can inhibit their action. For example, others looking unconcerned and remaining passive often stops us from acting. We also help them realize how much power they have to influence others. I found in one of my studies that just by saying something like, "This seems bad, maybe we should do something," can strongly influence another person's actions.

To raise caring children, it is important to work with adults. Warmth and affection by adults, combined with guiding children to understand caring values and to act according to them, are very important. And to act in caring ways not only to people close to them, but toward everyone.

CONNECTING WITH THE PAST: THE FIRST HIDDEN CHILDREN'S CONFERENCE

ES: Around 1990, maybe a little earlier, there was this first hidden children's conference in New York, a big event, something like 2,000 people showed up. I had no intention of going. A couple years before, I met Paul Valent in San Francisco at the ISTSS, International Society for Traumatic Stress Studies meeting. He's an Australian psychiatrist, also a child survivor from Hungary, and he was leading a child survivor group in Australia. He immediately acted as if we were friends, and I responded and we became close. He and my wife persuaded me to go with him to New York. I said okay I will go for 1 day, then I stayed, it was 2 days, maybe 3 days. I stayed for the whole thing. I had the sense that, I think somebody described this in one of your papers, that I was with others who understood each other. We understood each other's experience. You didn't have to explain. These are people who knew. Then, when I went home I started to talk to my children about this. I talked to them earlier as well, but I did not think I talked that much about my experience. But I'm often surprised, I am not aware that I talked about some aspect of my life, and they seem to know. So I talk more than I think sometimes.

REMEMBERING THE END OF THE WAR

ES: Yes. The end of the war I remember quite vividly. I remember my father was hiding with us in that house, so at some point we saw some men running down the street and there was street fighting, and my father said, "Those are Russian soldiers," and a couple days later a Soviet tank pulled up in front of the building and we were liberated. I was sick with something and I remember I was bundled up and somebody carried me upstairs, and I remember seeing a couple Russian soldiers standing there and some people talking with them, including my father who was a prisoner of war in Russia in WWI. Pretty soon we heard that people were looting stores, and I remember that my oldest cousin, I don't know if it was any of my other cousins as well, my oldest cousin went off and saw what was going on to see if we could get some stuff. He came back without anything but vividly described people taking things. Of course, nobody had a thing at that time. I wanted to go with him just to see what was happening, but I was too young and they wouldn't let me.

Then I remember moving back into our apartment. We were told it was used first by the Germans and then it was used by Russians, and apparently the Soviets took up horses, it was on the mezzanine, so the horses had to go up some steps. They took horses into the apartment. There were these hoof marks in the floor.

NG: Now that fascinates a child!

ES: I don't know how many days passed, but I remember going out. We had this little store near the apartment where we lived before the war. My parents were selling trousseaus. There was a big pile of bricks in front of the building where the store was, and I remember I was moving bricks away, and I remember walking down the street and there was no bread. There were some people selling cornbread on the street.

NG: It's really in your mind; it was an important thing.

ES: Well, I mean, it was huge! We were going to die, I mean, that was the sense that, you know, there was a clear sense for a long time that our life was in danger. These little pieces of letters of protection, I mean there were raids on the house and people were being taken away, and it seemed very shaky. So, and then we were liberated! You know, we didn't have to fear for our lives. It was a very big deal.

MM: You go from living in a state of fear and terror to a state of freedom.

ES: I don't remember that actively, the terror, but now as I'm talking about it I remember this kind of vague sense of anxiety that we had all the time. It was a miracle that they didn't find my father and take him away. Apart from that, we never felt secure there. So, yeah, I mean that was a very big event, the Soviets arriving.

WE HAVE TO ASK AGAIN: HOW DOES GENOCIDE HAPPEN?

ES: Well, there are a number of charts and a number of descriptions in different ways in my books. Different social conditions, what I call difficult life conditions, whether it's severe economic conditions, political disorganization, or great social change are starting points. They usually go together, not always, but often go together. While nobody is invulnerable, usually we have some feeling of invulnerability. When events frustrate, that contributes. Then there is a history of devaluation of another group who is defined as different from the major cultural group. As I mentioned, some group, usually an already devalued group, is scapegoated for life problems. In addition, people create a vision of a better future, an ideology that is destructive because it identifies another group as an enemy, usually this already devalued and scapegoated group. Sometimes the starting point is conflict between two groups. The conflict can be over land, or water rights, or over power and privilege in society. But if it persists, and if it turns violent, usually each group sees the other group as responsible, as immoral. So the other group is an enemy, and seen in a very negative light.

Whether the starting point is difficult life conditions or group conflict, of often their combination, as you begin to harm the other, that changes you. And you move on and take more harmful actions. Devaluation turns to discrimination, and discrimination turns to small acts of violence, and then to greater violence. All this is supported by the ideology, and the people who become part of the ideological movement. Ideologies, visions of a better future, also develop in group conflict. The passivity of people who don't even say this is wrong encourages perpetrators. So there is this unfolding of increasing violence, and everybody changes along the way. The perpetrators are transformed. They come to see killing these people as the right thing to do. Albert Bandura, an important psychologist, has this concept of moral disengagement, but I think that he is only partly right. At the beginning there may be moral disengagement, but mostly it is moral transformation.

NG: Your work takes our understanding of trauma and witnessing to an additional level. It is very painful, it's very difficult, scary, and there are wonderful things you can do. You really can do things. You can go into a classroom and help children know how to behave as active bystanders; you can be alert and have your government and groups alert to watching this continuum begin and know that it can be effectively interrupted. I mean, this will give me a way to talk to my grandchildren about why, why bother to know about the Holocaust and other terrible things going on in the world.

ENDING OUR CONVERSATION: SAYING GOOD-BYE

At this point, we were all aware that it was time to stop, to say good-bye. We had to reverse our direction and go back to the airport on the return trip. Being together, telling and receiving stories makes for an intimate and enriching experience. The power of witnessing brings emotion. We were all feeling close, sad, and vital. We together were facing genocide and creating the living surround where our minds and hearts could feel alive. We were grateful. We did not want to let go of Ervin and his plenitude of scholarship and personal presence as witness and intervener. We also knew that this was our last chapter; we were ready to finish our journey into the world of the power of witnessing.

MM: I think it is reflected right now that we are confronting the reality that there is so much more that we could talk about and the recognition that it's never done. In the book we are so aware of that—there are so many other places we could go.

ES: Well you know there is a famous writer who, in either a short story or part of a novel, writes about a painter who wants to paint the perfect picture. He is painting it and repainting it, and this is all done, all it needs is one little touch, and then he does one little touch, and now it's all wrong. … So the fact is at some point you have to say, this is the project, life continues and there are going to be other projects.

We were able to say good-bye.

REFERENCES

Staub, E. (1989). *The roots of evil: The origins of genocide and other group violence.* New York: Cambridge University Press.

Staub, E. (2003). *The psychology of good and evil.* New York: Cambridge University Press.

Staub, E. (2011). *Overcoming evil: Genocide, violent conflict and terrorism.* New York: Oxford University Press.

Staub, E. (2012, in preparation). *The roots of goodness: Inclusive caring, moral courage, altruism born of suffering and active bystandership.* New York: Oxford University Press.

Postscript: A Goodbye

Nancy R. Goodman and Marilyn B. Meyers

We are now closing the book. Without exception, our contributors were willing to plumb the depths of their own psyches in order to show how the power of witnessing brings forth a living mind. Their generosity is stunning. We were struck over and over again by the hope expressed that knowledge of the Holocaust would provide lessons to bring the power of witnessing to all individual trauma as well as to contemporary and future genocides and atrocities.

We are deeply indebted to all of you, the readers, who join with us and accept our invitation to continue to bear witness.

Index

Children
adoption of Jewish, 212
in hiding, 333
responsiveness to Holocaust
narratives, 95
teaching about inhumanity,
343–345
as witnesses to Holocaust memoirs,
94–95
Children of survivors, 9, 146
anger among, 98
denial responses in, 146, 205
dream analysis, 290
effects of silence on, 155
internalization of Holocaust
experiences by, 98
memoir of parents, 167
Miklós Roth narrative, 173
musical performance by, 194–195
narrative of mother, 177
psychological witnessing by,
145–157
revivification of self, 292
as translator between generations,
298
typical survival fantasies, 173
untreatability of, 71
Children's brains, and experience of
trauma, 151
Chorus of the Rescued, 223–224
Civic responsibility, listening as, 82
Civilization, lies of, 165–166
Clinical vignettes, 295
9/11 attacks, 306–311
9/11 first anniversary, 314–317
aftermath of 9/11 attacks, 312–314
fragments, 295–296
life theme, 296
metaphor use, 297
transference phenomena, 296–297
Clothing, confiscation from Terezín,
198
Collaboration
by European countries, 100
French denial of, 101
in Vichy France, 92, 100, 101
Collective consciousness, of memory,
261
Combat neurosis, 300
shame over, 301
stigma and shame of, 302

unacknowledged in WWII, 300
unmet psychological needs, 301
in Vietnam, 301
Compassion fatigue, 145
Composers, deportation from Terezín,
192
Composure, as reality and façade, 65
Concentration camps, 67, 90, 105,
122, 189
arrival experience, 48
childhood experiences of, 61–64
deportation of Hungarian Jews to,
174
GIs witnessing, 36
hiding after escape from, 105
Holocaust museum exhibitions,
132
Mauthausen, 171
novels about, 164
return to, 174
revisitation, 137
trauma on part of liberating forces,
300
in Vichy France, 91
visit by children of survivors, 176
visits to, 240
Consequences, educating about, 344
Conspiracy, 50
Conspiracy of silence, 37
Consumerist activism, 327
Contact, making during witnessing,
3, 4
Containment, 4–5, 290
Contemporary genocide, 319
challenge of, 320
defined, 320
Converted Jews, 106
Core metaphor, 7
Core pain, 24
Countertransference, 292, 315
after 9/11 attacks, 318
effects of 9/11 on, 305–306
to patients' trauma, 252
to trauma, 8
Creativity, 109, 294
growth-enhancing properties, 115
as means to healing, 112, 113
sculpture of lost father, 209–210
self-healing through, 116–117
symbolic representations, 196
in Terezín Ghetto, 191

Specificity, loss of, in emotional
  responses, 290
Spiegelman, Art, 248
Spielberg, Steven, 247
Split-screen video, 148, 345
  analyzing trauma experiences
    through, 152
Srebrenican genocide, 328
St. Ottilien monastery, 134
Staub, Ervin, 32, 333–334
Stein, Jiri, 258, 259
  transport to Dachau, 260
Stigma, of combat trauma, 302
Stone quarry camp, 61–64
Stones of remembrance. See Memorial
  stones
Storytelling
  as coping mechanism in genocide,
    330
  documentary, 235
  drive to, 129
  establishing narrative of genocide
    by, 330
  moral obligation to, 264
  restorative nature of, 82
  as survival mechanism, 133
  survival of memory through, 256
  through arts, 255
  through needlework, 236
Strom, Margot, 343
Stutthof concentration camp, 122, 127,
  130
Sudetenland, annexation, 182
Suffering, as source of caring, 340
Survival
  amazement at, 165
  competition for, 336
  intergenerational transmission, 297
  profound gratitude for, 162–163
  role of memorable moments, 179–190
  through hiding, 296
Survival fantasies, in children of
  Holocaust, 173
Survival in Auschwitz, 47, 88
Surviving the Americans, 134, 135
Survivor families, 96–99
  effects on, 96–99
  in Rwandan genocide, 328
Survivor guilt, 137, 205, 336
  9/11 attacks, 306
  in poetry, 219, 225–227, 229,
    230–232

Survivor identity, conflict with
  continued living, 329
Survivor interviews, 36, 38
Survivor parents, 10
  difficulty with witnessing children's
    trauma, 153
Survivor persona, 189
Survivor testimonies, 9
Survivors
  internal anti-train, 54
  re-interviewing, 21
  seeking and shunning, 29
Sutzkever, Abraham, 222, 225–227,
  228, 274
Svenk, Karel, 201–202
Symbolizing capacity, 12
  traumatic destruction of, 79
Sympathy, 257
  versus empathy, 256–257
Systems creation, in evolution of
  genocide, 341

T

Talent, 116
Teachers, survivors as, 84
Terezín, Voices of, 260–262
Terezín Anthem, 201–202, 349
Terezín Ghetto, 37
  2006 homecoming, 194–195
  as anteroom to hell, 191
  death toll, 191
  deceptive Red Cross visit, 198–199
  documenting artistic life of, 255
  laughter in ruins of, 202, 203
  as model ghetto, 198
  Verdi's *Requiem* performance
    reenactment, 192–195
  waste of lives at, 261
Terezín survivors, 348, 350, 351
  interviews with, 258
Terror
  ability to eclipse all else, 65
  acknowledging patients', 305
  after 9/11 attacks, 309
  annihilation through, 46, 65
  childhood, 65
  facing with witnesses, 69
  overcoming through witnessing, 3
  as response to 9/11 attacks, 310
Terrorism, 306
Testimonial alliance, 82–83